Rule by Aesthetics
World-Class City Making in Delhi

D. Asher Ghertner

OXFORD
UNIVERSITY PRESS

Oxford University Press is a department of the University of
Oxford. It furthers the University's objective of excellence in research,
scholarship, and education by publishing worldwide.

Oxford   New York
Auckland   Cape Town   Dar es Salaam   Hong Kong   Karachi
Kuala Lumpur   Madrid   Melbourne   Mexico City   Nairobi
New Delhi   Shanghai   Taipei   Toronto

With offices in
Argentina   Austria   Brazil   Chile   Czech Republic   France   Greece
Guatemala   Hungary   Italy   Japan   Poland   Portugal   Singapore
South Korea   Switzerland   Thailand   Turkey   Ukraine   Vietnam

Oxford is a registered trademark of Oxford University Press
in the UK and certain other countries.

Published in the United States of America by
Oxford University Press
198 Madison Avenue, New York, NY 10016

© Oxford University Press 2015

All rights reserved. No part of this publication may be reproduced, stored in
a retrieval system, or transmitted, in any form or by any means, without the prior
permission in writing of Oxford University Press, or as expressly permitted by law,
by license, or under terms agreed with the appropriate reproduction rights organization.
Inquiries concerning reproduction outside the scope of the above should be sent to the
Rights Department, Oxford University Press, at the address above.

You must not circulate this work in any other form
and you must impose this same condition on any acquirer.

Library of Congress Cataloging-in-Publication Data
Ghertner, D. Asher.
Rule by aesthetics : world-class city making in Delhi / D. Asher Ghertner.
pages cm
Includes bibliographical references.
ISBN 978–0–19–938556–0 (hardback : alk. paper) — ISBN 978–0–19–938557–7 (pbk. : alk. paper)
1. City planning—India—Delhi. 2. Slums—India—Delhi. 3. Urban renewal—India—Delhi.
I. Title.
HT169.I52D446 2015
307.1'216095456—dc23
2015001740

1 3 5 7 9 8 6 4 2
Printed in the United States of America
on acid-free paper

Rule by Aesthetics

CONTENTS

Acknowledgments vii
Note on Translation and Transliteration ix

Introduction 1
1. World-Class City Making 23
2. Gentrifying the State: Governing Through Property 45
3. Nuisance Talk: From Sensory Disgust to Urban Abjection 78
4. Aesthetic Criminalization: The Nuisance of Slums 99
5. World-Class Detritus: The Sense of Unbelonging 125
6. The Propriety of Property: Resettlement and the Pursuit of Belonging 158
Conclusion 183

Notes 199
References 233
Index 247

ACKNOWLEDGMENTS

I have accrued many debts in the course of completing this book, the deepest of which is to the residents of the place I call Shiv Camp. Shiv Camp families invited me into their homes, shared stories about their lives and losses, and built an enduring bond in the face of the unnerving threat of eviction. Their voices shaped the political commitments that underlie this project and animate the pages that follow. Elsewhere in Delhi, I am grateful to Dunu Roy and Rohan D'Souza for serving as early mentors. Amita Baviskar has been a constant source of encouragement and insight for understanding the city. I benefitted immeasurably from the comradeship and political inspiration of Lalit Batra, Pritpal Randhawa, Supriya Chottani, Sanjay Kumar, and Nithya Raman. I also thank Ramendra and Anita Juneja and the organizers at the *Dilli Shramik Sangathan* for helping me learn to listen for voices of struggle that have not yet found the larger political platform they warrant.

This book began as a dissertation at the University of California, Berkeley and was blessed by the critical oversight of my wonderful committee: Michael Watts, Gillian Hart, and Ananya Roy. I hope this text honors their commitment to engaged scholarship. I am incredibly fortunate to have shared the company of a rich intellectual community in and around Berkeley. I owe special thanks to Mike Dwyer, Malini Ranganathan, Sapana Doshi, Tracey Osborne, and Rozy Fredericks—members of "the peeps" writing group—for constant inspiration, critique, and merriment, as well as to coconspirators Kamal Kapadia, Matthias Fripp, Amol Phadke, Mayuri Panditrao, and Rahul Parson.

I will be eternally grateful for the careful attention that Sharad Chari, Jenny Robinson, Sharon Zukin, and Mazen Labban took in reading the manuscript in its entirety. For their helpful contributions to this project in various capacities, I also thank Lalitha Kamath, Diya Mehra, Mike Levien, Rena Searle, Costas Nakassis, Jon Anjaria, Thomas Blom Hansen, Nikhil Anand, Vinay Gidwani, Gareth Jones, Akhil Gupta, Anne Rademacher, Janaki Nair, Shehzad Nadeem, K. Sivaramakrishnan, Meheli Sen, Anjali Nerlekar, Corin Golding, David Lunn, Gautam Bhan, Austin Zeiderman,

Romola Sanyal, Jia-Ching Chen, Trevor and Jessica Birkenholtz, Rick Schroeder, Daniel Goldstein, and Hudson McFann. Mike Siegel of Rutgers Cartography produced the map of Delhi. I have benefitted tremendously from the support of colleagues and graduate students in the Department of Geography at Rutgers and former colleagues and students at the Department of Geography and Environment at the London School of Economics. I owe great thanks to Dave McBride, my editor at Oxford University Press, for his insights and patience in taking this project forward.

Many of the arguments presented here benefitted from feedback I received from audiences at Stanford University (the Center for South Asia), the University of Chicago (Anthropology Monday Seminar), the University of Pennsylvania (South Asian Studies), UC-Berkeley (Global Metropolitan Studies), Durham University (Geography), University College London (Geography), the London School of Economics (Anthropology and Geography), Dartmouth College (Geography), the Rutgers Center for Historical Analysis, the University of Hong Kong (Institute for the Humanities and Social Sciences), and the Centre for Policy Research in Delhi. Some of the evidence contained here was published in earlier form, especially chapters 2 and 3 in the *International Journal of Urban and Regional Research* and *Antipode*, respectively.

This book was made possible thanks to the generous financial support I received in the form of a Social Science Research Council International Dissertation Research Fellowship, a Fulbright-Hays Doctoral Dissertation Research Award, an American Institute of Indian Studies Language Fellowship, a National Science Foundation Doctoral Dissertation Research Improvement Award, a National Science Foundation Graduate Student Research Fellowship, a Mellon/American Council of Learned Societies Dissertation Completion Fellowship, a grant from the London School of Economics Faculty Seed Fund, and a Rutgers University Faculty Research Council Grant.

None of this would have been possible without the constant support of my family. Nancy, Lory, Robin, and Zoë Ghertner and Venk, Usha, Priya, and Sunita Mani helped keep me honest about this project and why it matters to the world. Preetha Mani's love, intellect, and patience have made me the scholar I am today. She has read and improved every page of this text; she is my best editor; and she has taught me to read, write, listen, and care.

NOTE ON TRANSLATION AND TRANSLITERATION

Unless otherwise noted, all translations of Hindi conversations and texts are my own. For the sake of readability, and to avoid filling the pages with diacritical marks, I use diacritics for Hindi words only the first time they appear in a chapter, where I follow the system in R. S. McGregor, *The Oxford Hindi-English Dictionary* (Delhi: Oxford University Press, 1993). This system allows readers to distinguish between short and long vowels (e.g., a and $ā$, i and $ī$), as well as dental and retroflex (e.g., t and $ṭ$, d and $ḍ$) and unaspirated and aspirated (e.g., p and ph, $ḍ$ and $ḍh$) consonants. For simplicity, I deviate from this system in two areas: I use sh instead of $ś$ and $ṣ$; and for place names, personal names, and well-known Hindi words, I retain their popular spellings in Roman letters without diacritics (e.g., chai instead of $cāy$). Where I translate from Hindi to English, English-language words that were spoken in Hindi sentences are shown in italics. Hindi terms are pluralized in the English manner, by adding an s.

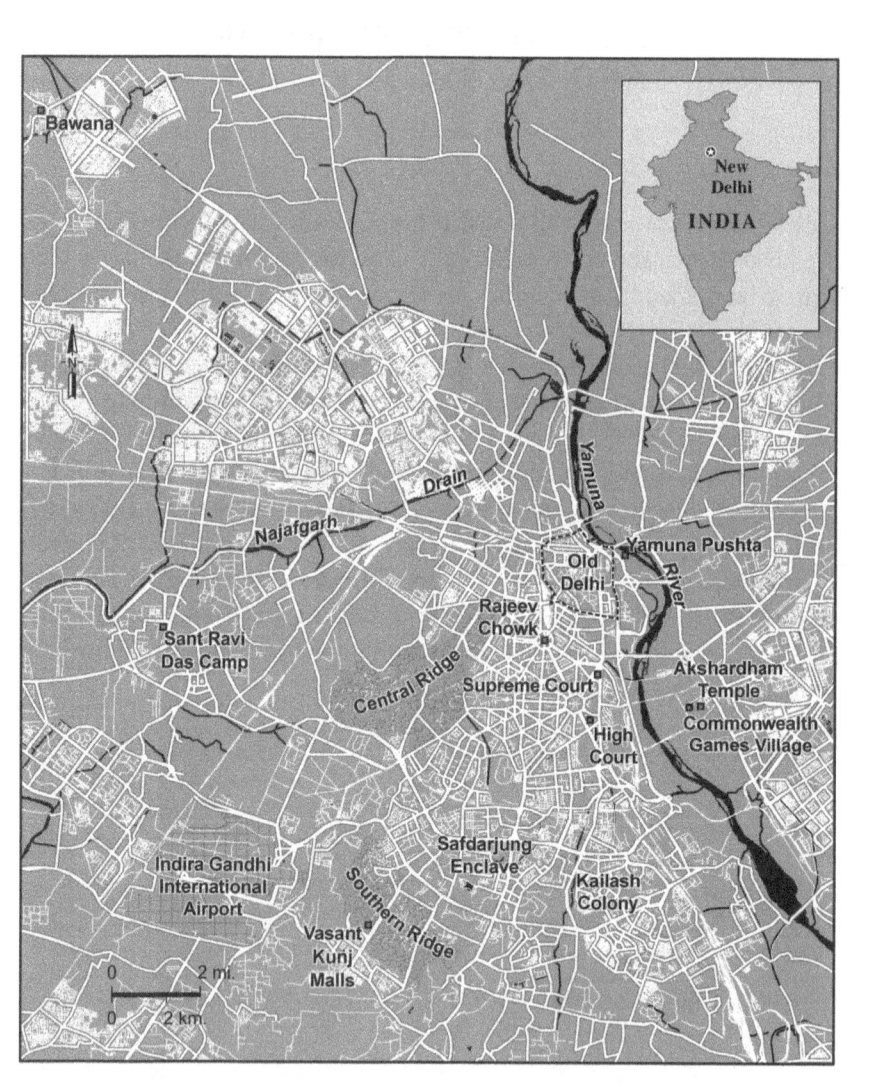

Introduction

More than a billion people live in squatter settlements today, a population that global development institutions nervously project could triple in size by 2050. Scholars have interpreted this future "planet of slums" as "the growth of a population outside state control."[1] Using the case of Delhi, the world's second largest city, my aim in this book is to challenge conceptions of the Third World megacity that emphasize a lack of state control and spatial discipline.[2] Instead, I focus on how the management of slums there forces us to rethink the epistemological foundation of government—that is, to rethink how it is that a state knows and directs its object.

Slums, squatter settlements, or *jhuggī jhoṁpḍī* (shanty) colonies, as they are called in Delhi, are often considered "informal" for the fact that they lie beyond the realm of state authorized maps, plans, and statutes. Their presumed ungovernability or unruliness, experts suggest, stems from the absence of cartographic and statistical simplifications of their territory. In this book, I trace how the production of an aesthetic normativity replaced maps and statistics as the key mechanism of rule in millennial Delhi. Specifically, I show that Delhi's attempt to transform itself into a world-class city—represented most vividly by the construction of seventy new shopping malls, the fivefold increase in land prices, and the displacement of a million slum dwellers in the first decade of the twenty-first century[3]—is occurring not solely through a legal redefinition of property or an economic calculus of cost-benefit, as most accounts of globalized urbanization suggest. Rather, it also requires the dissemination of a compelling vision of the future—what I call a world-class aesthetic—and the cultivation of a viewing public that takes part in that very vision—the making of world-class

(1)

subjects. I begin with three scenes from millennial Delhi to sketch this aesthetic project.

SCENE 1

In 2003, a local environmental group submitted a petition to the Supreme Court of India challenging the construction of India's largest shopping mall complex for being built on Delhi's southern ridge, a protected green space according to the Delhi Master Plan. Expert testimony by the Delhi Development Authority (DDA)—the agency that drafts and is legally bound to implement the Master Plan—defended the project in the Court for being "planned" and thus legal because of its high-quality construction and its strategic function in boosting Delhi's architectural profile. Showing glossy, artistic renderings of the proposed development and describing the mall as a world-class commercial complex (see Figure I.1), the DDA argued that the visual appearance of the future mall was in itself enough to confirm the project's planned-ness (just look at it!). The Supreme Court, despite acknowledging that the project constituted a "flagrant violation" of planning law, sided with the DDA, allowing the mall construction to go forward.[4]

During the course of the mall proceedings, an adjacent multigenerational *jhuggi* colony that conformed with the land use designation of the Master Plan was declared unplanned and illegal for being a nuisance to the upscale neighborhoods nearby. Based on a set of photographs showing the unsightly conditions in the colony, and despite the absence of a survey

Figure I.1. An artistic rendering of the DLF Emporio, the most expensive mall in India and one of the seven malls in the disputed shopping mall complex located in Vasant Kunj (Dewan, 2007). Image reproduced with the permission of DLF Limited.

or scientific evaluation of its so-called nuisance-causing activities, the DDA demolished the settlement without compensation, an action upheld by the court.⁵

In these two examples, "planned-ness," an attribute of urban space key to the determination of legality, was defined as that which *looks* planned, regardless of its formal standing in planning law or any correspondence between actually existing urban development and expert paper representations of the city. Here, it was a land use's relationship to a particular world-class aesthetic (conformance in the case of the mall, divergence in the case of the *jhuggi* colony) that determined the appropriate governance response. How did this world-class aesthetic come to stand in for maps, plans, and statutes?

SCENE 2

On a hot May afternoon early in my fieldwork in Delhi, I rode an air-conditioned elevator up the Vikas Minar to the office of A. K. Jain, the commissioner of planning in the DDA. Perched inside Delhi's tallest building, whose name literally means "development tower," Jain has a nearly panoptic view of the city he governs, and at the time of our meeting Jain was in the midst of guiding his agency in redrafting a document with an equally panoptic vision: the Delhi Master Plan. A statutory document that provides comprehensive planning guidelines for the city, the Delhi Master Plan is updated every twenty years to meet new mandates. According to planning law, Jain and his staff of 26,000 engineers, clerks, and field workers are required to conduct a comprehensive civic survey before any master plan revision can begin. Excited to have secured a meeting with Delhi's top planning official, I opened my notebook to the first of a long list of questions I had prepared on planning practice and began with: How did you survey the city?

Jain's answer that day fundamentally changed my understanding of planning in India: "We didn't do a survey. Well, we did a 'windshield survey': I sent some engineers out in cars and had them look and see how things were. If people knew we were measuring them, things would get too political. We know what needs to be done without having to survey. We know what a world-class city should look like."⁶ Forgoing precise surveyance, here was a planning regime that built a governing vision not through intricate calculations, but rather through the gaze itself. How can a planning authority design and administer a plan without first physically assessing the territory and population it would govern?

SCENE 3

Gopal is a resident of Shiv Camp, a *jhuggi* colony nestled in the midst of a burgeoning middle-class neighborhood in Delhi's most rapidly growing western district. As shopping malls and five-star hotels opened, west Delhi witnessed some of the most aggressive slum demolitions in millennial Delhi. I spent a year in Shiv Camp, examining how men and women like Gopal responded to the threat of demolition. A quarter of Shiv Camp homes had been bulldozed a few days before I first spoke with Gopal. Yet despite the fact that the government's bulldozers had arrived unannounced, without a legal notice, the demolition made sense to Gopal; it seemed part of a plan:

> *Sarkār* [government] has made a new map that shows how the new city will look. There will be nice clean roads, big buildings; it will be beautiful; it will be clean and maintained. There will be less [traffic] *jam* and filth. . . . They are making Delhi like Paris, clearing all these *jhuggis* [shanties].⁷

When I asked Gopal how he knew what the map looked like, he replied matter-of-factly, "well, we haven't seen the map. That is only for officials to see, but they tell everyone about it. They say that the city will look beautiful and have all these nice things. The newspapers tell us about it, and we read those and learn about the map slowly." While Gopal made implicit reference to the Master Plan, a document being widely discussed in newspapers at the time, the map he described was more like a picture than a calculative grid of land use zones, infrastructure codes, and development norms. What gave this imagined map—a map without the calculative underpinnings so often presumed of cartography—such authority to Gopal?⁸

These scenes introduce key components of what I call "rule by aesthetics," a mode of governing space on the basis of codes of appearance rather than through the calculative instruments of map, census, and survey. Scenes 1 and 2 suggest that the judiciary, state planners, and the media share a common vision of a world-class city, even without a rigorous, technoscientific basis for defining such a city or evaluating progress toward its realization. Scene 3 shows that *jhuggi* dwellers—often depicted as obstacles to the world-class city—also participate in this vision, even when it appears against their interest to do so. These scenes thus animate the two motivating questions of this book: In the absence of statistical and cartographic techniques of rational planning, how are coherent ways of seeing put in place for identifying order and disorder? And, what compels marginalized populations to appropriate these same ways of seeing as their own? Phrased through the above scenes, how does not just A. K. Jain, but also his staff of 26,000 workers, know what the world-class city looks like? And, why do Gopal and his neighbors—those being displaced to make way for the world-class city—look upon themselves through the gaze of the planner and his map?

AESTHETIC GOVERNMENTALITY

The question of how populations and territories are seen, ordered, and rendered governable—and subsequently come to see and govern themselves—has been a central concern of social and political theory. The French philosopher Michel Foucault, in his famous lectures at the Collège de France, for example, argued that a modern form of power, what he called governmentality, emerged in the late eighteenth century that operated by cultivating a normative disposition within broad population groups, thereby guiding them "to do as they ought" without requiring direct intervention or recourse to disciplinary mechanisms, like the police.[9] Famously summarized as "the conduct of conduct," governmentality, Foucault argued, works by constructing social categories that were once illegible, such as the rate of economic growth or the occurrence of a disease, and problematizing those categories such that they appear to require active improvement—for example: growth is too slow, disease is too prevalent. By training individuals to take up these categories in their own lives, governmental programs direct the habits, aspirations, and beliefs of the governed toward what Foucault called "convenient ends": a growing economy, a healthy society.

According to Foucault, it was the rise of statistics, a scientifically rational procedure of recording the surface attributes of the population—such as the birth rate or disease incidence—that became "the main technical factor" of modern governmentality.[10] This argument has led others to insist that "to govern a problem requires that it be counted."[11] In James Scott's well-known account of state simplification schemes and the legibility they seek to secure, a state's ability to see into and intervene in otherwise ungovernable space is the product of careful measurement and calculation: "Whatever the units being manipulated, they must be organized in a manner that permits them to be identified, observed, recorded, counted, aggregated, and monitored."[12] In British India, the East India Company and subsequently the colonial state invested tremendously in technologies of census, survey, and cartography under "the belief that they were creating the perfect map. . . . Rule in India was dependent on the creation of a space within which a systematic archive of knowledge of this space might be created."[13] Modern government across diverse contexts, in other words, is thought to depend on rigorous technoscience, what Ian Hacking calls an "avalanche of printed numbers" and calculative techniques.[14]

When I met A. K. Jain (Scene 2), I was looking for maps and the avalanche of printed numbers according to which urban government operated in Delhi. His insistence that planning practice in Delhi required no such records made me realize I needed to pay more attention to absences than presences. Indeed, when I looked closer, I found a conspicuous absence of accurate and up-to-date maps and statistics on either the population or the territory. For example, a comprehensive statistical summary of the size and distribution of Delhi's slum population has not been reported since 1998. The Delhi government itself is unaware of the total number of *jhuggi* colonies in Delhi and therefore continues to report 1998 numbers as if they were valid to this day.[15] Early in my fieldwork, when I held out hope that such records existed, I submitted a number of right to information requests to the DDA asking for summary statistics on the number of *jhuggis* demolished in Delhi in each district since 1990. Although I received a handwritten reply from one of fifteen districts, including the responding officer's own provisional, handwritten arithmetic, the final reply to my request said, "there is no such compiled record/information."

If modern cities are supposed to be built through technoscientific procedures of urban planning and government such as maps, censuses, and surveys, the conspicuous absence of such techniques in the world-class redevelopment of Delhi raises the question of how rule there is achieved. If we apply familiar models of government and planning, this absence of synoptic maps and numbers might look like a type of failure.[16] But the above scenes suggest that this is not about failed government. Rather, millennial Delhi came to be characterized by a different mode of governing space, one in which intensely political decisions about who and what belongs in the city took place primarily on the basis of codes of appearance, not documents and records. As I show in the pages that follow, under conditions of such aesthetic rule, social order is inscribed in public modes of viewership as much as it is secured through reasoned injunctions, systems of belief, or statutory command. Saying this is not to deny the significance of the rational or the calculative; it is rather to insist that any form of rule draws on variable applications of each, and that certain ostensibly calculative technologies—such as a survey exercise or a numerical chart—can have equally important aesthetic functions, capable of training a particular way of seeing as much as they convey information or organize thoughts.

[Bernard Cohn long ago turned our attention to the aesthetic underpinnings of political rule. In his classic studies of what he called the "investigative modalities" used to assemble knowledge and build the imperial capacity to govern, Cohn noted that in addition to survey and enumerative modalities such as mapping and census, what he termed an "observational modality" was central to colonial government in India. Cohn argued that this observational modality operates by creating expectations for how space looks and how it should look. He discussed this drawing from records of how new colonial visitors to India were trained to see "India" through an already narrated experience. By following set itineraries and patterns of movement, the colonial eye was directed to view strange sites/sights in familiar, preinformed ways: Calcutta as a city of slums, Bombay as a city of traders, Banaras as a Hindu city.[17] As a method of training a particular way of seeing—for example, by guiding the eye to identify "the slum" as illegal or to associate shopping malls with progress—this modality can put in place what Jacques Rancière calls a "community of sense," or a shared mode of aesthetic engagement with mutually recognizable visual markers of order and disorder.[18] When a strong narrative of moving through and seeing space becomes dominant within a population—that is, when it prompts the viewing public to identify with the state's vision—then how one sees that space becomes the basis for assessing what that space is, positively, and what it should be, normatively.

Whereas Cohn studied how this observational modality was used to differentiate between the native and the modern and to categorize, simplify, and essentialize native forms of life under colonial rule, the above scenes indicate how it enables the easy visual identification of what does and does not belong in contemporary urban landscapes. Malls appear planned even if they violate planning law; slums look unplanned even if they conform with land-use plans. India is of course not alone here: we need only think of the reliance on visual identifiers of blight in American cities or the beautification drives that took place in the slums and *favelas* of Beijing and Rio de Janeiro in preparation for the Olympic Games to note the widespread use of aesthetic markers of unbelonging in the governance of contemporary cities. Yet while there is growing interest today in the informal means by which urban systems function beyond grids, cadastres, and zones, much of this work presumes that when these calculative devices are missing or unused, government either disappears as a coherent conceptualization or else descends into ad hoc and localized systems of arbitrary rule.[19]

For example, in his highly influential reading of the African city, AbdouMaliq Simone argues: "Vacuums of authority or excessive expressions of it are unable to consolidate strong overarching perspectives capable of putting bodies and objects in 'their' place." For Simone, under- and disinvestment in "order," by which he means technologies of "zoning, cadastre, property and administration," create a scenario in which the very possibility of putting in place a coherent urban vision, what he calls a "common future," only exist through pirate practices "cut off" from formal state systems. As he writes: "Despite all of the development regimes that attempt to bring order and efficacy to African cities, they continue to be, in many respects, virtual cities," impossible achievements.[20] In Delhi, the lack of synoptic maps and statistics does not signal an absence of an overarching perspective, and limitations on rational planning technologies have not reduced order. Instead, what we find there is a situation in which it is the virtual city itself—an imagined future city—that produces the common future toward which collective energies are directed. In other words, as in so many postcolonial cities where development remains indexed to clearly felt, even while unmeasured, standards of order and appearance, it is those standards themselves that direct action in Delhi. This global index is what planners, politicians, and citizens in India call the world-class city.

IMAGINING THE WORLD-CLASS CITY

The project of world-class city making in Delhi, as in other emerging market contexts, is marked by a strong normative drive to reach globally indexed targets of development: to host prestigious international events, to house Fortune 500 companies, and to offer lifestyles capable of attracting global consumer classes. In millennial Delhi, this project transformed the long-standing postcolonial anxiety around catching up—the sense of temporal lag imposed first by colonialism and then the gradualism of fifty years of modernist planning after Independence[21]—into a far bolder fantasy futurism. This futurist disposition is indeed central to what I mean by millennial Delhi, a moment of market triumphalism beginning in the late 1990s that sketched the world-class city as an imminent break from the perceived inefficiencies and encumbrances of the more socialistic, planned city of the past—state-regulated housing, restrictions on business, bureaucratic red tape, and the regular deferral, for the elite at least, of individual advancement in the name of the collective. The world-class city thus operates as a future-oriented technology, shifting collective horizons toward the long run and projecting the norms of appearance and civility of the future city across the existing landscape. While world-class city making continues in Delhi to this day, I mark the end of Delhi's millennial moment at 2010, the year the city hosted the Commonwealth Games, a mega-event that the state used as a primary justification for massive physical transformations of the city, but the execution of which eventually led to corruption charges that, in ways that I turn to in the conclusion, have contributed to a shift in the nature and surety of world-class city making. Throughout this book I therefore refer to "millennial Delhi" in the past tense, and the world-class city and world-class city making in the present tense.

Delhi came to be characterized in its millennial moment by a new extroversion, or an attempt to index the city's imagined future to other global cities. It was thus common to hear Delhi residents—from *jhuggi* dwellers to wealthy bungalow owners—distill the diverse changes taking place around them into the claim that "Delhi will look like Paris."[22] While Paris has long held symbolic significance as the "capital of modernity"—including among planners and administrators in urban India—the world-class city differs from the modernist impulse characteristic of earlier periods.[23] Rather than upholding a single city or urban model as an ideal—the modern—and extracting measurable design or infrastructural attributes from it that can be benchmarked and achieved (aha! We are modern now!), the world-class aesthetic operates as a regime for partitioning visual attributes of space on the basis of both locally rooted quality of life concerns as well as globally circulating and ever-shifting images of world-class spaces. The question the world-class aesthetic asks then is not "Does Delhi look sufficiently like Paris?"; rather, it asks whether the space in question would be acceptable in a world-class city, where any other iconic city might just as easily stand in for Paris. The world-class city is thus the aspirational target toward which world-class city making is oriented. It operates as a diffuse signifier, training a particular way of seeing and putting in place an aesthetically grounded form of power/knowledge—the world-class aesthetic—that inspires among its potential subjects a will to participate in its discourse and to make its visual criteria their own. Gopal evinced this when he said in response to ongoing slum demolitions that Delhi would become beautiful.

It is precisely this vague sense of an improved, more beautiful urban future, without planning benchmarks or even mutually agreeable definitional criteria, that gives the world-class city its efficacy: the excitement of stepping into an air-conditioned, stainless steel carriage on the Delhi Metro, or the pride of living near a shopping mall with more marble than the Taj Mahal, give world-classness a sensory self-evidence. Amita Baviskar captures this experience well: "We may not have been to Singapore or London, but we know when we are in the presence of something 'world-class.' Like obscenity or divinity, 'world-classness' provokes a response from within, an instant shock of recognition."[24] I refer to a world-class aesthetic, then, to signal the sensory knowledge that allows for the easy differentiation between what is or is not world-class and the associated visual criteria that set the boundary between what does or does not belong in a place with world-class ambitions.

Like other utopian projects, world-class city making is oriented toward not progressive improvement, but an already known conclusion. It thereby sketches the interim as but a medium for reaching the anticipated future, casting elements of the present not suitably world-class—most notably the slum—as anachronistic. In India, this is not the same anachronism that characterized the earlier developmentalist era of five-year plans, socialistic housing policy, and inclusive planning targets. In this developmentalist dispensation, which lasted through the Nehruvian era (1947–1989) and which was only slowly replaced by a more market-oriented dispensation through the 1990s, slums were seen as labor camps housing the working class—the builders of the modern city. Such areas were anachronistic in the sense that planning discourse registered them as insufficiently developed—lagging areas yet to have benefited from the modernizing and civilizing impulse of the urban. They needed to be ripped out of the village past, upgraded, and civilized through physical and social planning.[25] In the millennial moment, the slum shifted from labor camp to undercapitalized public resource, and slum dwellers were rescripted as encroachers obstructing the full realization of the world-class urban dream.[26]

World-class city making hence needs to be seen as an inherently speculative project, premised on an almost prophetic temporality in which the present is wagered on the future. This speculative disposition was trained in millennial Delhi through persistent state, media, and business narratives declaring Delhi's (and India's) impending transformation. It was also performed through the circulation of images that hubristically projected a picture of the future already known—from artistic renderings of the future cityscape that real estate firms plastered around town on massive advertising hoardings, to the celebrated *Delhi Master Plan 2021*, which begins on page 1 with its goal of making Delhi a world-class city. I explore one especially potent future-making technology in chapter 1: mathematical projections of India's class structure that depict a poverty-free future and that provide a narrative wherein clearing slums to make way for luxury real estate appears a most inclusive endeavor. The speculative disposition of the world-class city thus cannot be dissociated from a deeper speculative turn in the urban economy.

Since the mid-1990s, beginning shortly after the advent of the pro-market reforms known as India's New Economic Policy, India's land market has been gradually liberalized, opening up new territories for private investment and prioritizing real estate profit regardless of its social or productive function. Foreign direct investment in real estate more than quadrupled in the late 2000s, with profits so high that companies with no history in property development began diverting profits from core business activities into the purchase of "land banks."[27] Speculative land development and the rentiership with which it is associated hence transformed real estate into the vanguard segment of the Indian economy, a speculative vehicle for generating private profit and state revenue, and casting nonprofit-generating land uses as inherently out of place (I discuss this further in chapter 1).

The Delhi government participated in this project by gradually shifting public finances away from education, public housing, health care, and food subsidies toward highly visible infrastructure works such as the Delhi Metro Rail; more than fifty new flyovers; two new toll roads to Delhi's posh satellite cities; and the Commonwealth Games Village[28]—prestige projects built "to dispel most visitors' first impression that India is a country soaked in poverty."[29] Similarly, it approved $100 million, which it later retracted after cost estimates almost doubled, for building a signature bridge modeled after London's Millennium Bridge, and liberalized building bylaws and development norms to allow for denser and taller commercial development across the city—all steps to demonstrate the city's world-class ambitions and to encourage rising land prices. The flip side of these efforts to upgrade undercapitalized areas of the city was the need to remove or redevelop areas of the city not deemed suitably world-class. It thus became no secret that, as the Chief Secretary of Delhi declared, "a world-class city means a slum-free city."[30]

INCALCULABLE SLUMS AND THE RISE OF AESTHETIC RULE

Despite the strong mandate to remove slums by the early 2000s, the practical means of doing so were limited at the time. Since the establishment of the postcolonial planning apparatus and lasting through the 1990s, the decision to remove a slum lay almost entirely in the hands of the state agencies upon whose land slums were settled. If a settlement on DDA land was to be removed, for example, the DDA was charged with completing a complex chain of bureaucratic work: it had to notify the settlers, survey the households to determine resettlement eligibility, collect fees from those eligible for resettlement, purchase or allocate the necessary land for a resettlement colony, obtain support from the police for protection during the demolition, hire the demolition team for the appropriate day, and coordinate the resettlement exercise with the Municipal Corporation. Not only was each of these steps bureaucratically challenging, but the elaborate patronage relations extending from settlements into the lower bureaucracy made the assembly of accurate survey registers—a requirement before a demolition could be carried out at the time—nearly impossible.[31] Surveys were tampered with, false names were appended, and between the time when the survey was completed and when the agency obtained the necessary clearances and land appropriations (usually years), the number of people residing in the settlement had changed, thus demanding a new survey and setting much of the same process in motion again. The complex inscriptive chains necessary for bureaucratic surveillance, in other words, became equally complex chains of social influence, implicating actors and purposes that far exceeded those of the state.

The significance of these inscriptive chains stems from the fact that they are the precise means by which the state is made continuously present in low-income neighborhoods: it is through its written signature, Veena Das argues, that the state finds its way into everyday life. Reports, surveys, identification cards, and other civic insignia bring the state into the life of such neighborhoods by tying social statuses and subjectivities to state categories—such as below poverty line or pre-1990 resident—which are then linked to particular social entitlements, such as subsidized food or an eighteen square meter plot in cases of eviction. But these documentary circuits also embed the state in popular society, thereby giving forms of life without legal standing a position from which to not only manipulate records, but also make citizenship claims.[32] Procuring a locally registered ration card, receiving an official electricity bill addressed to one's *jhuggi*, or registering a neighborhood welfare association through the Co-Operative Societies Act provided proof of legality by nature of these documents' incorporation into normal bureaucratic circuits, even though these documents in themselves have nothing to do with housing tenure.[33] Politicians and bureaucrats acknowledged *jhuggi* dwellers' document-backed occupancy claims historically both to cultivate vote banks, as well as because those documents implicated the state in the formation and life of their settlements: settlement histories are also state histories.[34]

By the dawn of the new millennium, government as "rule by records" hence faced an avalanche of numbers, lists, and records produced with state imprint, but mobilized to rework the state's very order.[35] That those living in *jhuggis* are often Muslim, Dalit or from so-called other backward castes, or otherwise socially depressed, and hence constitutionally protected, meant that even when *jhuggi* colonies were threatened with demolition, the judiciary could easily be moved to issue stay orders—which postponed demolition, often indefinitely—to protect the "right to life" of the community, or by noting that slums were actively settled by state agents and were the product of a planning system that failed to provide the low-income housing mandated by the Master Plan.[36] As a result, despite sustained state efforts to reduce the growth of *jhuggi* colonies through the 1990s, their number almost doubled over this period.

In the early 2000s, however, there was a huge increase in public interest litigations (PILs) filed against settlements by resident welfare associations (RWAs)—property owners' associations mobilized around quality of life and neighborhood security issues.[37] Combined with the announcement of Delhi's successful bid to host the 2010 Commonwealth Games, which the chief minister declared Delhi's top priority,[38] this placed land agencies under increasing pressure from both above and below to clean up the city. In the late 1990s, the courts increasingly took notice of "the dismal and gloomy picture of such jhuggi/jhopries coming up regularly,"[39] and in 2002 observed that "it would require 272 years to resettle the slum dwellers" according to existing procedures.[40] This set of conditions was incompatible with Delhi's imagined world-class future, so the courts—which had begun to endorse explicitly the vision of making Delhi a showpiece, world-class, and heritage city at the time—responded to the increasingly frequent demands of RWAs by intervening in slum matters and rebuking state agencies for failing to address the "menace of illegal encroachment" and slums.[41]

However, when the courts pushed state agencies to more aggressively clear slums, judges were befuddled by messy ground realities, missing government records, and incomplete surveys. The courts found themselves in a position where they were unable to even assess the size of the problem, not to mention issue informed action orders. For example, in a case against a *jhuggi* colony in South Delhi, the High Court stated: "There are several controversies, claims and counter claims made by the learned counsel for the parties. The records are, however, scanty and the said claims and counter claims cannot be decided on the basis of existing material and documents on record."[42] In many instances, the ownership of the land occupied by settlements itself was ambiguous, putting the court in the strange position of being prepared to order a demolition, but not knowing which agency was obligated to carry out the order.

Such an absence of cadastral precision was widespread in slum-related cases, which led to the absence of a synoptic vision by which upper-level bureaucrats and the courts could "survey a large territory at a glance" and govern from a distance."[43] For the sociologist of science Bruno Latour, such "action at a distance" relies on a "cascade" or relay of measurements and inscriptions (e.g., survey registers) that can be combined and simplified into more generalizable and thus legible representations of the territory (e.g., maps and statistical tables) as they move up the chain of administrative command to "centers of calculation," such as courtrooms and centralized government offices.[44] The absence of accurate baseline surveys in Delhi, however, broke this cascade, rendering knowledge of slum space highly localized rather than abstractly knowable and manipulable from above. Until accurate visual simplifications of slum space were secured (i.e., until the cascade of inscriptions was complete), bureaucrats sitting in state offices and judges in courtrooms had their hands tied, or so it seemed.

Compounding these calculative challenges was the fact that according to the Municipal Corporation, 70 percent of Delhi was "unauthorized," meaning that it violated land use codes or building bylaws in one way or another.⁴⁵ If the court were to begin removing all unauthorized land uses, most of Delhi would have to be razed, including many developments central to Delhi's world-class ambitions—such as the Vasant Kunj shopping mall complex described in Scene 1 above. Thus, strict enforcement of the Master Plan or development codes, which had been avoided for almost fifty years, would lead to not just a slum-free city, but also a business-, mall-, and industry-free city. Recognizing this dilemma, the Municipal Corporation submitted in the High Court that the problem of unauthorized constructions and slums is "mammoth in nature—and cannot be controlled by simply dealing under the existing laws or under the provisions of [Delhi's] master plan."⁴⁶ [Rational bureaucratic procedures and calculative planning, in other words, were not up to the task of world-class city making.]

The courts responded to this dilemma by abandoning the system of rule by records, which was based on the requirement that state agencies upon whose land *jhuggis* were settled create map- and survey-based simplifications of the occupied land. Instead of requiring these complex and increasingly politicized calculative procedures, the courts started using a surrogate indicator to identify illegality: the "look" of space. That is, the judiciary started to adopt the position that settlements of *jhuggis* were illegal not just because they occupied public land, a position that had proven ineffective in remedying the growing menace of slums, but because they violated the world-class aesthetic.

I explore the conditions that made such aesthetic judgments possible in chapters 2, 3, and 4. Chapter 2, "The Power of Property," examines an urban governance experiment called Bhagidari—a word meaning "participation" in Hindi—that gave RWAs and the property owners they represent increased access to state decision-making channels in Delhi. If the urban poor have been able to secure housing historically by using documentary and patronage ties to implicate themselves in the spaces of the local state, then Delhi's Bhagidari Scheme, I show, had the effect of gentrifying the state by tuning these same spaces to the quality-of-life and civic demands of RWAs. Despite being celebrated for enhancing citizen-government partnership, this scheme empowered property owners, allowing them to use state channels to extend their codes of civility and appearance beyond their homes and neighborhoods and across the whole of urban space. The world-class city is thus founded on not only speculative theories of ever-rising land prices (the focus of chapter 1, "World-Class City Making"), but also the glorification of property ownership as a foundation of urbanity.

In chapter 3, "Nuisance Talk," I consider how propertied codes of civility and appearance became normalized into a popular aesthetic sensibility in millennial Delhi. I do so by tracing how property owners' everyday depictions of the nuisance and incivility of slums moved from neighborhood lay talk into an organizing lens for remaking the city. As this nuisance talk—a type of speech rooted in localized, class-specific habits and appropriations of space—was taken up by the media, the state, and the judiciary, it helped consolidate an aesthetic consensus concerning who and what belongs in the world-class city. Slums in this new aesthetic discourse were self-evidently out of place.

Nuisance, an inherently aesthetic category used to identify sensory revulsion, is a long-standing type of descriptive utterance in India: "that slum is gross," or "that street stinks." Yet as seemingly benign, descriptive statements of slums as nuisances—statements even slum residents would be unlikely to dispute—entered state and judicial discourse, they acquired performative effects that allowed the simple identification of unsightliness to carry statutory force. I document this process in chapter 4, "Aesthetic Criminalization." Reviewing court documents in slum-related cases in Delhi from the past thirty years and drawing on detailed observations of court proceedings and the practical means by which judges "see" and classify distant territories, I here show how the judiciary was able to order the massive demolition of slums based on their affront to world-class aesthetic codes. Specifically, by reinterpreting the category of public nuisance to include not only objects or actions but also entire population groups, the judiciary increasingly classified slums, for the first time in postcolonial India, as nuisances, the remedy for which became removal—the same as might apply to an overflowing dumpster or sewage pond.

Chapters 2, 3, and 4 together aim to show how a certain world-class aesthetic was put in place in millennial Delhi—a "distribution of the sensible," to borrow Rancière's phrase, that delimited sensory experience, setting the boundary between order and disorder, the visible and the invisible, and thereby allowing the city's "governors," be they planners, politicians, or elite neighborhood associations, to rule by aesthetics.[47] The remainder of the book turns to the complex ways in which *jhuggi* dwellers have appropriated the world-class aesthetic, turning it in another direction.

AESTHETIC POLITICS

To explore the contradictory process by which codes of appearance are both imposed externally and appropriated through inner faculties, I use an analytic of the aesthetic that treats sensory experience as a vibrant site of political contestation that while informed by rationality is not reducible to it. According to Rancière the aesthetic is "a system of *a priori* forms determining what presents itself to sense experience," although the a priori here is not founded on a transcendental sublime, as is the case for Immanuel Kant, but rather in social structures that appear or are handed down *as though* they are fixed and natural.[48] For Kant, when "we find ourselves concurring spontaneously in an aesthetic judgment, able to agree that a certain phenomenon is sublime or beautiful, we exercise a precious form of intersubjectivity, establishing ourselves as a community of feeling subjects linked by a quick sense of our shared capacities."[49] Yet Kant's community—a "community of sense" in Rancière's language—while potentially emancipatory, can easily slip into a means of hegemony. This is because the aesthetic takes root in the sensuous immediacies of the individual while simultaneously bonding them to a greater whole—the "community of feeling subjects." What through social and perceptual training strikes one as individual taste—rooted in one's own inner faculties—is, in a hegemonic order, the affective material that secures our sometimes unwitting promotion of a common good defined through hegemonic norms.

Recall the example of Gopal from Scene 3 above, who said, in the face of his own possible displacement, that the world-class city will be beautiful. What is profound about Gopal's utterance is that while it was his own aesthetic judgment, it simultaneously seemed to have an objective rooting, as if it were inscribed on a map that anyone could look at and agree on. This is what Rancière means when he defines the distribution of the sensible [*le partage du sensible*] as "the system of self-evident facts of sense perception that simultaneously discloses the existence of something in common"—a shared aesthetic disposition—as well as "who can have a share in what is common to the community."[50] For Gopal, the beauty of the world-class city was a self-evident fact, known just by looking; even while he recognized that the settlement that housed him had no part in that community (the world-class city), he participated in what was common to it. In this way, what I am calling rule by aesthetics consists not just of the deployment of standardized aesthetic sensibilities for partitioning and ordering things—the work of the state, the judiciary, political elites, or broadly defined governors—which is the focus of the first part of the book. It also stems from the complex ways in which these aesthetic sensibilities are established among a community of sense—including those who have no ostensible part in *le partage*—shaping what they see and can say, even when they might disagree otherwise.[51]

The English phrase "the distribution of the sensible," from the French *le partage du sensible*, is somewhat inadequate, even awkward, due to the fact that the French *partage* can have two opposite meanings: "to have in common, to share" or "to divide, to share out."[52] Despite this awkwardness, what I find compelling about Rancière's theory of the aesthetic as the "distribution of the sensible" is that the *partage* (as the dividing up and sharing out) of parts and positions that it puts in place also shapes, as he says, "the manner in which something in common *lends itself to participation* and in what way various individuals have [or do not have] a part in this distribution."⁵³ In other words, it sets what is shared—what lends itself to participation—even by those with no share: the politically abandoned, the "part with no part." This is the question Gopal's statement motivates us to ask: Why does he participate in the language of authority? Why does he partake in the world-class aesthetic—a particular regime of partitioning the beautiful from the ugly, that which belongs from that which does not—when it seems against his interest to do so? What I take Rancière to be arguing, and what I find Gopal and his Shiv Camp neighbors instructing us to notice, is that any social order—the distribution of parts and positions in a community—produces and is produced by an aesthetic order—the distribution of the sensible—which shapes how differently placed individuals see and what they can say, what gets recognized as speech and what is heard as mere noise, and thus who has the talent to speak in sensible terms. In the latter part of the book (chapters 5 and 6), I explore the performative possibilities in *jhuggi* dwellers' appropriation of dominant aesthetic codes, arguing that statements like Gopal's—statements by the excluded that seem to take up dominant norms of appearance—should be read not as descriptive statements of belief or signs of resignation, but rather as experiments in the seeable and the sayable aimed at garnering recognition as legitimate subjects of discourse: they are efforts to *take part* in order to *have a part*.

But before getting there, let me make clear the degree to which *jhuggi* dwellers' political demands were rendered mere noise in millennial Delhi, for it is only with an understanding of the constrained environment within which they found themselves that these experiments make sense. As I mentioned above, through the 1990s settlers and their advocates found great success preventing or postponing displacement by intervening in the documentary circuitry of the state or, when all else failed, by appealing to the judiciary to protect their right to life. The Supreme Court opened the door for this type of plea when, in a landmark decision in 1985, it challenged the Bombay Municipal Corporation's eviction of pavement dwellers for violating their right, as citizens, to livelihood, a component of the right to life.⁵⁴ In 1997, the Supreme Court strengthened the occupancy rights of the urban poor further, stating that "Article 19(1)(e) [of the Indian Constitution] accords right to residence and settlement in any part of India as a fundamental right."⁵⁵

The reinterpretation of nuisance law I describe in chapter 4, and the form of aesthetic rule that it codified, fundamentally transformed how the right to life was recognized in millennial Delhi. Specifically, the classification of *jhuggi* dwellers as nuisances redefined them not as a depressed social group whose right to life was subject to great risk, but as themselves sources of risk to property-owning citizens' right to life. My review of legal judgments here specifically shows how the basic statement "slums are illegal" and reference to *jhuggi* colonies as "illegal encroachments"—common, almost taken-for-granted utterances in millennial Delhi—gained widespread circulation in judicial discourse only after the equation of slums with nuisance in the early 2000s. From this point on, *jhuggi* dwellers became objects—nuisances, encroachers—to be managed, not citizens warranting equal protection.[56]

There are numerous examples of this new judicial position, but the case of Nangla Machi is particularly instructive for the boldness with which the Supreme Court turned down the right to life plea of the 2,800 households that once lived in this multigenerational settlement. Nangla Machi was located in central Delhi, not far from the Supreme Court building, and it predominantly housed Dalit laborers.[57] The Special Leave Petition submitted by Nangla Machi's lawyer made note of this fact, and it shared all the other features of previous, successful right to life petitions: "The citizens have a right to life, a right which cannot be exercised without [a] proper place to live," and "the demolition of said slum without ensuring proper relocation of its poor residents is in total violation of their fundamental right of Right to Shelter, enshrined under Article 21 of the Constitution as interpreted by this Hon'ble Court in its various judgements [*sic*]."[58] The Bench responded definitively in 2006: "When you are occupying illegal land, you have no legal right, what of talk of fundamental right, to stay there a minute longer."[59] Residents of *jhuggi* colonies in millennial Delhi hence found themselves self-evidently out of place, cast as outsiders in a city they had considered home for decades, and relegated to a state of abandonment—a condition in which, Agamben writes, one "is not, in fact, simply set outside the law and made indifferent to it but *abandoned* by it, that is, exposed and threatened on the threshold in which law and life, outside and inside, become indistinguishable."[60]

This is the context in which I entered the settlement I call Shiv Camp. During the course of my fieldwork, a court case was being heard in the Delhi High Court over the settlement's status, and on two separate occasions during the twelve months that I spent visiting Shiv Camp in 2007 and 2008, state bulldozers descended upon the settlement, razing around a quarter of its *jhuggis*. Like settlers elsewhere in Delhi, Shiv Camp residents found limited scope for judicial redress; similarly, they found that the documentary credentials of belonging they had so carefully assembled over the previous years went unrecognized: politicians and bureaucrats, after all, had little power in the face of orders from India's upper courts. How, then, were they to stake their claim to the city?

I was initially unprepared to address this question. My entry point into the complex and charged field of land politics and slum demolitions in Delhi was a network of slum-based organizations and unions called Sajha Manch (Joint Platform). During my initial research in 2005, I was involved in the legal analysis and documentation of slum demolitions with the Hazards Centre, the research and support NGO associated with Sajha Manch. The vibrant group of activists with whom I interacted in my early months in Delhi (and who helped keep me abreast of events across the city throughout my following twenty-four months of fieldwork) had been incredibly successful over the preceding years in mobilizing settlers and utilizing patronage, documentary, and judicial channels to prevent demolition. I learned from this inspiring and eclectic group of slum-based youth, Gandhian old timers, radicalized social workers, and ultra-left and communist student leaders what a community meeting looked like, how to do the right *nāre-bāzī* (sloganeering)—*sangharsh hamārā nārā hai, sangharsh hamārā nārā* (struggle is our slogan)—and what true *sangharsh* (resistance) consisted of.

When I entered Shiv Camp shortly after the Municipal Corporation demolished over a hundred of its *jhuggis* in an unannounced raid in 2007, such *sangharsh* was notable for its absence. In fact, like Gopal, most residents described their possible eviction as a necessary step to beautify the city, even adopting the nuisance talk activist property owners used to characterize slum incivility. To many of my activist comrades, this signaled the lack of *jāgriktā* (awakening) they saw holding back a true political movement. Delhi's slum-based activists were not alone in offering this reading. Prominent scholarly accounts also question the "historical agency" of the global slum dweller.[61] Javier Auyero and Debora Swistun, in their study of a polluted Argentine shantytown, describe the absence of collective resistance as an effect of environmental uncertainty and the "confused and mistaken beliefs people hold," a status of degraded life that hinders their ability to imagine a world otherwise—what the authors call a condition of "hopeful submission."[62] In Loïc Wacquant's influential study of "advanced marginality," he argues that the American black ghetto and the French *banlieue*—and he extends his argument to informal settlements through a brief discussion of Brazilian *favelas*—are functionally disconnected not just from the global economy, but also from politics, operating as "mere warehouses for supernumerary populations that no longer have any identifiable economic or political utility."[63] Such narratives, I argue in chapter 3, sustain the territorial stigmatization of slums and those who live in them. But even literature that aims to recover subaltern political agency through a focus on the organizational capacity and collective resistance of the urban poor offers little sense of what politics look like when traditional patronage, documentary, and judicial channels of claims-making are foreclosed, as is so common in places that face economic pressure to insert vernacular land markets into global capital circuits (see chapter 1)—what some call the globalization of gentrification.[64]

While acts of heroic resistance—of bodies strewn before bulldozers and mass arrests—do take place and are to be celebrated, when viewed through the rhythms of everyday life in a settlement they prove to be exceptional, the outcome of concentrated outrage mediated through far more mundane struggles over what it means to belong to a place and over the materials for convincing others of that belonging. In this sense, the presence or absence of collective protest or insurgency is a strange basis for explaining political struggle in settlements.[65] Shiv Camp residents, for example, did encamp en masse in front of the office of their elected Member of Parliament; they did block the Municipal Corporation bulldozers set upon razing their *jhuggis*; they did do their *nare-bazi*, file a court petition, and launch a hunger strike against the demolition—all actions that we would tend to count as *sangharsh*. But these actions explain little of how settlers actually cultivated the capacity to be heard in a city that no longer wanted them. I therefore turn to the everyday doings and sayings of Shiv Camp residents who, like Gopal, took the world-class city up in their own imagination. Just as under the earlier, calculative mode of government when settlers appropriated the normative workings of the state by implicating themselves in its inscriptive chains, I suggest that partaking in the normative workings of dominant aesthetic codes offers a similar way to implicate everyday life in the workings of power, transforming it toward other ends. In other words, I turn to a domain of subaltern aesthetic politics often glossed over by scholars and activists as consent or resignation.

I make this argument in chapter 5, "World-Class Detritus," beginning in the immediate aftermath of a demolition raid in Shiv Camp. Recording residents' diverse characterizations of their own settlement as an aesthetic eyesore, I show how the world-class aesthetic became the implicit ordering framework residents used to explain their precarious position. Yet rather than treat such statements of unbelonging as a sign of resignation or inner belief, I trace their usage into a number of different performative settings—from the home, to the courtroom, to public forums—showing their entailments to be far more complex than we might initially expect. While these statements at once upheld the vision of a sanitized, slum-free city, they simultaneously allowed residents to make their aspirations intelligible on terms sensible to the world-class city. By taking part in the world-class aesthetic, they seek to become part of the collective city-visioning process, positioning themselves to potentially—against all odds—turn the city imagined in another direction.

After examining the performative possibilities of taking up the world-class aesthetic in their everyday speech and public engagements in chapter 5, I turn in chapter 6, "The Propriety of Property," to the specific terms on which settlers imagine and speak of the future city. Specifically, I trace how residents adopted a particular "slum future"—government resettlement—and invested it with ethical force aimed at transforming how those who live in a world-class city, even on its margins, are placed. In light of the state's celebration of property ownership as a pathway to legal recognition and the speculative profits the land market promised, Shiv Camp residents often entered a speculative register in describing resettlement, transforming it from a geography of banishment into a geography of hope. Yet while a refined vision of resettlement provides a foundation for settlers to make claims and assert their place within the world-class city, it also reinforces a model of propertied citizenship that stigmatizes and further excludes those who continue to rely on public and common land.

The conclusion thus traces the rise of new policies of inclusive growth aimed at transforming slum land into legible and monetized property markets. In the wake of a series of corruption and governance crises in the aftermath of the Commonwealth Games, and a more general tarnishing of the image of the world-class city, a period that marks the end of millennial Delhi, the Delhi government rebranded Delhi as "the caring city." Amidst popular calls for enhanced systems of public accountability, inclusive growth emerged as a new paradigm of development in which the property market was construed as the core technology for allowing the urban poor to—in the language of the Ministry of Urban Housing and Poverty Alleviation—"create and share in the wealth of the nation." Along with a renewed commitment to calculative techniques for monitoring population and territory, such as biometric ID cards and comprehensive digital land maps, inclusive growth aims to use land titling to transform property markets into mechanisms of both financial and political inclusion for the poor. But under conditions of such market rule, the urban poor find that the propertied citizenship on offer is accessible only by submitting to displacement and resettlement. As a result, inclusion ironically comes at the expense of a place in the city. The contradiction at the heart of the world-class city hence lies in the fact that its future depends more than ever not on middle-class and elite buy-in, but rather on the participation of the urban poor—the very group being expelled to the margins—in the now anemic housing market.

While recent events in Delhi have precipitated an attempted return to a more calculative mode of government, the dream of the world-class city goes on, albeit in a far less confident form. And, like all popular imaginaries, the world-class city emerges only through the collective vision of its adherents. It is a loosely defined sense of what the city is and ought to be, and it gains material traction only to the extent that it is adopted and elaborated in residents' daily practices and habits. As an aesthetic idealization, the world-class city clarifies what does and does not belong, but it leaves considerable room for different meanings to be applied to it. Oriented toward producing aesthetic, not ideological, consensus, the world-class city tells us little, in other words, about how to reconcile competing world-class interests: shopping malls and high-rise towers as much as secluded neighborhood parks or heritage monuments fit the world-class "look." Yet the different real estate, amenity, and heritage interests these physical structures represent rub up against each other in the actual process of world-class city making.[66] In other words, while the world-class city forges an aesthetic consensus, there is considerable room for difference in its operationalization. The place of the informal settlement remains problematic throughout, yet as the shifting terrain of city making in Delhi makes clear, aesthetic politics profoundly shape how the urban future is understood and fought for. *Rule by Aesthetics* argues that aesthetic politics not only provide a powerful foundation for governing space and populations under conditions of rapid growth and spatial transformation, but also will play an increasingly integral role in how the twenty-first century metropolis is shaped. Who participates in the aesthetic imagination of the future and how the capacity to participate in such politics is cultivated among those historically excluded are perhaps the key political questions confronting India's increasingly urban future.

1

World-Class City Making

PICTURING THE FUTURE

In millennial Delhi, talk of the world-class city was everywhere. The new Delhi Master Plan emerged with the explicit goal of transforming Delhi into a world-class city. The chief minister inaugurated every state ceremony with reference to this imagined future, and city residents were constantly reminded of this impending transformation of self and city through the media's campaign to prepare them for the 2010 Commonwealth Games, hosted by Delhi, and other mega-events promised to follow. But how do you make a world-class city?

According to A. K. Jain, the commissioner of planning in the Delhi Development Authority (DDA), "making Delhi a world-class city means building high quality sports facilities, creating a clean environment, and beautification of the city."[1] The minister of state for finance and planning proclaimed: "The urban planning of Delhi entails providing the city with adequate and quality urban and civic infrastructure to bring it on par with most developed metropolises of the world." Broadly construed, a world-class city is an idealized vision of a modern, privatized, and slum-free city assembled from transnationally circulating images of other so-called global cities. "Delhi might one day compete with the urban waterfront of London or Paris," read one headline. "Delhi will be among world's top 10 cities, says Mayor," pronounced another.[3] As Partha Chatterjee writes, "this idea of the new post-industrial globalized metropolis" was heavily influenced by "the intensified circulation of images of global cities through cinema, television, and the internet as well as through the Indian middle classes' far greater access to international travel."[4]

But the world-class city is more than a mental image. It is also a set of material processes, part of a speculative project of attracting capital investment and fixing it in (and in turn fixing) the city. In India, this is a project executed largely through the valorization of the land market and by constructing urban real estate as an undervalued asset, ready to be tapped as a frontier of capitalist growth. It is thus no coincidence that state officials and politicians began articulating the goal of turning Delhi into a slum-free city and giving it a world-class look at the precise moment when the government sought to liberalize the land market by converting what it called "underutilized" public land, including that occupied by informal slum settlements, into commercially exploitable private property.[5]

This chapter discusses the processes underlying this transformation of land-as-the-material-basis-of-shelter and -production into real estate—a financial instrument for producing profit through the commodification of space.[6] But to draw in an audience willing to invest in Indian real estate, the government's claim of underutilized land had to be referenced to a higher potential use. That is, a vision of a higher value future was required to transform action in the present. I focus here on a powerful technology that the real estate industry and the Indian state has used for picturing such a future: poverty projections.

In recent years, private think tanks and consulting firms, most notably McKinsey & Company, have used proprietary economic models to produce figures predicting an imminent boom in the size of what they call "the great Indian middle class." These figures have circulated widely in investor reports, the business press, and mutual fund prospectuses, presenting a predicted decrease in poverty as a sign of rising consumer demand. Poverty projections, like all predictive models, are devices that organize thoughts, feelings, and actions by constituting fields for future intervention.[7] Predictions of future income levels and consumer purchasing power hence create visions of economic possibility, encouraging real estate developers and investors to make risk calculations according to their current market position. Expectations of rising consumer demand suggest that current supply is inadequate or will become inadequate in the near future. This reading of scarcity in the present triggers rising land valuations and pressure to increase land supply—slums are bulldozed, public land auctioned, and urban peripheries expanded. While economic conditions in the present are the presumed foundation of projections of the future, it is the vision of that possible future, crystallized in the image, that directs present action. In other words, as the possibility of a foretold outcome takes shape, affect accrues in the projections themselves.[8]

As this occurs, a strange displacement can unfold: the importance of present economic conditions, which presumably undergird the projection, recedes. What matters now is the future, and how present action is oriented toward that future. Simply put, the projected image (e.g., a curve showing falling poverty, rising mortgage rates, or inverted bond yields) seems to stand on its own, *pointing to the future*, not to the conditions of its making. This is especially true when the measures of present conditions are difficult to interpret on their own, are opaque or concealed behind complicated technical exercises, are produced by bodies of experts whose calculations are considered reliable, or are based on large and complicated datasets that are updated only every so often.[9] Such is the case with poverty projections, which require massive datasets and chains of assumptions to generate a stable picture of poverty, and which expert bodies spend months or years assembling. Given these conditions, the picture in question, once formed, stands almost on its own, with even greater affective intensity than other images: it has an underlying meaning (its presumed relation to the data that produced it), but that meaning is either inaccessible to the viewer or, at the least, secondary to the larger story it tells. In the case of poverty projections, it is the connection between field measures of material conditions in the country, such as the nutritional status of the population, and the picture of poverty that recedes, while the story that picture tells—of a prosperous economic future, for example—expands, like a myth.

This chapter proceeds by describing recent changes in India's land market and the importance of poverty trends in shaping confidence in this market, after which I turn to this almost mythical character of poverty projections—that is, the way they become unanchored from their original referents and point to the future. By contrasting McKinsey's figures predicting a poverty-free future with estimates based on government surveys that show persistent deprivation, I show poverty lines to be aesthetic as much as they are calculative. This points to how central image work is to the project of world-class city making, the various contradictions of which I turn to in the rest of the book.

REAL ESTATE AS SPECULATIVE VEHICLE

Until the late 1990s, Delhi's land was managed by a policy of socialized land. As codified in the Delhi Master Plan, this policy had three main components. First, according to the Delhi Development Act (1957), the DDA was granted monopoly control over the acquisition, development, and disposal of all urban land. This defined land in Delhi as *public* and was arguably the largest land nationalization program in the history of urban India.[10]

Empowering the DDA to acquire more than 35,000 acres of land through the Land Acquisition Act, the policy was initiated specifically to prevent forms of land speculation that had begun to impede new emigrants' access to affordable housing. Second, Delhi had no formal private property system, as all land was leased from the state, and all private land sales had to be deemed to be in the public interest before receiving approval. Third, the Master Plan entitled the poorest income classes to 25 percent of residential units in the city.[11]

In 1991, India began a gradual process of economic liberalization, devaluing the rupee, lifting import restrictions, privatizing state-run enterprises, and more generally dismantling the instruments of the command economy. In the mid-1990s, the World Bank, the Asian Development Bank, the US Agency for International Development, and a host of private consultancies began publishing reports highlighting the central role of the land market in putting India on track to a high-growth future. By deregulating this market and inserting once-public land into the marketplace, the Indian economy, so these institutions argued, would not only be able to mobilize a huge reserve of untapped capital, but also attract foreign investment—a necessary step to finance cities' world-class infrastructure needs.[12] The World Bank's India Urban Strategy Paper thus states that the preliberalized system of land administration "effectively 'froze' large blocks of the urban capital stock," creating "a shortage of basic infrastructure capital." It did not, however, acknowledge that this "frozen" land, outside of a formal system of property and therefore largely inaccessible to property developers, housed more than 50 percent of Delhi's population in squatter and unauthorized settlements—a pattern similar in most Indian cities.[13]

Making Indian cities more bankable—that is, transforming urban land into capital—required aggressive land reform, the only means by which India would be able to meet and sustain high rates of GDP growth (the stated goal of the central government since the mid-1990s was maintaining an annual growth rate of at least 8 percent).[14] As the World Bank wrote, "idle GOI [Government of India] land holdings or constraints on land usage in many cities—such as public land holdings or encroached infrastructure—often represent an enormous 'implicit tax.' This tax corresponds to the foregone imputed rent that could have accrued to residents of the city." Public land, so the story went, was undervalued and underutilized; this "forgone imputed rent" represented a new investment frontier, a new source of potential profit that could be capitalized. Generating capital in the city—and thus national economic growth, since urban centers contribute more than 60 percent of India's GDP—required privatizing urban land.[15]

The McKinsey Global Institute, the economic research arm of McKinsey & Company, a management consulting firm that is one of the major players in economic reform debates in India, took this argument a step further when it published a more than 700-page, bottom-up study of "the barriers to productivity and output growth" in India. Noting, in 2001, that India's GDP "is growing at a mere six per cent a year, compared to China's ten per cent," McKinsey argued that "with the right new policies, GDP growth of 10 per cent per year is within India's reach." Shunning common economic arguments about the causes of restricted growth rates, McKinsey's report, titled *India: The Growth Imperative*, claimed that product and land market barriers were the greatest hindrance to India's growth—not the country's fiscal deficit, capital market distortions, restrictive labor laws, or poor infrastructure, as economists commonly argued.[16]

Emphasizing the need for land market deregulation, the report, the advisory committee for which included high ranking members of India's Ministry of Finance, claimed that across all industries, "we found that product and land market barriers are four to five times more likely than government ownership to constrain output growth" (82). Overall, McKinsey calculated that "land market distortions account for close to 1.3 per cent of lost [GDP] growth a year" (7). These distortions included unclear ownership, counterproductive taxation and inflexible zoning, and rent and tenancy laws. Boosting its overall argument, the report gave the example of the retail sector, asserting that "allowing FDI [foreign direct investment] and removing land market barriers will allow retail supermarkets to increase productivity more than four-fold from the current 20 per cent to almost 90 per cent of US levels in 10 years" (69). It further showed that 75 percent of the barrier to labor productivity in the construction sector was caused by land market distortions (111).

One of McKinsey's major recommendations logically extended from this analysis: to make land procurement easier for private firms, which would increase investment and competition in *all* economic sectors. Coupled with other deregulations, it said that land privatization "will allow India to achieve a growth rate of 10 per cent a year" (182). The sentiment that land-use laws stifled urban development was (and still is) widely shared within the real estate industry, which read the state's policies to protect the poor from displacement from public land as a misplaced subsidy that detered the true driver of poverty reduction: growth. As Rajiv Singh, the vice chairman of DLF—India's largest developer, which also built the DLF Emporio mall shown in Figure I.1—announced:

> The whole system was not and still is not geared to rapid provisioning of infrastructure. There's too much political freedom, too many legal rights, too much media. By contrast, I was in Shanghai recently and one day passed a bunch of huts beside the road. The next day they were all gone. The third day there were a bunch of guys rolling out sod and

planting trees. And on the fourth day they inaugurated a park. In India they first debate everything.¹⁷

In a more technocratic register than Singh's flippant call to replace slum huts with parks, McKinsey justified the need for capital generation via land privatization through a diagram titled "International Benchmarks for Investment Rates," which it used to imply that India's relatively low rate of GDP growth (5.8 percent) through the 1990s was related to its low level of investment as a percentage of overall GDP (24.5 percent). China (32.9 percent), Indonesia (27.5 percent), and other emerging markets on a higher growth trajectory, it showed, had much higher rates of investment. Increasing investment, and foreign direct investment in particular, was necessary to increase GDP, and privatization and monetization of the land market was one of the most important strategies to bring this about.¹⁸ A. K. Jain of the DDA echoed this sentiment when he said of Delhi, "until land is used as a resource—a precious commodity—we won't achieve the goal of planned development, meaning a city free of slums."¹⁹ McKinsey more recently affirmed that land monetization must be a central strategy for funding urban investment in India, given the country's low per capita income and municipal tax revenue, if it is to avoid urban crisis.²⁰ It is in this light that a series of land market reforms initiated in the late 1990s and deepened in the 2000s should be seen as efforts to transform land into a new financial instrument: real estate.

Once the goal of spurring economic growth and competing for foreign investment with other emerging markets had been solidified as both national and city-level policy priorities, land market liberalization began in Delhi. In 1999 the DDA launched its first commercial auctions, selling un- or underused land (e.g., parks, vacant land, wedding grounds) that it had acquired for public purposes in order to generate revenue and to encourage capital investment in the city.²¹ In 2000, the DDA initiated its Freehold Conversion Program, which allowed leaseholders to obtain legal title to their land, thereby setting in place a system of private property relations—that is, land could be bought and sold in an unregulated market—for the first time since the DDA was established. In 2001 the DDA passed a new Cooperative Housing Society Policy, which created a direct avenue by which land allocated to associations of private users at below-market rates could be sold on the market. In 2003, the chief minister of Delhi proclaimed that the World Bank's "vision document" would become the guideline for urban governance in Delhi, which called for a rapid increase in foreign investment into real estate. Finally, in April 2005 the central government opened the real estate and construction sectors to 100 percent foreign direct investment, previously capped at 40 percent. When the Delhi Master Plan 2021 was approved in 2007, stating "Vision-2021 is to make Delhi a global metropolis and a world-class city," it cleared the books of the last remnants of the policy of socialized land by deleting the central passages mandating land reservations for the urban poor.[22]

CONJURING THE WORLD-CLASS FUTURE

Besides creating the conditions through which investors could access the land market, constructing this market as one ripe for high growth required the mobilization of new speculative discourses.[23] Markets run on hype and fear as much as fundamentals, and, as in all speculative enterprises, "profit must be imagined before it can be extracted; the possibility of economic performance must be conjured like a spirit to draw an audience of potential investors."[24] How was a high-growth future conjured for the land market and the Indian economy more generally?

Conjuring a world-class future requires putting in place a compelling urban vision that will attract foreign capital, encourage rising valuations of existing capital stock, *and* produce a citizenry desirous of cities in which they can enjoy the benefits of world-class consumption and lifestyle. As economists George Akerlof and Robert Shiller write, "high confidence tends to be associated with inspirational stories, stories about new business initiatives, tales of how others are getting rich."[25] Indian GDP, as a result of the economy's structural makeup and demographics, is overwhelmingly driven by private consumption; it made up approximately 60 percent of GDP in the mid-2000s, a much higher number than in other developing countries, such as China (~40 percent).[26] The most logical means to construct compelling growth stories favorable to long-term capital appreciation thus lay in depicting long run increases in domestic consumption. Herein entered the role of the middle class and a dominant narrative of socioeconomic transformation in India.

The story—told consistently in newspaper accounts, by politicians, and by economists banking on the Indian boom—goes something like this: India has historically been a poor country, with cripplingly high rates of poverty leaving most of the population living hand to mouth. In 1991, India began a gradual process of economic reforms, leading to a jump in economic growth for much of the 1990s and an additional boost in growth by the mid-2000s, which led it to surpass all other nations except China. With growth, so too has come a decline in poverty, and the poor are gradually morphing into a new middle class that is poised to catapult India into the ranks of the world's economic leaders. As one report proclaimed, "the Indian economy is growing from strength to strength. The fast-paced economic growth is bringing about a change in India's socioeconomic fabric. It is creating more jobs, fuelling aspirations and leading consumers to spend more."[27] Rising middle-class consumption in such accounts both symbolizes the positive effects of economic liberalization and serves as the anticipated driver of future growth. Prime Minister Manmohan Singh invoked the booming middle class in an effort to woo Saudi investors when he said: "Today, India's economy is on the move. For three years, we have witnessed growth rates of between 7.0 percent and 8.5 percent. A growing market, with a large middle class, abundant raw materials, highly trained and skilled manpower, especially in the field of science and technology, is thirsting for new investment."[28]

Leading the charge in narrating an impending explosion in the growth of the middle class were a series of proprietary datasets that constructed scenarios relating India's class composition to GDP growth. Prominent among these was the National Council of Applied Economic Research's (NCAER) report called "The Great Indian Middle Class," which was based on a marketing survey that divided the Indian population into eight income groups called the Deprived, Aspirers, Seekers, Strivers, Near Rich, Clear Rich, Sheer Rich, and Super Rich. The NCAER's rhetorical slight of hand should already be evident, as four of the eight group names included the word "rich," three signified upward mobility, and only one ("the deprived") suggested poverty. In 2005, the four categories of the rich added up to less than 1 percent of total households, making clear the irony of the NCAER's imagined class hierarchy (see Table 1.1).

Despite the near numerical absence of rich people in India, the NCAER's decision to switch away from standard income quintiles or deciles (i.e., evenly distributed categories) and to depict most class categories as

Table 1.1. THE GREAT INDIAN MARKET?

NCAER Name	Annual Income ('000 rupees)	1995 (%)	2002 (%)	2005 (%)	2010* (%)
Deprived	<90	80	72	65	52
Aspireres	91–200	18	22	26	34
Seekers	201–500	2	5	6	10
Strivers	501–1,000	0.4	1	2	3
Near Rich	1001–2,000	0.11	0.29	0.55	1.07
Clear Rich	2001–5,000	0.04	0.11	0.22	0.47
Sheer Rich	5001–10,000	0.01	0.02	0.05	0.11
Super Rich	10,000+	0.00	0.01	0.03	0.06

Source: NCAER. 2005. "The Great Indian Market: Results from the NCAER's Market Information Survey of Households." New Delhi: National Council of Applied Economic Research.
*Data for 2010 were projected.[83]

yet-to-be-filled and rich represented the first of what would be a series of rhetorical steps to conjure the image of an upwardly mobile future. One of the NCAER report's main findings thus read: "The rapid rise in incomes will lead to an even faster increase in demand for consumer durables. . . . What will power this is the increased usage [and purchase of these consumer goods] in different income classes coupled with the rise in the size of the Great Indian Middle Class."[29] Yet the middle class—which the NCAER defined as the seekers and strivers, or households that earn between 200,000 and 1,000,000 rupees per year (around $4,500–22,000 at 2000 exchange rates)—made up just over 8 percent of the population in 2005. If the growth potential of the Indian economy was largely gauged by future middle-class demand, and if the middle class was but a small minority of the overall Indian population, as these data suggest, then how could the Indian growth story sustain itself?

In 2007, McKinsey fed the NCAER's data through a proprietary econometric model to predict India's class distribution in 2025. Its report, called *Bird of Gold: The Rise of India's Consumer Class*, claimed that "over the next two decades, the country's middle class will grow from about 5 percent of the population to more than 40 percent and create the world's fifth-largest consumer market." It went on to say: "The same furious energy that made India a world-class provider of software and business services is creating a huge urban middle class."[30] McKinsey simplified the NCAER income categories by renaming the four categories of rich into a single group that it termed Globals, but did so in a way that generated results even more favorable to a rising middle class. Whereas the NCAER had found that the deprived made up 65 percent of the population of India in 2005, McKinsey claimed:

> In 1985 93 percent of the population lived on a household income of less than 90,000 rupees per year [the deprived], or about a dollar per person per day; by 2005 that proportion had been cut nearly in half, to 54 percent. We project that if India can achieve 7.3 percent annual growth over the next 20 years, 465 million more people will be spared a life of extreme deprivation.[31]

As the chart called "Escaping Poverty" shows (reprinted here as Figure 1.1), McKinsey predicted that these 465 million people would move up the imagined income ladder, swelling the ranks of the middle class and leaving only 22 percent of the population deprived by 2025. According to this model, then, the vast pool of low-income people in India today represents a future investment opportunity: poor people are portrayed as future rich people. As McKinsey wrote, investment "opportunities will blossom as millions of first-time buyers step up to cash registers," causing aggregate

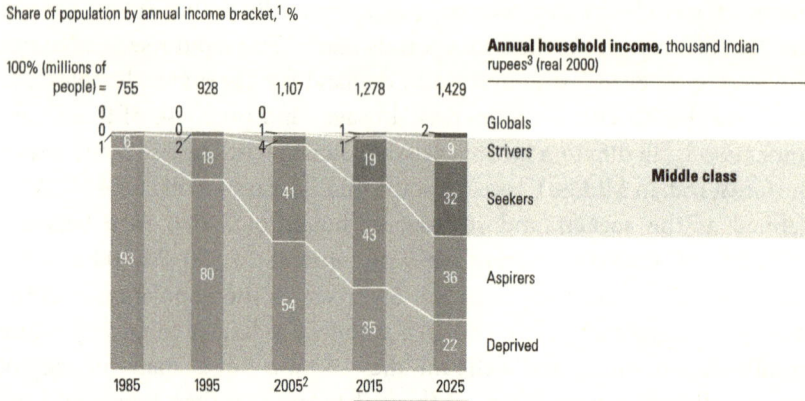

Figure 1.1. Exact reprint of exhibit 2 from "Tracking the Growth of India's Middle Class," McKinsey & Company (2007). Reprinted by permission.

consumer demand to quadruple by 2025.[32] Incorporating the NCAER's definition of the middle class (i.e., the seekers and strivers), McKinsey's model found that:

> By 2025 a continuing rise in personal incomes will spur a tenfold increase enlarging the middle class to about 583 million people, or 41 percent of the population. ... About 400 million Indian city dwellers—a group nearly 100 million people larger than the current population of the United States—will belong to households with a comfortable standard of living.[33]

According to McKinsey, the ranks of the aspirers and seekers, those households earning between 90,000 and 500,000 rupees per year, had swelled to 45 percent of the population by 2005, whereas the NCAER had found only 32 percent. Despite the fact that the NCAER data include estimates for 2005, McKinsey chose to ignore this most recent time point and instead deployed its own 2005 numbers—again, the model producing these numbers was proprietary, making it unavailable to public scrutiny. The rapid fall in the size of the deprived from 1995 to 2005 allowed McKinsey to project even more positive future trends, painting a picture in which India's poor masses were on the verge of transforming into a new consuming class—one with the means to leave their *jhuggis*, tenements, and joint family homes in favor of monthly mortgage payments in new private developments. As Llrena Searle notes, the NCAER and McKinsey data were widely reproduced in the media and in real estate prospectuses through the mid-2000s, spinning this imagined demographic transformation as one of India's growth fundamentals, what *BusinessWeek* called a "seismic wave of income growth."[34]

And, according to investment numbers, the conjuring of a future middle class worked. By 2007, the "animal spirits" of private corporations—a term John Maynard Keynes used to account for "the spontaneous urge to action" premised on confidence and belief "rather than mathematical expectations"—had awoken, sending the share of investment in overall GDP growth up to 40 percent (from 25 percent in 2001), with the influx of foreign direct investment (FDI) making up a staggering 16 percent of GDP growth.[35] The real estate sector was on the forefront of this trend, accounting for 26 percent of FDI in 2007,[36] with economists even describing the possibility of "mak[ing] India a property-driven stock market."[37] In the wake of DLF launching the largest initial public offering (IPO) in the history of India in 2007, the company's chairman said in a speech to shareholders:

> I would go so far as to say that the institutional investment from overseas has been of such high quality that it is clear that global investors, knowing fully well that the growth of India is closely linked to real estate and infrastructure development in the country, have chosen your Company to express their faith in the future of the Indian economy . . . [and this] reflects investor confidence in the DLF growth story.[38]

According to Jones Lang LaSalle, one of the world's largest real estate firms, India became the cutting edge in global real estate investment: "Total retail mall stock has been doubling every year, from a meagre one million sq ft in 2002 to a staggering 40 million sq ft in 2007 and an estimated 60 million sq ft by the end of 2008," and "office rental rates went up almost 73 percent from 07–8, and capital values went up 72.4 percent."[39] The chairman of Jones Lang LaSalle's Indian subsidiary said: "On an average, we've been growing over the last three years by 60 percent to 70 percent. . . . Even as of today, there is [a] 20 million dwelling units shortfall on the residential, so the pent-up demand is huge. That needs to be caught up."[40] Where did this estimation of pent-up demand come from? What fueled these animal spirits?[41] Again, the estimation was based on anticipated future demand, "an ever burgeoning middle class," and what were called "favourable demographics," described as an "emerging youthful, urban and relatively affluent Vanguard Class that is the driving force behind consumer spending . . . This group includes circa 120 million people and continues to expand."[42]

STATISTICAL CONJURING, MYTHIC TREND LINES

In the above quotation, DLF noted investor confidence in what it calls its "growth story," while I have been using the word "conjure" to describe the fabulous reinvention of the poor as a future elite. To conjure: "To invoke by supernatural power, to effect by magic or jugglery"; "to bring, get, move, convey, as by magic."[43] What is the conjurer's trick in these speculative stories? The premise of the NCAER and McKinsey reports is a downward sloping poverty curve, for it is the transformation of the poor into the rich that pads the promise of a sustained profit margin and ever-rising land prices. India's official poverty estimates, published by the Planning Commission, also read a gradual increase in income levels across India, with the percentage of Indians living below the official poverty line falling from 44.7 percent in 1985 to 36.2 percent in 1995, and all the way down to 27.5 percent by 2005.[44] But, as the economist Utsa Patnaik argues, this is an act of "statistical trickery": "No amount of full-page advertisements by the government in newspapers ... can alter the fact that in reality ... this country remains a Republic of Hunger."[45]

Patnaik has been arguing in recent years that the Planning Commission, the central government body that establishes the official poverty line for the country, has abandoned its own standards of poverty estimation to conceal what is in fact an increase in the incidence of poverty throughout India during the economic reform years. To understand the basis of her claim, we must briefly foray into the methods of poverty estimation in India, for it is only with a basic understanding of nutritional norms that we can begin to see the trick by which India's hundreds of millions of poor people are read as an opportunity for investment.

Since the early 1970s, poverty estimates in India have been based on establishing a poverty line defined as the monthly expenditure per person required to ensure the daily per capita consumption of 2,100 calories of food in urban areas and 2,400 calories in rural areas. Those spending below the poverty line are considered poor because they do not consume enough calories. While this is obviously a minimalist definition of poverty, including no norms for nonfood expenditure (e.g., shelter, clothing, education), it is the standard the government of India has used to define poverty for forty years, and in this line—in its trajectory (up or down) and in who lives below and above it (more people or less)—lies the image of future India. Every five years or so, the National Sample Survey Organization (NSSO) surveys hundreds of thousands of households across India, measuring total household expenditure and total food consumption, with smaller-scale surveys conducted annually. These surveys are summarized in tables that present a population distribution according to per capita monthly expenditure groups in one column alongside the daily per capita calories of food consumed by each of those groups in another. Such data are compiled for India's major cities and at the state and national level. Poverty levels can be directly observed on the NSSO's tables because they show the percentage of households whose monthly per capita consumption expenditure is not enough to meet minimum caloric norms: anyone spending at or below the expenditure level necessary to eat enough food is counted as poor.

In 1974, the Planning Commission used this very approach—called the method of "direct observation"—to establish rural and urban poverty lines of 49 and 57 rupees per person per month, respectively. This established the incidence of poverty, which was 56 percent across India. The National Sample Survey (NSS) has been completed annually since 1974. However, rather than following this method, the Planning Commission simply applies a consumer price index adjustment to the 1974 poverty line, assuming that the pattern of consumer expenditure has remained unchanged with time. This method of "indirect estimation," as Patnaik calls it, leads to widely divergent poverty numbers from those derived from the method of direct observation. This is because it fails to consider changes in consumption patterns caused by such things as a decline in common property resources and payment in kind, both of which supplement household consumption.[46] The shift away from measuring poverty based on food intake in favor of a simple price adjustment has resulted in a delinking of official poverty estimates from the Planning Commission's own nutrition norm. Official poverty trends, as a result, now reflect only the changing price of food, not households' ability to access it.

Patnaik, using the direct observation method drawn from the NSS, finds that the Planning Commission's 2005 poverty line provided enough money to consume only 1,820 and 1,835 calories per person per day in rural and urban areas, respectively—far below the 2,400 and 2,100 norms. That is, she argues that in India, there is a large and growing percentage of the population that is malnourished and *not* considered poor.[47]

After acquiring the NSS data from 1983 to 2005, I calculated the poverty rate using the direct observation method (described in Patnaik (2007, 2008)), which I then compared with the official Planning Commission estimates. I did my own calculation instead of reproducing Patnaik's data because she provides poverty estimates only for the large-sample years (1994, 2000, 2005), whereas I wanted to present annual results on the same terms as McKinsey (whose data end at 2005). My results, which I present in greater detail when I return to McKinsey's figures below, closely resemble Patnaik's findings. Like Patnaik, my numbers show that poverty in India, according to official nutritional norms, has been steadily increasing over the past twenty years. Whereas official estimates show that poverty numbers have fallen from more than 40 percent in the early 1980s to 27.5 percent by 2005, direct observation shows that the percentage of Indians with too little food has jumped from just over 50 percent to 80 percent over the same period. It is not hard to locate the source of this huge gulf in findings: for 2005, the official poverty line, as reported by the Planning Commission, was 356 rupees per person per month (~$8.2 at 2005 exchange rates) for rural areas and 539 rupees (~$12.5) for urban areas, whereas meeting minimum nutritional norms, according to my calculation using the NSS tables, actually required 890 rupees (~$20.5) for rural areas and 930 rupees (~$21.5) for urban areas.[48] This means that to be officially considered poor one had to consume less than 12 rupees (1/30th of the monthly 356 rupee poverty line, equivalent to about 27 US cents) a day in rural India, and less than 18 rupees (~42 US cents) a day in urban India.[49] Based on my calculation, the Planning Commission's estimate rendered invisible more than a half billion people who did not eat enough food every day.[50]

The political implications of the Planning Commission's statistical trickery are massive, including their use in justifying a reduction in food subsidies to the poor in the face of documented increases in malnutrition. But I offer these figures not to claim that my numbers are the truest. In 2007, a government report estimated India's poverty rate at 77 percent, while a second government committee, in 2009, using different poverty measures, came up with 38 percent.[51] This huge range in estimates, each effecting a different picture of poverty, confirms that what we might think of as long chains of assumptions are a part of all poverty measures.[52] So, rather than weigh in on poverty "truth,"[53] my aim is to examine the representational work that poverty trendlines perform, as well as the narrative afterlives of these graphic artifacts once they take on their own form and signification.[54] What happens after the complex political translation of material deprivation into a line on a page? What happens once, as Robert Chambers wrote more than twenty years ago, "poverty becomes what has been measured," once the chain of assumptions and value judgments translating "reality out there" into a line on a page recede?[55]

POVERTY MYTH

John Harriss writes of the social science of poverty measurement: "Narratives, some of them almost myths, drive the collection and interpretation of data."[56] Myth, according to Roland Barthes, is a type of depoliticized speech that produces statements that go without saying. It does so by giving them a "natural and eternal justification ... a clarity which is not that of an explanation but that of a statement of fact."⁵⁷ In this light, consider the Planning Commission's *India Vision 2020* report:

> The compounded effect of achieving the targeted annual GDP growth rate of 8.5 to 9 per cent over the next 20 years would result in a quadrupling of the real per capita income and *almost eliminating the percentage of Indians living below the poverty line*. This will raise India's rank from around 11th today to 4th from the top in 2020 among 207 countries given in the World Development Report in terms of GDP. Further, in terms of per capita GDP measured in ppp [purchasing power parity] India's rank will rise by a minimum of 53 ranks from the present 153 to 100. This will mean India will move from a low income country to an upper middle income country. This is a very real possibility for us to seize upon and realise.⁵⁸

This passage reads rising per capita GDP as a sign of poverty reduction, presenting the link between declining poverty and economic growth as a statement of fact requiring no explanation. While the report briefly acknowledges that "in spite of enormous progress in food production, nearly half the country's population still suffers from chronic undernutrition and malnutrition," it proceeds to divorce hunger from the concept of poverty in presenting a glorious Indian future in which poverty is no longer an economic problem.⁵⁹ Hunger in the present is anachronistic, the present is fixed as an already anticipated future without poverty, and the poor do not need to be, and in fact cannot be, read as poor. This is the myth of economic growth.

To Barthes, myth is a metalanguage that speaks about an already established language-object, or a sign. A sign is made up of a linguistic chain linking signifier to signified, form (a word, photograph, chart, etc.) to content (the concept with which the form is associated). In the case of poverty numbers, we might consider this sign to be the chain of assumptions linking various formal measures of deprivation (nutritional status, the frequency of meals eaten, etc.) to the concept of poverty. In other words, nutritional and expenditure data are the signifier and the statement "the number of people spending less than 539 rupees a month has decreased" is the signified.⁶⁰ Together, these two elements make up a linguistic sign ("poverty has decreased"), the raw material upon which mythical speech operates.⁶¹ Myth then takes hold of that initial sign (the signifier-signified link: nutritional data-"poverty" in this case) and treats it as itself a signifier pointing to a new concept—what Barthes calls a mythical concept.

In the case of poverty numbers, the original signified "more people spend 539 rupees a month"—a statement with a stable reference to field measures—is transformed into the new meaning "the poor are becoming rich." This is where the mythical concept of economic growth appears.

A decrease in official poverty numbers, even if that decrease ignores rising hunger, signifies that economic growth solves poverty, and the picture of more people spending at least 539 rupees per month, confirms what we already know: poverty will disappear. Here again is a report by the Planning Commission, which extrapolates the fall in the official poverty rate (1.08 percent decline per annum) forward to claim: "*Poverty in India would be eliminated by 2020*, when India would be a Middle Income Country."[62] As in the above block quotation from the Planning Commission, this statement does not refer to the content of poverty (i.e., expenditure and nutritional data), making clear that "poverty," as a sign of economic conditions in India, is shorn of reference to its origins.[63] This can be visualized in Figure 1.2 as the distance between "2 Signified" and "II SIGNIFIED," which is the gap between the meaning established through the linguistic system and the mythical concept that picks up and works upon this meaning. In the mythological system, meaning derived from the linguistic system is reduced to form as it becomes the first term of the mythic sign. Meaning has value because it is the product of an initial linguistic reading: in our case, expenditure data allow us to understand that people are spending more money. When it is reduced to form, such as a line on a graph, however, that meaning loses its value and only "the letter remains."[64] Or, in our case, only the line remains, and the knowledge that rising expenditure does not necessarily mean decreasing poverty loses its value.

McKinsey's report on future consumer demand works through the same mythical concept of economic growth, constructing, this time through more visual form, the category of the deprived as a holdover from an earlier era—a remnant of an inefficient, planned economy. To visualize the mythic nature of McKinsey's celebration of India's middle-class future, I plotted the percentage of Indians who do not meet minimum nutritional norms (based on the direct observation method outlined by Patnaik 2008) on top of the McKinsey chart depicting India's escape from poverty, as shown in Figure 1.3.[65] As the figure shows, the percentage of what I have labeled the "absolute poor," which represents the undernourished, in India makes clear the image work that goes into the myth of middle-class India.

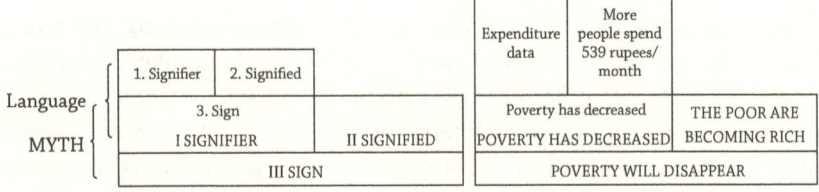

Figure 1.2. Mythic signification, as represented abstractly by Barthes (1972) on left and as is specific to Indian poverty discourse on right.

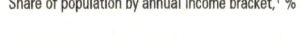

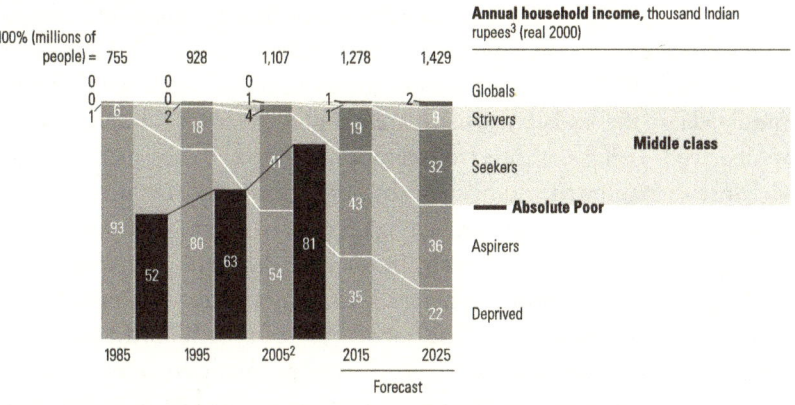

Figure 1.3. Deconstructing growth. Estimation of the percentage of absolute poor in India overlaid upon McKinsey's mythic presentation of a future without poverty.

The absolute poor, a category based on the largest survey of households across India (the NSS), shows that the era of economic reforms has, in contrast to McKinsey's claims, led to a massive increase in poverty. The rise in farmer suicides, the burgeoning population of urban slum dwellers, the decline in per capita food grain absorption, and the persistence of high rates of stunted growth in children in India throughout the 2000s all confirm this startling trend, yet the measure of malnourishment or the observation of real purchasing power do not figure in the magical incantations of middle-class growth found in McKinsey's table, for this is an image less concerned with referencing an existing reality than producing its own reality.[66]

In McKinsey's report, the actual numbers backing its figures—the chain of assumptions that produced the picture of rising incomes—are not presented. This makes it clear that the figures, as graphic artifacts, lack a stable relationship between discourse and things in the world; they point not to the numbers that ostensibly produced them, but rather to a different meaning: growth will eliminate poverty. This move from an internally referenced linguistic function—premised on a claim of representational adequacy—to an unreferenced yet naturalized meaning is what Barthes means by mythical speech. McKinsey's figure hence works more like a picture than what we typically think of as charts or figures. As Barthes says: "Everything happens as if the picture *naturally* conjured up the concept, as if the signifier [of myth] *gave a foundation* to the signified."[67]

Another McKinsey chart (see Figure 1.4), called "Winds of Change," represents an even more dramatic effort to paint poverty as an anachronism. Focusing only on urban households, McKinsey suggested that the poor were already a small minority of the urban population and that sometime around 2013 the largest income group in Indian cities would be the middle class (the seekers), when barely 6 percent of city dwellers would be deprived. Using the direct observation method, I have included atop McKinsey's graphic the number of absolute poor in Indian cities between 1985 and 2005. The trend here yet again reveals the means by which the urban poor are misidentified as an already emergent middle-income group in McKinsey's presentation. Whereas McKinsey claimed that only 13 percent of the urban population of India was deprived as of 2005, the method of direct observation suggests that more than 40 percent were poor, a number that steadily increased over the previous twenty years. [Yet in India's aspiring world-class cities, the suggestion that the middle class is *not* the most rapidly growing class would strike almost anyone as absurd: the media had already declared the English-speaking, air-conditioned car-driver the harbinger of "India rising," and the urban form in these cities was already being constructed as a playground for consumption and tourism. Slums, the traditional settlement of the urban poor, are hence anachronistic, a housing type obsolete in light of the emerging middle-class future.]

While the central government claims that India "needs to reach an economic growth rate of at least 8 percent in order to significantly reduce the incidence of poverty,"[68] McKinsey's graphics and the rhetorical strategy of narrating an impending middle-class future show that the symbolic and physical displacement of the poor—through the denial of their very

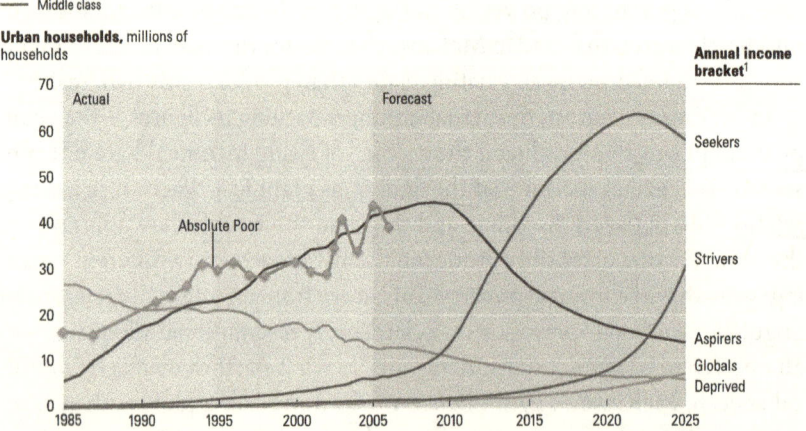

Figure 1.4. Calculation of number of "absolute poor" urban households in India plotted on top of McKinsey's (2007) exhibit from "Tracking the Growth of India's Middle Class." Reprinted by permission.

existence and through the large-scale displacement of urban squatters to attract capital investment into supposedly underutilized and vacant land—might better be read as a condition necessary to attain these rates of economic growth in the first place. In other words, these figures, by conjuring away the poor, perform economic growth.[69] The question of removing the poor would be one thing—a form of what Michael Watts calls "silent violence" driven by the goal of maximizing economic growth, regardless of the human cost.[70] But the narrative of world-class India, and especially of its world-class cities, is premised on an even more insidious equation: the poor not as obstacle, but asset; not the disappeared poor, but the consuming and entrepreneurial poor transforming themselves through the magic of economic growth. An article in *Newsweek* that appeared in February 2009, for example, during the height of the global financial meltdown, praised India's potential to lead a global recovery on the backs of the consuming poor:

> India boasts an unlikely growth driver all its own: legions of poor whose incomes have risen just enough in recent years to create powerful demands for basic goods and services.... The idea that Indian backwardness is a plus may sound absurd... [But, s]uch a large population subsisting at so low an economic base is a powerful economic driver.[71]

This vision, common in real estate prospectuses and market projections, "manages to transform even the absence of development into a sign of possible growth."[72]

In the introduction, I argued that government in Delhi works despite the absence of a comprehensive statistical picture of territory and population. I have here shown how numbers deployed for governmental ends—figures meant to educate desires and configure habits and beliefs—require no equivalence between the record and the world. They rather operate more as aesthetic objects—as pictures aimed at *performing a different reality*, not reflecting or corresponding to it. Poverty figures, I have shown, are meant to shape investor confidence, to maintain the influx of billions of dollars of foreign direct investment, to sustain the speculative rise in land prices, and to construct economic reform and land market liberalization as part of a nation-building project in the interest of the population as a whole. And, in millennial Delhi, state officials have joined this performance, ignoring material deprivation in the country, accepting McKinsey's numbers, and speaking through these images to describe the gated communities and private penthouses cropping up as housing stock to meet the demand of India's emerging consumer class. That is, the exclusive homes being built with the massive influx of investment money are not just for the wealthiest 5 percent of the population, it is claimed, but rather for the future everyday Delhiite. The growing number of people living in slums with insecure tenure and unable to afford housing elsewhere do not fit into this picture. They are anachronistic, the poor yet to disappear.

CONJURED FUTURES

This book is about the aesthetic politics of a world-class future, the way in which such a future is conjured into existence, deployed and circulated through diverse political technologies, received and practiced as a normative framework for self-government, and lived and contested in everyday life. In Scene 3 from the introduction, Gopal described his faith in the integrity of an imagined map, a faith that his potential displacement was part of a broader project of urban improvement—that his eviction would somehow make the city a better place and maybe, just maybe, a better place *for him*. Investor confidence in India's growth story, too, is based on a faith, a faith that land values will steadily climb along with the rise of India's consumer class. Each of these faiths is sustained by what I am calling aesthetic rule, a means of eliciting, fostering, and promoting a particular set of convictions and dispositions in a population through a compelling image. While the conjuring of India's "great middle class" constitutes a quite distinct set of practices of calculative expertise, it thus shares with the three scenes with which I began this book a powerful form of image work: a discursive and material mobilization of an image of the future intent on transforming the desires and dispositions, habits and habitus, affects and aversions of its consumer.

Poverty curves, I have shown, function as indicators of future economic strength. Yet while all instruments of economic prediction indicate what may come, the mythic projections offered by McKinsey elide the uncertainty of the indicated future. By "elide," I do not mean "lie." Rather, the particular picture of poverty on offer arises only through the contingent chain of assumptions that generated it. Different assumptions, as discussed above, would produce different pictures. Yet McKinsey's presentation asks us to query not this relationship, but the implications for present action of the picture supplied. This is what I meant in the introduction when I said that the world-class city is offered as an already known conclusion; it is cast in a prophetic temporality. The picture of the future is, more or less, fully supplied. What matters is not debating how present action will shape the emergent future, but rather how present action can be aligned to prepare for what is to come.[73]

The numerical conjuring of the middle class encourages the anticipation of a prosperous future and draws in an audience to evaluate existing conditions on the basis of that future. Discourses of Delhi's imminent transformation into a world-class city likewise put in place the vision of an attainable and inherently good future, allowing diverse viewers to evaluate existing uses of space on the basis of this future matrix. Like the industrial steel towns built as idealizations of the nation under India's earlier developmentalist dispensation, world-class city making and its diverse representational vehicles "visibly showcase the promise of the as-yet-unrealized future."[74] Yet while this earlier, Nehruvian city-making project elevated the worker-citizen as the ideal national subject—a subject valorized for his role in state-directed economic production, in the world-class city—the worker of yesteryear is recast as a consumer whose assent to citizenship is gauged by his contribution to ever-rising property prices.

In the National Capital Region, which includes Delhi and its surrounding satellite cities, the average price of a new flat today is more than a hundred times the mean annual income of Delhiites. Fifty-four percent of Delhi is poor,[75] yet the bulk of new housing is built for the superrich. If in Delhi, as in the rest of India, the middle class remains but a small minority, then who is buying the thousands of new penthouses being constructed every year? Real estate insiders concede that approximately 70 percent of buyers in the National Capital Region are investors, who typically purchase the properties before a single brick is laid, with only digital renderings, scale models, and vacant plots of land to assure them that their castles in the air will one day materialize.[76] These investors, in many instances the property developers themselves, purchase with the intention of flipping their properties—a practice typically repeated many times before construction is finished—as soon as prices climb enough, often packaging sets of flats together to be sold to larger institutional investors.[77] Only very late in the game, if ever, does the question of who might actually live in such flats enter the equation. With one in five completed houses lying vacant in the booming areas of the Delhi National Capital Region in 2010, real estate agents noted that "vacant stock simply shows profiteering at play in an era of exorbitant property prices" wherein builders and investors do not mind foregoing rental income—and avoiding actual end users—because of anticipated increases in property prices.[78] This is millennial Delhi, a city that had a housing shortfall of 1.3 million units in 2007, but over nine hundred thousand vacant houses.[79]

This is speculative urbanism, where the promise of a world-class future sustains the material transformation of the present, even when the roots of the future projection are forgotten. Empty income projections produce empty apartment buildings; invisibilized poverty trends make the replacement of slums and low-income land uses by properties few can afford appear inclusive. As William Cronon observes of speculative boosters during Chicago's rise, "fictive lots on fictive streets in fictive towns became the basis for thousands of transactions whose only justification was a dubious idea expressed on an overly optimistic map."[80] As in nineteenth-century Chicago, so in twenty-first-century Delhi; frontier growth begins with the image of a future city, which, when projected onto the present, creates a vision of economic possibility. Despite uncertainty as to whether the urban future pictured in the overly optimistic map or speculative poverty projection will ever materialize, these graphic artifacts guide action and thought, constituting a field for action. As we will see in the following chapters, the world-class aesthetic similarly operates as a projection across existing space, allowing viewers to assess the merits of existing land uses on the basis of expected future appearances.

Even in the wake of the global economic meltdown that began in 2008, real estate investors remained hot on India—for as long as the future Indian middle class could be conjured into economic prospectuses and shareholder reports, the upswing in the income curve (and the downswing in the poverty line) was able to secure investment. As one annual report for a real estate fund read in late 2009: "The current velocity of growth in the world's emerging markets should provide significant opportunities in Brazil, China, India, Indonesia and other countries, where 6 percent to 8 percent plus GDP growth should enable middle-class expansion and underpin demand for real estate."[81]

This chapter has also shown that in the face of its quantitative insignificance, the middle class has been accorded great symbolic power. The middle class is, we have seen, the world-class city's talisman, inhering the power to propel Indian cities onto the global stage and to maintain the torrid rise in urban property prices. While it should now be clear that the price of property is the engine of world-class city making, Marx has shown us that this rent is also the expression of the social power of landed property.[82] It should come as no surprise, then, that rising ground rents and the rising symbolic significance of the property-owning middle class comes with an equal rise in the political power of landed property. It is to the conditions through which the power of property grew in millennial Delhi that I now turn.

2

Gentrifying the State

Governing Through Property

"R-W-WHAT?"

Before 2000, the acronym RWA would have left almost any Delhi resident guessing. A middle-class man in his mid-thirties who I interviewed early in my fieldwork, quite out of touch with current events in the city, may well represent what was the common view just five years earlier: "R-W-what? I don't know what that is."[1] When I said it was a neighborhood association—the resident welfare association—that exists in residential colonies like his, his response was "Yeah. My dad's in one of those. It's for senior citizens, right?"

A senior citizen club, a retiree's group, a social committee for the elderly: combine that with a bit of neighborhood volunteer work, and you have the picture of how RWAs functioned in Delhi until the early 2000s. Primarily made up of retired men, many with military or bureaucratic backgrounds, RWAs had little if any influence beyond their immediate colonies and typically had minimal say in the workings of even their own residential blocks. As one RWA old-timer recalled, thinking back to his earlier days as his RWA's secretary: "It was a type of timepass, a way to socialize with neighbors in a meaningful way." Typical RWA activities included hiring and managing the *caukīdār* (watchman) and trash collectors, maintaining the community garden, coordinating tree planting campaigns, and installing street signs.

RWAs play a radically different role in Delhi today. Often considered by the media, government, and judiciary to be the de facto voice of citizens—or "the residents' voice," as the *Hindustan Times* has emblazoned on its weekly section covering neighborhood affairs—RWAs in millennial Delhi acquired veto power over development projects in their areas, held sway over local budgetary decisions, and directly influenced land use and development policy across the city. As I discuss in the following two chapters, RWAs lobbied vociferously in millennial Delhi for the removal of slum settlements, using the mass media and the courts to establish new criteria of social respectability and new aesthetic standards for evaluating Delhi's urban form. Visions of a world-class Delhi have since been forged increasingly through the aesthetic sensibilities of the property owners RWAs represent. Before discussing how this aesthetic consensus was consolidated and deployed, however, I examine in this chapter how RWAs—emblems of the property-owning middle class—took the political leap from bystander to political juggernaut.

I do so through an institutional ethnography of an urban governance experiment called Bhagidari, launched by the Delhi government in 2000 as a citizen-government partnership. By moving with RWA members and state officials through the spaces of urban governance they came to share under Bhagidari, I argue that the power of the property-owning middle class emerged not from a political awakening within this class itself, as is argued in studies of the new middle class, nor did it emerge to fill the space left by a hollowed-out state enfeebled in its service to global capital, as studies of neoliberal governance might suggest.[2] Rather, it was consolidated through the machinations of the local state. In particular, I show how this widely praised "good governance" program, conceived by the chief minister of Delhi, created a parallel governance mechanism, divorced from the electoral process, that provided RWAs with privileged access to both upper- and lower-level state workers. If gentrification consists of the usurpation of formerly lower-class spaces by the upper classes, then Bhagidari, I argue, achieves nothing less than the gentrification of state space, or of the channels of political participation more generally. Specifically, by creating venues in which low-level state workers, whose ethico-political duties were once harnessed to the needs of the poor, are required to address the demands of RWAs, Bhagidari displaced the unpropertied poor to the periphery of state space and empowered property owners to extend their aesthetic codes into the apparatus of urban government.

Before detailing how Bhagidari reengineered state space, however, we must first clarify the contrasting political channels through which the elite and subaltern classes have accessed the state historically in India and locate these channels of state access within Delhi's specific administrative context.

How did *jhuggi* dwellers secure political protection for so long despite the best efforts of state planners and property owners to repurpose the land they occupy, and what explains the millennial shift that closed down channels of state access, thereby facilitating mass slum demolition?

PASSIVE POLITICS

The starting point for most studies of local politics in India is the observation that the modalities through which one can exercise political agency are highly determined by socioeconomic status. In other words, the manner in which a wealthy English-speaking homeowner "problem-solves" differs starkly from the manner in which a Hindi-speaking *jhuggi* dweller "fixes." Scholars of Indian state form have thus long observed a broad division of how different categories of society access the state.[3]

Sudipta Kaviraj, for example, notes the inability of the modernizing bourgeoisie at the time of Independence to exercise cultural leadership.[4] While Independence in 1947 freed the nation from the reins of colonial rule, it failed to put in place the cultural instruments necessary for translating the state's new development priorities (e.g., social reform, economic redistribution) into the nation's vernacular spaces—a term Kaviraj uses to describe areas where social life remains structured predominantly by family, kin, caste, and community and where, as Satish Saberwal argues, state institutions lack "the normative support necessary for their reliable, effective functioning."[5] Yet the central and state governments depended precisely on these vernacular spaces to implement policy.[6] As the planning and governance apparatus sought to extend control over "larger areas of social life, it had to find its personnel, especially at lower levels, from groups who did not inhabit the modernist discourse."[7] Thus, with the extension of the state into more vernacular spaces and with the incorporation of bureaucrats of different class, caste, and (non-English) linguistic backgrounds into the modern state apparatus, a concomitant expansion took place in the gap between elite bureaucrats who inhabit the modernist discourse of bureaucratic rationality and lower-level personnel "whose 'everyday vernacular discourses' were not structured around principles of formal rationality at all."[8] Because the state had what Kaviraj terms "feet of vernacular clay," elite bureaucrats found their mandates "reinterpreted beyond recognition" by the time they reached the implementation stage "very low down in the bureaucracy."[9]

Postcolonial governance thus produced an arrangement in which upper and lower level bureaucrats not only interpret the meaning of policies differently, but are also embedded in contrasting ethico-political and linguistic contexts. As a result, the ties between India's elite classes and the upper level bureaucracy are not just ones of economic stature and influence; they are also based on shared cultural formation, language, and positionality. Similarly, subaltern classes' ability to extract benefits or exercise influence over lower-level bureaucrats is not a secondary game of spoils, but rather a different cultural space in which the poor are more equipped to establish shared meanings and obligations with state agents.[10]

[Partha Chatterjee premises his treatment of postcolonial politics on the same disjuncture between a more formalized domain reserved for culturally equipped citizens and a sphere marked by a more "paralegal," fluid, and vernacular mobilization of demands.] He refers to the former as "civil society," which is premised on the ideals of democratic liberalism under which all citizens are considered equal before the law. The latter he calls "political society" and is a political realm in which all those denied access (either legally or culturally) to the formal protections of civil society must tread, relying primarily on more makeshift mechanisms of political patronage, bribery, and sometimes outright coercion in order to negotiate political benefits.[11] This "politics of the governed" is made up of efforts by groups denied rights and protections under the law to draw on their cultural and political affinities with low-level bureaucrats and locally embedded political representatives to gain access to shelter, employment, or other material and symbolic resources.

India's highly centralized planning system accentuates the divide between central planners who sit far from the territories they govern and local politicians and bureaucrats, who have little input into plan conceptualization yet face constant pressure from constituents—especially from those not recognized by plans—to extend infrastructure, ensure tenure security, and prevent evictions. These local figures accede to these demands and reinterpret planning rules for different reasons: politicians in exchange for votes; bureaucrats to avoid scorn from elected officials, to earn extra income through petty bribes, or on the basis of camaraderie arising from their own semilegal residential arrangements. State-produced letters, ration cards, electricity bills, and survey registers that record the state's past involvement in the life of a settlement—what Veena Das calls "the signature of the state"—often provide the material infrastructure for exerting such pressure. Although such stealth procedures are not the only way to interact with the local state, Solomon Benjamin suggests that the majority of India's urban population—mostly those without formal property rights—use these channels to access land and employment, an arrangement he calls India's "porous bureaucracy."[12] Such channels are available to these otherwise marginal classes at least in part because the poor in Indian cities vote en masse, vastly outnumbering the voter turnout of wealthier residents. Locally elected representatives therefore have to at least entertain the demands of the urban poor; this does not hold for upper level bureaucrats and state planners, who see *jhuggi* colonies as illegal for falling outside the formal domain of planning.

During my time in Delhi's settlements, I heard stories and in some cases witnessed instances of residents deftly negotiating established political networks. When illegal electricity connections were cut, for example, the delivery of a case of top whisky to the right worker in the local power substation was enough to reestablish service. To secure an informal stay of a demolition, the elected councilor could be coaxed into calling in a favor from the assistant commissioner of police, who would in turn withhold support for the demolition by deploying his forces to the wrong settlement on the requested day by the Municipal Corporation. Although such informal channels of state access were structured by seniority, gender, caste, and party affiliation and were often mediated by unelected *pradhāns* (headmen), they nonetheless make visible the way in which vernacular state spaces had been attuned historically to the pressure of the poor.[13] As we will see, Bhagidari severely constricted these spaces. Throughout my fieldwork, I consistently heard *jhuggi* dwellers describe how politicians and state contacts had abandoned them in recent years, offering far less support than in the past. What did the spaces of Delhi's porous bureaucracy look like, and what allowed RWAs to subvert them so effectively in millennial Delhi?

"POLITICAL SOCIETY" AND SLUM PREVALENCE IN DELHI

Figure 2.1 shows a simplified version of Delhi's administrative structure, including an illustration of the zone of negotiability (labeled "political society") in which the urban poor have historically been able to exercise political claims to the city.

Because Delhi is India's capital and only city-state, it has a unique administrative structure with municipal, state, and federal bodies overseeing different—although sometimes overlapping—administrative functions. Delhi does not have full statehood, which means that the Government of India (that is, the central government) retains direct oversight over state and municipal government. For example, the Legislative Assembly, the legislative arm of the Delhi (state) government, is constrained by the fact that any act it tables must first be approved by the lieutenant governor, who is appointed by the Government of India. There is thus a dual executive wing in the Delhi government: the unelected lieutenant governor, who is a senior officer in the Indian Administrative Service, and

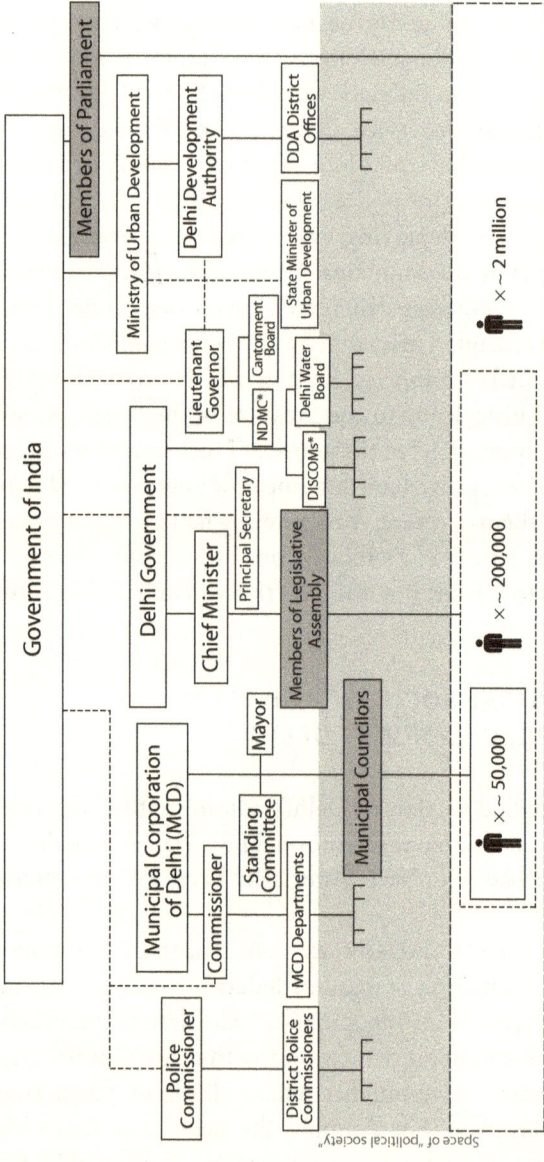

Figure 2.1. Simplified administrative structure for the National Capital Territory of Delhi.

Solid lines within the figure indicate direct bureaucratic hierarchy; lower boxes are subordinate to those higher on the figure. Dashed lines indicate that a given administrative position is directly appointed by a superordinate body (usually the Government of India). For example, Delhi's State Minister of Urban Development is appointed by the Ministry of Urban Development from among the Members of the Legislative Assembly (MLAs); Delhi's lieutenant governor, directly appointed by the Government of India, also serves as chairperson of the DDA; and, although the chief minister is chosen by the ruling party of the Legislative Assembly's 70 MLAs, her chief secretary is a senior bureaucrat appointed by the Government of India. The shaded boxes represent directly elected positions; the population boxes at the bottom show the approximate number of citizens represented by each elected official. Branches of the diagram hanging below the lowest designated position in any given hierarchy that lack titles indicate the domains in which lower-level bureaucrats operate. The large shaded area indicates the state space in which Chatterjee's (2004) "political society" is strongest. The degree to which a branch or box falls in this space represents how prone it is to the pressures of "political society."

* "NDMC" stands for the New Delhi Municipal Council, which serves the same function as the MCD, only in the more geographically confined administrative areas of New Delhi; the Cantonment Board is the municipal body that oversees Delhi's Cantonment area; "DISCOMs" stand for the electricity distribution companies, which are regulated by the Delhi government.

the chief minister, chosen from the elected Members of the Legislative Assembly (MLAs). Within the municipal government, the elected councilors, who choose a mayor, constitute the deliberative wing of the Municipal Corporation of Delhi (MCD)—a primarily consultative role that frames thematic committees and has limited financial control—whereas the central government-appointed MCD commissioner heads the executive wing, which drafts the budget.[14]

Local electoral politics are further removed from executive and planning decisions as a result of the fact that the central government retains control over the domains of police, social order, and land management and planning in Delhi. Thus the Delhi Development Authority (DDA), which is responsible for the acquisition, development, management, and disposal of land, operates under the central government. This means that the elected MLAs (the state government) and the councilors elected into municipal government do not have any direct input into urban planning in Delhi. All of this is to say that the bureaucratic chains linking high-up planners and low-level implementers are indirect or discontinuous in many sectors in Delhi, which leads to considerable negotiability in how plans are implemented.

The presence of informal settlements itself is the outcome of the negotiable boundaries between centralized plans and localized implementation. Since 1957, the DDA has been assigned the task of preparing and implementing a master plan for the development of Delhi land, a key component of which was a 25 percent residential land reservation for the poorest economic classes. While the DDA has effectively acquired the bulk of land notified through the Master Plan, land disposal has proceeded at a much slower pace due to delays in land allocation, cost overruns, and competing interests across Delhi's vast and often overlapping federal, state, and municipal governments. This is especially true for low-income housing, less than a third of which had been completed by 2010.[15] As a result, *jhuggi* dwellers, who constitute approximately one-third of the city's population and mostly fall in the lowest income group (referred to as the economically weaker section), occupied less than 3 percent of city land by the early 2000s.[16]

The DDA's failure to provide adequate shelter for the city's poor did not, however, dissuade new migrants from coming to Delhi. In 1981, according to the Census of India, of Delhi's total population of 5.7 million people, 1.8 million lived in *jhuggis*. The number of *jhuggi* dwellers had risen to 2.25 million (out of a total of 8.4 million) by 1991 and to 3.25 by 2001 (out of a total of 12.25 million).[17]

In common state usage, *jhuggī jhompḍī* clusters, often called "slums" colloquially in English, are areas with substandard housing whose residents do not formally own or lease the land on which they reside.[18] This land can be private or, more often, public. Because the DDA is by far the largest land-owning agency in Delhi, most *jhuggis* are located on land that it controls. While, according to the Delhi Master Plan, the low-income population occupying *jhuggis* are entitled to far more land in Delhi than they actually occupy, the DDA deems them unplanned encroachers because they were not formally allocated the land they occupy. However, due to the vast underprovision of low-income housing and to the wide availability of vacant public land, the urban poor have historically settled on vacant land with little difficulty. It is important to emphasize here that this does not constitute an unsolicited act of squatting, as it is commonly depicted. Rather, most existing *jhuggi* colonies were settled deliberately by state or private labor contractors in the late 1960s, 1970s, and 1980s. These contractors, who are located lower down in the state hierarchy, recruited and hired laborers from the neighboring states to build the new planned areas of the city, while the DDA consistently failed to meet the Master Plan's provisions for low-income housing. Instead, contractors created labor camps on government or private land beside their worksites.

This type of squatting, then, took place with government approval in the majority of cases: *jhuggi* colonies arose as planned violations of the Master Plan. Because many of the construction projects at the time consisted of building up entire residential colonies (municipal infrastructure, roads, buildings, and so on), the labor camps became semipermanent. As these camps grew, local politicians (councilors and MLAs) recognized the possibility of mobilizing the laboring population for their own electoral advantage. Thus bureaucrats and local politicians seeking to solidify their influence or expand their electoral base offered ration cards to *jhuggi* residents, usually within the first few years of the establishment of a settlement, in exchange for political support. Until the late 1980s these ration cards—which formally entitle households below the poverty line to subsidized food and cooking oil—were the sole requirement for exercising the vote. As the only identification card that listed the address of one's *jhuggi*, ration cards performed an important semiotic task at the time: linking a head of household to the physical address written below (almost always) his name and headshot. The initial distribution of ration cards often coincided with the formal extension of state-registered addresses into settlements, deepening the association between the possession of these documentary artifacts and residential permanence. Throughout the 1990s settlers, elected officials, and local bureaucrats thus treated ration cards as proof of legal residence, with settlers believing (and being told) that such proof provided tenure security and the right to public services.[19] After ration cards, voter ID cards, which were first issued in the late 1980s, performed the task of tying households to a state-registered location. The presence of ration card, voter, and other registration lists, which were accompanied by survey registries carried out periodically under various slum improvement schemes, allowed DDA, Delhi government, and municipal officials to see into and know the space of the slum. These same lists and registries also implicated the state in the everyday life of the settlement: old ration cards, for example, confirmed continuous occupation of land, giving settlers greater protection against uncompensated eviction. The judiciary thus holds these land-owning agencies doubly responsible for slums: first, as the parties culpable for public land encroachment in the first place and, second, as the bodies responsible for protecting the life and livelihood of settlers.

In Shiv Camp, the settlement I discuss in detail in chapters 5 and 6, a private land developer purchased land from the Delhi Development Authority in the mid-1960s to build Krishna Garden, the planned residential colony in which Shiv Camp is located.[20] The developer hired laborers and settled them on a small portion of the land he purchased. In 1981, having sold individual plots to private buyers, he turned the land over to the Municipal Corporation to maintain the area's public infrastructure. Because local politicians in both the state and municipal government depended on Shiv Camp residents for their vote and because the land was on the periphery of the city at the time, when the land developer handed the colony over to the Municipal Corporation, there was no question of whether the settlement would remain. Therefore, at the time when the Municipal Corporation took over the administration of the land, the residents of Shiv Camp were never threatened with demolition and were in fact never officially told that the land had been transferred.[21]

Despite the fact that Shiv Camp violated the Master Plan—it is located on land designated for government institutional use—its residents had negotiated secure tenure with the support of elected representatives and state bureaucrats: ration cards, voter ID cards, and a Municipal Corporation toilet block confirmed as much. While upper-level bureaucrats in the state and central governments deride this divide between the plan and the city's actually existing residential geography, which they attribute to political corruption and failed plan implementation, this system benefited the local state, Shiv Camp residents, and, it must be added, the city as a whole through the availability of cheap labor subsidized by low-cost slum housing.[22] Thus a highly favorable reading of this arrangement would suggest that in the absence of the resources to develop formal low-income housing, India's developmental state extended the right to occupy public land to the working poor as a type of social welfare. These arrangements, however, did not solely benefit the poor; according to the Municipal Corporation, 70 percent of all land development in Delhi—by *jhuggi* dwellers and wealthy property owners alike—violates the Master Plan.[23] Indeed, most of the privileged few in

Delhi who own private land received it at highly concessional rates from the government. Furthermore, the vast majority of the land used outside of the formal oversight of the state is occupied by the wealthy.[24]

The point, then, is not to romanticize the bureaucratic negotiability that occurs in the local state, but to recognize that only through these arrangements were India's unpropertied poor able to secure the tenuous access to the city they enjoy today. The porosity of the lower bureaucracy and the multiple, fluid channels of accessing the local state have hence prevented the complete embourgeoisement of the city. Efforts by planning officials in the DDA and in the Delhi government to rationalize land use in the city, which increased in the 1990s as land prices climbed and more profitable opportunities for urban land development arose, were thus consistently thwarted. These arrangements, however, rapidly deteriorated in millennial Delhi. The pace and scale of slum demolitions increased starkly in the early 2000s, conservative estimates suggesting at least a tripling of the pre-2000 pace.[25] According to most scholars, the increasingly antipoor orientation of Indian cities arose because of an emboldened new middle class. This class indeed played a key role in the drive to transform Delhi into a world-class city, but not for the reasons widely affirmed.

BOURGEOIS CITIES: THE RISE OF THE NEW MIDDLE CLASSES

If the ethico-political bonds between the lower classes and the lower bureaucracy militate against the urban elite's best efforts to impose rational order on Indian cities, what explains the upswing in slum demolitions in millennial Delhi? How have bourgeois visions of the urban future gained enough political traction to reshape these cities' physical landscapes despite their prolonged stubbornness for change, or "feet of vernacular clay"? These are the underlying questions motivating Partha Chatterjee's highly influential essay "Are Indian Cities Becoming Bourgeois At Last?" and a spate of recent scholarship on the new middle class in India.

Chatterjee starts by charting the gradual thickening of "political society" that put in place new paralegal arrangements that directly benefited the burgeoning ranks of the urban poor. While the poor were gaining political ground throughout the 1980s, Chatterjee argues, the middle class retreated and disengaged from the messy politics of the city. In the 1990s, however, "the tide turned" and those cordoned off in "civil society" fought back:[26]

> There has been without doubt a surge in the activities and visibility of civil society. In metropolis after Indian metropolis, organized civic groups have come forward to

demand from the administration and the judiciary that laws and regulations for the proper use of land, public spaces, and thoroughfares be formulated and strictly adhered to in order to improve the quality of life of citizens. Everywhere the dominant cry seems to be to rid the city of encroachers and polluters and, as it were, to give the city back to its proper citizens.²⁷

From where did this shift in civil society arise? The triggering event, for Chatterjee, occurred when "a new idea of the postindustrial city became globally available for emulation." Somehow, according to Chatterjee, the sudden exposure to the image of a postindustrial city not only spurred a political awakening among the elite, but also endowed those in civil society with the capacity to put pressure on the local state to stop "helping the poor subsist within the city" and instead move Indian cities in the direction of this new image—the image of the world-class city.²⁸

Chatterjee, in his book *The Nation and its Fragments*, critiqued Benedict Anderson's argument in *Imagined Communities* for suggesting that "the historical experience of nationalism in Western Europe, in the Americas, and in Russia had supplied . . . a set of modular forms from which nationalist elites in Asia and Africa had chosen the ones they liked."²⁹ It is thus surprising to find Chatterjee's explanation of the new Indian city stemming from a simple borrowing of Western modular forms ("the post-industrial global image"). Regardless of the origins of world-class aesthetic discourse in contemporary India, which I discuss in detail in the following chapter, the middle class's mere adoption of a particular aesthetic sensibility does not tell us if and how such an aesthetic became hegemonic.

In describing the role of the Calcutta middle class in establishing a hegemonic nationalist project in the early twentieth century, Chatterjee writes:

> It was this class that constructed through a modern vernacular the new forms of public discourse, laid down new criteria of social respectability, set new aesthetic and moral standards of judgment, and, suffused with its spirit of nationalism, fashioned the new forms of political mobilization that were to have such a decisive impact on the political history of the province [West Bengal] in the 20th century.³⁰

In making this observation, however, he details the specific institutional channels through which the middle class achieved such political power: its position within the colonial bureaucracy and educational system (a "mediating" role, as Chatterjee calls it), its command of English as a leadership quality necessary to confront British colonial policy, its importance as a highly visible and "civilized" class capable of countering British claims of Indian savagery, among others. His comments about the contemporary urban middle class, however, leave the political channels by which it was able to disseminate hegemonic aesthetic standards unspecified.

If Chatterjee's brief consideration of the making of bourgeois cities is but an appeal to turn greater research attention to how middle-class power is consolidated, then more elaborate studies of this class have done little to elucidate any further the concrete practices by which the gains of the urban poor were slashed. For Leela Fernandes, who has engaged in by far the most in-depth study of India's new middle class, the remaking of Indian cities is driven by "new suburban aesthetic identities and lifestyles that seek to displace visual signs of poverty from public space."[31] Like Chatterjee, Fernandes sees middle-class power arising from new urban visions and demands within this class itself. But if, as Fernandes says, "this social group has in fact historically been concerned with the assertion of civic order, a quest that has tended to rest on the exclusion of marginalized social groups that have threatened to disrupt this order"[32]—that is, if middle-class aesthetic sensibilities are not new—then what is new about the rise of middle-class power?

Just as Chatterjee argues that "organized civic groups have come forward to demand" a new type of city, Fernandes suggests that "the rise of a new middle class identity begins to take the form of organized associational activity as segments of this social group form civic and neighborhood organizations in order to reclaim public space and consolidate a style of living that can adequately embody its self-image as the primary agent of the globalizing city and nation."[33] For both authors, it is not just an emboldened middle-class vision that is remaking the Indian city, but also the organization of that vision into new associational practices. But once again, the spur to the remaking of Indian cities is seen to emanate from internal changes within the middle class, while an account of how these new visions are imposed on the lower levels of the bureaucracy remains missing. State power figures in this analysis only once middle-class demands are secured and given official sanction, but the authors give no sense of how this class and the local state intersect to transfigure the linkages between the lower-level state and the lower classes. For example, Leela Fernandes and Patrick Heller argue: "The growth of civic organizations represents an emerging trend in which the NMC [new middle class] has begun to assert an autonomous form of agency as it has sought to defend its interests against groups such as hawkers and slumdwellers." They go on to call this a "de-representation of politics, as the middle class has shifted its political practices from representative structures to making representations through civil society structures."[34] Their argument, hence, is that the elite has asserted authority over the city by *disengaging* from the state. This argument seems to endorse the view of middle-class activism held by the middle class itself: as a Delhi-based monthly magazine covering civic associations suggests, "middle-class anger pays. The louder you scream the better."³⁵ The problem with this view, however, is that the middle class has been screaming for years, but nobody had to listen. Current analyses provide little insight into what has brought the megaphone to their lips, to continue the metaphor.

In contrast to these positions, I argue that only through a reconfiguration of urban governance structures—that is, a respatialization of the state—was the middle-class vision of urban space able to gain traction and become hegemonic.³⁶ I now turn to how this respatialization contributed to the rise of middle-class power.

GENTRIFYING PARTICIPATION

Delhi's administrative context throughout the 1990s continued to be defined by a wide gap between residents and their elected representatives on the one hand, and the planning mechanisms of the state on the other. In 2000, however, Delhi's system of urban governance took a radical turn. Sheila Dikshit, the chief minister of Delhi and a member of the ruling Congress Party, launched an ambitious program called Bhagidari, which means "participation" or "partnership" in Hindi. Bhagidari was conceived, according to the Chief Minister's Office, to respond to

> the deteriorating condition of environment, traffic, and public utilities. . . . "Delhi" was synonymous with overflowing sewers, littering on public places [sic], poor roads, long traffic jam coupled with vehicular and industrial pollution. To make matters worse, the administration was overburdened, and the conventional methods of problem solving were not yielding the desired results.³⁷

These conventional methods were the existing system of fragmented governance—that is, the space of political negotiability between the planning apparatus and the ground of implementation that had enabled the poor to subvert official plans and policies. Dikshit's vision since taking office in 1998 has been to transform Delhi into a world-class city, a term that she introduced into popular discourse in Delhi at the time and a key component of which, as I described in the introduction, is the removal of slums. Garnering legitimacy and popular support for slum removal and ensuring full buy-in from the lower branches of the state—a weakening of the political ties in political society—however, required a restructuring of the state itself. This is the context out of which Bhagidari emerged, the goal of which is "to build a 'clean, green, hassle-free quality of life' in Delhi, and transform Delhi into a 'world-class capital city.'"³⁸

In 2000 the chief secretary of Delhi, S. Regunathan, developed the concept of Bhagidari. Reflecting back on the chief minister's enthusiasm for his proposal, he told me in an interview:

> Citizens were unhappy with the state of the city, but all they did was complain to the government. What could we do? Colonial rule and rule by kings before that created a psyche that government had to do everything. . . . Bhagidari was created to tell people, "you are a part of government and have equal duties and responsibilities." It is a change management process . . . Bhagidari tries to establish a structural and formal relationship with the government and people.[39]

After the chief secretary's initial idea to create a new institutional mechanism to bring citizens directly into the governance process through workshops and consultations, the chief minister hired the Asian Centre for Organisation Research and Development (ACORD), a consulting organization specializing in "change management, strategic planning, and human development" that has worked for industrial organizations, corporations, and local governments to design efficient organizational structures.[40] After initial consultations with ACORD, a Bhagidari Cell was created inside the Chief Minister's Office that was envisaged as the center for recruiting participants, called "Bhagidars," and for coordinating Bhagidari programs. The Bhagidari Cell and ACORD quickly defined three primary stakeholders: market and industrial associations; bureaucrats across Delhi's various departments; and RWAs based in officially planned residential colonies, membership in which is open only to property owners. This meant that residents of slum settlements and unauthorized colonies were excluded from the citizen-government partnership—the voices of which, the Delhi government claimed, were represented by RWAs, the so-called grass roots citizens associations.[41]

From the beginning, Bhagidari was an elite "invited space," designed as an instrument to incorporate the voices of property owners into urban governance without similar inclusion for the unpropertied.[42] As Regunathan said, "its [Bhagidari's] goal is to make RWAs more powerful and responsive." Despite declarations made by politicians (in both the opposition and ruling parties) that Bhagidari had become elitist, its exclusion of the 69 percent of the population living in slum settlements and unauthorized colonies did not waiver in millennial Delhi.[43] When I asked the secretary to the chief minister (one rank below the chief secretary) who oversees the Bhagidari Cell why Bhagidari was not open to slum residents, she began by describing the legal and administrative challenges of working in such areas, but concluded by saying, "in the end, the city shouldn't look like a slum."[44]

Despite Bhagidari's overtly exclusionary basis, its bureaucrats and documents depict it as an inclusive program aimed at fostering good governance. As a Bhagidari brochure states:

> A change process was required to bring the citizens into the centre of governance. Thus the scheme of "Citizen-Government Partnership: Bhagidari" was formulated to develop a democratic framework wherein citizen groups can interact and partner with government functionaries for resolution of simple, day-to-day civic issues. It encourages citizen volunteerism and sharing of responsibilities between the government and its people. It facilitates public scrutiny of government functioning and works towards policy interventions in support of popular empowerment and betterment of civil society.

The first goal of Bhagidari is to incorporate citizen concerns into the practice of government by training RWA members through workshops (described below) and the public more broadly through publicity campaigns to see themselves, and to act as, government. In addition to this effort to produce participation, Bhagidari arose out of a second—and perhaps more deeply felt—need: to change the organization and operation of the state bureaucracy itself. The secretary to the chief minister said, speaking about the inefficiencies of the bureaucratic process:

> Government workers don't respond to the demands of citizens. They don't follow directives outside of their immediate command either, and they sometimes don't even follow those. . . . We saw the need for Bhagidari to coordinate the demands of citizens, so citizens wouldn't have to negotiate the maze of different departments and so those departments would become more responsive. . . . This was difficult early on because it was difficult to get government bureaucrats to move. Over five years now, there's been a change of mindset so that initial barriers are overcome.

Bhagidari seeks not only to transform citizens into the eyes and ears of government, as its bureaucrats like to say, but also to rearrange state space so that bureaucrats respond more directly to the demands of RWAs and the interests of property they represent. I now turn to three primary Bhagidari activities through which this takes place.

Bhagidari Activity 1: The Membership Workshop

The first activity of Bhagidari is a three-day workshop held approximately three times a year in which new Bhagidars are inducted into the program and undergo training on how to participate. These workshops are held in large, air-conditioned, decorated conference halls with dozens of round tables seating a mixture of bureaucrats and RWA representatives. The workshops are inaugurated by the chief minister of Delhi and followed by comments by the chief secretary and the director of the Bhagidari Cell, who proclaim in increasingly celebratory language the importance of the new Bhagidars in the efficient administration of the city. In one workshop I attended, the director followed the chief minister by saying:

> It is time to showcase the city, to showcase the country in the city. The Beijing Games came before the Commonwealth Games in Delhi, and China showcased its economic and military power. This is what countries do. The 1986 Asiad Games [hosted in Delhi, in 1982 not 1986] did this for Delhi. The city's first two flyovers came then. Color TV first came to India then. Now, we will construct twenty-four new flyovers before the Commonwealth Games. . . . Sports offer a stimulus to get any upgradation done: wider roads, the Metro, new stadiums—improving the city. We are here today to make sure this happens, to help make Delhi the best city, a world-class city.

The director thus began by establishing the vision of the world-class city as the national goal of citizens and government alike. He proceeded to describe how the relationship between Bhagidars and the state is formalized by laying out the structure and organization of the Bhagidari process. Bhagidars, he explained, have four primary points of contact with the state.

First, monthly Bhagidari meetings are held in each of Delhi's nine revenue districts, in which member RWAs and lower-level bureaucrats as well as a district nodal officer—a top ranking bureaucrat—from all relevant government departments meet under the chairmanship of the deputy commissioner, who is the officer in charge of the District Office. I describe the details of these meetings below, but in the Bhagidari Membership Workshops, these monthly meetings are described as the first line of contact between RWAs and the state. In addition to these monthly meetings, RWAs can directly contact the Bhagidari Cell, which then forwards the aggrieved RWA's request to the relevant department. The third line of contact between RWAs and the state is in Bhagidari Thematic Workshops, which address a single issue (e.g., water delivery, street encroachments) over the course of a three-day workshop. The fourth line of contact between RWAs and the state is through direct communication, usually via telephone or office visits.

The Bhagidari Cell insists that a major goal of Bhagidari is to open lines of communication by which residents can call the relevant department workers when there is a leaking pipe, a downed power line, or a truant waste collector. As the chairman of ACORD told me during a workshop, "a lot of bonding takes place [in Bhagidari]. New friendships are made.

People exchange phone numbers. Then, when RWAs have problems, they can just call up officials and get things fixed up."[45] Indeed, extended lunch and tea breaks in both the membership and thematic workshops created a shared middle-class cultural space in which the casual style of interaction, the attire of participants, and the mixed English–Hindi conversations helped reduce the divide between citizen and government worker.

Bhagidari workshops next break into individual sessions, wherein Bhagidars are taught the administrative structure in their district, who works for whom, and the procedures by which they can access and communicate with various branches of the state.

In addition to holding small group sessions where new RWA Bhagidars interact with bureaucrats to understand the nature of their future interaction, membership workshops have two other primary functions. The first is to instill in Bhagidars a set of norms and expectations as to how the city should appear and function. While RWAs join Bhagidari with a preformulated set of civic concerns and actually existing neighborhood problems, these workshops, via communication from Bhagidari staff scattered throughout the hall and written activity instructions, sketch out broader urban problematics that are supposed to be shared by all legitimate urban residents: residents should pay taxes, discourage littering and public urination, prevent electricity and water theft, ensure that residents in an area are registered with the police, report suspicious individuals to the authorities, help Delhi become world-class, support the planned development of the city and the project of "greening" Delhi, and discourage encroachments on streets and public land. While the workshop organizers repeatedly raise these challenges over the course of the workshop, a key way in which a normative picture of Delhi emerges is through a small group exercise in which Bhagidars are asked to identify positive things as well as negative things in Delhi.

In these exercises, Bhagidars from diverse locales across the city are placed in groups of around ten people and instructed to debate the best and worst aspects of Delhi, and which citywide civic problems should be tackled on a priority basis. At the end of the session, the Bhagidari staff collects written recommendations and priority problems from the small groups, so these can be summarized and discussed in the large group by the day's end. The summary sheet shows Bhagidars what the consensual positives and negatives are in Delhi. During one workshop, the top positives included the Delhi Metro, new flyovers and highway construction, Green Delhi, and the Commonwealth Games. Top negatives included uncontrolled population growth; unauthorized occupation of parks, roads, and public places; water and electricity supply; and the lack of cleanliness.

Over the course of the workshop days, a handful of problems are selected, and training sessions are run to show Bhagidars how past problems have been resolved within neighborhoods. In these sessions, groups of eight to ten are put in mock situations that ask the RWA members, in conjunction with the bureaucrats at their table, to write up a proposed solution to the problem at hand. The answers discussed in each small group are then shared with the large group and written responses are collected by Bhagidari staff so that they can be summarized for the next day. These summaries are then passed out to all new Bhagidars, who are shown the consensus strategies that should be adopted for the particular problems discussed. This establishes procedural protocols for civic action, guiding RWA concerns and conduct toward certain problem areas and predefined improvement strategies.

A related function of these workshops, thus, is to define RWAs as governors, to train them to conduct themselves and attempt to conduct the conduct of others in a way amenable to Delhi's world-class ascent. Bhagidari becomes in part an exercise of cultivating a pattern of self-government among the middle class, but, more importantly, of instilling a set of civic concerns within a privileged segment of the population, which can demand adherence to world-class standards from the lower branches of the state—via Bhagidari itself as well as in the media. After membership training, RWA representatives return to their neighborhoods and are expected to pursue the problem-solving strategies learned. They are handed workshop summaries broken down by problem type, and they are given a final instruction sheet on how to educate other RWA members and neighborhood residents.

Bhagidari Activity 2: Thematic Workshops

Bhagidari coordinates up to a dozen thematic workshops each year, taking up issues as diverse as "Water Problems in Delhi" and "Future Delhi: 2020," which was a collective exercise to define how Delhi should look come 2020. Bhagidari thematic workshops are structured around a principle of large-group dynamics that ACORD drew from management practice, systems theory, and psychoanalytic research. Broadly concerned with the relationship between large-group and individual identity, ACORD applies this approach in an effort to overcome institutional "inertia and resistance to change."[46] As the president of ACORD told me during a Bhagidari thematic workshop, "bureaucrats have never had a reason to listen to the citizen. There was no way to foster such an interaction. We have to find ways to bring all levels into this so that everyone sees the need for change."[47] Building on the chief minister's idea of using Bhagidari to bring about a transformation in the operation of the state, ACORD designed the Bhagidari workshops, which it calls "large group interactive events," in order to make the bureaucracy more attuned to RWA demands, especially at the ground level. The workshops begin this process by bringing a mix of three to four hundred RWA members and bureaucrats across departments together to "engage in intensive and participatory dialogue" on problems and solutions in the city.[48] Bhagidari literature describes this approach in the following terms:

> In a Large Group Interactive Event/"Bhagidari" workshop the large group is further fragmented into 25–40 identical "small groups," each small group constituted of members from various stakeholders of an area/locality. Each small group works in a large group environment on specific issues identified by the stakeholders themselves and evolves consensus solutions. During the workshop, the suggestions, views and outputs of each group are fed back to all the small groups so as to keep everyone involved in the process intimately. This energises the large group as well as the small table groups, and creates a momentum for implementing change. This helps generate surprisingly common grounds, common interests, common solutions among all the small groups and hence a common ownership of the change process. The small table groups . . . give specific commitments to these agreed solutions. . . . "Action teams" are formed on the concluding day of the workshop for implementing the agreed solutions within a timeframe. . . . These action teams are given a mandate, by the Large Group itself, as well as by the "senior leadership group" to go ahead and implement the workable solutions.[49]

The workshops therefore take up particular themes and draw the diverse opinions of RWAs and bureaucrats together to develop consensus solutions. The idea is that because the final solutions are based on the input of the small groups, which are collaborative efforts between RWAs and bureaucrats, all participants will buy in to the proposed changes. ACORD's interpretation of large-group dynamics insists that these events

> must span at least two-and-a-half days (if not three) with two nights in between. This is based on interesting findings from sleep research, that during sleep, the day's discussions and experiences in the small and large group are "processed" by the participants [*sic*] "subconscious minds. Only after such "sub-conscious" processing . . . does the phenomenon of "paradigm-shift" (or "change in the mind-set and attitude") take place in 80 percent to 90 percent of the participants at the "experiential level."[50]

Further, the report notes, "since people do not function based only on logic and reasoning, the LGIE [workshop] smoothly processes both *reason and feeling* simultaneously, to create 'consensus' and 'ownership.'" ACORD thus designed Bhagidari workshops as a forum in which participants, RWAs, and bureaucrats alike, would be inculcated with new urban governance norms and priorities.

In a workshop focused on improving public service delivery, bureaucrats from more than sixty government departments, along with RWA members, discussed strategies to increase government responsiveness to citizen demands. After the heads of various departments spoke to the large group on the importance of adapting to twenty-first century governance styles, all tables were handed a sheet that specified seven parameters for improving public service delivery, and stated: "We need to translate the vision of 'citizen-centric administration' into a reality." The seven parameters, predetermined by ACORD and the Bhagidari staff, included such things as reducing citizens' time and effort; improving attitude, language/communication, and behavior of officials; achieving honest, clean, service delivery; and getting and utilizing continuous feedback from citizens. These distinctly middle-class concerns—many of which have to do more with the style than the content of service delivery—hence structured the conversations throughout the workshop, precluding certain topics of bureaucratic procedure (e.g., equity) and elevating the relevance of others (e.g., courtesy and politeness). These parameters were framed in response to the RWA criticism that bureaucrats do not behave as if they are educated and do not express concern for citizen problems. As one RWA member commented, "anybody can just push to the front of the queue. It isn't like in other [corporate] offices where you are attended to and given a number."

Over the course of the workshop, hour-long sessions were run in small groups to identify possible solutions to improving each of these seven areas. Small group discussions specifically treated the seven parameters as part of an effort to minimize the type of back-office, under-the-table interactions typically negotiated among the urban poor, bureaucrats, and politicians—operations connoted by the phrase "dirty politics." Of the final recommendations shared with the large group and summarized in a list of agreed upon action points, five of the seven parameters led to recommendations to increase interaction with RWAs, which reinforced the importance of specifically RWA–government, not the more broadly construed citizen–government, interaction.

While bureaucrats from the lowest to highest levels of office participate in Bhagidari, only low- and midlevel bureaucrats sit at the tables with RWAs. Top officers sit together at the front of the conference hall and respond to the final recommendations made by the small tables. While Bhagidari workshops are intended to guide bureaucrats toward taking charge of improving the city and the government on their own accord, the oversight and monitoring mechanisms put in place via Bhagidari and implemented by their seniors make it clear that bureaucratic change is a requirement of the job, even if there is not buy-in. A bureaucrat from the Delhi Water Board alluded to the tension between bureaucratic initiative to improve government responsiveness versus a simple tightening of the chain of command when he told me over lunch, "how am I supposed to do my regular work when I have to say all this 'please and thank you' and answer all these calls?"

In addition to broader efforts to develop bureaucratic responsiveness to RWA demands, Bhagidari workshops construct mutual agreement between RWAs and bureaucrats on the future direction of the city. In the "Future Delhi" workshop, participants agreed that top goals necessary for Delhi to become world-class include removing/rehousing slums, discouraging begging, removing encroachments on public land, increasing greenery in the city, and reducing litter. A clear bureaucratic vision emerging out of this and other workshops was thus that slums represent obstacles to Delhi's progress. In a workshop on "Citizens Partnership in Governance," small-group sessions focused on the role of RWAs and the Municipal Corporation (MCD), respectively, in keeping the colony and its surroundings clean and improving the quality of urban public space. Here too, final recommendations had a distinctly antipoor bias: a final recommendation was to give RWAs authority to certify work done by staff of the MCD, to encourage RWAs to be vigilant about illegal land use, and to create a regular line of communication between RWAs and the head of department of the MCD. Specific attention was given to various security concerns, with multiple sessions devoted to fostering RWA–police cooperation, verification of the status of servants, creating lists of authorized service providers (e.g., hawkers, repairmen, sweepers) to prevent unauthorized people from entering the colony, and reducing the security threat of slum clusters. While bureaucrats with whom I interacted did not seem to experience the change of mindset that Bhagidari officers and ACORD anticipated, they did recognize that RWA interest in cleaning up Delhi had become an official bureaucratic mandate, a situation that laid the ground for the normalization of propertied criteria of civility and aesthetic standards of judgment.

Bhagidari Activity 3: Monthly Bhagidari Meetings

The third and most important Bhagidari activity is the monthly district-level meeting. These meetings bring the highest-ranking officer (the district nodal officer) from each government department at the district level to the district office once a month for a two-hour meeting, during which all RWA Bhagidars from that district can attend and raise neighborhood grievances. Monthly Bhagidari meetings were institutionalized through an executive order from the chief secretary of Delhi, which required each department in the Delhi government to designate a nodal officer to meet RWA Bhagidars on a monthly basis to design action plans "to be implemented within the department's budgetary provisions for the year."[51]

The deputy commissioner (the highest ranking bureaucrat in the Delhi government at the district level) chairs these monthly meetings and begins each session by asking about progress in addressing the problems from the previous meeting. If problems have been resolved to the satisfaction of the concerned RWA, they are removed from the list. If not, then the commissioner asks when work to solve the problem will begin and what progress has been made, which usually leads to a discussion of timeline and the proposed remedy. If the RWA is dissatisfied with the response, which is often the case, this can push the commissioner to apply pressure on the officer at hand. As a result, RWAs have a tremendous amount of influence over problem definition and resolution. RWA concerns are taken seriously in these meetings, and if a satisfactory solution is not reached after several months, the officers in charge often face some sort of public embarrassment or reprimand from their superiors. For example, in one case where an RWA had complained about water logging in a park that had not been addressed in three months, the commissioner picked up his mobile phone and called a more senior official in the Delhi Water Board, asking him why the drain had not yet been cleared when the officer present knew about the problem for so long. In this instance, the officer in the meeting quickly promised that he would take care of the issue by the next month.

By forcing low-level bureaucrats to directly address the concerns of RWAs under the watch of higher-level bureaucrats and by creating a common space in which RWAs can engage all the relevant government departments, Bhagidari monthly meetings significantly reconfigure the organizational space of the state.

NEW STATE SPACES

As Figure 2.2 shows, Bhagidari created a centralized governance space in which cross-departmental and cross-sectoral decisions and concerns are deliberated upon and to which only a privileged segment of society—RWA representatives—is given access. Via Bhagidari, RWAs are elevated above the common citizen and placed within what Neil Brenner calls a "new state space" that gives them direct access to governance decisions.[52] The idea behind Bhagidari was that creating a space to bring upper- and lower-level bureaucrats together would eliminate the need for the complex political negotiability through which abstract plans have been reworked historically

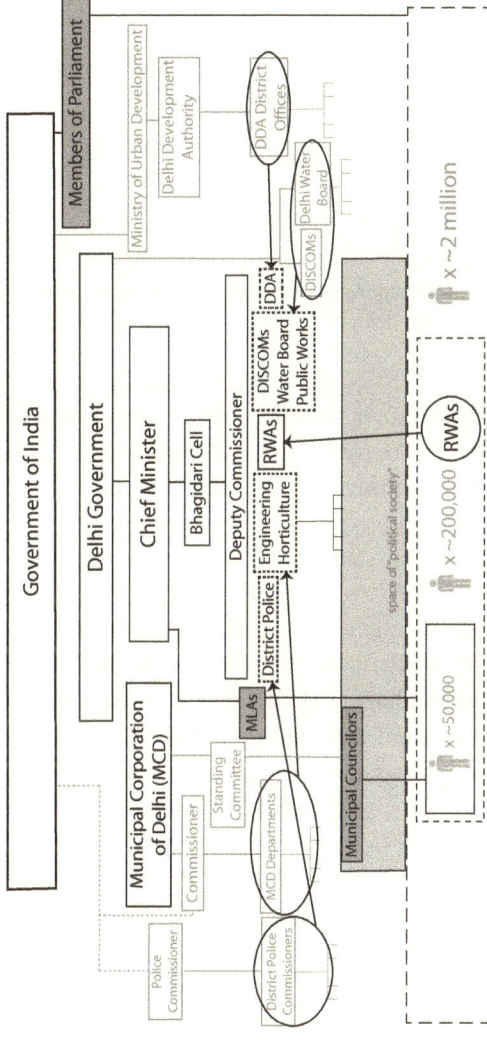

Figure 2.2. Reconfigured administrative hierarchy under the Delhi government's new Bhagidari Scheme. The figure shows a new state space within which the deputy commissioner, the highest-ranking official in each district of Delhi, oversees monthly meetings in which nodal officers from various MCD Departments (Engineering and Horticulture are shown here), DDA divisions, and public works, water, and other service providing agencies (DISCOMs) join RWAs, a privileged group of citizens, to discuss urban governance issues. This reconfigured state space makes the space of political society both shallower—i.e., those in political society cannot reach high enough up into the state to access the bureaucrats that have bent rules historically in their favor—and narrower—i.e., they now cannot access as wide a range of government departments.

to meet local needs, since plans, it was thought, would be designed from the beginning to address the problems faced by low-level state workers. However, Bhagidari has not eliminated the space of political negotiability (labeled "political society" in the above figures). Rather, it has gentrified it in two ways.

First, Bhagidari created a parallel governance mechanism through which RWA interests earn the special attention of government officials. Whereas those outside of Bhagidari have to go through the existing grievance redressal process, RWAs have direct access to the relevant officials, both in monthly meetings and through personal communication. As the president of ACORD told me:

> Everyone starts at the local office, and if that doesn't solve their problem, then they go to the district office. If this doesn't work for Bhagidars, they go to their monthly district meeting and talk directly with the nodal officer, who is in a much higher position than the district officer.[53]

RWA members often skip the first steps described here—going to the local, then to the district offices—and instead go straight to a higher officer, either by phone or through the monthly meeting. In a survey I carried out with twenty-five RWA members involved in Bhagidari, twenty-two said they agree or strongly agree with the statement "because of Bhagidari, you know more government officials and contact them more often."[54] I often asked RWA members and bureaucrats if they had each other's phone numbers stored in their mobile phones to confirm this increased familiarity. Without fail, bureaucrats involved in Bhagidari had the names of secretaries from the most active RWAs on hand and said they were in regular contact.

Bhagidari monthly meetings also establish a direct line of communication between RWAs and the Chief Minister's Office, giving RWAs a platform to indirectly influence policy decisions and to frame debates on urban issues. As the supervisor of the South Delhi District Office told me, "ultimately, if a problem isn't addressed it'll go to the CM's Office. . . . If we have a problem we can't address, we tell the CMO and they call high-level meeting in chairmanship of the CM with the highest officers. This is how bigger issues get addressed."[55] For example, consistent complaints by RWAs in west Delhi about the unresponsiveness of district officers in the Municipal Corporation led the Chief Minister's Office to send a request to the Municipal Corporation District Office to officially investigate officer performance. The chief minister or Delhi Cabinet also calls occasional special meetings with RWAs to address contentious issues, ranging from the fee structure for cable television to the government's approach to water privatization to the policies on mixed land use and land commercialization.[56] In the case of charting out the government's policy on mixed land use, a contentious issue that had led thousands of businesses in 2006 and 2007 to be sealed by Supreme Court order, the chief minister said the recommendations received from RWAs would be summarized and forwarded directly to the group of ministers charged with devising the central government's policy on the matter.[57]

Bhagidari monthly meetings are a forum in which any RWA can develop a one-to-one relationship with public officials. They also directly introduce RWAs to those most capable of implementing change at the neighborhood level. As the secretary of a high-income neighborhood in south Delhi said, "we no longer see them as some *babu* in a government office; we understand their constraints and are assured that our problems will be resolved. And they are resolved most often."[58] Bureaucrats also prefer to discuss problems directly with the RWA rather than having to face scrutiny in monthly meetings—this creates a regular dialogue between officials and powerful residents. As the above-quoted RWA secretary said, "they [MCD officers] give us numbers, sometimes personal cell phone numbers; we know who to call for our water problems or for maintaining roads, or our garden. Earlier we wasted all our time being redirected from one office to another to register our complaints. This was definitely a change."[59] The secretary of a middle income RWA from north Delhi expressed a similar point: "We have a close relationship with the DC [Deputy Commissioner] thanks to Bhagidari. Before we'd try calling an officer and his PA [personal assistant] would say he's busy or in a meeting. Now, we know these officers well. Bhagidari has made a huge difference in our ability to make our point and voice heard. . . . We are the government now!"[60] As another RWA leader said, "my RWA business card has the most powerful logo in the city, the Bhagidari logo. It opens doors, makes officials sit up and listen."[61]

Twenty out of the twenty-five RWA members who completed my survey, all of whom were active in Bhagidari, agreed with the statements "RWAs have been empowered because of Bhagidari" and "because of Bhagidari, government departments listen to you more."[62] Officers in various departments in the Delhi government confirmed that they personally knew the leaders of RWAs in their area, found out about problems in RWA neighborhoods more quickly, received more complaints from citizens, and solved RWAs' problems more quickly thanks to Bhagidari. Most bureaucrats further confirmed that they spent more time engaging with RWAs due to Bhagidari.

The frequency and intimacy of RWA-bureaucrat interactions make monthly meetings a context in which property-owners' sensibilities enter the day-to-day culture of governance. As bureaucrats learn common RWA concerns and perspectives, their priorities shift to accommodate RWA civic sense. Although not all RWAs in Delhi perceive the same threats and challenges to healthy neighborhoods, the removal of slum settlements and encroachments on public land emerged in millennial Delhi as a cross-RWA platform considered essential to improving the city. While I discuss the manner in which antislum views are culturally expressed and discursively consolidated in the following chapter, copies of monthly district meeting summaries, as reported to the Bhagidari Cell, show that RWAs regularly raised this issue. I obtained these summaries for four of the nine districts in Delhi for three consecutive months in 2007. Each summary showed at least one grievance related specifically to a slum, with at least 15 percent of problems in each meeting pertaining to encroachments (e.g., slums, hawkers, illegal parking) on public land or roadsides. For example, one states, "road on south of Soami Nagar Colony and MCD flats from Savitri Nagar corner upto [sic] Chirag Delhi nala [drain] is heavily encroached by jhuggis," and it reported that the Slum Wing of the MCD had been deputed to address the issue. Bhagidari thus represents one important site in which slum removal gains official recognition—a point that deputy commissioners confirmed in interviews with me.

The deputy commissioner of Delhi's Eastern District, for example, described how Bhagidari had broken down the people–government divide and specifically, in her district at least, led her to take up the issue of slum removal:

> We listen and respond to the needs of people more directly. So, because we have to meet RWAs every month, we have to at some point show progress on their wishes. We can't just keep saying *"dekh lenge"* [we'll see]. At some point we have to actually do the work, and now we are beginning to understand [the] *mentality* of the people and act more proactive. This is why I really want to work on the slum rehabilitations, to improve the district and address the needs.[63]

When I asked if she specifically follows up on RWA requests to remove slums, she replied, "as long as their claims have some evidence, we pursue them." One of the main reporters for the *Hindustan Times Live*, a weekly supplement that covers RWA activities and concerns, concurred with the view that RWAs have new power over slum removal decisions:

> The councilor is the head of the MCD for that area, so his opinion is important if the slum is on government land. If you can convince him to remove the slum, or the DC [Deputy Commissioner], then you can get the slum removed. Bhagidari has made the link between RWAs and the DC and the councilors closer. . . . They are getting things done today.[64]

RWAs' antislum views are further translated into the public arena and official policy discourse through the Annual Bhagidari Utsav, a three-day festival during which approximately ten thousand RWA members, bureaucrats, politicians, and citizens display and celebrate the achievements of Bhagidari throughout the year. In addition to the display of model slum upgradation and removal schemes, Bhagidari gives out awards to the best citizen groups, in an event featuring prominent guest speakers that is widely covered in the English and Hindi media. Bhagidari awards in millennial Delhi frequently went to RWAs that successfully had neighboring slums removed, with these RWAs showcased in Bhagidari print materials circulated for others to emulate.

In addition to strengthening RWAs, incorporating their problem definitions as part of the mentality of government, and giving them privileged access to upper- and lower-level state workers, Bhagidari's second form of gentrifying the state is the weakening of the electoral process and forms of bureaucratic fixing upon which the urban poor have historically been most dependent. That is, whereas on the one hand Bhagidari builds new bonds and strengthens old ones between the propertied classes and the state, on the other it weakens the linkages between residents of slum settlements and the lower-level bureaucracy and diminishes elected councilors' influence over the bureaucracy. If we examine Figure 2.2, we see that the lowest branches of most government departments are now pulled into the sphere of the Bhagidari Cell, which elevates the concerns of RWAs above all others and reconfigures the chain of command such that low-level bureaucrats, who have typically been effective fixers in negotiating benefits for *jhuggi* residents, now face more regular oversight from senior officers. The shaded area in Figure 2.2, marked "political society," indicates the effect of this. On the one hand, this space has been narrowed, which means that the urban poor can access fewer state departments now, as these departments' primary citizen contacts have been formally defined as RWAs. On the other hand, this space of political negotiability has become shallower, which means that the urban poor now have to traverse a greater distance (an often impossible task) in order to reach the same level of the state, and their elected representatives have less influence over state workers who have been drawn into the Bhagidari fold and pulled higher up the state administrative hierarchy.

That Bhagidari led to an enervation of representative democracy in millennial Delhi is perhaps best illustrated by municipal councilors' views of it. Bhagidari's first couple of years of operation led to conflicts between the MCD and the Chief Minister's Office, the former claiming that the latter was encroaching on its political space. As *The Hindu* reported in 2005: "Interestingly, the Congress [the ruling political party] Councilors have from the very beginning opposed the *Bhagidari* scheme, describing it as an attempt to clip the wings of the elected representatives."[65] The councilors had earlier claimed that the chief minister was trying to run the MCD "through a remote control called the 'Commissioner' and implementing her plans in the name of *'Bhagidari.'*"[66] This led councilors to demand that "MCD's Zonal [district] staff be stopped from attending the district-level 'Bhagidari Workshops,'" because while they were at the workshops, the zonal offices were empty for addressing regular public grievances.[67] This sidelining of elected representatives and weakening of the avenues by which the non-Bhagidar public can access the state are points that were celebrated by many active RWAs. As the president of one RWA told me:

> Before, only the poor people voted and had voice. Politicians lived off these vote banks. Middle class didn't vote. Because of Bhagidari, middle class has come up and expresses its right. And, we now have very active participation in government policies. . . . RWAs are platforms for this movement against illegal activities of the land mafia: commercialization and slumification; these are what we stand against. . . . We perform the duties of the active representatives.[68]

Here, RWAs' increasing role in neighborhood- and district-level governance is viewed as a positive step toward increased efficiency, transparency, and equity in government, despite the entirely unrepresentative nature of RWAs.

Adding fuel to the debate over representative structures and democratic process, in 2004, the Bhagidari Cell first proposed extending five million rupees (~$125,000) to each district that would be allocated to RWAs on the basis of project proposals. Elected politicians (both councilors and MLAs)—who rely on the dispersal of their annual development funds (7.5 million and 20 million rupees, respectively) to garner political support—claimed that this proposal was "not only undermining the role of the legislator but also throwing up a parallel administration by creating a new system and a new set of administrators."[69] Although this proposal was finally approved and implemented in 2007 (with funds rising from five to twenty-five million rupees per district in 2012),[70] the leader of the opposition Bharatiya Janata Party perhaps best summarizes the implications of this program:

> This shows that Ms. Dikshit [the chief minister] has been trying to bypass the deliberative wing of the MCD. . . . This is undemocratic. . . . This is an insult to the MCD. . . . We as responsible opposition cannot let this happen as this is nothing but an attempt to throttle grassroots democracy in the Capital.[71]

By extending almost as much development money to RWAs as the elected councilors have for their wards, this fund, called the My Delhi, I Care fund, further established RWAs as the de facto representatives of wards and neighborhoods and bestowed middle-class, propertied development norms with official sanction. For example, in justifying the need for this general development fund, the chief minister said one of the key activities for which it would be put to use consisted of the "protection of vacant public land in the colony"—that is, discouraging slum settlements and encroachments.[72] As *The Times of India* reported after the final approval of the fund, "the Delhi government seems to be going in sync with what the citizen groups have been advocating."[73]

THE POWER OF PROPERTY, GENERALIZED

While Bhagidari went to great lengths to recalibrate the gears of government to the demands of propertied interests, perhaps Bhagidari's most important effect was to increase the status and influence of RWAs in the eyes of the judiciary, state, and media. In addition to the financial backing Bhagidari provides to RWAs, RWAs have gained quasi-official authority as units in the governance structure through the actions of the judiciary and various state departments. For example, the MCD floated a scheme to invite RWAs to take over its responsibilities in maintaining neighborhood parks.[74] The Delhi government also directed executing agencies to "supply a copy of the estimates of all civil works awarded to contractors to the RWAs of their locality" and "a brief summary of the project report in layman's language highlighting the nature of works proposed to be undertaken."[75] Individual departments have made similar efforts to incorporate RWA interests and energies explicitly into neighborhood level development and oversight activities. For example, the police commissioner described an initiative during a Bhagidari meeting to involve RWAs in minor dispute resolution and crime assessment and monitoring, despite the fact that official magistrates are meant to fulfill this very role.

RWA influence on local development decisions is best reflected by their empanelment on what are called district development committees.[76] Whereas these committees were intended to consist of elected representatives, the top district-level officers from all government agencies, and elected community members, three RWA representatives assumed the role of community representatives in millennial Delhi.[77] These committees, which control key district-level budgetary decisions and deliberate over local land use, economic development, and infrastructural planning, hence came to treat RWAs as de facto citizen representatives.

In addition to this influence over local- and district-level development, RWAs enjoy considerable power in citywide policy formulation and in setting standards of urban progress. A. K. Jain, the commissioner of planning in the DDA, for example, said that RWAs had "preparatory input" into the review process that preceded the drafting of the most recent Delhi Master Plan: "Interaction with RWAs as 'stakeholders' took place prior to drafting of the plan and showing it to the public."[78] Over the course of some of the most vitriolic battles over land use the city has ever seen regarding how to address the 2006 Supreme Court order to close down all shops operating commercially in noncommercial areas of the city, the Delhi Cabinet engaged in high-level negotiations with RWA members, while the Supreme Court's Monitoring Committee formed to deal with the matter held multiple meetings with RWAs to solicit input on how to proceed, treating them as the de facto stakeholders presumed to represent residential interests in the city.[79] The Ministry of Urban Development followed suit and "ruled out relaxation for allowing commercial activities in posh 'A' and 'B' category colonies except on recommendations by residents' welfare associations of these areas,"[80] giving RWAs effective veto power over the course of commercial development in wealthy localities. In "nonposh" areas, it declared that recommendations for changes in local land use categorization would be "entertained only if more than 50 per cent of the RWA office-bearers back the proposal."[81] Furthermore, the Supreme Court appointed an *amicus curiae* (friend of the court) specifically to represent the RWA position on the question of mixed land use and commercialization. No other interest group was assigned such a court representative. During the course of a long-running case in the Delhi High Court dealing with unauthorized land use (including land use violations, slums, and building code violations), the Court appointed court commissioners to monitor the ground situation and report back during court hearings. The commissioners soon after issued a public notice saying, "RWAs and individual citizens can send their written complaints regarding unauthorized construction on public land and other unauthorized constructions, as well as commercialization of residential premises/misuses, preferably along with photos, to the Court Commissioner of their respective zone." While the commissioners' relationship with RWAs started as a mere information collection strategy, it soon became more of a collaborative effort to identify slums and unauthorized areas. As *The Hindu* reported in May 2007:

> A pilot project for removing encroachments from government land will soon be launched at East of Kailash in South Delhi. During the project, residents' welfare associations and nongovernment organisations will work closely with the Delhi High Court-appointed Monitoring Committee.... During the meeting, the residents had put forth their concerns about growing encroachments on government land in various parts of Delhi. It was then decided that RWAs and NGOs would aid and assist the panel in

removing encroachments from government land. For this purpose, they will develop a list of prioritised actions required in their area for maximum impact in the shortest period of time and place it before the Monitoring Committee.[82]

The secretary of the East of Kailash RWA told me that the purpose of this project was to increase the pace with which slums and unauthorized constructions were removed from the area:

> We will bring the Court Commissioner to each colony after RWAs make their complaints. He'll bring the demolition squad and take one colony at a time. He can demolish on sight because he is empowered by the court. . . . This is how the court comes to the grassroots. The court commissioners become the voice of the court. They interact with RWAs, get views then tell the court and direct the MCD and police how to respond.[83]

In an interview, the court commissioner for the South District confirmed the role of RWAs in launching not only this special pilot project, but also the Monitoring Committee itself: "This is the first committee dealing with unauthorized constructions on a city-wide scale. It is the first committee that is permanent. . . . RWAs were the catalysts for it because they were the ones who were most affected, but there was a confluence with the court view on this."[84]

While the RWA members acknowledge Bhagidari's initial role in spurring RWA activism, the program came under heavy criticism in millennial Delhi for not transforming the city thoroughly or quickly enough. These RWAs specifically complained that Bhagidari did not produce real results and that they themselves had to lobby to make things happen. As an RWA member told me, "Bhagidari is a bit of a disappointment. Bhagidari monthly meetings tend to be dominated by discussion of single areas. . . . Bhagidari is too slow."[85] Harsher criticism came from RWAs not actively involved in Bhagidari, especially supporters of the opposition Bharatiya Janata Party. As one RWA president said, "it is just a game for the Chief Minister. If you want to get anything done, you have to do it yourself. Nothing happens in those meetings."[86]

Criticism of Bhagidari had a surprising effect, however. While it certainly weakened the public's perception of the ruling Congress Party, such criticism treated Bhagidari only in the limited sense of its official workshops and meetings and ignored the larger reconfiguration of governance structures that Bhagidari put in place. While the Chief Minister's Office imagined Bhagidari as a way to inculcate a middle-class, consumerist modernity, Bhagidari is in fact a product of this very middle-class experience of the urban. People coming to Bhagidari already endorse the dream of making Delhi a world-class city. Bhagidari was so successful in reconfiguring state space, even though this was rarely acknowledged, because it presented its *premise*—a consolidated, property-owning class ready to intervene into state practice—as its *outcome*—an activist citizenry. Even when criticized, Bhagidari reinforces the vision and desire for a world-class city because criticism of Bhagidari is based on the claim that it does not implement this vision fast enough.

In provoking this criticism, though, Bhagidari simultaneously provokes the demand for greater RWA power, which is precisely its goal. That is, Bhagidari effectively governmentalizes the state, fostering the sentiment among elite RWAs that they should be Delhi's governors. As the secretary of one of Delhi's largest RWA federations said, "Bhagidari isn't working very effectively, but it has brought authorities closer to RWAs. Now, the government can't ignore RWA issues. This is largely because RWAs are getting more media attention. The newspapers have even appointed special RWA correspondents."[87] Here, the suggestion is that RWAs have sprung up and taken charge, forcing the government to respond; the causal arrow points from RWAs to the state. But as I have shown, this empowerment of RWAs was Bhagidari's very intention. RWAs in millennial Delhi saw their governing role as natural and necessary, operating outside of, but upon, the state. The fact that a reconfiguration of state space itself had given rise to this rationality was consistently elided in RWA accounts, especially among those less active in Bhagidari. As a journalist for *The Times of India*'s weekly RWA supplement said of the effect of Bhagidari, "it was as if all of a sudden people started seeing governance, seeing their lives, and seeing space in the city differently: new concerns emerged in a very short period that all of a sudden were considered noteworthy and important to people."[88]

Delhi's property-owning classes were certainly well-positioned to stamp their vision upon the city, but Bhagidari consolidated their critique of urban disorder, cultivated their desire to act upon this critique, and granted them access to previously restricted state channels through which they could extend their standards of public order and appearance across the whole of urban space.

PROPERTIED CITIZENSHIP

Bhagidari was justified as a program to increase government transparency, reduce corruption and bureaucratic inefficiency, and produce good governance in Delhi. It won the 2005 UN Public Service Award on the basis of its performance in these areas and has been cited in other Indian states as an example of participatory best practice.[89] High-level state officials, the media, and nongovernmental organizations have celebrated

Bhagidari for its effectiveness in rooting out vote bank politics and corruption, even while acknowledging that it made property-owning residents of Delhi, who represent less than 25 percent of the population, de facto citizen representatives. [It did so by forging multiple new state spaces—including monthly citizen meetings and thematic workshops—in which low-level bureaucrats are put into direct contact with property owners' RWAs and held accountable for implementing their visions of urban change. Whereas it is the unpropertied poor who have historically enjoyed close cultural ties to these low-level officials—ties that provided the foundation for the poor's hard won, if paralegal, tenure security—Bhagidari reengineered Delhi's administrative hierarchy, loosening these ties and creating a parallel governance mechanism accessible only to RWAs. If gentrification is broadly defined as the displacement of a lower class from a space into which a wealthier class is entering, then Bhagidari brought about nothing less than the gentrification of state space.]

[The irony is that under Bhagidari the same forms of bureaucratic contact—forms of fixing that operate through pressure, threats, and embarrassments on low-level state workers—that are called "dirty" and "corrupt" when practiced by the poor are celebrated as "efficient" and "transparent" when exercised by the elite.] As an RWA correspondent for *The Times of India* said while praising the merits of Bhagidari, "the conclusion is obvious: transparency, anticorruption and good governance lead to more money, more power and control for the middle class."[90] I next turn to how RWAs used this power to standardize their expectations of public appearance and civility into a world-class aesthetic sensibility.

3

Nuisance Talk

From Sensory Disgust to Urban Abjection

INTRODUCTORY BOUNDARIES

Mr. Jindal called me to his two-story bungalow in west Delhi after we met at a Bhagidari workshop on neighborhood parks. Jindal was new to Bhagidari, the governance scheme I discussed in the previous chapter that enhanced property owners' access to state decision-making channels in millennial Delhi. In the workshop, he had enthusiastically offered a number of ideas on preventing *jhuggi* dwellers from entering residential parks, and he invited me to visit his resident welfare association (RWA) after I inquired further about his efforts.

Jindal's house benefited from a recent facelift, adorned with new marble cladding and a faux-Grecian balustrade skirting the roof. Jindal had been working to improve his neighborhood's image through more than personal architectural flourish, though. He had also convinced everyone in his RWA to chip in for tall iron gates at all neighborhood entry points, each to be manned by twenty-four-hour security personnel. Children from a local slum had been freely using the park, which he considered a security problem that he was driven to address after having stepped in human feces during his morning walk a month earlier. Through our conversation that afternoon, Jindal slowly elaborated a theory of the slum shared by many RWA members I would meet over the next year, polishing his argument with what seemed a well-rehearsed aphorism: "Slums are the culmination of unwanted elements."

This chapter examines how activist property owners such as Jindal translate their local anxieties around the presence of slums into a larger politics of urban abjection. Abjection has been understood primarily as a psychic process by which the self encounters and affectively registers the other. According to Julia Kristeva, the abject is everything that the subject seeks to expunge in order to maintain the symbolic division between self and other, inside and outside, and, in her psychoanalytic framing, it is at the same time the bodily reaction to those things that must be expunged.[1] Yet as Jindal's statement indicates, city making involves a politics of abjection that extends well beyond intimate aversions to include larger spatial processes of exclusion and expulsion: erecting iron gates, kicking out shitters, clearing slums.

Building on scholarship that examines abjection as a social process that both casts out and throws down unwanted social groups, I here explore how everyday depictions of slums as dirty, uncivil, and out of place—what I call "nuisance talk"—travel into and gain legitimacy in popular representations and state visions of urban space.[2] In other words, I'm interested not so much in how a shit-free neighborhood is made, but more importantly in how social and geographical membership in a "proper" neighborhood, in a modern society, and in a world-class city is produced and maintained through the active designation of those things that do not belong—the shit, the slum, the nuisance—and through the processes of expunging them from the social order. Activist property owners, in talking about slums as abject outsiders and in disconnecting slums from public space, were simultaneously engaged in a larger spatial politics of abjection: one that constructed slum removal as a process of urban improvement, a positive form of violence necessary to "clean and green" Delhi and further the city's march toward becoming world-class.

Nuisance plays a special role in defining both the objects of repugnance—the abject—and the processes by which they are to be remedied in urban India. As I shall argue, it operates as the key principle according to which discourses of the slum are both organized in everyday speech and translated from the neighborhood into a broader rationality for governing space. As a lay term, "nuisance" is widely used to identify forms of aesthetic impropriety or private annoyance. The simple statement "that slum stinks," for example, is a seemingly descriptive utterance grounded in a locally specific experience of sensory disgust. Through its circulation across different geographical settings, however, nuisance ties together a larger geographical imaginary, allowing speakers and audiences in different local settings to understand the disgust of *that slum* without ever seeing or smelling it: [I know the stink of *that slum* because I have smelled *this slum*; your abject is also my abject. In other words, your enunciation of *that* and my experience of *this* indexes an urban abject that we must expunge collectively.] In the context of aggressive efforts to build a "Clean Delhi, Green Delhi"—the Delhi government's millennial tagline, nuisance talk began to garner a larger coalition of speakers and consolidate a sensory vocabulary concerning who and what belongs in the city. The first feature of nuisance talk, then, is this ability to spread and consolidate: it has a gravitational force that, as it spreads, pulls diverse experiences into its enunciative orbit.[3]

Because nuisance statutes provide the foundation of environmental law in India and have purview over both public welfare and the defense of private property, nuisance operates discursively as a catchall category allowing a diverse array of private grievances, often pertaining to the defense of private property, to be expressed in terms of environmental welfare and the public interest.[4] As such, the widening depiction of slums as nuisances—that is, as illegal environments—reworks the public–private divide, inserting codes of civility once restricted to the home and neighborhood into the core of public life. [Through its geographical circulation, as well as its circulation between lay and official discourse—from a conversation among neighbors into a Bhagidari meeting or courtroom, for example—nuisance talk propels into public space a tacit grammar for interpreting the city's defilement. At the same time, it puts into play a charged lexicon of resonant terms that signal bodily disgust (such as: foul, ghastly, disturbing, intrusive) or civic impropriety (such as: filthy, unsanitary, infectious, injurious) that appeal to others for redress or sympathy.] In other words, I want to suggest that nuisance talk is a type of utterance that moves easily from being a medium for expressing taste or opinion into the bearer of force:[5] when an audience shares in nuisance talk, it doesn't just agree on the meaning of what is said; it also agrees on, or at least grants authority to, what is to be done about the object described.[6] This is why nuisance operates as abjection, for in the simple act of identifying aesthetic annoyance or sensory disgust, it already points to what is to be done about it: revulsion tends toward expulsion. [Utterances that assert or enunciate, in other words, begin to intend more, even if those aren't the intentions of the speaker uttering them. This is the second feature of nuisance talk: to not just agree on an abject object, but to initiate a political and material process of abjection.[7]]

In order to introduce nuisance talk, I begin in the next section with an extended ethnographic vignette of my first encounter with an RWA actively mobilized against a slum. This vignette shows how intimate aversions around hygiene and class difference link up with state and judicial anxieties over security and environmental order, while subsequent sections trace how wider circulations of nuisance talk consolidate a grammar of urban abjection that provides the governing vision, or aesthetic sensibility, that undergirds mass slum removal. The following chapter analyzes the judicial logic that translates the identification of nuisance into a legal mechanism for demolishing slums.

SANT RAVI DAS CAMP

I had visited Sant Ravi Das Camp numerous times until its eventual demolition in May 2006 (see Map at the front of the book). In the days before its demolition, I watched Delhi Development Authority (DDA) surveyors enumerate the settlement's households and eventually saw the bulldozers roll in and raze the more than eight hundred *jhuggis* settled there. When I came back to Delhi six months after Ravi Das Camp's demolition, I returned to the site, curious to see what the DDA had done with the open space (see Figure 3.1).

A thick, concrete fence had been erected on all sides of the empty land, with yellow signs staked in the ground saying "Property of the DDA: Do Not Enter." Dotted with mounds of rubble and scattered brick, the site lay vacant, except for a Hindu temple still nestled in the corner of the lot (see Figure 3.2). After I had parked my scooter and pulled out my camera, a shopkeeper approached me from the housing society across the street. We began talking about the scene before us.

Figure 3.1. The left and right photographs show two settlements, outlined in black, before (September 2004) and after (September 2006), respectively, the DDA demolished them on May 4, 2006. The larger of the two settlements, located on the left side of each of the two photographs, is the site of Sant Ravi Das Camp, and the smaller settlement located on the right side of the photographs is the site of what was known as Sanjay Camp. The small "x" on the photograph on the right shows the position from which the photograph shown in Figure 3.2 was taken.
© Google 2009.

Figure 3.2. Former site of Sant Ravi Das Camp, which was demolished on May 4, 2006. The temple is visible in the top right of the image. Photograph by the author.

I told the shopkeeper that I had visited months before when a *basti* (settlement) was here and wondered what had happened. With this subtle prompt, he launched into a tirade:

> Those people were a major problem in the area. They made lots of noise, spread filth, and disturbed the area. They screamed a lot and made all kinds of noise. They were always drunk and would fight for no reason. The space was such a mess. There were a thousand jhuggis here and many thousands of people. They were such dirty people. . . . But, don't think they were poor. They just occupied the land, took rent on it, and got rich. . . . We filed a petition in court, and the court had them removed. The place is better now, no?[8]

Pointing across the vacant lot, he asked me how things looked. I was not sure what to say. It appeared quite ruinous, with the foundations of huts and other signs of the previous inhabitants still visible. "Seems okay," I said, to which he quickly shot back a succession of adjectives: clean, peaceful, quiet. "There is no filth, no more noise and troubles," he said. "The air is totally clean. It's beautiful, no?" He then offered to walk me around and introduce me to his neighbors.

The first person we met as we strolled toward the society's faded yellow apartment buildings was a man in his early seventies, perched against the society's boundary fence. The shopkeeper addressed him as "Uncle": "Uncle can tell you about all the problems we had." "*Ofo,*" Uncle began, "these people troubled us so much. They would, *yūṁ hī,* just come into our park and *ease* themselves," as he looked over his shoulder to a small playground. "There was filth everywhere. We couldn't use our own park. It was so bad we wanted to sell our homes and leave, but we couldn't sell. The price fell so much, and it took a lot of time. As soon as anybody saw the jhuggis here, they weren't interested. The stench of fish and meat destroyed the atmosphere," he said, an explicit reference to caste impurity and the olfactory dimension of untouchability.[9] Uncle said the value of his flat had increased threefold after the demolition, "but, what's the reason to leave? Now this will become a *posh* area."

Our next encounter was with a carpenter who was renting a flat in the housing society and who had rented a *jhuggi* in Ravi Das Camp for storing his supplies before the demolition. The shopkeeper joked that the carpenter, like the *jhuggi* dwellers, had earned excessive profit through his slum business, a claim the carpenter disputed along with the shopkeeper's repeated suggestion that the *jhuggi* residents were actually rich due to the free government services they received. As a participant in the slum economy, this man challenged the shopkeeper and Uncle's effort to draw a sharp distinction between the residents of their lower-middle-class housing society and the slum: "I have lived here for 32 years. I came here to build for the Asiad [Asian Games in 1982] and applied for an LIG [Lower Income Group] flat, like here. But, it wasn't in my fate. You had good fate. Maybe I'll get one some day."

The shopkeeper and Uncle's housing society was made up of Delhi Development Authority (DDA) flats constructed by the earliest residents of Ravi Das Camp, who were predominantly Dalit laborers recruited, employed, and settled by a government contractor in the early 1980s.[10] Through the 1970s and 1980s, applying to the DDA housing lottery was the primary way to access land legally in Delhi, but the DDA failed to build the number of flats mandated by the Delhi Master Plan, leading to the gross underprovision of planned housing in the city, especially in what are known as the Lower Income Group (LIG) and Economically Weaker Sections (EWS) categories—the two lowest income classifications in India.[11] These income categories set the income level below which one is eligible for a particular type of state housing: EWS is a one-room set, with an attached kitchen; LIG has a single, separated bedroom; middle-income group (MIG) has two bedrooms, and so forth. Due to the shortage of housing, competition to obtain a DDA flat was (and still is) fierce; fewer than 10 percent of applicants receive flats. Most lower income households denied DDA housing either rent rooms in planned neighborhoods or move to *bastis* and unauthorized colonies, which together house more than 40 percent of the total population. The carpenter's "bad" fate, he hinted, was based on this fact. If Uncle and the shopkeeper had not been in the lucky 10 percent, they would have been like the carpenter and *jhuggi* dwellers: unpropertied.

After Uncle and the carpenter took their leave, the shopkeeper walked me through the gate into the housing society, where we met three men who had just returned from work. The shopkeeper introduced me and said I wanted to know about the old *basti*. Again, with little prompting, they began describing how much their lives had improved after the demolition. One of the men pointed at my scooter and told me that had I left my helmet unlocked, as it was, before the demolition, it would have been stolen right away: "You couldn't have even parked there! I wanted to buy a car, but had no place to park it safely. Out there anything could have happened."[12]

The four of us sat for tea on plastic chairs directly in front of the large iron gate that enclosed the society's inner road from the main street, our backs to the playground where Uncle had been standing, and the former site of Ravi Das Camp a stone's throw away. The shopkeeper retreated to his shop. After introductions, we returned to the topic of the *basti*. One man began, "before, we wouldn't have been able to sit here like this. There would have been so much crowd. Those people walked straight in and used our park and bothered us so much. Our own children couldn't play here."

The three men looked out over the empty lot: "It is so clear. The weather is also nicer now. You feel the wind, right? Before, we didn't have such wind," a middle-aged Sikh man who was a sales manager in a furniture store said.

When I asked what the society had done to avoid the trouble of the *basti*, the men said they had installed the gate to prevent the *jhuggi* dwellers from entering, but threats by the Ravi Das Camp leaders had forced them to keep it open during the day. The man hosting us, whose flat was on the ground floor and just two doors down from the main road that abutted the former *basti*, pointed at the iron grilling in front of his veranda and said he had built this wall with a roof and locking gate to prevent theft (see Figure 3.3): "I have valuable things out there. Without this, those people would have just taken it all. . . . For security, I built this cage and locked my own family in, like animals, but the real animals were out there!" Turning to the other men, he laughed at his joke. The other men nodded in approval, awaiting my laughter at what seemed a familiar line to them.

Later in our conversation, I asked about the temple still erect on the empty plot. One of the men said the DDA could not clear it because of its religious significance, an excuse he did not buy, noting the high value of the land and describing the priest's side business: "They run a guesthouse out of it so people from Bihar can come stay. The people who run it are Bihari. Now they are making their own little Bihar here! The rest of the people, we had them thrown out. They lived in trash; wherever they went, our roads, our parks, filth also came. . . . They were filth. We had them tossed."[13]

Figure 3.3. "I built this cage and locked my own family in." Photograph by author.

While Ravi Das Camp had been cleared many months before, the symbol of the slum continued to operate in these narratives as the constitutive outside against which property-bearing and middle-class selfhood is defined. Against the filth and disorder of the slum, the housing society emerged as "posh." Against the violence and decay of slum life, the men found a caring and secure home. The stories the shopkeeper and his neighbors told me that day had been recited time and time again, supplying a generative symbolism for distancing self from slum. This was a division that had to be actively maintained, lest the distinction between the inside and outside break down, as was shown by the ambiguous status of the carpenter, who was of the same economic class as the housing society residents, lived in the housing society, but had deep ties to the slum.

I begin with an extended description of this encounter because it highlights [the metonymic associations RWAs in Delhi frequently make between dirt on the one hand and slums and the defiled bodies they house] (e.g., "they were filth") on the other, as well as how such associations are used to enforce the social and physical boundary between private property and slum. Scholars have long noted how talk of dirt and excrement is used to represent residual people and places: "Excrement and its equivalents (decay, infection, disease, etc.) stand for the danger to identity that comes from without."[14] The history of struggles over urban space in colonial and postcolonial India confirms, as Dipesh Chakrabarty argues, how constructions of middle-class selfhood have been "replete with these themes of the enclosed inside and the exposed outside" and the "protective power" inhering in the symbolic and material boundaries dividing these two domains. Chakrabarty thus contends that the "outside," at least for middle-class Hindus, "always carries 'substances' that threaten one's well-being" and "produces both malevolence and exchange between communities and hence needs to be tamed."[15] This "unattainable desire to expel or control those things which threaten the boundary" between inside and outside has been well studied as a psychic process of abjection (revulsion, disavowal, fetishism).[16] What is so striking about millennial Delhi is how these highly localized and intimate aversions, often rooted in a caste-based habitus of purity and pollution, were translated into a type of urban abjection—a politics of expulsion that draws legitimacy from notions of public welfare and environmental health but that remains rooted in necessarily localized experiences of nuisance.

Nuisance, as the neighbors of Ravi Das Camp suggest, begins as an embodied category based on shared local experience: it is the olfactory annoyance of rotting fish or the discomfort of seeing naked, raggedy children occupy "your" park. Without the immediate evidence of the nuisance of Ravi Das Camp, the shopkeeper and his neighbors relied on a rich, sensory language—of foul smells, disturbing sounds, and intrusive bodies—to evoke the slum as a threatening category. But although most speakers engage it only in this way, nuisance talk proves to have a more complex trajectory. As it circulates and gains a larger coalition of speakers, nuisance talk consolidates a sensory vocabulary that influences the terms on which space and bodies in the city can be described. That is, nuisance talk lays out a sensory framework that provides the basis for identifying order and disorder, as well as determining the credibility of claims to public space based on how a speaker is positioned inside or outside the corresponding social order. Nuisance talk, in other words, is the discursive foundation of the world-class aesthetic.

Consider, for example, the legal case against Ravi Das Camp. The men with whom I sat that day were members of the local RWA that, along with two neighboring RWAs, had filed the public interest litigation (PIL) in the Delhi High Court that led to Ravi Das Camp's demolition. I obtained a copy of the RWAs' petition later, through which the same vocabulary of slum filth was brought into the domain of the judiciary:

> The encroachment [Ravi Das Camp] ... has now grown and taken a mammoth shape threatening the natural environment in the area and has started jeopardising the life of the residents of the area by posing problems ... like pollution of all sorts, health hazards, insanitary conditions due to garbage dumping ... blocks of roads ... and also giving rise to social problems like theft, robbery etc. and has threatened the security of the residents.

As in the men's comments to me, the slum emerges in this petition as an illegal environment based purely on its aesthetic impropriety and the nuisance it causes to property-owning residents of the city. Yet as I demonstrate in the following chapter on nuisance law, since the early 2000s the judiciary and planning branches of the state have accepted such arguments about the nuisance of slums as a legitimate basis for issuing demolition orders. In this particular case, the High Court concurred with the RWAs' nuisance argument, ordering the slum's demolition on the basis of a nuisance logic by stating that Ravi Das Camp "deprives the rights of citizens of Delhi" to civic amenities and degrades public space.[17]

How does nuisance talk, a particularistic set of speech acts expressing local environmental anxieties and social aversions, move from everyday neighborhood conversation into state discourse and urban policy? How do such specific statements of disgust circulate and gain official legitimacy? To answer these questions, we must begin with nuisance's circulatory power—its capacity to build a coalition of speakers, before turning to how it consolidates a broader politics of city making.

TALKING NUISANCE

After my encounter with the RWA members adjacent to Ravi Das Camp, I began contacting other active RWAs in Delhi to ask them about their mobilization against slums. Most RWA members were enthusiastic to meet me, calling me to their homes or offices after I reached them by phone. Upon meeting, I usually initiated conversation by describing my research, where I studied and lived, and my interest in neighborhood and urban governance. In most cases, my interlocutors would follow not with a response to my research interests, but rather with their reflections on the contrasting civic culture in Delhi and abroad, usually the United States. In fact, we rarely even began talking about RWA matters until they had sufficient time to display their knowledge of and, in many cases, admiration for the West. As one man said, "oh, California, such a lovely place! Where do you live, San Francisco, LA? . . . I took a trip there while visiting my son in Arizona. . . . When I first went there—it must have been ten years ago—Delhi was some thirty-plus years behind. Today, we have caught up so much. We must be only ten years behind now. Much better, but still a way to go." Such comments provided an opportunity for me to ask about their perceptions of Delhi, as in, "in what ways do you think Delhi is behind?"

Across a diverse array of neighborhood-specific concerns, most RWA members, especially those in wealthier south Delhi colonies, expressed a clear desire for Delhi to become world-class. When I asked what a world-class city meant to them, they often gave examples of the Delhi Metro or a new shopping mall, but they most often expressed a general sense of a clean, comfortable, and nuisance-free public life. Regardless of how optimistic they were that Delhi would become world-class, residents agreed that Delhi required a significant upgrade in infrastructure, services, and visual appearance.

All RWA members with whom I spoke stressed the value of their neighborhood-specific efforts in terms of their contribution to increasing the quality of life in, and appearance of, Delhi as a whole. For example, the secretary of an RWA in one of south Delhi's wealthiest colonies said, "our goal is to maintain and enhance the posh character of [the colony]," an effort that he directly linked with the image of greater Delhi:

> I had a friend whose boss was visiting from Germany. They were driving in [the colony], and he had just told his boss how [it] is one of Delhi's poshest areas. Just then, some pigs crossed the street. He was so embarrassed! No matter what we do, this city is still a mess. We have to do more to change things and put the proper systems in place. Everyone needs to get together and make Delhi look like a planned city.[18]

One of the main problems his RWA worked to solve in both his colony and in Delhi as a whole was the presence of hawkers and other "street encroachments," as he called them:

> The hawkers that operate under the Tehbazari scheme [a license program granting temporary vending rights] are a big problem. They aren't supposed to cook in the open, but they do. They create filth, causing danger to human life and making the colony unsightly. They sit in an unauthorized way, cook, and create filth. . . . Near D-block . . . 20-25 rickshaws stand there and eat breakfast. People taking morning walks have to see this. It's not a pleasant sight to see auto drivers eating their breakfasts and then easing themselves, just taking a leak on the street. We aren't against the poor people trying to live, but are against the creation of filth and unhygienic living conditions.

This statement makes clear how grievances of a primarily aesthetic nature—the hawkers as eyesores, as stains on an otherwise posh landscape—gain expression through a rhetoric of hygiene and public nuisance. His main complaint was not about illness in the neighborhood or a noxious environment, but rather an unpleasant scene. This statement also demonstrates the manner in which RWAs frequently depict their interventionist efforts to structure and discipline public life as a struggle to secure the inside from the alien and impure threats of the outside. This RWA secretary moved on to say, "overall, we are against traffic flow and outsiders entering into the colony unnecessarily," thus marking his move from the identification of an abject object—hawkers—to the formulation of a spatial politics of abjection, displacing outsiders in order to maintain and enhance the posh character of the colony.

Most RWA members similarly attributed neighborhood deficiencies to external forces, whether visible or remote. After I asked a south Delhi RWA member, a retired man in his seventies, what the main problems his RWA faced were, he responded with his own question: "Did you smell the *nālā* [drain] on your way in?" I had noticed the strong smell of sewage in his otherwise upscale neighborhood of Safdarjung Enclave (see Map),[19] but was unsure whether I should conceal this fact out of courtesy. I hesitated, and he proceeded: "There is a *nala* outside our boundary wall, and slums and their fecal matters and foul materials ruin things here." I asked him where the slum was located, and he said his RWA had won a three-year court battle that eventually led to the slum's demolition earlier in the year:

> The problem was that the DDA was letting people occupy the land. In the city there are 35 lakh [3.5 million] slum dwellers. . . . This has given rise to crime because they are mostly unemployed and coming from all states. A car was stolen here even. . . . They occupy public land, set up *jhuggis*, and create [a] health hazard. Because the infrastructure in the city isn't even enough for [real] inhabitants, so they should stop immigration from these countries: Nepal, Bangladesh, West Bengal, Bihar.

Flicking the fingers of his left hand away from his body, he continued, "these [slum] people used to roam into this area; their children played here. Our children couldn't even go outside. These people are a different lot."

He went on to describe how neighborhood crime had gone down after the slum's removal and how the quality of public services in the city would only improve by demolishing the city's remaining slums. When I asked him why the stench of the *nala* remained even after the slum's demolition, he conceded that the environment of the colony had not improved with the removal of the slum, but attributed the sewage not to other planned colonies, most of whose sewage flows untreated through twenty-two open *nalas* across the city and directly into the Yamuna River, but rather to an upstream slum: "The root cause for the filth is the slum. Delhi is infested by this problem." Referring to the problem of open defecation, he continued, "just travel by train and you'll see along the tracks how people behave. It's shameful."

Despite the physical distance between slums and his residence, this man attributed waste in his social environment to the slum problem, bolstering his claim by referring to the aesthetic impropriety of the poor who, in their compulsion to openly defecate, he argued, were the source of urban decay. When I asked him about the legal basis for his RWA's court petition against the old slum, he replied, "basically, these people do not belong in Delhi.... They ruin Delhi's environment. They don't follow any of the rules and create so much nuisance. This is a posh colony. How can we have such slums nearby?"

Even in colonies with no nearby slum, RWA members often described slums as a source of disease and danger that, if not controlled, would spread into purer spaces like neighborhoods and homes. One man exemplified this in describing how a scorpion had crawled out of the drain in his kitchen sink while his wife was using it: "She was very frightened. This is a dangerous thing! I mean, it can't kill you, but it's dangerous. Now how does a scorpion come out of a drain like that?" Responding to my confusion, he proceeded to answer his own question, "all these sewers are connected. Our waste flows into them, and the slum waste flows into them before ours. It is all mixed. This scorpion just climbed through the sewer and came into our house." Here, he was signaling the invisible risk of the slum through the city's subterranean and public infrastructure. The scorpion represented a violation of the inside, the perceived threat that the sanctity of the home could be punctured at any moment by external risks. Even the boundary walls, security guards, and dogs dividing his home from the street could not tame the disease that overflows from slums. Whereas this man had begun his conversation with a partial recognition that the degraded state of slums was the product of social conditions for which slum residents were not themselves responsible—namely, a shortage of low-income housing—the social origins of slum degradation were quickly elided in his move to refer to the natural, animal essence of the slum. It is here, in stories about invasion and savagery, that the metonymic association of filth with slums was often displaced by a metaphoric language of the slum dweller as animal, a theme that emerged in a number of my interactions with RWA activists. As Jindal, who I introduced at the beginning of the chapter, proclaimed, "these people live with dogs and pigs. Of course their habits will be like that only." "Slums," he continued, "aren't part of society; they aren't integrated. And, anything not integrated into society can't last forever.... They have to be removed. They are all bound to be relocated." When he saw my look of surprise, he shifted his phrasing: "Slum people are used to going from place to place. It's natural for them." Animalized slums, naturalized dispossession.

If not through the transgression of the boundary separating human and animal, then RWAs seeking to justify their aggressive stance vis-à-vis slums invoked transgressions of "natural" boundaries dividing the urban from the rural, educated from uneducated, and Indian from foreign. As one RWA president told me, "the people who have encroached on parks here by habit don't develop a taste for sanitation. . . . We haven't yet changed the culture of these people to be urban. We need to change the rural mindset. We need to change the attitude to cleanliness and responsibility. All people in Delhi were once migrants. These people need to change or else they don't belong in the city."

This type of neighborhood speech is not in itself new; upper-caste Hindus have long invoked caste imaginaries of purity and pollution to leverage colonial law and later postcolonial technologies of planning to maintain and increase spatial exclusion.[20] What is significant about nuisance talk is the way in which everyday speech is molded into a larger spatial politics as it is taken up by the media, state, and judiciary. That is, nuisance talk becomes part of a discourse of world-class city making, where the category of nuisance provides the key pivot combining bourgeois claims to the moral and aesthetic value of private property with an environmental and civic claim to public welfare. Nuisance talk hence articulates with and is picked up by other ongoing interventions to civilize public space, such as heightened state concerns about crime and public order, as well as increasing middle-class worries about the origins of domestic servants and associated police efforts to monitor the floating population of itinerant workers. As a result, nuisance talk often slides through these different registers, depicting slums as spaces of environmental, economic, and social decay.

It is in this way that the trope of the slum-dwelling migrant unhabituated to urban life dovetails with a more deeply rooted neo-Malthusian concern about resource scarcity and overpopulation, as well as upper-caste anxieties about the plebianization of the public in the wake of what is known as "the second democratic upsurge" of backward caste influence in electoral politics.[21] Delhi's second largest RWA federation, called People's Action, hence staked out an explicitly anti-immigrant political platform, drawing popular support from the widespread belief that shortages in electricity and water supply are caused by overpopulated slums and not rising middle-class consumption. As Sanjay Kaul, a savvy media professional and the spokesman for People's Action, told me in an interview in his office, "the biggest problem for Delhi is that 500,000 people come here every year. . . . Delhi can't become world-class if it lets 5 lakh people in tattered clothes come to the city. . . . It can't be world-class without security." He continued: "In Delhi, those who legitimately own land, pay taxes, and those with papers are getting pushed out of the city to the satellite cities because the prices are going up so much from letting illegal occupation go on for political benefit. . . . The culture of illegality is crowding out the good, working man who buys land and pays taxes. . . . You are marginalized if middle-class and educated."[22] This "culture of illegality," according to Kaul, contaminates not only physical space, sullying neighborhoods and street sides, but also political space, producing vote-bank politics and corruption. The response to the slum problem, then, requires measures both to insulate important decision-making processes from the poor (the role of the Bhagidari scheme I discussed in the previous chapter), as well as to bolster physical security within colonies.

NUISANCE ON THE MOVE

A primary strategy that RWAs deployed to reclaim "their" city was to fortify and securitize their neighborhoods by building fences, closing colony entrances at night, and increasing the number of hired security guards. Such efforts are considered necessary to ensure neighborhood security, a primary RWA concern. Jindal, for example, stated that the main goal of his RWA was to turn his residential block, a pocket of four hundred houses and approximately 2,000 residents, into a subcity—a vision of a privatized, urban utopia shared by many RWAs:

> We would have our own small market with only approved vendors and shops so the residents don't have to go outside for daily requirements. There would be a food supplier, a *dhobī* [clothes washer], milkman, daily rations, all these things. We would have the colony fully developed and maintained by the RWA only. We would be in charge of services and oversight. We would build gates and have permanent security guards to monitor who could enter and when. . . . We are now trying to work with the police to start a checking system for security enhancement.

Unlike other cities that experienced deepening segregation and fortification in the wake of economic liberalization, millennial Delhi did not see a marked increase in violent or property crime.[23] After asking Pankaj Agarwal, the secretary of Delhi's RWA Joint Front, which is the largest RWA federation in Delhi with over four hundred member RWAs, about why there is so much opposition to slums, he said, "they drain resources, create security problems, and create [a] negative impression in the minds of tourists when they see beggars on the streets. . . . You see, today, a house costs some three to four crore rupees [~$750,000–$1,000,000]—for a small house. The middle class has to pay so much to live here, and then to have all these security problems. The middle class is discriminated against." I interjected and asked what security problems slums cause, and he replied, "the feeling is there that crime is a problem, even if it is not true. It is a psychological feeling."[24]

These feelings are enhanced by sensational media coverage of violent crime and dangerous slums, which depict an increasingly violent and decayed city in need of securitization, despite a significant decline in crime in the first decade of the new millennium.[25] Without questioning the credibility of the police analysis—such as the absence of a sociological study to back the police report—or interviewing criminologists with competing hypotheses, the *Hindustan Times*, for example, reported that the "police's annual crime report attributes the incidence of sexual abuse to a number of sociological factors, including mushrooming of JJ [*jhuggī jhompḍī*] clusters and subhuman living conditions. Last year, about 80 per cent of the accused belonged to the poor strata."[26] It further drew upon the fallacy of rising crime to justify RWA securitization when it stated, "with murders and burglary increasing by the day, security concerns have led RWAs to build more gates around colonies."[27]

Police support for neighborhood securitization further fuels RWA rhetoric of outside intruders, blending the nuisance-based sensory vocabulary of slum unsightliness with security concerns over social deviance and criminality. As the police chief said during a Bhagidari meeting:

> The attacks that took place in Ayodhya were organized by people staying in Delhi.[28] There are many antisocial elements that stay in Delhi, its slums, and unmonitored places. We have to watch out for suspicious people, terrorists, and criminals. This is the duty of RWAs. RWAs need to restrict and control this movement with security to remove antisocial elements and security risks.[29]

The discursive resonance between the police chief's statement and common RWA anxieties about the degradation of public spaces shows that discussion of slums as criminal, polluting spaces became a routine part of public speech in millennial Delhi. A south Delhi RWA president justified his successful court petition to demolish a nearby slum on the same terms, saying the slum was inhabited "by illegal immigrants and antisocial elements. They had big brawls with the cops and a month and a half back stole a cop's gun. They also could have been involved in the terrorist issues. There were many Pakistanis and Bangladeshis there."[30]

Unlike the case of Ravi Das Camp's neighbors, these statements indicate how the inside is read beyond home and neighborhood and comes to include the whole of the city. Thus, whereas in Ravi Das Camp nuisance worked as a relational, localized category that emerged with reference to community-specific grievances and discomforts (an encroached park, the stench of fish), nuisance talk's circulation into the domain of urban security puts in place increasingly standardized metrics of disorder, which are visually (and sensorially) calibrated to propertied notions of the public as a space intended to supplement the moral and economic attributes of the private—a vision at the very core of the world-class aesthetic.

THE PROPRIETY OF PROPERTY

RWA members consistently raise concerns about slum sanitation and cleanliness by arguing that behavior they consider distinctly private—for example, washing, bathing, drinking, and defecating—is unpleasant, morally degrading, and harmful when conducted in public. Seeing public land as the material foundation for urban order and an aesthetically gratifying life, property owners oppose the use of public land for subsistence purposes, a claim echoed in city planning documents that emphasize the importance of a clean and green streetscape amenable to circulation, tourism, and leisure. As Pankaj Agarwal told me, "we want gardens in front of our houses, but there's all kinds of filth there now. They [slum residents] wash clothes there. How can I enjoy my balcony?" Thus, while couched in the language of danger and insalubrity, RWA members' nuisance talk often betrays more of a concern with property value and the quality of their private life than with environmental risk or crime. A wealthy south Delhi RWA member candidly conveyed this sentiment while giving me a tour of his house:

> We have a back entrance also. It was on the side [of the house] with the jhuggis, so until we had them removed we never even opened the door.... Why would someone in a posh colony want to walk that way [near the slum]? This house is worth so much, and to just see these people squatting on free land! One wants to be reminded of the value of his property, not faced with encroachment and nuisance.

Here, nuisance signifies a theory of value as much as it indexes biological risk, resembling colonial applications of the concept under British rule that had fallen out of favor in postcolonial India. As "the coercive arm of property rights," the doctrine of nuisance under the British "was closely wedded to a regime of private property ... affording [property owners] a promise of protection against extrinsic interferences."[31] The law of nuisance also "played an important role in the appropriation and reconstitution of a specifically 'public' social space," curtailing previous modes of common access by introducing a new spatial order premised on a sanitized and leisure-based mode of using public space.[32]

The logic of nuisance in millennial Delhi, for the first time on a citywide scale in postcolonial India, returned to its earlier, colonial origins, making nuisance a mechanism for sequestering and removing culturally coded signs of decay and defending the symbolic and economic value of private property. As a full-time RWA activist responsible for organizing some of south Delhi's most well-covered media events told me: "You have to create space for the rich. I don't know what you think about the US, but we think capitalism isn't a bad word. Rich people only spread goodness. Poor people spread dirt." Arguing against the Master Plan's approach to densifying residential space, he continued: "It [densification] will squeeze out the rich, making posh colonies too tight. They want to make the whole city for the poor. You need to encourage rich people to live here because they bring good things.... If you make things too tight, they'll go outside the city and it will crumble like a slum." In his framing, the "good" of the rich depends on their separation from the poor—value accrues through the sequestration/abjection of degraded people, or as Vinay Gidwani and Rajyashree Reddy write, "wasteful 'natures'—bodies, spaces, things, and conducts—have to be territorialized for ordered 'society'—the society of law that safeguards property and value—to be possible."[33]

While such stark binaries of wealth-virtue and poverty-degradation may appear extreme, the media and government have launched various public campaigns couched in similar terms, explicitly drawing upon the discourse of nuisance. The Delhi government's Clean Delhi, Green Delhi campaign, for example, was a citywide public information drive aimed at instilling a sense of civic pride in the city's cleanliness and appearance, primarily through aesthetic projects such as roadside landscaping and park rejuvenation that do little to address underlying sources of environmental stress.[34] The Clean Delhi, Green Delhi phrase was used specifically to criminalize public urination and to fence and beautify road medians to remove space for begging and hawking. Under the guise of cleaning up Delhi in preparation for the 2010 Commonwealth Games, the DDA similarly sought to ban approximately 300,000 vendors of street food, and the courts demanded the removal of all beggars from city roads. As the Delhi government's advertisement shown in Figure 3.4 attests, the discourse of infestation not only circulates from the middle class to government, as discussed above, but becomes a part of official problematizations of urban poverty that are conveyed to the public at large. Because nuisance talk establishes a pattern of identifying its problem objects (the slum, the beggar, pollution) as sources, not products, of urban decay, the reader of this advertisement is asked to inhabit a subject-position with a particular bourgeois stance vis-à-vis the poor. By drawing upon a shared affective response (guilt, discomfort, abjection), the advertisement interpolates its subjects, hailing readers to respond on the aesthetic terms with which they are familiar. As the advertisement's text brazenly reads: "For all you know, your alm may cause ... Traffic Jams.... Unemployment.... Alcohol. ... Heroin. ... Robbery. Rape. ... Murder. ... Slums." Here, readers are positioned in an automobile, a distinctly bourgeois inside space, facing the onslaught of social ills listed in the text, their senses educated for later embodied encounters with poverty and disorder. The message is clear: the source of social decay is the urban poor, donations to whom encourage their illicit conduct and inhibit urban progress.

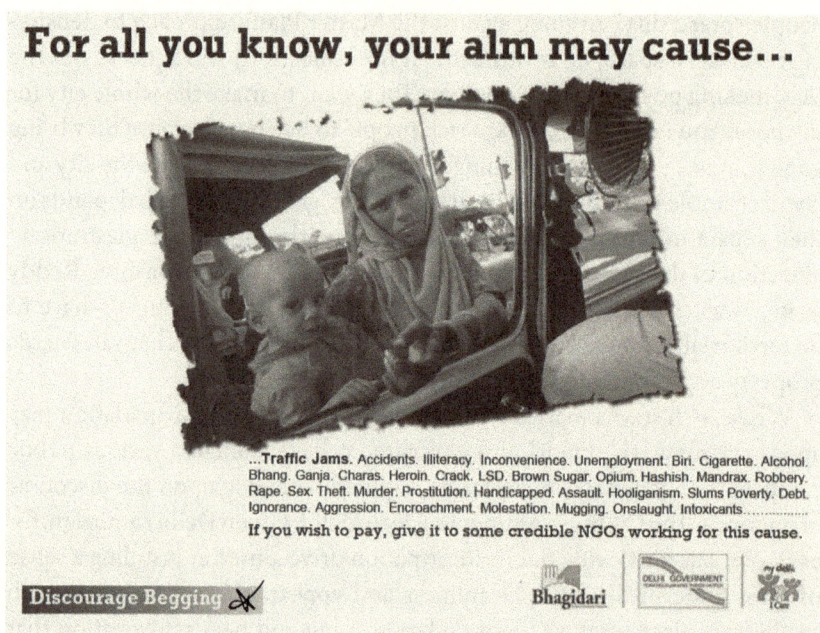

Figure 3.4. Delhi government advertisement appearing in the *Hindustan Times* on November 25, 2006.

The government advanced this message perhaps most aggressively in attributing high pollution levels in the Yamuna River to the presence of slums, despite the Delhi Water Board's public acknowledgment that the main cause of pollution is the twenty-two open drains [*nalas*] that carry untreated sewage from mostly middle-class residential colonies across the city directly into the river.[35] The managing director of the Delhi Metro Rail Corporation thus wrote in an editorial, responding to resistance to the plan to model the Yamuna on the Thames in London by clearing all slum settlements in sight, "a handful of self-styled environmentalists is stalling this idea. The result is rampant encroachments on the riverbed by jhuggis[,] which catch fire at regular intervals every summer, often burning alive a few people. Sewage and untreated industrial waste are let into the river without treatment."[36] The chief minister similarly held "the slums responsible for the condition of the Yamuna," even though the Central Pollution Control Board found "no improvement in the quality of water" following the removal of 40,000 *jhuggis* housing approximately 200,000 people from its banks.[37] In the case of the Yamuna River, the evidentiary basis for proving slums are the source of environmental stress and public nuisance is not a technoscientific or calculative rationality—nor, as I argue in the following chapter, is it based on legal precedent or statutory law. Rather, the fact of slum pollution and illegality is known via a shared aesthetic disposition, acquired through subjective engagement with nuisance talk.

PERFORMING NUISANCE

Property owners in Delhi and the RWAs that represent them mobilize diverse geographic imaginaries of transgression. These imaginaries operate across scales from the neighborhood, to the city, to the nation, and engage anxieties and aspirations traversing the material, symbolic, and sensate. Nuisance proves to be equally transmutable, taking on ecological and economic registers and allowing for the easy identification of the abject outside. As it circulates beyond local settings, becoming incorporated in public service announcements, the mass media, commercial advertisements, judicial orders, and government proclamations, nuisance talk shapes the terms on which poverty and urban space can be described in the city. By designating objects of urban disorder and calibrating individuals' perceptions of that disorder to a broader, class-based program of social action—world-class city making—nuisance-as-aesthetic clarifies and confirms the unsightliness of poverty, disclosing its inherent structure to be as it appears: out of place, disturbing the natural order, illegal. Slums are known to be polluting and illegal because they look polluting and illegal; slum removal is a necessary process of urban improvement because it contributes to a more beautiful city.

By routing residents' affective response to urban disorder through an aesthetic field defined through the image of the world-class city, nuisance talk establishes its own rules of order, hierarchies of meaning, and legitimate opinions. Because nuisance talk makes certain types of disorder visible (e.g., pollution caused by open cooking) and not others (e.g., automobile exhaust), those entering into this aesthetic field embody certain visual dispositions in order to gain membership in communities defined in terms of the field. In the case of the lower-middle-class residents adjacent to Ravi Das Camp, membership in this community is sought through efforts to claim middle-class status. In the case of elite RWA members, it is membership in a global community of world-class citizens, or a more general desire to catch up with the West. As I explore in chapters 5 and 6, *jhuggi* residents also seek membership via this field, at times adopting nuisance talk to construct themselves as potential world-class citizens, deserving of government resettlement and critical of the nuisance of slums.

All acts of naming—whether they bestow the title of doctor, declare something to be a nuisance, or call someone an idiot—aim to impose a more or less authorized way of seeing the world. I know who to call if I am sick, where to avoid when going for a walk, and whose advice to pay no heed based on these acts of nominalization. Pierre Bourdieu differentiates two types of naming practices: those that involve common nouns with a well-understood meaning—for example, the statement "it is winter"—on the one hand, and "acts of institution" on the other, whose efficacy in imposing their visions of the social world rests on claims to symbolic authority—for example, a judge proclaiming someone to be guilty.[38] The former class of naming acts principally describes reality, whereas the latter has greater performative effect, meaning such acts modify, and do not just describe, that reality. The performative efficacy of "acts of institution," Bourdieu argues, is proportional to the power of the institution backing them, where "institution" means not just formal rules, but also the symbolic authority delegated to the speaker.

Nuisance talk, on first glance, consists of descriptive utterances: "Slums are dirty." But nuisance talk has a linked performative dimension that in practice structures social perception by placing slums on the outside, beyond accepted standards of civility. This is what I mean when I say nuisance moves from being a medium for expressing taste or opinion into the bearer of force. Nuisance talk acquires this force, in part, by gaining the institutional authorization of the media, police, and government departments—in other words, as institutions with greater symbolic authority incorporate nuisance into their accounts of urban space. But, more importantly, nuisance talk gains popular legitimacy through the aesthetic consensus it builds around seemingly nonpolitical descriptions of local urban environments. Through its capacity to spread, it pulls diverse clusters of statements about local aesthetic annoyances into its enunciative orbit, identifying something larger than its parts: the urban abject. The increasing use of nuisance-as-lay-term to describe local hassles and aesthetic annoyances ("that slum stinks") gains performative force when it acquires the power to name what is proper and improper, what belongs and does not belong: the abject that must be expunged.

4

Aesthetic Criminalization

The Nuisance of Slums

PUBLIC NUISANCE, PRIVATE PURPOSE

At the turn of the new millennium, the pace of slum demolition in Delhi increased starkly, leading to the displacement of as many as a million *jhuggi* dwellers by 2012. Until this time, the decision to raze a slum had been the almost exclusive domain of Delhi's various land-owning agencies, in particular the Delhi Development Authority (DDA). In millennial Delhi, these wings of government had little say in determining the legal and political status of such settlements. Instead, court-issued demolition orders became the primary mechanism of slum removal, in most cases issued in response to resident welfare associations' (RWAs) petitions requesting the removal of neighboring slums. Whereas in the previous two chapters I considered how RWAs and the property owners they represent gained the authority to define slum removal as a necessary step in Delhi's millennial march toward becoming a world-class city, in this chapter I identify the legal mechanisms of slum demolition. I do so through an analysis of the orders and judgments of the Delhi High Court and Supreme Court of India related to slum demolition over the past thirty years, as well as the civil writ petitions filed that directly led to the demolition of dozens of settlements in millennial Delhi.

By highlighting key words and phrases that arise within the proceedings of slum-related cases, I set out to show how the basic statement that "slums are illegal" is part of a very recent juridical discourse, despite its widespread circulation in India at the turn of the millennium. I further argue that proving this statement in the courts rests on a different and less rigorous evidentiary procedure than other types of truth claims: to prove a slum's illegality, one must demonstrate that it appears to be a nuisance—an inherently aesthetic category grounded in Indian civil and criminal law, but, as I argued in the previous chapter, also a rich terrain of popular speech. I find that the recent criminalization of slum settlements in general, and the rise of court orders to demolish settlements in particular, occurred because of a reinterpretation of nuisance law, the main component of environmental law in India. Specifically, in the early 2000s, the judiciary extended the broad enforcement powers related to public nuisance into matters of private nuisance. In doing so, it reconstituted the meaning of "public interest," defined distinctly private interests as public matters, and allowed the nuisance talk I described in the previous chapter to circulate through the courts, projecting a vision of urban order—a world-class aesthetic—founded on property ownership. Nuisance thus became the key legal principle driving slum demolitions in millennial Delhi and has been incredibly influential in resculpting both Delhi's residential geography and how the city's future is imagined.

After describing the roots of nuisance law in India, I turn to how the crisis of calculative governmentality I described in the introduction led to a reproblematization of the slum as a nuisance in the early 2000s. I follow by describing how the courts consolidated a new discourse of nuisance that codified world-class aesthetic norms in law and provided a visual basis for removing slums and visible signs of poverty. Based on fieldwork inside the courtroom, I find that photographs and other simplified visual representations allow judges to look at a building, plot of land, or population and, without knowing its location or history, determine its legality by drawing upon world-class aesthetic codes. Obviating the need to simplify messy ground realities through careful inscriptive procedures like mapping and surveying—slow and complicated techniques that have prevented judges from making swift decisions historically—judges rule by aesthetics. Rule in the form of individual court judgments clearly differs from the broader treatment of rule as the more diffuse practice of shaping perceptions and habits discussed elsewhere in the book. However, as I show, individual High Court and Supreme Court orders, which set precedent across the whole of India, form the juridical node of aesthetic governmentality, both laying down a rule and punishing those who violate it as well as reinforcing and codifying the world-class aesthetic that more diffusely shapes popular perceptions and behaviour.

THE FOUNDATIONS OF NUISANCE LAW

A nuisance is legally defined as "any act, omission, injury, damage, annoyance or offense to the sense of sight, smell, hearing or which is or may be dangerous to life or injurious to health or property."[1] In common law, nuisances are of two types: public and private, the former an "unreasonable interference with a right common to the general public" and the latter a "substantial and unreasonable interference with the use or enjoyment of land."[2] In the Indian legal system, the primary statutes that provide channels to redress nuisance are Section 133 of the Code of Criminal Procedure (hereafter Cr. P.C.) and Section 91 of the Code of Civil Procedure, both of which derive their definitions of nuisance from British common law. In postcolonial India, Section 133 Cr. P.C. has operated as the primary statute for matters of public nuisance, the aim of which is to provide an independent, quick, and summary remedy to public nuisance by empowering a magistrate to order its removal.[3] The nuisances referred to in Section 133 include: obstructions to a public place or way, trades or activities hazardous to the surrounding community, flammable substances, objects that could fall and cause injury, unfenced excavations or wells, or unconfined and dangerous animals.[4] Nuisances are thus limited statutorily to two categories: (i) objects or possessions, and (ii) actions.

The landmark case pertaining to slum-related nuisance, which affirmed the enforcement powers of Section 133 Cr. P.C., was decided in 1980 in *Ratlam Municipal Council v. Vardichan*. In this case, the Ratlam Municipal Council was directed by a magistrate, empowered under Section 133 Cr. P.C., to construct and improve drains in a municipal ward to eradicate nuisance caused by stagnant, putrid water. The Municipal Council subsequently filed an appeal, which eventually came before the Supreme Court. The Supreme Court defended the magistrate's initial order, affirmed the statutory nature of Section 133 Cr. P.C., and declared that it was the primary remedial mechanism for dealing with public nuisance: "Wherever there is a public nuisance, the presence of Section 133 Cr. P.C. must be felt and any contrary opinion is contrary to law."[5] The judge further stated that Section 133 Cr. P.C. should be the main channel by which courts ensure that municipal bodies carry out their duty to provide clean and safe environments for city residents.

In the Ratlam judgment, the court further clarified that the municipal authorities and *not* slum dwellers are the party responsible for nuisances arising from slums with inadequate municipal services. The judge explained:

> The grievous failure of local authorities to provide the basic amenity of public conveniences drives the miserable slum-dwellers to ease in the streets, on the sly for a time,

and openly thereafter, because under Nature's pressure, bashfulness becomes a luxury and dignity a difficult art.... Providing drainage systems ... cannot be evaded if the municipality is to justify its existence.

The removal of public nuisance in slum-related cases, then, was to occur through the application of positive technologies, such as building drainage systems or toilet blocks. That is, instead of removing, disciplining, or punishing those denied adequate sanitation services, the governance of nuisance should operate through positive means to manage and mitigate waste and effluent, and thus improve the population subjected to these conditions. Throughout the 1980s and early 1990s, the Ratlam decision set a precedent for upholding the statutory duties of municipal authorities to ensure public health, particularly that of slum residents.[6]

To better grasp the influence of this statutory foundation of nuisance law, it is useful to examine the character of petitions filed during this same period by private RWAs seeking judicial intervention to address slum-related nuisances, the type of petition that became the primary instrument of slum demolition in millennial Delhi and that I examine in detail below. As an example, take the case of *K. K. Manchanda v. the Union of India*, a matter that appeared before the Delhi High Court regularly until 2002 and that became the lead petition in a summary ruling of sixty-three related slum matters that I discuss below.[7] The petitioner, the Ashok Vihar RWA, located in northwest Delhi, submitted that residents were aggrieved by the squalid conditions of a vacant piece of land in front of their colony that, according to the approved zonal plan, was supposed to be a green belt-cum-community park. The petition states that the primary source of grievance is public nuisance and health hazards created by nearby slum dwellers' use of this land as an open public lavatory: "Adjacent to this Green Belt ... there are large number of jhuggies and jhompries [huts] situated in the said vicinity ... [and] people residing in these jhuggies ... all of them ladies, gents, their offsprings make use of this Public Ground ... for easing themselves throughout the day [sic]." The petition goes on to say that this made the lives of the RWA residents "miserable" and "transgressed their right to very living" because "thousand of people easing themselves pose such uncultured scene, besides no young girls can dare to come to their own balconies throughout the day [because] obnoxious smells pollute the atmosphere [, thus] the entire environment is unconducive to public health and morality [sic]."

The petition thus states clearly that the source of public nuisance faced by the petitioner was slum dwellers' misuse of public land. Yet because the petition was written in a context structured by the Ratlam decision and the statutory definition of public nuisance described above, the petition does not target the slum itself, as similar petitions filed a decade later would do. Rather it states that the petitioner was aggrieved "because the inaction on the part of the Respondents [the government agencies, including the Municipal Corporation of Delhi and DDA] has posed various problems like public indecency, public immorality, health hazard etc. which the Respondents are statutorily liable to control." Following the norm set forth in the Ratlam decision, the petition thus states that the slum residents were forced to ease themselves on public land because "there is no provision of latrines (Public Toilets) for the people residing in these jhuggies." Again, the blame for the public nuisance fell on the authorities, as is clear from the petitioner's request that the court order the authorities to build a community toilet near the slum, develop the vacant land into a community park, and control access to the park by building a boundary wall. In August 1992, the court disposed of the petition while ordering the Municipal Corporation of Delhi (MCD) to prevent the slum residents from defecating in the park, implying that it should fulfil its statutory duty to improve sanitation in the area.

The problem defined and targeted in this case did not pertain to the legal basis of the slum as such; rather, it merely concerned the nuisance-causing activities of the community living there. Furthermore, nuisance law was used here as a mechanism by the courts to provide municipal services to slum dwellers.

While cases through the late 1990s continued to rely on the Ratlam decision in dealing with slum-derived public nuisances, a new problematization of the slum began to emerge at the same time, a trend that would portend how slums would come to be seen by the beginning of the next decade. This trend began to surface in *B. L. Wadehra v. the Union of India*, a case addressing the problem of inadequate waste disposal throughout Delhi.[8] Whereas the original petition concerned the failure of the MCD to dispose of municipal waste across the city, and whereas the final orders issued by the Supreme Court directed the MCD to fulfil its statutory duties to "collect and dispose of the garbage/waste generated from various sources in the city" by increasing the efficiency of waste collection, the judgment makes occasional mention of a growing problem of the slum. The MCD in particular presents slums as a key problem obstructing it from carrying out its duties, stating in its affidavit that because of "problems of Jhuggi Jhompri Clusters [and] floating population and for various other reasons, it is not possible to give the time schedule regarding the cleaning of Delhi as directed by this Court." While this type of statement did not yet target *jhuggi* clusters for demolition, it forms the basis on which future decisions equating slums with nuisance would rely. The Wadehra case further indexes both the rising visibility of municipal pollution as an urgent public matter and, as we shall see, a creeping sense that long-standing records- and survey-based procedures for reducing public nuisances were not up to the task of world-class city making.

SLUM CLEARANCE AS ENVIRONMENTAL IMPROVEMENT

As the goal of transforming Delhi into a world-class city was increasingly enshrined into official planning and policy documents in the early 2000s, and as cases pertaining to municipal waste and slum-based nuisances started to mount up, the judiciary began to show increasing frustration with state agencies for failing to reply to its broad orders, issued in the Wadehra judgment and elsewhere, to clean up the city. In 2000, in *Almrita Patel v. the Union of India*, the Supreme Court held: "In Delhi, which is the capital of the country and which should be its showpiece, no effective initiative of any kind has been taken by the numerous governmental agencies operating there in cleaning up the city."[9] Without a single mention of the Ratlam decision, this judgment begins by referencing the MCD's failure to comply with the orders of the Wadehra case: "The insanitary conditions of different areas of Delhi does not in any way show that requisite effort has been put in or the required time spent in the cleaning operations." However, the judgment quickly introduces a new problem in addressing the citywide problem of cleanliness: "When a large number of inhabitants live ... in slums with no care for hygiene, the problem becomes more complex." The judgment thus displaces the source of the problem from a lack of proper sanitation and services to the innate character of slum dwellers.

These words set the tone for the following paragraph, wherein the distinction between slums and slum-derived waste is blurred:

> Instead of "slum clearance" there is "slum creation" in Delhi. This in turn gives rise to domestic waste being strewn on open land in and around the slums. This can best be controlled at least, in the first instance, by *preventing the growth of slums*. The authorities must realize that there is a limit to which the population of a city can be increased, without enlarging its size. In other words the density of population per square kilometre cannot be allowed to increase beyond the sustainable limit. Creation of slums resulting in increase in density has to be prevented. . . . It is the *garbage and solid waste generated by these slums* which require to be dealt with most expeditiously. (emphasis added)

And so emerged the new, millennial definition of nuisance: nuisances in the city, the judgment states, originate from the growth of a population "with no care for hygiene"—not from the government's failure to provide municipal services, as the Ratlam decision had affirmed, and not from its failure to provide low-income housing as required by the Delhi Master Plan. Examining the two italicized word clusters shown above, we find that this paragraph not only radically redefined nuisance, but also proposed a new solution to it: "Waste generated by these slums" can be dealt with "by preventing the growth of slums."

The statutory definition of nuisance, as provided by Section 133 Cr. P.C., includes only particular categories of *objects* possessed or *actions* performed by an individual or group, whereas the new interpretation in the Almrita Patel judgment includes *individuals* or *groups* themselves as possible nuisance categories. This vastly expanded the range of procedures that could be administered to remedy nuisance: no longer simply regulating the nuisance-causing behaviour of individuals, nuisance law would soon be used to remove individuals themselves. Order number six in the Almrita Patel judgment sets the stage for this very strategy in future cases: "We direct [the respondent authorities] to take appropriate steps for preventing any fresh encroachment or unauthorized occupation of public land for the purpose of dwelling resulting in creation of a slum. Further appropriate steps be taken to improve the sanitation in the existing slums *till they are removed and the land reclaimed*" (emphasis added). Here, it is clear that the court saw the need to remove all slums in order to resolve the problem of municipal waste in the city. Thus, within the space of a few paragraphs, the strategic implication of nuisance law shifted from a positive technology of building municipal infrastructure to a negative and disciplinary technology of elimination and displacement. The MCD's lackadaisical approach to installing public waste bins, the main problem raised in the original Almrita Patel petition, led to a court order to eliminate the residential spaces of the working poor.[10]

The statement "slums are illegal" and reference to slums as "illegal encroachments" gained widespread circulation in judicial discourse only after the Supreme Court's equation of slums with nuisance in the early 2000s. Petitions and court matters filed before the main orders from Almrita Patel were issued, such as the Manchanda petition described above, show little to no mention of slums as illegal encroachments. Where accusations of encroachment or misuse were leveled, they were typically buoyed by concrete evidence related to a land use violation. This was because the question of slum legality had been grounded over the previous fifty years of postcolonial jurisprudence in land-use records and planning documents, the technical underpinning of the system of rule by records I discussed in the introduction. When it came to the question of public land occupation, the calculative epistemology that underpinned government had relied specifically on slum surveys and land occupancy records, which by the late 1990s were becoming vastly outdated. These records and the slum survey registers compiled to render the space of the slum intelligible had further become increasingly prone to the interference of slum dwellers, who were able to mobilize their own documents, records, and political connections to modify and bend state rules and plans to their own ends.[11]

As the judiciary came under increasing pressure to address the problem of the slum at the turn of the millennium, and as it explicitly embraced the strategic goal of making Delhi world-class through its frequent invocation of Delhi being a showpiece or show window to the world, it increasingly bumped up against the inefficiencies of rule by records. For example, in a case pertaining to the clearance of slums along the Yamuna River, which I discuss below and which ultimately dispensed with the long-standing requirement for calculative knowledge of slums by using the nuisance logic to order the slums' removal, the High Court observed: "In spite of repeated directions no progress has been made by the DDA as the DDA has not submitted area-wise sketch plans showing clusters of jhuggis and other structures on various parts of [the] Western embankment of the river Yamuna. It seems that the DDA itself does not have [a] plan."[12] As a result of the overall absence of a records-based synoptic vision of the territory, the judiciary began to put increased pressure on the DDA and other land-owning agencies to improve their calculative records.

The first means the court adopted was to order the DDA, MCD, and related land-owning agencies to follow their own calculative procedures better. It did so by reaffirming the DDA's statutory duty to implement the Delhi Master Plan, requesting detailed information on occupied land in pending cases, and threatening to levy penalties and hold responsible officers in contempt of court. However, as RWA petitions continued to mount up and state agencies only partially adhered to the court's orders, the court deemed the calculative efforts of the state a failure and began appointing its own special committees and court commissioners to do ground-level field assessments in place of the state bureaucracy.[13] But producing calculations capable of guiding the population and administering the law required extensive field knowledge not only of the current ground reality, but also of the history of such spaces. These court-appointed surveyors ended up producing equally (or more) flawed calculations of the ground reality, a point raised by slum advocates. A civil writ petition contesting a court committee's recommendation to demolish a slum in north Delhi is indicative of this type of challenge:

> It is apparent that the inspection and scrutiny performed by the Learned Court Commissioner appears, at best, perfunctory . . . [and contains] marked discrepancies about the area and size of the basti [settlement] . . . [The Committee's report] is also incomplete, cursory and factually inaccurate. [The letter by the Court Commissioner]

requests the Court to give directions for removal of encroachments without clarifying what are considered encroachments.... Further the Monitoring Committee also differs from the Learned Court Commissioner in its assessment of the size of the basti.... The authorities appear to be unclear even to the extent and demarcation of the land area in question—the land of two Khasras [plots] ... are shown in the Revenue record as merely Government land, without designating a specific land owning agency.[14]

In this case, the legal boundary between planned developments and encroachments did not accurately reflect the mixed land uses found on the ground—the MCD had itself placed the so-called encroachers on vacant lots as part of a temporary housing policy in the 1970s. The effort to parse dynamic and amorphous tenure arrangements into this clear binary produced factually inaccurate simplifications.[15]

[In response to the increasingly complex and unruly ground situation and the inability of existing calculative practices to render that ground sufficiently intelligible to the courts and upper-level bureaucrats, the courts in the early 2000s began declaring the existing procedures of governing slums incompatible with the world-class city making project. As the Delhi High Court stated in a 2002 order, "it would require 272 years to resettle the slum dwellers" according to existing procedures.[16] This is the context in which the judiciary turned to the more aesthetic foundation for the adjudication of slum matters, as offered by the new interpretation of nuisance inaugurated by the Almrita Patel judgment and further codified as a legal mechanism through a parallel case being heard before the High Court until 2002, which I now discuss.

EQUATING SLUMS WITH NUISANCE

While the Almrita Patel judgment, in breaking from the statutory definition of nuisance laid down in Section 133 Cr. P.C., marked a key discursive shift regarding slum-based nuisance, it was a case proceeding before the chief justice of the Delhi High Court in the early 2000s that cleared the way for the more aesthetic judgments that would characterize millennial Delhi. In 1999, the petitioner in the Manchanda case introduced above filed a contempt motion against the municipal authorities for failing to improve the environment in its neighborhood.[17] The updated judgment in this case would extend the nuisance logic introduced in Almrita Patel, clearing the way both for a weakening of the urban poor's right to shelter and for the legal codification of world-class aesthetic codes.

Prior to the continuation of the Manchanda matter, RWAs across Delhi had flooded the Delhi High Court with petitions targeting slums, which the ruling bench would later describe as "mostly filed by various resident associations of colonies alleging that after encroaching the public land, these JJ [*jhuggi jhompdi*] clusters have been constructed in an illegal manner and they are causing nuisance of varied kind for the residents of those areas."[18] Responding to this broad concern, having observed that "a city like Delhi must act as a catalyst for building modern India. It cannot be allowed to degenerate and decay," the court lumped the sixty-three related petitions together while embarking on the stated goal of taking up "the larger issue of removal of unauthorized JJ clusters from public land which were in the vicinity of various residential colonies."[19] This represented a stark contrast with the court's approach to the Manchanda case in the early 1990s. The introductory comments to the judgment (hereafter called the Pitampura judgment) issued in September 2002 clearly enunciate the purpose behind bringing these sixty-three cases together: to rid Delhi of the persistent nuisance of slums. An interim order passed in January 2002 justified this goal by invoking the problem of overpopulation in controlling slum-related nuisance: "The agencies . . . have not taken any effective steps to check the growth of these jhuggies which are still mushrooming on public land."

However, the task of removing the more than 25 percent of Delhi's population living in *jhuggis* required a far more complex assemblage of justificatory and legal argumentation than the simple description of their uncontrolled growth. This is so because Delhi's more than one thousand JJ clusters did not crop up surreptitiously (like mushrooms) in Delhi's shady, vacant corners. Rather, as outlined in previous chapters, they have a complex legal and political history that includes formal entitlement to 25 percent of residential land, only a fraction of which they were provided.[20] Further, the Delhi government's various resettlement policies at the time protected slum residents from demolition without compensation. In fact, just months before the drafting of the final judgment in this case, the Planning Commission of India published a report explaining Delhi's slum problem as the direct outcome of the DDA's failure to implement the mandatory 25 percent housing provision for the Economically Weaker Sections—the central government's lowest income classification. How, then, was the court able to flout the poor's legal and regulatory protections in favor of the more recent and seemingly offhand remarks of the Almrita Patel judgment?

The Pitampura judgment of 2002 begins by dividing the problem of the slum into two individual dimensions: "One is the removal of JJ clusters and the other is their rehabilitation." Because the question of rehabilitating residents of JJ clusters was being heard before a different bench of the High Court in parallel with the Pitampura case,[21] the bench set itself the task of focusing on the removal of JJ clusters alone. Uncoupling Delhi residents' entitlement to land and right to life in the city from their present place of residence was an unprecedented twist in logic. In hindsight, however, this uncoupling was the only way that the court could simultaneously sustain the position that slums are nuisances *and* that slum dwellers are entitled to land and livelihood. Once the question of the entitlements of the urban poor to public land (i.e., the question of "rehabilitation") was bracketed off, the court could easily proceed to summarize the entire history of slum settlement in a single sentence:[22] "There is large scale encroachment of public land by the persons who come from other States." That is, slum dwellers are alien, come from other places, and deprive the true residents of Delhi of what is rightfully theirs. Despite forty-five years of the DDA's existence and a longer history of slum settlements in Delhi, the court disregarded the messy conditions that led to the development of slums and declared: "There is no denying the fact that no person has right to encroach public land.... It is the statutory duty cast upon the civic authorities ... to remove such encroachments."[23]

Following this logic, the question of a settlement's legal status would henceforth ignore (i) the economic and political context that led to the use of public land for informal housing; (ii) the manner in which residents of these spaces have been de facto formalized by receiving various forms of residence proof from the state (e.g., ration and identity cards, registration tokens) and by enjoying state-funded infrastructure improvements (e.g., government-run schools); and (iii) the patent failure by the DDA to fulfil the statutory housing provisions of the Master Plan. Separating the question of entitlement from one's present residential status, then, did not treat these two issues as logically distinct, as the tone of the judgment suggests. Rather, this discursive separation made accessing one's housing entitlement incumbent on his or her current settlement status.

The judgment next briefly acknowledges the second aspect of the slum problem—slum dweller's entitlement to public land—but denies its relevance by referring to the broader logic of nuisance: "No doubt, shelter for every citizen is an imperative of any good government, but there are *cleaner* ways to achieve that goal than converting public property into slum lords' illegal estates" (emphasis added). "Cleaner" is of course the key word in this sentence, here used as if it referred to a specific legal code. One might think that the legal procedure for addressing cleanliness would derive from nuisance law, but the entire judgment makes no reference to Section 133 Cr. P.C., the key statute dealing with public nuisance. Rather, this word, "clean," derives its efficacy from the broader judicial mandate to "clean up" the city, as expressed through the earlier Wadehra and Almrita Patel judgments that had initiated the discursive linkage between municipal pollution and the problem of the slum. That is, "cleanliness" became a symbolic code of settled meaning within judicial discourse, a constative element of speech agreed upon without explication of its origins or legal foundation. It is part of a lexicon of resonant terms for interpreting the city's defilement and part of what in the previous chapter I described as the unspoken grammar that allows nuisance to shift seamlessly between constative and performative registers and to thereby give statements that seemingly merely describe reality the force to change that reality. This is precisely the power of nuisance in the Pitampura judgment, wherein descriptions of slum uncleanliness acquired the performative effect of declaring them illegal—as the final orders in the judgment would affirm. While it seems preposterous to say a settlement is illegal because it is not clean enough, this is precisely what the judgment enforces, for there is no other justification provided in the judgment for clearing slums; there is no mention—implicit or explicit—of any of the statutes governing displacement: not the Public Premises Act, 1971, or the Land Acquisition Act, 1894. The statutory laws for dealing with the cleanliness of urban space are distinct from those for displacing a population. However, these two procedures were melded in the Pitampura judgment.

The judgment's final paragraph before the bench's orders are recorded further clarifies how nuisance provided the underlying logic on which the bench's final demolition order would rest:

> The welfare of the residents of these [RWAs'] colonies is also in the realm of public interest which cannot be overlooked. After all, these residential colonies were developed first. *The slums* have been created afterwards *which is the cause of nuisance* and brooding [sic] ground of so many ills. The welfare, health, maintenance of law and order, safety and sanitation of these residents cannot be sacrificed and their right under Article 21 [of the Indian Constitution] is violated in the name of social justice to the slum dwellers. Even if the government and civic authorities move at snails pace and take time at their own leisure for the rehabilitation of these clusters, this is no excuse for continuing them at the given places [sic]. (emphasis added)

This paragraph provided the logic upon which dozens of JJ clusters would be demolished in the subsequent decade. The declaration that slums are the cause of nuisance completed the discursive reworking of nuisance and established a new legal precedent for the territorial administration of informal settlements.

THE NEW NUISANCE DISCOURSE

The Pitampura judgment provided the foundation on which RWA and property owners' everyday nuisance talk, as written into the petitions flooding into the Delhi High Court, would acquire the performative force of law. Before tracking how this lay speech was transformed into judicial discourse and how the aesthetic codes that underpinned this speech were codified in law, however, let us first highlight three concrete components of the Pitampura judgment's discursive work. First, following the logic initiated in the Almrita Patel judgment, we see in the above block quote how the judgment divides the public into two categories: residents and slum dwellers, the former owning private property and the latter occupying public land. Based on earlier text in the judgment, the court makes it clear that these two categories of settlement and the regulatory arrangements that support them are at odds. Therefore, the judgment states that because those in the former category own their property, came first, and suffer from the nuisance of the latter's presence, their "right to life" under Article 21 of the Constitution should trump the latter's. This marked a change in the interpretation of rights away from a framework envisioning the even distribution of rights across a population and in favor of a zero-sum conception of rights in which the enhancement of one's well-being necessarily detracts from another's. As Mariana Valverde notes, the "enjoyment" of land "that is the guiding star of nuisance and quasi-nuisance law is not a right that persons have (in which case it would have to be equally distributed) but rather a privilege that flows from one's links to property."[24] It is in this vein that the judgment defines slum dwellers as a secondary category of citizens whose social justice becomes actionable only after the fulfilment of the property-based privileges of residents of formal colonies: the true citizens of the city.

Legal scholars Kevin Gray and Susan Gray note of common law jurisprudence, on which the Indian legal system is based, that property often has more in common with propriety than with entitlement. In this usage, "the word 'property' reflects its semantically correct root by identifying the condition of a particular resource as being 'proper' to a particular person." They further note: "The notion of a 'property right' may ultimately have more to do with perceptions of 'rightness' than with any understanding of enforceable exclusory title."[25] The Pitampura judgment conforms with this "symantically correct root," codifying in law the inherent "rightness," or propriety, of property. It affirms this position by reversing the prevalent interpretation of the "right to life" in Article 21 of the Indian Constitution regarding slum dwellers that had been established almost twenty years earlier in the landmark judgment of *Olga Tellis v. Bombay Municipal Corporation*.[26] Whereas Olga Tellis emphasized the right of the working poor to occupy public land to fulfil their livelihood requirements—"the right to livelihood is an important facet of the right to life"—the interpretation advanced in the Pitampura judgment elevates the quality of life and enjoyment of land for propertied citizens over the livelihood of slum dwellers.

This transformed interpretation of Article 21 has been lamented widely by critical legal studies of slum demolitions in India, largely because of public interest lawyers' success through the 1980s and 1990s in preventing or postponing demolitions by invoking Article 21.[27] As I described in the introduction, these same lawyers confronted a judiciary that by the mid-2000s summarily dismissed these same pleas, finding that *jhuggi* residents had no legal right to the city.[28] The Pitampura judgment clearly shows that it is only through the mechanisms of nuisance law—a particular elevation of the propriety of property—that the reversal of Olga Tellis was practically enacted. That is, the reinterpretation of Article 21 is a legal effect of the new nuisance discourse, not its cause, as these studies suggest. This is the case because, once it was established, this discourse contained a set of assumptions about (i) what defines the proper citizens of a city—residence in "planned" colonies; (ii) who constitutes the public in whose interest public interest is defined—private property owners; and (iii) the elements of a world-class city—an urban milieu that is clean, nuisance-free, and thus slum-free.[29] Nuisance discourse became so powerful, then, precisely because in performing the simple semiotic task of transforming what everyone knows—slums are dirty—into the new truth that slums are a nuisance, it simultaneously performed much deeper ideological work. By rendering the statement "slums are nuisances" acceptable, it reoriented the terrain of citizenship, social justice, and access to the city—categories that would typically fall in the domain of Article 21.[30]

The second component of this new nuisance discourse, which derives from the first, was a blurring of the distinction between public and private nuisance. If we return to the above quoted paragraph from the Pitampura judgment, it becomes clear that the court (following the petitioners) was concerned with removing impediments to the welfare of the private residential colonies. This concern overlaps perfectly with the legal definition of *private* nuisance—a "substantial and unreasonable interference with the use or enjoyment of land," meaning private property.[31] Yet each of the cases under discussion was filed as public interest litigation (PIL), a requirement of which is that the matter affects the broader public, not only a private party. Whereas the cases in question were ostensibly treated as matters of *public* nuisance, many of the actual grievances fall under the strict definition of *private* nuisance. It is thus apparent that the distinction between public and private was breaking down in the course of these hearings, allowing—for the first time in postcolonial India—nuisance law to follow its earlier, colonial logic as "the coercive arm of property rights," defending private interest in the name of public purpose.[32]

To better grasp the significance of the blurring of private and public nuisances, and to understand how this blurring allowed distinctly propertied aesthetic sensibilities to be applied to broader matters of public space, let us return to the distinction between citizens and slum dwellers, which the court in the Pitampura judgment argued rests on the variable of property ownership. This position was affirmed even more categorically in the matter proceeding alongside the Pitampura case concerning the issue of slum rehabilitation.[33] In quashing the Delhi government's slum resettlement policy, the judgment in this case made a clear distinction between "those who have scant respect for law and unauthorisedly squat on public land" and "citizens who have paid for the land."[34] Once land ownership was established as the basis of citizenship as such, the preservation and prosperity of private property became an elevated concern. That is to say, when the public became defined by its ownership of property—and conversely when those without private property were excluded from the category of the citizen—the minimization of private nuisance and the defence of private property became matters of public interest. Thus, whereas the first effect of this judgment was to divide the public into two categories—property-owning citizens and encroachers, one with the special privileges of property and one defined by the absence of those privileges—the second effect was to reinvest the public with the attributes and interests of the first of these groups. This consisted of nothing less than the juridical embourgeoisement of Delhi—that is, a privatization of the definition of public interest and the affirmation of a propertied form of citizenship.

This construal of "the public" had stark implications for the prosecution of nuisance and the overall manner in which land use was legally treated because, as Shyam Diwan and Armin Rosencranz say in their review of environmental law in India, "the test which has always been found to be useful in distinguishing ... [whether or not a nuisance exists] is the test of ascertaining the reaction of a reasonable person according to the ordinary usage of mankind living in a particular society in respect of the thing complained of."[35] That is, nuisance is defined as conduct that the court determines to be outside the range of what a "reasonable person" would do. Once a reasonable person and "ordinary usage of mankind" were defined in terms of property owners in planned residential colonies, the conduct of slum dwellers could easily be labeled deviant and unreasonable, be it even their mere existence. Whereas the Ratlam decision discussed above sympathized with the compulsion slum dwellers face to defecate in the open, this same act in millennial Delhi's legal environment represented the behavior of a population with what the Almrita Patel judgment called "no care for hygiene";[36] a clear affront to urban order; and, as the Delhi High Court declared in the Pitampura judgment, an impediment to the "building of modern India."[37] This construal of legality flows from the view that the protection of private property is a component of public nuisance prosecution.

Coming to the third component of the new nuisance discourse put in place by the Pitampura judgment, we find that once slum dwellers' lives were defined as outside the normal range of citizen conduct, their access to representation and formal appeal was also brought into question. For if they are "outside" of normal citizenship, then the procedures for administering their conduct also falls outside the normal domain of civil society. It is in this capacity that the final order of the Pitampura judgment states: "We may also note at this stage that some petitions were filed by various occupiers [slum dwellers] against whom Orders for removal were passed. . . . Since they are encroachments of public land . . . they have no legal right to maintain such a Petition." This statement militates against the position established by the Supreme Court in 1996: "When an encroacher approaches the Court, the Court is required to examine whether the encroacher had any right and to what extent he would be given protection and relief."[38] Here, the possibility that an encroacher has a right to occupy public land was maintained, a right that historically would have been built up incrementally and piecemeal, over time, through settlers' assembly of ration cards, voter ID cards, and registration tokens on the one hand, and deepening patronage ties on the other—both of which affirmed the state's direct involvement in the life of the settlement. However, the definition of citizenship did not extend as far in millennial Delhi as it did in 1996, for the new nuisance discourse had adjusted the procedures of justice. As a result, slum residents became objects to be managed and disposed of, not citizens with rights.[39]

NUISANCE DISCOURSE AS MECHANISM

In the previous section I tracked the consolidation of a new nuisance discourse and how it recalibrated the factors used to determine slum legality. I now turn to how petitions filed by RWAs used depictions of the nuisance of slums to demand the removal of settlements in millennial Delhi. Specifically, by submitting petitions characterizing how neighboring slums violated world-class aesthetic codes, petitioners were able to bypass the earlier calculative and records-based procedures of eviction, transforming nuisance-based petitions into the most powerful mechanism of slum demolition in millennial Delhi. To analyze the factors that drove this nuisance-based demolition mechanism, I examine five original civil writ petitions filed in the Delhi High Court, each of which relied on the new nuisance discourse, was filed by an RWA, and led to a slum demolition.[40] What is striking in these petitions is how directly their depictions of the slum problem borrow from the everyday nuisance talk explored in the previous chapter. For example, while discussing the details of her case, the vice president of the Kailash Fraternity RWA told me that the general secretary of the RWA had written most of the petition himself, while the lawyer "only changed some words to fit the argument to the finer points of argument and law."⁴¹ To illustrate the extension of everyday nuisance talk into writ petitions, I quote at length from the Kailash Fraternity petition, one of the five petitions I analyze below:

> The unhygienic conditions are created by the dwellers in hutments as they excrete, urinate and throw garbage just along the residences, which create hazardous health risks.... The situation is aggravating with the increase in number of hutments and also the garbage dumping grounds created by them in the locality. The petitioner submits that the park is being used by the encroachers for mass celebrations. Their functions cross all noise pollution limits. Loud sound blasting forth from TVs, music systems and high pitched drunken brawls and fights between themselves, which are part of daily nuisance, continues in midnight. It is submitted that men and women folk also indulge in unlawful activities ranging from thefts of private and public property, hideouts of criminals and illegal immigrants.... The many hutments have even been converted into double storied permanent brick and mortar dwellings with all amenities like illegal power connection and abundant free use of ... water meant for the colony.... This has created serious hindrance to the civil amenities like sewage, rainwater drainage and supply of tap water choking up, meant for residents of the Colony.... The smoke of firewood envelops the entire area and settles heavy measure especially in winter, which is harmful and injurious to health of the residents of the society [sic].

Most petitions against slums begin with similar descriptions, which are usually repeated in more elaborate detail throughout the text. To show how the new nuisance discourse was activated in the courtroom, transforming lay nuisance talk into legal edict, I begin by briefly identifying discursive devices—turns of phrase aimed at producing a specific audience response—common across the petitions. These reveal the patterns by which nuisance was identified empirically and summoned as a key term for transforming the identification of slums as dirty into the legal claim that slums are nuisances.

The first discursive device all five petitions use is reference to slums as a problem of overpopulation: "The area has virtually turned into a slum and the illegal and unauthorized encroachments has not only double, tripled over the years but has attained mammoth proportions and is threatening to burst at its seams [sic]."⁴² The words "bursting," "infesting," "infectious," or "mushrooming" are invariably used to evoke neo-Malthusian fears shared by many activist RWAs, the English media, and prominent political figures, introduced in the previous chapter, that the poor's mere presence will endanger the welfare of society at large: "The slum dwellers are living in highly infectious and contagious conditions thus exposing themselves as well as the residents of the society to epidemics."[43] The language in three of the petitions goes so far as to dehumanize slums by using the word "slum" not as a noun, but an adjective. Slums are then not places in this discourse; "slum" is a condition or a disease that infects certain spaces and must be eliminated, lest it spread to purer places. One concrete discursive device that plays upon this fear of society becoming slumified is the emphasis in four of the petitions on the special problem of slum dwellers' open defecation; two of the petitions go so far as to include photographs of residents caught in the act: "These people defecate in the open creating ghastly scenes and spreading foul smell and infection."[44] Overall, the overpopulation device is used to show the uncivic conduct of slum dwellers and the importance of removing them to enhance Delhi's world-class image.

The second discursive device shared by all five petitions is the description of the dual categories of citizenship discussed above: one is the rightful, tax-paying citizen who owns property or rents from property owners in planned colonies, and the other is the unlawful resident of slums, the encroacher. Four of the petitions bolster this viewpoint by explicitly relying on the narrow, millennial interpretation of Article 21 that prioritizes the right to life of private property owners over all others. Further alluding to the second-class status of slum dwellers, four of the petitions describe formally nonevictable actions like slum dwellers' unmetered use of electricity or hosting of mass celebrations that deprive RWA residents of resources and tranquility as a justification for slum removal. Three of the five petitions also argue that slum dwellers are alien by citing the presence of antisocial or criminal elements and people of Bangladeshi origin in slums. These common discursive devices reveal the petitioners' anxieties over urban environmental order, but more importantly show the channels by which slums are equated with nuisance in petitions.

To see how the presence of a nuisance is calibrated to a legal framework that requires slum demolition, consider the basis on which illegality is adduced in the petitions. Each of the five petitions makes reference to "illegal slums/JJ clusters" or describes "illegal/unauthorized encroachers" more often than it provides any specific details or discussion of what makes the slum in question illegal. None of the petitions state an explicit statutory basis for eviction. Three of the petitions only vaguely mention the MCD Act, Delhi Development Act, or Delhi Master Plan, the invocation of which, in itself, does not justify demolition. So, although "illegal" is used as if it were a precise term, it does not actually carry any statutory precision. Therefore, to determine what these petitions infer when they describe slum illegality, I conducted a line-by-line analysis, marking lines in the petitions' text based on the justification they provide for requesting demolition. Because the primary statutory basis on which slums can be, and historically have been, demolished is their violation of land-use codes, I tracked lines in the petitions that make explicit mention of *land use* as a basis for the petitioner's demolition request. The second category I tracked consists of lines referring to the *slum as a nuisance*. Before presenting the results from this analysis, let me clarify that the argument here is not that nuisance was the only basis for slum demolitions cited by the courts in millennial Delhi.[45] The land-use category of the land on which slums were settled continued to play a role in slum demolition cases. However, petitions targeting slums for land-use violations were filed regularly before the millennial round of accelerated slum demolitions. What was *new* and of an overriding influence in this millennial moment was the import accorded to nuisance—the discursive hinge that codified in law world-class aesthetic codes that were otherwise circulating in the public sphere.

In the five petitions analyzed, lines referring to land use as the basis for demolition appear 139 times, whereas lines referring to slums-as-nuisance appear 346 times, or two and a half times more frequently. In all of the petitions, nuisance-based lines appear at least 50 percent more frequently than land use–based lines. This shows that these five petitions rely most forcefully on nuisance-based argumentation for declaring slums illegal and that the declaration of slums as a nuisance performs their illegality.

The converse is as true: declaring slums illegal presumes their ontological status as a nuisance. This is evident in each of the five petitions' extensive use of photographs *showing* slums-as-nuisances. These photos appear in the petitions as annexures and show both the presence of the slum as well as what the petitioner considers the ill effects of the slum's presence: accumulated trash, standing water, stray animals, open defecation, children playing in and taking over the streets. The manner in which the petitions describe these photos makes it clear that the petitioner expected the court to agree that the photos demonstrate a need to remove the slum. As one petitioner wrote of a photograph showing standing water in front of a cluster of *jhuggis*, "the acuteness of the situation can [be] seen clearly from the photographs of the affected area."[46] All of the petitions' bold, dehumanizing claims about slums as spaces of filth are given moral license upon the presentation of a few photographs. It is useful to note here that the Manchanda petition I examined above, an example of an early petition submitted by an RWA pertaining to slum-based nuisance prior to the rise of the new nuisance discourse, did not make use of such photographs.[47] The visual depiction of slums-as-nuisances had become a new visual technology in millennial Delhi that put judges in a position to see slums and slum-derived nuisance as one in the same.

The power of this technology is evidenced in the case of *R. L. Kaushal v. Lt. Governor of Delhi,* the petition for which differs from the five nuisance-based petitions just described in that it neither requests the removal of a slum nor uses any of the above discursive devices. This petition was submitted "for better civic amenities and for nuisance caused by open wide drain [*sic*]" in Safdarjung Enclave in South Delhi (see Map),[48] but does not mention *jhuggis* or a settled slum. Only in the petition's annexures containing letters to elected representatives and photos of the drain with such captions as "Jhuggi dwellers defecate in nallah [drain]" was it revealed that a slum existed beside the drain. Nonetheless, the court observed that "photographs were filed of the area showing the filth at site and encroachments in and around the nallah" (see Figure 4.1) and ordered that "the area should also be cleaned and the encroachments removed."[49] Without initiating an inquiry into the settlement's size, location, history, or legal basis, the court ordered the slum's demolition.

Each of the five petitions I examined above, in addition to the Kaushal petition, was met with a positive response by the Delhi High Court, which not only ordered the demolition of the neighboring slums, but in many cases also adopted the language of nuisance in emphasizing the priority basis on which the demolitions should take place. As the court stated in an interim order in the Vikas Puri case, the same order that led to the

Figure 4.1. Photograph of the "deep and dangerous pit/gorge on both sides of the said open drain," a "nuisance to the posh locality" of Safdarjung Enclave (see Map).[63]

demolition of Sant Ravi Das Camp, the settlement I discussed in the previous chapter:

> The encroachment has not been removed and it is this lackluster approach of the DDA which has resulted in unscrupulous elements to make encroachment on government land. . . . We only observe that on the one hand a citizen has to pay handsome price for acquiring land . . . for his habitat and on the other hand unauthorized encroachment and habitat on government land is allowed to go on, [which] . . . deprives the rights of citizens of Delhi to water, electricity and other civic services. The right of honest citizens in this regard cannot be made subservient to the right of encroachers [sic].[50]

Here, we see the same process of dehumanization found in the RWAs' petitions repeated by the bench: slum residents are called "unscrupulous elements," whereas RWA members are called "citizens." And, in constructing the second sentence quoted above in the passive voice (i.e., without a subject), the court completely erases the slum subject from the order. This makes the solution to the problem of the slum appear purely technical, despite its deeply ethical and political nature. In reiterating the reasons for needing to remove the entire slum in question, the order further states:

> We have seen from the photographs filed as to how illegal electric connections have been taken, the Delhi Vidyut [Electricity] Board has been used as a junk yard, service lane has been completely blocked [by carts and supplies], the encroachment has been made on road and footpath. . . . The whole area has been converted into a garbage landfill. No legal right is vested in the encroachers [sic].[51]

With the exception of "the encroachment . . . on road and footpath," none of these activities statutorily permit the removal of the slum. The huts built on the roads and footpaths, as shown in the drawing submitted by the petitioner, made up less than 10 percent of the total area of the slum and were the most recently constructed. However, the court lumped the entire settlement together in passing its demolition order. The court's other observations here must then provide the basis for clearing the entire settlement. On what grounds do these activities—illegal electricity use, blocking a service lane with carts, and using vacant land for dumping garbage and scrap material[52]—add up to a demolition notice? "Illegal electric connections," according to the Electricity Act of 2003, require imposing a fine. The remaining activities are nuisances whose removal is governed by Section 133 Cr. P.C., which nowhere states that the party responsible for a nuisance is to be displaced. However, nuisance law in millennial Delhi clearly acquired new legal and moral coordinates.

The overall thrust of these five petitions shows that nuisance had become the predominant justification for slum demolitions in millennial Delhi, even when a land-use violation was also identified. Further, even in the absence of petitions that specifically target slums for demolition, such as the Kaushal petition just described, the courts themselves took up the task of identifying slums-as-nuisances and issued demolition orders. This pattern emerged in the proceedings leading up to the demolition of Yamuna Pushta, a heterogeneous cluster of settlements housing more than 150,000 people on the banks of the Yamuna River (see Map). In March 2003, the High Court arbitrarily took cognizance of the problem of pollution in the Yamuna River, despite the lack of any mention of the issue in the original petition. While referring to other causes of pollution, the bench quickly identified the true source of the problem: "In view of the encroachment and construction of jhuggies/pucca structure in the Yamuna [river] Bed and its embankment with no drainage facility, sewerage water and other filth is discharged in Yamuna water [sic]."[53] In the total absence of any evidence demonstrating Pushta's contribution to the Yamuna's pollution levels, the court passed its demolition order. And, like the RWA petitions just reviewed, the most "scientific" evidence the court used to justify this claim was a set of photographs submitted by the Ministry of Tourism—part of its proposal to develop the site of Pushta into a riverside promenade and tourist attraction—ostensibly showing slum dwellers as polluters and carrying captions indicating the unsightliness of slums for foreign visitors and dignitaries.[54]

Following this order, the Delhi High Court continued to target slums as the primary source of Yamuna pollution by launching its own *suo moto* case and setting up an expert committee tasked not with monitoring the Yamuna's environmental quality, the basis for slum clearance in the first place, but rather with ensuring that other encroachments on the river were removed apace.[55] Between 2006 and 2008, an additional 10,000 huts were cleared under the watchful eye of the monitoring committee, with 30,000 more identified for future removal.[56] In the immediate aftermath of these demolitions—what the court labeled a "clean-up" drive necessary to prevent the conversion of the Yamuna "into a huge sewage drain"—the Central Pollution Control Board showed "no improvement in the quality of water. Instead, it had deteriorated over the years and several crore [1 crore = 10 million] rupees spent by the Government on the Yamuna Action Plan has virtually gone down the drain."[57]

While the final judgment in this case does refer to the fact that Pushta existed on the Yamuna floodplain and thus violated the layout plan for the area, a handful of other developments with a different, what we might call world-class "look" than Pushta—including the Akshardam Temple (a high-tech theme park and the world's largest Hindu monument), the Commonwealth Games Village, an information technology park, and a Delhi Metro Rail depot—similarly fall on the floodplain. The fact that the court targeted Pushta and ignored these developments proves that the nuisance logic formed the strongest basis for the demolition. The Pushta case further confirms that the courts did not have anything close to what could be called a sound calculative basis for assessing whether a slum was a nuisance or not. Rather, if a slum *appeared* to be polluting or filthy, based on a judge's aesthetic view of acceptable, clean conduct, then the slum was deemed polluting, a nuisance, and therefore illegal.

COURTLY VISIONS, FROM BENCH TO *BASTI*

RWAs and their advocates recognized the legal opening created by the new nuisance discourse. In speaking with the general secretary of the Kailash Fraternity RWA, whose successful petition I discussed in the previous section, he told me, "from the very first hearing, the judges were very responsive. On that day itself they gave an order to MCD to clear all the *jhuggis*." Later, a lawyer representing Kailash Fraternity confirmed this: "The MCD didn't dispute the facts of the case, so it had to just accept the order of the judge." When I asked her about the legal basis for the demolition order in her case, she said:

> Our strategy was to highlight the nuisance caused by the slum. This is what the court responds to, and indeed the court took cognizance of this problem and made the order to clear the slum. The courts now recognize the growing problem of encroachments. This problem has been growing for the last 20 years, so the courts have changed their approach to dealing with this. Now if we show how an encroachment is reducing the quality of life of colony residents, the courts respond favorably.[58]

To see for myself how slums were viewed by judges passing judgments from their benches, I began attending slum and encroachment-related cases in the Delhi High Court, where I took detailed notes on the statements delivered, recorded the duration of each hearing, and, when possible and for cases that seemed particularly significant, spoke with the parties informally after the hearing. While I observed more than fifty cases (and many more with no relationship to slums), I present the details of one case here, which appeared before the Chief Justice of Delhi, to exemplify the extent to which world-class aesthetic codes became codified in law in millennial Delhi. In this case, an RWA in the south Delhi colony of Kalkaji was demanding the removal of a transit camp that the MCD had intentionally settled in 1980 as temporary housing for slum residents, but which had since expanded onto neighboring land that the RWA argued was meant for a park. This complicated matter, in which the MCD and DDA were the main respondents, had produced six independently filed civil writ petitions, one review petition, and six contempt motions, all lumped together as a single court matter.

On the day of the hearing, after the judges concluded their discussion of the previous case, a veritable army of lawyers representing the different parties involved, each with tall stacks of paper tucked under their black-robed sleeves, shuffled to the front of the courtroom to plead their case. The lawyer representing the DDA began by reminding the judges that the case pertained to the transit camp/slum located in the colony of Kalkaji. When she said this, the secondary judge (who sits on the bench beside the primary judge, who was the chief justice in this instance) briefly recounted a slum case, perhaps to remind the chief justice of the case details, or perhaps to ensure that he had the right case in mind (this was a common practice across cases I observed). Nobody objected to the judge's quick description of the settlement, and the legal arguments began. The RWA's lawyer first raised the question of granting the original transit camp residents freehold tenure rights, an issue that had been discussed in the previous hearing. The chief justice responded abruptly, "how can freehold be a question before us? These are slum dwellers?" The lawyers stood frozen for a moment, likely wondering how the judge could have changed his mind so drastically since the previous hearing. The DDA lawyer, noting the judges' confusion, then corrected the judges, eventually determining that the judges were thinking of a different slum located nowhere near Kalkaji, the case for which would not be heard for another month.[59] After further details of the Kalkaji case were discussed, the DDA lawyer requested additional time to respond to the freehold question, which the judges granted. This entire interaction took only four minutes.

I recall this brief incident not to question the precision of judicial knowledge in Delhi, but rather to provide a sense of the conditions under which judges form interpretations of slum space. High Court judges, on most days, see between twenty-five and forty cases, one following the other from around 10 a.m. until 5 p.m., punctuated by an hour-and-a-half lunch break. If thirty matters are seen in a day (which, after subtracting the time it takes to transition from one matter to the next, means around five working hours), each matter, on average, receives ten minutes of time. On this particular day, I observed twenty-five matters. The longest matter I observed lasted thirteen minutes, the shortest only one minute (where one of the main lawyers was absent), with a mean hearing time of eight minutes. If orders were passed, the main judge spent a couple of minutes dictating to a typist, further reducing the time for adjudication.

Prior to hearing these matters, the judges are presumed to have reviewed all documents submitted by the parties related to the case. The original petitions (which are not public record) for the cases I obtained, including annexures, often surpassed 150 pages in length. The affidavits, counteraffidavits, and supporting documents submitted by the numerous respondents (usually between five and ten state agencies) were often as long as the petitions. Judges are thus expected to compress a minimum of 600 pages of material (some of it no doubt superfluous), often much more, into a simplified vision of the case so that they can, in eight minutes or so, ask the relevant questions, weed through the verbal testimony and explanations provided, confer with each other, and, if ready, pass an order. The vast majority of cases extend across multiple hearings, granting more time to the parties to assemble their arguments and to the judges to make decisions. But, follow-up hearings usually take place weeks or months later. It is also common for matters to be moved to alternate benches, where the case details have to be looked at afresh by new judges.[60]

What does this imply for the adjudication of slum-related cases? The Kalkaji case shows how judges must necessarily pare down diverse residential geographies into an easily intelligible typology of space in order to keep track of the huge number of cases they see. In addition to sometimes blurring the details of specific cases (a simple and correctable error), judges must form simplified mental images of slum space, allowing them to quickly locate (both spatially and cognitively) the case and make a decision. Given the lack of details at their disposal and the speed with which they have to act, it is no surprise that heterogeneous slum spaces are conflated into a single geographical imaginary, as the judge in the Kalkaji case inadvertently demonstrated.[61] It is also perhaps no surprise that simplified visual representations of slums, such as the photographs presented in RWAs' petitions, media portrayals, or the everyday neighborhood talk discussed in the previous chapter, help judges index individual settlements to a broader image of the slum. It is here, then, in the interstices of legal norms and the popular urban imaginary, that the discourse of nuisance circulates. In the context of the severe limitations of calculative government that the judiciary confronted in millennial Delhi, nuisance law, with its aesthetic foundation for evaluating and assessing space, offered a far more efficient and summary mechanism for world-class city making.

This chapter has shown nuisance to be the legal and political concept through which the world-class aesthetic is codified in law, extending subjective judgments about what does and does not belong in the city into legal mechanisms for putting in place exclusionary geographies. Yet world-class city making requires more than a recalibration or state and judicial visions of the city. As Franco Moretti writes, "it is not enough that the social order is 'legal'; it must also appear *symbolically legitimate*. . . . It is also necessary that, as a 'free individual', not as a fearful subject but as a convinced citizen, one perceives the social norms as *one's own*."[62] For the world-class aesthetic and the sanitized social order it calls forth to be taken up by diverse residents of Delhi, including those who do not own property—that is, for these individuals to enter into the world-class "community of sense"—they must appear natural, universal, in line with standards of justice, and in accordance with a sense of the public in which they feel sympathy. This is the point at which law becomes aesthetic, when it is authorized by the very subjects over which it rules, and when people recognize and submit to law out of a spontaneous recognition. How this spontaneous recognition takes place among slum residents—those deemed nuisances in the world-class city—is the subject to which I now turn.

5

World-Class Detritus

The Sense of Unbelonging

SLUM UNBELONGING

[Rule by aesthetics is a process of translating broad aesthetic codes into a governing lens for organizing urban space.] Land uses that conform to dominant aesthetic codes thus appear as sensible features of the urban landscape, even if they violate the law. In contrast, land uses that defy these codes appear out of place, deemed spaces of relegation. Shopping malls and five-star hotels rise; slum settlements fall. In this way, rule by aesthetics sets in place a certain "hegemony of form"—what I have been calling a world-class aesthetic in Delhi.[1] Yet for such a system of rule to be effective it must not only work as an observational grid for ordering space, but also be internally appropriated by the population it would govern; its vision of social order must be imprinted on their sensibilities, inscribed in their senses. In what follows, I examine this process by turning to one of those spaces of relegation deemed outside the world-class aesthetic—a multigenerational slum settlement called Shiv Camp that was partially demolished on two separate occasions after the Delhi High Court declared it a public nuisance.

I first entered Shiv Camp two days after the first of these demolition exercises, when residents were still sifting through the rubble of their demolished homes. Prem, a forty-five-year-old woman who moved from her village in Rajasthan to mud-trodden Shiv Camp after her marriage in 1980, was helping her neighbors stack bricks when we met. Although Prem's home was on the edge of the demolition zone, spared by the bulldozers on this occasion, it was close enough to the destruction that her future was in limbo. Prem, like her neighbors, was enraged by the demolition: "*Dhokhā diyā*, fucking dogs! They gave us land before, but now are running us out!" she said of the Municipal Corporation, whose bulldozers had showed up unannounced. Yet when I asked Prem why the demolition took place, she suggested that Shiv Camp did not belong: "Delhi is improving so much. Look around. All you see are big *koṭhīs* [private bungalows] and cars. Where is there room for *jhuggīs*?" For Prem, who would later lay an assortment of documents out before me to explain what she considered her legal entitlement to live in Shiv Camp, this unbelonging was not something easily categorized. It did not, for example, require the same documentary evidence she used to discuss such things as legal rights or eligibility for government resettlement. Rather, it was something simply grasped, a self-evident fact known just by looking.

In this chapter I examine the modes of aesthetic apprehension by which Prem and many of her Shiv Camp neighbors grasped and made sense of their unbelonging. To do so, I turn to the everyday narratives and forms of habitation through which large-scale state violence was greeted with nonconfrontational responses. How did Prem and her neighbors know slums were out of place? What did the seeming inevitability of slum removal imply for how they imagined and prepared for their future in the city?

As an opening proposition, I want to suggest that statements such as Prem's, in which the constative meanings expressed ("there is no place for *jhuggis*") are at odds with the speaker's material interests ("I don't want to be evicted"), allow us to discern the aesthetic dimensions of rule—to see how dominant aesthetic dispositions become the shaping perceptions for how we see ourselves and our world, even when we might otherwise disagree with the material consequences of those perceptions. By taking statements like Prem's on their own terms, we are able to see the conditions under which marginalized populations are compelled to speak through, identify with, and perform aesthetic dispositions that reinforce their own subordination. Shiv Camp residents, as we shall see, identified with the world-class aesthetic; they spoke through and drew insight from the rapidly beautifying cityscape around them; and they often deployed the same nuisance talk that property owners, as described in chapter 3, used to identify the undesirability of slum settlements. To borrow the language of Rancière, Shiv Camp residents seemed to be partaking in a world-class "community of sense"—a grouping formed through spontaneous concurrence of what is beautiful and what is out of place.[2] Prem, for example, acknowledged that slums were out of place without having an explanation for it—a knowledge more imageric and sensory than ideational.]

But this initial proposition that aesthetic rule operates by drawing individuals into a dominant sensibility is not the same thing as saying that it produces consent on the level of belief. Indeed, Shiv Camp residents acknowledged that the world-class city, premised as it was on their exclusion, was against their material interest even while they partook in its very terms. To "partake" means to participate, but it also means to "take part," to make one's own, or to appropriate. In the introduction I described how settlers in Delhi were able to appropriate the normative workings of the state by implicating themselves in its bureaucratic procedures: by assembling state-supplied ration and voter ID cards, school lists, and survey registries, they were able to build a foundation for their right to occupy—a right built not on entitlement or legal status, but rather on the documentary implication of the state into the life of the community. [The shift that took place in millennial Delhi from a more calculative and document-based form of government to aesthetic rule led these same document-based claims to go unrecognized. Yet I want to suggest that partaking in the normative workings of rule by aesthetics offers a similar way for the urban poor to implicate themselves in the operation of power.]

Any aesthetic regime offers a particular viewing disposition, sensory vocabulary, and set of expressive material. Individuals partake in these sensible ways of seeing and speaking both because of the various symbolic merits and expressive powers it affords them, as well as when alternative sensory vocabularies and expressive intentions are denied[Yet to delimit the terms of sensibility—that is, to distinguish sensible statements from noise, legitimate political speech from nonsense—aesthetic rule must create the conditions for subjects to take them up as their own, discovering and appropriating them not as heteronymous law, but rather as internal inclination. For these terms of sensibility to be appropriated aesthetically, internalized through habit, they must thus be open to diverse meanings, making them prone to redirection and new political possibilities. [Shiv Camp residents, as we shall see, applied diverse, sometimes contradictory, meanings to the world-class city. While no political solution to the problem of slum removal was forthcoming, diverse appropriations of the world-class city allowed those subject to state violence to retain hope in an alternative future—to keep open what Arjun Appadurai calls the "capacity to aspire," the possibility, against all odds, that they might turn the urban imaginary in another direction, reshaping the city's horizons.] Less resistance or subversion, this is a story of appropriation and the political scope and limits it entails.]

I proceed in the next section by describing a situation of extreme constraint: the violence of demolition. While Shiv Camp residents were clearly opposed to their displacement, I here show how they nonetheless felt compelled to situate this experience in the larger context of world-class city making: slums were being removed to make way for a city of glimmering steel and glass megaliths; manicured parks to be looked at, not used; and bigger roads, bigger cars, and bigger people. World-class aesthetics became the implicit ordering framework for explaining Shiv Camp's predicament, which often led residents to characterize their own settlement as filthy, disorderly, and thus in need of improvement or elimination. On first glance, this adoption of a world-class aesthetic disposition and characterization of slum "unbelonging" might suggest an absence of contestation, a reading I aim to counter in the rest of the chapter. I do so by examining a set of aesthetic techniques by which world-class metrics of disorder were extended into Shiv Camp, constraining forms of speech and action, which I use to show how world-class terms of sensibility became commonplace in residents' everyday lives. Once demonstrating the extent to which political speech was constrained by the world-class aesthetic, I return to residents' statements of their unbelonging to rethink how we might interpret the act of partaking in dominant aesthetic codes. Whereas the growing literature on the slum and similar spaces of urban relegation tend to read the poor's participation in dominant discourses and sensibilities as a sign of resignation or consent—the end of politics—Shiv Camp residents treated it as the starting point of politics.

DISPLACEMENT

January in Delhi brings cold, heavy fog, leading people to hover over stoves and around fires in anticipation of the coming spring. On the evening of January 3, on a night when temperatures would dip as low as three degrees Celsius, a team of fifty policemen wielding cane shields and batons, four bulldozers, and a dozen Municipal Corporation officers descended upon Shiv Camp.[4] Women were fetching water from the community taps; children were playing in the streets, fighting the cold; and day laboring men had not yet returned from their construction sites. A child yelled "*sarkār ā gayī* [government has come]," and the group of officers stepped forward. While the demolition squad went for tea, Shiv Camp residents were told that in thirty minutes, the bulldozers and sledgehammers would begin their work: a High Court order had been issued to clear a forty-five-foot-wide path through the middle of the *bastī* [settlement].[5] People panicked: Which huts would fall, which would remain? What was going to happen to those displaced? Why was this happening?

The chief officer recommended that people remove the belongings from their homes, before turning to retrieve his cup of tea. People scattered, some shouted, while others followed the officer, begging for answers.

At five o'clock, in the final hour of daylight, the bulldozers began their work. With people running in and out of huts carrying televisions, bags of clothing, and cookware, the machines rolled forward, toppling walls and crushing bricks. Night fell, but they pushed on, razing 122 homes in two hours. People clamored, teenage boys pelted stones at the machines before running into the night to avoid the pursuing police, and three men were arrested for arguing with, and according to the police, slapping a Municipal Corporation officer.

At the end of the row of huts, a woman's scream pierced the cold night air as a bulldozer knocked the wall of her hut onto her two-week-old son lying inside. Shambu later said her yelp was like a thousand screeching frogs [*hazār meṇḍhuk kā phaṭā āvāz*]. The child died instantly due to blunt trauma, an autopsy report later showed.

Because of the infant's death, the demolition squad had not returned after the demolition raid to clear the land, so by the time I arrived two days later, residents whose homes had been razed were stacking bricks, living in makeshift tents, and considering rebuilding their *jhuggis* (see Figure 5.1).

Figure 5.1. Shiv Camp residents organizing their belongings in the aftermath of the January demolition. Photograph by author.

I entered Shiv Camp asking residents what had happened. Some mentioned a High Court order against the settlement, while many insisted that the neighboring resident welfare association (RWA) had simply bribed the police and Municipal Corporation to clear the area. Because few people heard the initial, terse remarks by the Municipal Corporation officers, and because many residents arrived on scene only after the demolition, memory, rumor, and conjecture mixed in people's efforts to make sense of the events that had unfolded. With this confusion came anger. As Deshraj told me,

> When we first moved here, the area was totally desolate. You could see all the way to [the nearby village, now a bustling market area]. There were only fields. Once the *koṭhīs* [private bungalows] came, all the owners had to do was raise a shout and we came and scared away the thief. We built their homes and ran off outsiders, and in return they are now running us off our land.... Sarkar says on the map there is a road here. Well, we've been here since before any maps and there was never a road in this place!

Feelings of betrayal were premised on both residents' direct labor contribution to the colony ("we built their homes") and an attachment to place ("we've been here since before any maps"). Prem, for example, found an argument that Shiv Camp residents attributed to the RWA—that the land upon which Shiv Camp was settled should be a local market—disingenuous: "For so many years we had to go so far to buy supplies at the market. Now, you can get everything you need around here. For forty years they never wanted to build a market, and now that all the space is gone and there are markets in all directions, they want to kick us out to build a market?" Motilal was still more piercing:

> A lot of these *baḍe log* [big people] are Panjabi, Sikh. After the Indira incident [*hādsā*—when Hindu mobs retaliated against Sikhs in Delhi after Prime Minister Indira Gandhi was assassinated by her Sikh bodyguard], these people were in great danger. What did we do? We are Hindu [implying piousness].[6] We went into the streets, and when people came looking for Sikhs, we said we live in this area and have taken care of everything. We protected them. Now look what we get in return!

Although the *pradhān* (local headman) had been informed of a pending High Court case against Shiv Camp, almost everyone was shocked by the demolition, grasping to assign meaning to the event. In the first month after the incident there was no word from the police or Municipal Corporation, leaving residents to speculate about their futures. Without an official signal from the state, anything could be taken as a sign of what was to come: a large corporate land purchase nearby or a newspaper report about park improvement for the upcoming Commonwealth Games signaled, as much as the *pradhan*'s decision to begin constructing a house on the land he had earlier purchased outside the settlement, that Shiv Camp's days were numbered.

Residents were afraid to leave Shiv Camp during this time, lest *sarkar* return while they were gone. Even those whose *jhuggis* had not been touched ensured someone was at home at all times, either to help others or out of fear that they might return to a demolished home. People lingered in the settlement, waiting for *sarkar* to act upon them—waiting for history to arrive and seal their fate.

Four days after the demolition, a group of Shiv Camp men organized a hunger strike on the main road in the adjacent middle-class colony of Krishna Garden and in front of the entrance to the nearest Delhi Metro station. Through a connection with the Janshakti Party, a national party with virtually no local presence in Delhi, they erected a large tent where eight men sat for three days fasting. Fifty other residents joined them on a rug—last rolled out for a Diwali celebration the *pradhan* had hosted—to shout slogans, deliver impassioned speeches, and denounce the injustice of the demolition.

An NGO receiving funds from a London-based charity for community empowerment in Shiv Camp had shown up a day after the demolition, offering to hire a lawyer for a fee of one lakh rupees. The de facto leaders of Shiv Camp—a collection of older, wealthier, or more educated men drawn equally from the Rajasthani and Bundelkhandi sides of the *basti*—liked the idea, but were suspicious of the middle-class women running the NGO, who appeared only twice a year, usually with white, foreign donors in tow, and never gave money to residents. After going door-to-door demanding contributions from their neighbors, the men managed to collect half that amount, enough to pay a local lawyer to represent them in their effort to prevent a future demolition. The men called the strike and the legal case the "grassroots battle" and the "paper battle" [*zamīnī laḍāī* and *kāgazī laḍāī*], respectively, adding to the resistance vocabulary already abuzz in Shiv Camp. This initial reaction to the violence of displacement, however, was shot through with the more embodied knowledge of their unbelonging that Prem displayed—a perception that they violated the city's emerging codes of appearance—and the unyielding sense that the future slum-free city was on its way.

"FILTHY SLUMS"

A few days after the hunger strike ended, I met Kishan, a man from the denser Bundelkhandi side of the *basti* with a penchant for a drink, a keen political acumen, and a sharp tongue.⁷ Kishan was the only Shiv Camp man (there were other boys) to have gone to college, and he liked to recite Sanskrit *shlokās* and historical trivia to remind his fellow construction workers of his superior education. Boys often huddled around Kishan to hear his stories, fondly calling him Pandit, a moniker he embarrassingly enjoyed. After I asked what would happen after the hunger strike, Kishan replied with a breath of Gandhian civil disobedience: "If you are going to do a hunger strike for only three days, what's the point? You have to do an unending hunger strike until your point is heard, otherwise you die. . . . A hunger strike is not about display or self; it is about getting the truth. *Bāpū* taught us this." He extended his combative tone into a discussion of the "paper battle" as a group of youth formed around us under the *pīpal* tree at the edge of the *basti*.

"These people have lived here for 15, 20, 30 years," he said. "Where was the MCD [Municipal Corporation of Delhi] that whole time? Why weren't they told then that this is the place for a road?!" Dhaniram, a recent high school graduate who helped the Shiv Camp leaders on legal and documentary matters, piped in: "There is a law that says sarkar cannot kick us out without resettlement." Others in the group agreed, but said even beyond the resettlement question, they had a fundamental right to live in Shiv Camp. Kishan elaborated: "All over India, if someone uses land and lives on it for three years, then they are given property rights [*mālikānā haq*]. . . . In Delhi though, this is not true. There is a different right here." I asked how long someone has to stay to secure this right in Delhi. "I don't know, but if someone is here for eighteen years like me, they have the right [*haq*]," he said. A boy added, "if you were here before 1990 you definitely have it, but anyone who stays here and sets up a house has it too."

1990 was the year that then Prime Minister V. P. Singh initiated a survey of all slums in Delhi, giving those enumerated a unique token, now known as the V. P. Singh token, which served as formal proof of residence. Delhi's slum policy was also modified at the time to grant any slum resident who could prove residence in Delhi prior to 1990—most easily by displaying a V. P. Singh token in their name—entitlement to government resettlement in case of a demolition. Most of Shiv Camp met this cut-off date, as the *basti* was first settled in 1968 by a land colonizer, a Panjabi man named Chaudhury who purchased a tract of low-lying, flood-prone land in two villages near the Najafgarh drain (see Map), which carries waste water from Delhi into the western plains. Once Chaudhury's layout plan for his proposed colony was approved by the development authority, he hired a labor contractor from the nearby state of Rajasthan, who brought a team of Dalit workers from his village to build the roads, buildings, and sewers for the planned colony of Krishna Garden. A 1977 flood led a second wave of around a dozen workers and their families, this time primarily from the Bundelkhand region of southern Uttar Pradesh and northern Madhya Pradesh, to Shiv Camp.

As the Rajasthani and Bundelkhandi settlements expanded, a single *basti* divided by geographic origin soon emerged. To this day, the *basti* is bisected along these same lines, a division now marked by the forty-five-foot-wide path the Municipal Corporation cleared through the middle of the *jhuggis* (see Figure 5.2). Once it was big enough to draw the attention of political parties and Delhi's Department of Food and Supplies—which gives out ration cards that entitle those designated below the poverty line to free and reduced-rate food staples and that, then, was the sole evidence required to vote—Chaudhury-the-colonizer gave the settlement, occupied entirely by Hindus at the time, the name "Shiv Camp."

In 1983, having sold off most of the individual plots in Krishna Garden, Chaudhury turned the entire area over to the Municipal Corporation, which provides municipal services (e.g., lighting, waste disposal, water connections) to the residents and businesses of planned colonies and maintains such areas' public infrastructure (e.g., parks, roads, sewers) once land colonizers have completed basic development works. To Shiv Camp residents, who by then had diversified their sources of employment and no longer worked for Chaudhury, this was an almost insignificant event. The Municipal Corporation did not challenge their settlement status, and most of the families, including the more recent migrants from Haryana and Bihar,

Figure 5.2. These three aerial photographs show Shiv Camp in September 2004, March 2007, and April 2007, respectively. The leftmost photograph shows the approximate peak density Shiv Camp reached, the middle one shows the extent to which residents had reconstructed their homes after the January 2007 demolition, and the rightmost shows Shiv Camp immediately after the Municipal Corporation had returned to clear the forty-five-footpath. The black lines outline the approximate boundaries of Shiv Camp, showing middle-class bungalows [*koṭhīs*] to the south, west, and east sides of the settlement. The rightmost image shows what appears to be a bulldozer (see arrow) parked in the path cleared through the settlement on April 19. © 2009 Google.

had received ration cards and voter ID cards that, in those days, confirmed their residential status.⁸ In the late 1990s, the Corporation enumerated 637 households in Shiv Camp on just over eight *bīghās* (two acres) of land, by then a densely packed settlement abutting a government sports college on one side and private *koṭhīs* on the others.

This history mattered to Shiv Camp residents: the initial approval they received from Chaudhury and later from the politicians who issued them residence proof endowed them with a deep sense of historical entitlement to their land—the right [*haq*] to which Kishan, Dhaniram, and the group of boys seated under the *pipal* tree that day had referred. This was a right not just known and felt, but also possessed in the form of the plastic folder-encased collections of ration cards, voter ID cards, tokens, school lists, and other civic insignia stored in steel cases tucked beneath beds. Who could question the residential status of an elderly man possessing a letter from the government school, addressed to his specific *jhuggi* number in Shiv Camp, confirming his daughter's enrollment in 1968? Such material histories, combined with residents' belief that the January demolition constituted a fundamental violation of their rights as citizens, led Kishan and the rest of the group to express great faith that the paper battle would lead this deeper sense of justice to prevail over any legal basis for the demolition, such as the rumored map showing a road through the middle of the settlement—a map residents never themselves saw.

Later, however, when the conversation shifted toward broader trends in the city, the group spoke without reference to this sense of historical entitlement, as if they stepped out of themselves and talked from a distant, disembodied perspective. For example, when I referred to the array of slum demolitions that were taking place across the city and asked what they meant for Delhi, a boy replied: "It means the city will become more beautiful and the roads will be better. More things like the Metro will come."

"So, because of the Metro, jhuggis are being removed?" I asked.

"Yes."

"So all this beautification is bad?"

"No," the group said collectively. "It is good for Delhi. Delhi will improve," the boy continued. Kishan interjected: "It is good because this is the capital of India and should be beautiful. People from all over the world come here."

"So on the one hand they are improving the city, but on the other this means they have to kick you out?" I continued, exploring how they reconciled what they considered the objective benefit of world-class redevelopment ("It is good for Delhi and India") and the violence this inflicted in their own lives.

"The *Olympic* game will happen in Delhi. They are preparing for that, fixing the city, making everything new. It is okay if we are *shift*ed outside of the city, but they have to give us the right to stay there," Kishan said, responding to my apparent confusion.

"So you think that you should be removed from the city?" I asked, using the verb *haṭānā* ("to remove or displace") instead of the English word *shift* to try to make the violence of this action, which they had been describing earlier, explicit.

"Yes," Kishan said, "it is good for Delhi if we are removed from the city. Look at this place. People here spread filth. The area is dirty. Anybody can see this. Such places are a problem for Delhi."

Their earlier reaction was to the violence of their removal [*haṭānā*], but they understood the necessity of being *shift*ed—a rationalized procedure, part of a larger urban improvement agenda. Whereas their earlier grievances, as expressed through the grassroots and paper battles, were framed in terms of defending a right [*haq*] to occupy their current land, and whereas these grievances confronted what they considered the fundamental injustice of their displacement, when framed in terms of the broader development of the city, they identified with the world-class city-building project, referring to common emblems of urban improvement and beautification, such as the Commonwealth Games (which residents commonly referred to as the "Olympic" or "international" game) and the Delhi Metro—what a prominent planner described "as the torch bearer of a resurgent India."[9] Thus, within the course of an hour-long conversation, they had invoked competing notions of entitlement and property: on the one hand, their inviolable right to occupancy, based on their length of residence, government approval and documentation, or their direct labor and political contribution to building the neighborhood and city; and on the other, a recognition of slum unbelonging and impermanence.

On first glance, the group seemed to be embracing contradictory positionalities—at once defending their stake as occupants of public land while simultaneously identifying slums as nuisances. As in the statement by Prem with which I began this chapter, the constative meanings the group expressed ("slum removal is good for Delhi") seemed to contradict their stated interests ("we shouldn't be removed"). In my first month in Shiv Camp, such moments utterly confused me.

One particularly confusing conversation occurred at the hunger strike while chatting with Lachmi, a fifty-year-old from Bundelkhand, a region with some of the highest rates of landlessness and caste discrimination in India. Lachmi moved to Shiv Camp thirty years earlier, when his family fled their village after an upper-caste landlord submitted a falsified police report that claimed Lachmi's father stole a water buffalo. Once in Delhi, Lachmi's uncle found him a six-rupee-a-day job as a head loader for a government contractor, and he had slowly worked his way up the construction ranks, now a small contractor himself.

Sitting on the rug underneath the protest tent, with billows of diesel exhaust sputtering in from the adjacent road, Lachmi pointed across the concrete landscape in front of us, proclaiming, "I worked for sarkar and helped build many of the big buildings in this area. The district center, the school, these offices, I made all of these things." Immediately in front of us was the elevated rail of the Delhi Metro, which he incorporated into his description: "Now that this has come, people want to get rid of us. People like this sort of thing, but with it comes ideas that everything should be clean, so they don't like us and want us to leave."

"Why don't people like you?" I asked.

"Because our clothes smell bad. They want order and cleanliness. The more this type of thing comes, the more they want to run us away," he said, an opinion reflecting his position as a slum resident threatened by a new vision of urban development in which he had no place. But without hesitation, his next sentence moderated this stance, embracing a more distant, nationalistic pride in this same urban vision: "But, I also like the Metro. Anyone in India will tell you it's a good thing. It brings you where you need to go quickly."

Continuing the theme of his contribution to the built environment, I asked Lachmi if he knew anyone who had worked to build the Metro, a hulking construction project built by a Japanese engineering company that employed thousands of local laborers. "No," he replied, "it was built by a company. Nobody here was involved. We learned how to build it from you [foreigners], and we then built it here," the "we" pronoun in this statement referring to Indian people as a whole. His words signaled an appreciation for the Metro as well as a simultaneous recognition of his exclusion from the production and consumption of this particular infrastructure and the model of urban development it represented: "All we want is to be given new land. Just put us somewhere outside the city. Or, just wipe all us poor out [*bas, ham garībom̐ ko golī mārnā cāhiye*]! Really. Then the city will be rid of us. We also won't have to worry about this all. But, if they are going to let us stay, then they have to give us land, and it is okay if it is far away, but they should put us near this Metro."

For the three days of the hunger strike I sat under the tent with the protestors, watching the Metro trains skim back and forth across the skyline and commuters hustle past the busy road in front of us. Each day the men took turns delivering speeches against the demolition, demanding a Central Bureau of Investigation inquiry, and launching into slogans denouncing the violence against them. The protestors used my presence strategically; one man proclaimed, "the Delhi Government says they are removing jhuggis to make Delhi beautiful for foreigners, but look here: here's a foreigner who stands with us!" More than a prop, I was invited to add into the chorus, one more voice to fill the oppositional airwaves. With nervous Hindi, I borrowed their same language of injustice, my American accent garnering the attention of a few additional onlookers. But attention was limited. A marbly five-star hotel was under construction on the far side of the road, behind the commanding Metro station that hovered above the divided road, and the sound of hydraulic drills limited the range of the protestors' megaphoned voices. In this small tent intent on making visible the violence of world-class city making, the world-class city barely returned a glance.

On the second day of the protest, I asked Lachmi if anyone from the neighboring RWA, which had filed the High Court petition leading to the destruction of his home, had come to see the hunger strike. "No. They will not come. They are like enemies and only want us removed," he said, again expressing anger toward the immediate actors mobilized against Shiv Camp. But Gopal—who sat beside Lachmi for those three days—a moment later described Shiv Camp from this very group's imagined perspective, wielding the quick, evenly cadenced logic a lawyer might use: "This place is dirty, right? We live on very small space. As people have children, the population grows. Therefore people have to do *latrine* outside, and this spreads filth. Because of this the whole area is dirty, so they want to clear it." Lachmi nodded in agreement.

Lachmi and Gopal were angry that their houses were destroyed. However, their broader contextualization of this event betrayed a recognition of and explicit engagement with the sanitized urban vision in widespread circulation in Delhi. When they spoke more broadly in terms of urban development and referenced this shared urban imaginary, Lachmi and Gopal spoke through the world-class aesthetic. After reviewing my field notes and returning to Shiv Camp the next day, I asked Gopal again why the government was trying to remove Shiv Camp. He replied matter-of-factly, "because we are dirty and make the city look bad.... Nobody wants to step out of his home and see us washing in the open or see our kids shitting." This "nobody" is described as a universal subject, yet one that is clearly not a slum resident: this subject has a balcony, and thus owns property, and observes the city from an elevated, removed position (see Figure 5.3). This is the exact type of nuisance-based argument RWA members made in justifying their efforts to remove neighboring slums (see chapter 3). Slum residents, to my surprise, were not only familiar with this nuisance talk, but in many instances deployed it in their own speech.

Consider the narrative of Shambu, one of the residents most actively involved in the paper battle to defend Shiv Camp. I met Shambu, a tall

Figure 5.3. "Nobody wants to step out of his home and see us"; *koṭhī* balconies overlook Shiv Camp residents on the streets during Navratri celebrations. Photograph by author.

Rajasthani man with a deep scowl, hard-won smile, and commanding presence in the *basti*, a month after the January demolition. I joined Shambu almost daily over the ensuing nine months, walking through Shiv Camp's narrow lanes, attending court hearings, or sitting in his turquoise *jhuggi* as people came to share local news. Many residents called Shambu by the name *Ṭhekedār* (contractor), even though the nature of his work had shifted after developing a heart ailment from organizing teams of laborers for construction projects to mobilizing them to vote for the right political party. That first day we met, Shambu explained the demolition as a mere whim of the government: "Sarkar wanted to build a road here," he put it, as we squatted, watching families rebuild their demolished homes with broken bricks and crumpled corrugated metal (see Figure 5.4).

I asked Shambu what these wealthier neighbors thought of Shiv Camp. "They think we are bad and want us to leave. We are insects to them," he said.

"Do you think your struggle is against them?" I asked.

"No, we have no animosity [*dushmanī*] with them. Why should we? They only want their own space. . . . It is like when you are eating and you get a stain on your face, you wipe it clean. That is what they are doing here. They see us as a stain. If you get something stuck in your teeth, you pick it out. We are the same for them. . . . This is happening all over Delhi. They want to make Delhi like Paris. They want it to be beautiful."

Figure 5.4. Reconstructed Shiv Camp homes in March 2007, two months after the January demolition. Photo taken from the same position as Figure 5.1. Photograph by author.

I wondered what beautiful meant to him.

"It means wider roads, cleaner neighborhoods, less traffic and crowd, removing jhuggis."

"Is this improvement [*sudharnā*]?" I asked.

"Of course it is improvement. Everyone will tell you that."

Here, Shambu, like Gopal and Kishan before him, spoke through the same world-class aesthetic that property owners and the judiciary used to characterize slum unbelonging: removing *jhuggis* is improvement, noted Shambu; slums make the city look bad, claimed Gopal; it is good for Delhi if slums are cleared, said Kishan. Were these moments of consent, of subaltern subjects unknowingly reinforcing exclusionary hierarchies through the language of taste?

Prominent conceptions of the aesthetic would lead us to just such a conclusion. Terry Eagleton, for example, writes that the moment when "moral actions can be classified chiefly as 'agreeable' or 'disagreeable,' when these aesthetic terms will do service for more complex distinctions," marks a point of aesthetic hegemony, a point at which "the sheer quick feel or impression of an object will be enough for sure judgment, short-circuiting discursive contention and thus mystifying the rules which regulate it."[10] While Eagleton alerts us to a more aesthetic, precognitive mode of apprehension, the power of the aesthetic here lies precisely in its ability to make dominant social imaginaries more ideologically effective—that is, to capture interests and beliefs. Choon-Piew Pow, writing about what he calls "the aestheticization of middle-class landscapes" in Shanghai, says that urban aesthetics "play an important role in the *masking* of class inequality and urban segregation."[11] Tim Hall and Phil Hubbard, in an influential description of city branding and image work, write that "city imagineering" is "an instrument of false consciousness by the elite in the advancement of their own entrepreneurial interests."[12]

Despite adhering to the formal constraints of world-class aesthetic discourse, Shiv Camp residents were not "mystified" or "masked": they did not in any straightforward way believe displacement was a good thing, and they understood very well that a world-class city meant a slum-free city. Consider, for example, a conversation between Kishani and two of her neighbors.

Seated on the ground in a paved patch of earth in front of Kishani's pink sherbet-colored *jhuggi*, the three women were discussing Kishani's plans to convert the ground floor of her two-story home into a provisions shop. I sat on the *chārpāī* [cot] beside them after they snickeringly offered me a smoke from the *hukkā* they were sharing—they had seen me struggle to smoke the milder *bīḍīs* their husbands offered me and knew I couldn't handle their powerful tobacco. With the threat of demolition looming, the women found Kishani's proposed home investment surprising. Kishani's *jhuggi* was one of the oldest and biggest in Shiv Camp, and it benefited from the shade of one of the only three living trees in the settlement, making it an ideal place to sell cigarettes and snacks. While the structure was more than two hundred feet away from the forty-five-foot demolition path cleared by the Municipal Corporation, and while Kishani possessed residence documents dating back to 1969, her neighbors knew that if the High Court case went the wrong way, all Shiv Camp homes would be removed. When I pushed this point, Kishani heard nothing of it: "I have lived here for thirty years. This is my home. It is wrong to remove us from here," expressing a clear opposition to displacement.

Later, the women started talking about the growth of shopping malls in Delhi, the topic of one of the pseudo-debates local Hindi news channels regularly aired on "local citizen matters." I asked the women what Delhi would look like once so many malls came up, and Kishani, pausing to exhaust two thin plumes of white smoke from her nostrils, responded calmly and without sarcasm, "Delhi will be a beautiful city, totally neat and clean. All the *jhuggis* will be removed, and there will only be rich people." If not mystification, masking, false consciousness, or trained desire, how else can we account for such a gap between residents' stated desire not to be displaced and their recognition that such displacement is a form of urban improvement?

The narrative shift Kishani conveyed—between a situated description of the personal injustice of demolition on the one hand, and a more disembodied expression of the common good on the other—was common in residents' discussions of the future city. While they would in one instance describe their experience in slums in the first-person voice, as when Kishani told me, "after we built our huts, we thought the land was our own," or in second-person voice, as when Kishani said, "when you are given a ration card, you become a permanent resident of Delhi," they would just as quickly shift and start talking about slums in general. Thus, while Kishani had earlier been describing her personal hardships and triumphs in Shiv Camp—the slow improvement of her home into a two-story, *pakkā* structure, the sudden death of her husband, the challenge of finding marriageable boys for her daughters—when I asked why slums were being demolished, she said, "jhuggis are dirty. They aren't permanent. Jhuggi dwellers don't live on their own land [*Jhuggīvāle apnī khud zamīn par nahīṁ rehte*]." As in Gopal's above description of the universal nobody who is disgusted by slum bodies ("nobody wants to step out of his home and see us washing in the open"), or Shambu's claim that everyone can see that slums are a problem for Delhi, Kishani here embraced a distant, third-person viewing perspective.

Unlike in Eagleton's mystification, the truth of the world-class city was not concealed from Kishani, yet she nonetheless spoke through and acknowledged the normative power of the world-class aesthetic. Why?

In each of Gopal, Shambu, and Kishani's statements, there was an abstract public—the everyone—whose authoritative position the speaker occupied ambiguously: I, Shambu, tell you that everyone sees that slums are out of place. On first glance, these words appear to be a descriptive statement of belief that slums are out of place. This is the primary way in which the voices of the urban poor—the slum subject, if you will—have been interpreted.[13] How else can we read such statements other than as signs of consent, compliance, or submission? For the remainder of this chapter, I want to try to address this question by shifting our normal mode of analysis. That is, I want to ask not what Shambu meant when he said "everyone knows" slums are out of place. Rather, I want to ask if Shambu was assigning himself to the category "everyone." In acknowledging the *unbelonging* of the slum, did Shambu *belong* to the everyone?

LANDSCAPE AESTHETICS

The world-class aesthetic became a near ubiquitous normative framework in millennial Delhi, giving the cityscape an aspirational quality. The Delhi government's billing of the preparations for the 2010 Commonwealth

Games as the city's top priority,[14] the constant media celebration of Delhi's glimmering new monuments of modernity, and the more diffuse effects of what William Mazzarella calls India's "consumerist dispensation" deepened and generalized an urban imaginary premised on polished steel, high automobility, and conspicuous consumption.[15] Indexed not through improvements in environmental health, urban livability, or human development, the world-class city became an ideal measureable through visual criteria, identifiable through an instant shock of recognition. The world-class city, in other words, came to operate as a symbol of progress and modernity, but also an object of desire in itself, regardless of the use value it might provide to residents. Delhiites, living in a city unmoored from its austere, centrally planned past, were thus enjoined to constantly observe themselves and others from the perspective of the future city and, in this way, implored to adopt a subjunctive disposition orienting the self-that-might-be to the city-that-would-be.[16] More concretely, the legal codification of the world-class aesthetic (discussed in chapter 4) extended bourgeois codes of appearance and order into the domain of official state practice, increasingly positing urban social relations in the binary terms of "public nuisance" and "private citizen." Those classified on the former side of this divide suddenly found themselves submitted to new social metrics and standards of belonging. In this section, I examine how the production of a world-class landscape constrains aesthetic sensibilities, modifying the sensory vocabularies and observational dispositions of Shiv Camp residents into what Pierre Bourdieu might call a world-class "scheme of perception," an authorized way of seeing put in place as "the world imposes its presence, with its urgencies, its things to be done and said, things made to be said."[17]

Following the increase in slum demolitions in the early 2000s, few large slums remain intact in Delhi, leaving scattered *jhuggi jhompdi* clusters, as they are called in official government reports, tucked along railroad tracks, wedged between planned residential colonies, and dotted across the rapidly expanding periphery. As a result, one sees few slums in Delhi while traveling its main streets, creating the sense, among slum and nonslum residents alike, that slums are anomalies, aberrations from the visual and legal norm. Shiv Camp residents, for example, insisted there were more *kothis* (bungalows) than *jhuggis* in Krishna Garden, as well as in Delhi as a whole. Demographic numbers do not confirm this visual experience: only a quarter of the city's population of seventeen million lives in formally planned residential colonies, the rest residing in unauthorized colonies, slums, resettlement colonies, urban villages, or the old walled city.[18] Nonetheless, the city's increasingly world-class look, combined with the intensifying enclosure and fragmentation of slums into denser settlements, perpetuates the overall sentiment that slums represent a visual affront to contemporary urban aesthetics.

This sentiment became especially strong in the wake of the steep increase in property prices that began after the liberalization of the real estate market in the 2000s (see chapter 1). On the urban peripheries, where this market was introduced to global investment flows for the first time, stories of decadal increases in home price of 1,000 percent were not uncommon. My middle-class landlord, a retired postal worker, for example, told me he purchased his flat for thirteen lakh rupees in 2000, grinning in 2008 as he said his neighbor's identical flat had recently sold for eighty lakh. As a local property dealer told me, after detailing how property prices near Shiv Camp had doubled instantly upon the arrival of the Delhi Metro in 2006, "by the time of the Commonwealth Games, the whole city will look different. There will be different buses, a different map, different buildings, and different people. People who earn 50,000 rupees per month will stay in Delhi. Everyone else will have to live outside. Delhi is changing like that. It will only be for that type of people."[19]

Because most Shiv Camp residents were involved in construction work, they were critically aware of this changing political economy, and they would often marvel at the spectacular changes taking place both in the built environment and in the price of land.[20] As Kishan told me, "look here. These kothis [surrounding Shiv Camp] are all worth two crore [1 crore = 10 million] rupees. The land here? None of us paid for it. They could sell this for crores. Of course they want to kick us off and sell it!" Others simply recognized that a world-class future—a program of urban development many summarized with the phrase "Delhi will become like Paris"—meant a deepening round of urban beautification and demolitions.

The sense of being outside of the aesthetic norm was especially strong in Shiv Camp for two reasons. First, three archetypical world-class monuments—the silver-bullet Delhi Metro; a five-star, blue-glass Hilton Hotel; and a twelve-story shopping mall with intergalactic, antennae-like towers—had recently been built or were under construction within a kilometer of Shiv Camp. As Susan Buck-Morss writes, such iconic and celebrated structures are historically "called upon to give visible 'proof' of historical progress," to inscribe into urban form both an expectation of transformation and a dividing line between what fits this imagined future and what does not.[21] The sheen of these structures' excessive mirrored glass and polished steel testified to their material modernness, making the brick, tin, and tarp of Shiv Camp huts incongruous blotches on the landscape. The look of the area's world-class buildings and spectacular infrastructure evinced a deeper economic rift that marked capitalized spaces from undercapitalized spaces: private land versus public land, planned *kothis* and flats versus *bastis* and *jhuggis*, *baḍe log* versus *mazdūr*, binary terms Shiv Camp residents used to describe the deepening social cleavages within their city.

This divide was further entrenched for a second reason. While for many years Shiv Camp grew and changed along with the surrounding colony of Krishna Garden, that colony had since grown to vastly surpass Shiv Camp in physical stature and area, with private *kothis* encircling and towering above Shiv Camp's tightly packed *jhuggis*. These *kothis* are three- or four-story brick and concrete houses, often with gates, carefully manicured gardens or boundary walls on their street side, and sometimes with façades embellished with fake columns, decorative arches, or vaulted windows sculpted out of cement in what one Delhi-based architect calls "Punjabi baroque."[22] One of the *kothis* abutting Shiv Camp was being rebuilt from the ground up during my fieldwork, while two others underwent exterior stylistic work to enhance their posh character. In contrast, Shiv Camp looked much like it did ten years ago, contributing to the sense among residents that they were anachronistic: remnants of the past, clinging to their place, outsiders in a city that has been home for decades. This experience of stasis in a sea of change, of anticipating a slum-free future, was enhanced by the absence of the homes razed initially in January, and again conclusively in April, as well as the complete demolition of two nearby *bastis* a year earlier.

In short, physical landscape transformations and spectacular infrastructure development meant the city's public spaces had come under an increasingly homogenized lens of aesthetic scrutiny, tuning the urban aesthetic field to the symbolic goal of attaining world-class city status. While projects of urban beautification are often characterized as efforts to "refashion the urban landscape for visual consumption . . . in the hope of producing real economic value," landscape aesthetics play an equally important role in refashioning urban subjects by linking criteria of appearance to criteria of belonging.[23] The twinning of a propertied regime of citizenship in Delhi with such class-based criteria of appearance hence has led to a fundamental reconfiguration of how public space and the vast population dependent on its use are perceived, as I now describe.

In Indian cities, the everyday habits and sensibilities of the lower and upper classes have been divided historically by unique appropriations of public space. In an infrastructure scarce environment such as Shiv Camp the biological compulsion to wash, bathe, and defecate in the open, for example, were routine practices that contributed to a habitus not informed by the clear demarcation of public and private.[24] As a result, residents' aesthetic sensibilities were not shaped by the bourgeois sense of propriety—premised on a functional divide between public and private—that would rise to prominence in millennial Delhi (see chapter 3). Walking to a community water tap to wash clothes and bodies was a normal, nonrebukable act, even if it offended the sensibilities of middle-class onlookers. While the sensory vocabularies and aesthetic preferences of the propertied classes no doubt carried great authority, they were limited in their ability to influence how the urban poor were symbolically represented and governmentally managed—public space through the 1990s retained a plebian character.[25] Recall here the Manchanda court petition I described in the previous chapter in which a Delhi RWA stated that open defecation in a neighboring slum made the property owners' lives "miserable" by creating an "uncultured scene."[26] When the petition was heard in court in 1991, the slum residents received no official rebuke, and because they were not themselves party to the case, they were likely unaware of the court's attention to the matter.

In millennial Delhi, however, what Bourdieu calls the "world imposed" shifted, as world-class aesthetic codes became codified as near-universal standards. This took place largely through the reinterpretation of nuisance law I described in the previous chapter, which led slum residents' same habitual practices (open cooking, washing, bathing) to be seen as public nuisances: distinctly private acts that fell beyond the bounds of civility when performed publically. With this gradual purification of the very meaning of the public, slum residents began to find their extant sensibilities incongruent with the world-class aesthetic—a situation that can lead individuals to feel "lost for words," condemned to silence within their social settings.[27] We here might recall those moments of seeming resignation when Lachmi, for example, said, "just wipe all of us poor out," or when Kishan said, "it is good for Delhi if we are removed from the city"—clear indications of residents' reduced capacity to influence the forms of their public representation.

World-class aesthetic codes became so coherent and well-codified in Shiv Camp that many residents assumed they were recorded, in some form or another, in the Delhi Master Plan. As Gopal told me shortly after the April demolition: "The government has made a new map that shows how the new city will look. There will be nice clean roads, big buildings; it will be beautiful and will be clean and maintained. There will be less [traffic] *jam* and without so much filth." Residents often described the Master Plan as a map showing how the future city would look. When I asked how Gopal knew what this imagined map looked like, he said, "well, we have not seen the map. That is only for government officials to see, but they tell everyone about it. They say that the city will look beautiful and have all these things [roads, bridges, malls]. The newspapers tell us about it, and we read those and learn about the map slowly."[28]

In light of the deep normalization of the world-class aesthetic, conveyed in the sense of its physical inscription in a map, residents were forced to respond to a scheme of perception that contradicted their own class habitus—similar to what Walter Benjamin once called "the standardization of perception."²⁹ In other words, as "filthy slums" were being demolished for violating world-class aesthetic codes, those dependent on subsistence uses of public space had to increasingly look upon themselves reflexively through the eyes of their better-off neighbors, as when Lachmi said "our clothes smell bad," Shambu said "they see us as a stain," and Gopal said, "nobody wants to step out of his home and see us washing in the open." What I am thus suggesting is that when aesthetic codes become so normalized and potent that they are seen to have the force of a map or written decree, statements such as Lachmi, Gopal, and Shambu's ought to be read not as constative statements of preference or belief, but rather as acts of recognizing the existing terms of sensibility. That is, rather than being condemned to silence, Shiv Camp residents often took part in the world-class community of sense, appropriating its vocabulary to avoid public humiliation, garner symbolic advantage, anticipate legal or political action, or deflect the stigma of life in a space of relegation.

It is with an eye toward the political possibility that lies in such an appropriation of dominant aesthetic norms that I turn in the next section to an ethnographic scene where Shiv Camp residents were put to the test, so to speak. I specifically seek to highlight how performing world-class aesthetic norms operated as a means of gaining symbolic legitimacy and holding open the possibility for reinterpreting those same norms, even though that performance maintained the power hierarchies those norms put in place.

PERFORMING SENSIBLY

In the course of my fieldwork, I spent a considerable amount of time with the group of men involved in Shiv Camp's legal defense (the "paper battle"), frequently joining them for court hearings and legal meetings. During its proceedings, the High Court determined that the land records for most of Shiv Camp were incomplete, so it appointed a court commissioner to mediate the dispute over land ownership.³⁰ I attended the mediation hearings in the High Court, where I listened as Shiv Camp residents, the Krishna Garden RWA that was demanding Shiv Camp's removal, and Delhi's multiple land agencies presented competing evidence and arguments.

Before the first of these meetings began, the parties sat around an oval table in the small mediation room flanked by their lawyers, awaiting the arrival of the commissioner. An absurd feature of many court cases against *bastis* is that the individuals whose homes and livelihoods are threatened are often not made party to the case: while elaborate legal proceedings against them take place in the center of the city, *basti* residents typically become aware of these cases only when a final demolition order is issued, as was the case in Shiv Camp on that cold January evening when the bulldozers arrived. Because these cases are usually fought between neighboring property owners and the agencies upon whose land the slums are settled, the residents remain mere objects of dispute, not active legal subjects—a part of the legal proceedings, but with no part in them.

After the January demolition, the Shiv Camp lawyer submitted a court petition, which led the judges to reluctantly grant them *locus standi*, which literally means a *recognized position*, or acknowledged right to participate in the legal proceedings. Yet even though Shiv Camp residents were made party to the case, they were far from active interlocutors in the proceedings, called upon merely to confirm or deny their stance—a position on the outskirts of the legal field (with weak *locus standi*) confirmed by their decision to sit not in the seats at the table, but in a row behind their lawyer.

During this first meeting, while waiting for the court commissioner to enter the mediation room, awkward chitchat opened up between the parties. One of the RWA members cut to the chase, stating that all he and his neighbors wanted was for Shiv Camp residents to receive resettlement plots. He continued, suggesting this was something everyone could agree on: "Look at the old resettlement colonies: Jangpura, Lajpat Nagar. No one would think they used to be *kaccā* [physically impermanent] or that there once were jhuggis there. The houses [*makān*] there are worth crores today and are better than our homes even." The lawyers, including the lawyer representing Shiv Camp, concurred, each adding personal anecdotes about friends or acquaintances whose families had received land in these post-Partition resettlement colonies, which were given to Hindu and Sikh refugees arriving in Delhi from the newly formed Pakistan and which have since grown into affluent middle-class neighborhoods. The lawyers then turned toward the Shiv Camp men, awaiting a response.

By contrasting *makān* and *jhuggī*, house and hut, the lawyers used a sensory vocabulary premised on a clear visual divide between formal and informal, private and public. These were sensible terms to them, put in place by the constraints of a court system that gave exceptional powers to property owners to defend their right to "the use and enjoyment of land,"[31] as well as the larger aesthetic field that equated *jhuggis* with disorder. These terms of sensibility also set the terms on which settlements could be represented, deeming the sensory experience and residential histories of those whose lives were ultimately at stake inadmissible.

Throughout the preceding months, conversations about the potential merits and risks of resettlement had peppered the open spaces throughout Shiv Camp. While resettlement appeared a best-case scenario to many residents, others were more skeptical of its merits. Motilal was among the latter. That very day, while riding the Metro to the High Court, Motilal had restated his worry that his construction business would fail were he to lose his foothold in Krishna Garden and the areas near Shiv Camp. In the courtroom, however, Motilal responded to the lawyers' glance with an approving nod, stating: "Everyone sees what is appropriate [*ucit*]. Where is there room for jhuggis in Delhi today?" The "everyone" here operated in the same third-person register residents often used to identify the map-like objectivity of world-class aesthetics, just as when Kishani and Shambu said "everyone knows" removing *jhuggis* is good for Delhi.

Soon after, the commissioner entered the room, laid out the terms of the meeting, and asked the lawyers if they objected to allowing the Shiv Camp residents to participate in the proceedings. Motilal and his neighbors looked nervously at each other, but no objections were raised. This initial meeting dealt little with substantive matters, and it finished with the commissioner calling all the parties, including the Shiv Camp residents, back for a follow-up meeting to present their positions, an outcome in no way certain at the outset of the meeting. Shiv Camp was here, even if provisionally, part of the everyone.

According to Bourdieu, "if one wishes to produce discourse successfully within a particular field, one must observe the forms and formalities of that field."[32] This self-censorship emerges as the practical competence of speakers to know how, and to be able, to produce expressions that will be valued within a given field—to speak *apropos*. In Motilal's case, this field was the courtroom, with its formal rules of representation, *locus standi*, and evidence, but it was also the broader aesthetic field in which his words were situated—a field that self-evidently equated *jhuggis* with disorder. Among a skeptical commissioner and group of lawyers, Motilal upheld the conventions of that field, exercised what Bourdieu calls the "the socially recognized capacity to speak and act legitimately,"[33] and found the language to confirm his place within the mediation room, garnering the approval of the lawyers and ensuring that his views would be consulted through the rest of the proceedings.

Too often statements such as Motilal's are interpreted either as signs of consent—true belief in the unbelonging of slums—or as dissimulation—a feigned statement uttered for calculated reasons. Yet this scene suggests that such "acts are not about stating facts and describing opinions but about doing things and opening new possibilities."[34] I here draw from linguistic anthropologist Alexei Yurchak, who argues in the context of the late socialist Soviet Union that following Stalin's death, the power to be recognized as a legitimate Soviet citizen was accorded only to actors "who correctly reproduced in form the acts and utterances of ideology."[35] Raising one's hand to vote for the sole candidate in a political contest, saying "yeh" in response to a committee's request for members' endorsement of a motion, or shouting a slogan of support during state-orchestrated rallies were ritual performances in which Soviet citizens participated without necessarily agreeing with or even understanding the meanings of their words or actions. Yurchak's insight is useful because it allows us to see that securing social status often requires correctly reproducing hegemonic form—making an appropriate expression, saying the sensible thing, upholding aesthetic standards—as much as it requires expressing a true meaning or belief.[36] Such acts thus defy simple categorization as resignation, conformance, or consent since they also can operate as symbolic attempts to open or keep open the opportunity to participate in a social field and to resignify the form of dominant speech.

In this light, Motilal's characterization of resettlement as appropriate might be read not so much as a description of things as it was a performative utterance confirming he and his neighbors as legitimate subjects of discourse. Responding less to the literal meaning of the language he reproduced—"jhuggis are out of place"—Motilal spoke to its pragmatic meaning: "I recognize the terms of sensibility I am to engage in the current context."[37] Motilal's Shiv Camp neighbors understood as much: after the meeting, the men were quite pleased with the proceedings. Motilal's statement, confirmed throughout the meeting, struck none of them as wrong or inappropriate, even though they had been speaking of how horrible resettlement might be on the Metro ride to the court just hours before.

To be sure, Motilal could have opposed the demolition outright, but the vocabulary and expressive material for doing so would have been perceived as utter nonsense within the mediation room. Recall here the systematic disregard judges had shown at the time for *basti* residents' legal appeals. In most cases since 2000, as discussed in the previous chapter, residents threatened by displacement are given no opportunity to present themselves in court—they are deemed outside the legal field. In the largest court case opposing demolition in Delhi, the Delhi High Court dismissed the injunctions of sixty-three settlements in a single order with the simple observation that the residents occupied public land.[38] In this light, Motilal and his neighbors' ability to secure *locus standi* should be read as a considerable achievement: a move from the status of an unrecognized population group to becoming a part of "the people."[39] I witnessed no other examples of the judiciary accepting slum residents' own documents as evidence of their residential history, or of judges asking residents to explain their tenure status, as occurred in the subsequent Shiv Camp mediation hearings.

During mediation meetings over the subsequent months, Motilal and his neighbors found opportunities to describe the life of the settlement directly: they described how during the 1971 flood Congress Party officials told them to flee to higher land, and how they were given ration cards addressed to Shiv Camp after setting up makeshift *jhuggis* there (a photocopied stack of which they brought with them to each meeting). Motilal described how a Municipal Corporation engineer had hired him to complete concrete work for the toilet block it was building in Shiv Camp in the mid-1980s. Others described how their children knew how to walk to school unaccompanied, how their lives centered on this neighborhood, and how resettlement would break up the community they had built. Partaking in the world-class aesthetic allowed Motilal and his neighbors to bring the life of the settlement into the space of the law. By entering into this space, their once differential demands, heard as mere noise, were posited on terms of equivalence; they were part of the world-class city.[40]

The commissioner offered no grand gesture of support and maintained that demolition was the most likely outcome, but he did see it fit to visit Shiv Camp, walk through its lanes, and witness the life of its community. The commissioner's final report to the High Court was ambiguous in its recommendations, although it did stress that Shiv Camp had been settled without any wrongdoing by the *jhuggi* dwellers. The legal dispute remained indeterminate—a constant source of uncertainty and anxiety for residents, yet an outcome far better than a summary demolition order.

PARTAKING AND APPROPRIATING

After I had become closely engaged in Shiv Camp's paper battle—through translating legal documents into Hindi and attending court hearings—residents began to regularly ask me for updates on the status of the case against them. In my early months, I was met with "will we be demolished [*jhuggī tūṭegī kyā*]?" which was often coupled with an unwillingness to accept displacement as a likely future. My field notes show this question to have gradually morphed into "When will we be demolished [*kab tūṭegī*]?" Five months after the April demolition, when the Municipal Corporation returned to clear the 122 huts it had first razed in January, residents started asking: "Will we receive a [resettlement] plot [*plot milegā*]?"—a question in which the possibility of *not* being demolished no longer figured. Displacement by this time appeared increasingly inevitable to most. As Lalaji said a week after the April demolition, "we have no faith in living here."

As in the courtroom, the world-class aesthetic similarly constrained expressive possibilities in everyday life, making it not only improbable that the settlement would remain, but also difficult to imagine a possible slum future. The increasing precarity of slum life, coupled with the enhanced privileges accorded to property owners, led resettlement plots, promoted by the government as a means to property ownership, to emerge as one of the few objects through which hope for the future could be expressed.[41] Yet although resettlement comes with state recognition, a precious attribute in an increasingly privatized and insecure city, it is no dream: located on the far outskirts of the city—beyond the outer ring road, the unauthorized colonies and the last Metro stop—resettlement plots spring up on recently tilled agricultural land, far from places of work, far from the city (see Figure 5.5).[42] Fear of snakebites, bandits from nearby villages in Haryana, and drowning in the adjacent canal, which people relied on for bathing due to water scarcity, were common among recent arrivals to Bawana, the most likely resettlement destination for Shiv Camp.

Many Shiv Camp residents rejected the merits of resettlement outright. But many others found creative ways of taking resettlement up in their visions of the future. While this might be read, like Motilal's statement of slum removal being appropriate, as a sign of submission, I here turn to how the act of making appropriate expressions, of upholding the world-class aesthetic, can function as a form of appropriation. In taking up resettlement in particular, residents laid forth a set of possibilities for how their vision might be articulated on terms sensible even to the most ardent promoters of the slum-free future. While in no way acts of resistance or even subversion, these practices nonetheless constituted something of an infrastructure of hope.

Figure 5.5. Bawana, Delhi's largest resettlement colony, where many of the residents of Sant Ravi Das Camp described in chapter 3 were relocated. Photograph by author.

To explore this ambiguous process of appropriating the world-class aesthetic, allow me to return to a conversation with Shambu, who had earlier characterized *jhuggis* as a "stain." When we met, the court had just alluded to a future ruling against Shiv Camp, which led me to ask Shambu, as I had done many times before, what he thought was going to happen to his settlement. Shambu responded, "look, one day we're going to have to leave this place. Such slums have no place in Delhi. Our future isn't here." Shambu had built his one-room, brick hut in Shiv Camp twenty-five years earlier, before his children were born and married, and well before residence in a *basti* was considered illegal. Even though this *jhuggi* nurtured his family and livelihood, he anticipated the day it would be razed to the ground. Here was one of those moments of seeming resignation to the private, slum-free city, an instance Bourdieu would describe as being "lost for words."

On this occasion, having previously heard various nonspecific iterations of this same response, I pushed Shambu, asking: "If your future isn't this hut, then what is it?" Switching from chai to *bīḍī*, and perhaps sensing that I wanted a more concrete answer this time, he said, "only God knows, but we hope it will be like this," as he turned to the back corner of his hut and pointed to a small paper poster nailed to the wall (see Figure 5.6).

The poster showed a house nestled in a surreal, computer-generated landscape, with an enhanced, orange sunset-like skyline, a cartoonish

Figure 5.6. "It is a proper house." Photograph by author.

foreground of landscaped trees and flowers, and something of a hybrid American ranch and Swiss chalet styled home depicted as its central object. In the backdrop to the left a second house is shown, making it clear that the main house is just one within a larger terrain of private, plotted homes. After asking Shambu what the poster shows, he replied, "it is a beautiful place. There is no noise or filth there. It is a proper [*sahī*] house." I sought clarification on what the word "proper" meant to him, and he said: "It is one's own house [*khud kā makān*]. A private [*nijī*] house."

I had noticed the decorative posters in Shiv Camp homes before. How couldn't you? They adorn the walls of most huts, with some enthusiastic interior decorators plastering more than a dozen across the walls of their squat, one-room homes. But the significance of the images displayed had never struck me. After Shambu indicated that his aesthetic choice to hang a poster of a house was linked to his desire for private property, I made sure to ask about such posters whenever I encountered them in Shiv Camp.

Many people, it turned out, displayed house posters, one among many popular styles of decorative poster art, and when I asked, most interpreted their house posters, like Shambu, as private property.[43] One man who had purchased a vacant plot of land in an unauthorized colony, but had not yet built a house on it, said the poster represented what he hoped his home would one day become when he had enough money to begin construction. A woman stated, as she nodded toward her poster, "rich people live in these houses. We also hope to live like that one day." Kishani said, while turning between me and her poster, "all these bastis, they're going away. The Delhi government is cleaning everything. It is making Delhi beautiful. If you want to stay here, you have to own such a house."

In these posters, the large houses appear as little more than a façade, an exterior inside of which private life takes place (see Figure 5.7). There are no people, the windows are opaque, and the viewer is positioned from a lower viewing angle, as if on the road looking up. This is, indeed, the manner in which slum residents see most private homes in Delhi: from the outside, looking up, and seeing people only enter and exit (see Figure 5.3). Those displaying house posters often explicitly contrasted the private houses shown in their posters with their more public *jhuggis*, frequently mobilizing world-class aesthetic terms to do so. Kishan, who had hung his two house posters over the previous Diwali—the Hindu festival of light, when most Shiv Camp residents clean, paint, and redecorate their homes—said: "It is our dream to someday have a private house. If we live there, all our problems will go away. You can live cleanly there." Deshraj told me, "these homes are beautiful. They have everything: cleanliness, peace, orderly life; no noise, no tension, no fighting. Not like here. Looking at them inspires us to live *ḍhang se* [properly]."

Figure 5.7. "We hope to live like that one day." Photograph by author.

One could certainly interpret Shambu, Kishan, and Deshraj's assessments of the beauty of the private home as a process of internalizing and culturally reproducing a bourgeois visual ideology—a process of the poor adopting an aesthetic unconscious that reproduces the conditions of their own domination.[44] This is what Eagleton's mystification or various theories of aesthetic masking would suggest. The appearance of perhaps the most powerful and enduring postcolonial symbol of private property—the bungalow—in the homes of those being criminalized for their lack of property ownership certainly lends itself to such a reading.[45]

But Shiv Camp residents also used house posters to enter a more speculative register, expressing desires enunciated on the terms of the world-class aesthetic, but in ways that sometimes exceeded its imaginative limits. As one man told me, pointing to his house poster: "This is what sarkar has promised us. This is what we should get. Maybe not this much [referring to the grand bungalow in his poster], but we need proper homes." As Shambu confided, "look. We will be sad if we're removed. That's that. But," he said, entering the subjunctive tense, a speculative mood used more often in Hindi than English for speaking of an uncertain future, "why shouldn't we also dream of a big life? Sarkar wants to make a big city. *We too* should become big [*Ham bhī baḍe hoṁ*]!"

As neighboring slums were demolished without compensation and as resettlement became one of the few terrains for imagining the future, Shiv Camp residents genuinely struggled to find terms on which to articulate their place in the city. They were often lost for words. Their claims of historical entitlement had been shot down in the courts; neighboring property owners were sick of hearing about the plight of the poor; and the price of land had reached a point where government officials were willing to bear the scorn of displaced slum dwellers in exchange for a piece of the real estate action. Slum residents, in short, face highly constrained political and imaginative conditions. In the city that *would be*, how can they articulate what instead *should be*? [handwritten: futurity restricts normativity]

Yurchak argues that in conditions where an hegemony of form is in place, which constrains expressive possibilities and delimits the terrain of sensible speech, constative meanings can become unanchored from hegemonic form, creating the possibility for a world of new meanings to emerge that nonetheless uphold that form. His example is of highly regulated Soviet discourse, where words, phrases, and images were constantly inspected for their conformance with Stalinist ideology. That Soviet subjects could apply diverse, even contradictory, meaning to their prescribed words allowed them to become fully prepared for postcommunist life even while never anticipating the collapse of the communist regime. Millennial Delhi's hegemony of form clearly differs from this, but it remains one in which, as I have argued in this chapter, sensory vocabularies, expressive materials, and what I have called the terms of sensibility are highly circumscribed, as in a courtroom. Shiv Camp residents hence confronted an almost unquestionable vision of a slum-free future, which made their views and desires politically unintelligible when cast outside of world-class terms of sensibility. Through their house posters, however, residents found a way to uphold the vision of a slum-free future while deriving diverse and politically polyvalent meanings from it. From Shambu's resigned statement "our future isn't here," he found the expressive capacity to switch registers and make a claim tinged with hope and political possibility: "*We too* should become big!"

Like Motilal's sensible performance in the courtroom, this was the appropriation of the world-class aesthetic, but one that seemed to turn it in another direction. The vision Shambu and his neighbors articulated was one not of wasteland on the outskirts of the city, but of bungalows and farmhouses, just like those desired by the elite. This was a vision not of expulsion from the world-class city, but rather of world-class citizenship. It was a vision of not only a transformation of habitation, but also of who inhabits the house. In this sense this act of appropriation can be seen as an aesthetic politics, which according to Rancière "invents new forms of collective enunciation; it reframes the given by inventing *new ways of making sense of the sensible*, new configurations between the visible and the invisible, and between the audible and inaudible."⁴⁶ Shambu and his neighbors attempted to find a new way of making sense of the sensible, upholding the world-class aesthetic while supplying it with new meanings. How this politics would play out in residents' lives was anybody's guess, but it was the only wager available to them, one that at least offered the symbolic footing to proceed with promise—to, as Shambu demonstrated, enter the same speculative register as the world-class city by turning resettlement into a geography of hope, not banishment.⁴⁷ This was no act of revolutionary politics. It was not resistance or even subversion. There was no certainty that the reimagination of resettlement as a process that should be world-class would lead to new solidarities or demands for improved services, entitlements, or political voice. But it nonetheless represents an accomplishment, a form of aesthetic politics with profound significance in the lives of its practitioners, for it allowed them to begin the process of inventing new forms of collective enunciation.

AESTHETIC EXPERIMENTS

Politics, before all else, is an intervention in the visible and the sayable.
Jacques Rancière, *The Politics of the Aesthetic*

I began this chapter with various ways in which residents in Shiv Camp, a settlement with a looming expiry date, took up the world-class aesthetic that framed *bastis* as out of place. On first glance this act of partaking in world-class aesthetic norms might be read as a simple form of compromise, of adjusting one's desires to a circumscribed political situation.⁴⁸ But if we take language to be not just a medium for expressing preformed views, but rather constitutive of those views, then we see that the appropriation of dominant forms and norms becomes central to the practice of opening up new political possibilities, not just making do with existing ones. This is because political alternatives are literally unthinkable outside of existing forms and norms. Thus, in Rancière's diverse writings, a feature common across all instances of politics is a particular kind of speech situation that invents new ways of seeing and saying and allows those excluded from the political order to stand up and speak for themselves. As he writes, "politics revolves around what is seen and what can be said about it, around who has the ability to see and the talent to speak."⁴⁹ Developing the talent to speak—the expressive capacity to make what was once mere noise audible as speech—is no easy task. It often fails, or even when that talent is cultivated, the claims the politically excluded put forward may still not be heard. This is why I say that the appropriation of dominant norms can operate as an infrastructure of hope, for it provides an expressive foundation from which the possibility of reimagining the city might emerge. When individuals like Motilal find that what remains to be said exceeds what they can presently phrase—when they confront the pain of silence—then such an infrastructure allows them to secure at least a position and vocabulary to begin the process of developing new expressive possibilities. The statements of slum unbelonging with which I began therefore cannot be evaluated straightforwardly as signs of consent, as is so often done. Rather, one needs to look at the ways in which such utterances can operate as expressive experiments in the visible and the sayable.

Part of what makes the world-class aesthetic so efficacious is its relative openness to meaning. A city with litter-free streets, glistening buildings, and spectacular architecture can be filled with radically different contents. The media and politicians' regular reference to cities as diverse as Paris, Singapore, and Dubai as emblematic world-class cities makes this evident. And it is precisely this openness that allows quite disparate political visions—from resident welfare associations' ideal of tranquil, low-density neighborhoods to shopping mall developers' pursuit of vertical growth—to share in the project of world-class city making. While these visions cohere around a set of minimum aesthetic criteria for the city, what this city might mean, practically, as far as distributions of rights and entitlements and conflict over residential, commercial, and symbolic uses of the city, is left ambiguous. In other words, the consolidation of an aesthetic consensus does not resolve the question of how the aesthetic ideal is to be reached or how the city's resources shared.[50] In this ambiguity lies the possibility for political change and reinterpretations of what the world-class city should be.

Residents of Shiv Camp, a slum with an unknown but foretold expiration date, faced this ambiguity constantly. Interested in improving their or their children's material conditions, they confronted an aesthetic field that located their future outside of the world-class city. Despite this predicament, they took part in the world-class aesthetic, holding open the possibility of participating in, and perhaps redirecting, the world-class city. There was no guarantee and little assurance that the future would emerge otherwise, but under highly constrained conditions, they acted to ensure a seat at the table. Rather than contest the world-class city, they pursued a part in it. I next turn to what their imaginations of a world-class future, or what the contents of an infrastructure of hope premised on the process of resettlement, practically entailed.

6

The Propriety of Property

Resettlement and the Pursuit of Belonging

LAND FETISH

In the previous chapter, I described how government-issued resettlement plots became the primary medium through which residents of settlements threatened by demolition could participate in the world-class urban imaginary. In this chapter, I move with residents from their idealized representations of resettlement—conveyed through the house posters of bungalows they displayed on their walls—to the practical entailments of assigning positive attributes to forced displacement. In shifting from the political possibilities that lie in appropriating and repurposing the world-class aesthetic to the lived contradictions of investing hope in an urban future wherein the slum has no place, I return to the relationship between property and propriety introduced in earlier chapters. There, I traced how property ownership became the primary foundation on which political belonging was recognized in millennial Delhi (chapters 2 and 4), as well as how propertied notions of civility and public appearance became codified into a dominant aesthetic sensibility (chapters 3 and 4). Property, in other words, was fetishized: elevated as a source of belonging and propriety and a requirement for securing substantive citizenship rights. Here, I examine how slum residents' investment in the resettlement process also fetishized property, investing it with a social power over its beholder.

Consider, for example, Ramkali, a middle-aged Bundelkhandi woman whose home had been spared by the Municipal Corporation's January and April demolition raids, but who expressed regular anxiety about her future. While I was attending the mediation hearings in the High Court concerning Shiv Camp's legal status, Ramkali frequently asked me about the status of things: "Will we receive a plot?" When I asked her what she thought a plot would provide, she responded:

> If we receive a plot, all our problems will go away. We will become big people, like the *koṭhī* owners. Our men will stop gambling and will find good work; our children will get good educations; our daughters will marry good boys. There, life will become good. We will have big houses and maybe even a car.

Like Shambu in the previous chapter, who had used his aspirational house poster to declare that "*We too* should become big [*Ham bhī baḍe hoṁ*]!", Ramkali tied possession of a resettlement plot to "big" social status. Her statement, however, links this status with the semantically correct root—"proper"—of property, in the sense of the rightfulness of property, and instructs us to explore further property's transformative power.

As we saw in previous chapters, lack of property became an index of the low social value, and skewed values, of slum dwellers in millennial Delhi. Slum dwellers unsurprisingly recognized this condition, often describing their exclusion from the world-class city as a symptom of their residence on the public land of a slum. In the context of deepening political exclusion and economic marginality, residents also recognized that obtaining property, even if that meant submitting to a process of violent resettlement, was a means to enhance their political standing in the city. As significantly, however, resettlement plots—assumed by most to share the qualities of private property—also promised to transform their possessors' inner states, making husbands less violent, daughters more marriageable, and neighbors more civil. I am here interested in how this particular form of property fetishism is tied to the broader property fetishism of the world-class city, or the speculative urbanism in which ever-increasing land prices and self-expanding value operate as the social premise, and the promise, of the world-class city (see chapter 1). Slum dwellers' speculative investment in resettlement, often in the face of strong indications that resettlement would reduce their quality of life, needs to be understood in light of this speculative urbanism. We must ask, in other words, how speculative and spectacular theories of value in the world-class city produce attendant speculations on the self.

For Marx, self-expanding value—the seeming "capacity for money, or of a commodity, to expand its own value independently of reproduction," which he labeled M–M', money becoming more money—was the most flagrant form of fetishism.[1] The fetishized form M–M' is an irrational formula: 3 = 4, money becoming more money, or, in its property form, land automatically producing value in rent. This representation, Marx argued, "metamorphoses the social, economic character that things are stamped with in the process of social production into a *natural character* arising from the material nature of those things."[2] In this sense, M–M' is "perverted" [*Verkehrung*] because the process that makes possible the transformation of 3 into 4—namely the exploitation of labor and the conditions of dispossession—disappears. For Marx, the full process was M–C–M', or more precisely:

$$M - C^L_{MP} \ldots P \ldots C' - M'.$$

In this process money (M) is used to buy labor (L) and means of production (MP), commodities (C) which are then transformed through production (P) into a different commodity (C') and later sold for profit. This process alone allows the transition from an initial value M to a greater value M'. In its reduced and speculative form M–M', a social relation (symbolized by M–L—the relation between capital and labor) is contained within a thing (M), thus bestowing it with "the motive power of the relations of production."[3] The surplus produced through this extended process (the difference between M and M') subsequently gets distributed in the form of interest to capital, rent to property, and wages to labor.[4] The fetish M–M' thus takes a specific form in relation to each of these couples.[5] In its interest-bearing form, capital demands its profit via interest. In its property form, land, Marx wrote, "gets on its hind legs to demand, as an independent force, its share of the product created with its help": land claims its M'.[6]

In millennial Delhi, land got on its hind legs and roared, a condition that could be observed through the way that the demolition of slums and the elimination of forms of life premised on public land occupation came to be seen as the outcome of rising land prices—property's presumed self-realization—and not as a socially necessary predicate, or condition, of its production. If in the early 2000s, as the World Bank argued, "idle" public land "such as public land holdings or encroached infrastructure [read: slums]" reduced real estate rents and restricted capital expansion in Delhi (M couldn't become M'), thus necessitating the social act of privatizing public land and clearing slums, then by the late 2000s it was rising rents and speculative property that seemed to automatically drive slum demolitions, as though this were the "natural character" of the land.[7] The removal of slums henceforth became inevitable, and the fate of slum residents seemed tied to an almost geological process rooted deep in the earth.

What I find useful about the concept of fetishism, despite the complications of all these formulas, is the way that it ties together two mysteries of property: the mystery of self-expanding value and the mystery of a mere thing (land in our case) transforming social relations and individual subjectivities.[8] In contrast to common notions of commodity fetishism that emphasize how the conditions of dispossession are concealed from those subject to them—a reading into which Ramkali's statement might appear to fit—I insist on tracking how subjects emerge at the intersection of these two mysteries.[9] Specifically, I argue that the experience of being subjected to speculative property opens a space for speculative subjectivities. While this is a process that aligns subjects with the conditions of dispossession—Ramkali, after all, responded favorably to resettlement—and can thus be seen as an effect of governmentality, or "the conduct of conduct," it also can transform the mysteries of property into promises.[10] If the promise of the world-class city is the promise of property, then Shiv Camp residents show it is also the promise of propriety: the promise of better work, better homes, and better lives. This, too, is the promise of the world-class city, and in millennial Delhi, it increasingly emerged as a demand of the urban majority. Rather than contest the fetish, Shiv Camp residents got with it.

MAGIC

I was seated among a group of boys at the edge of Shiv Camp, responding to questions about life in the United States, when Rajiv approached asking if there were tantrics there. I thought this was a lead-in to a question about sex in the West, a topic the boys liked to raise, but I misunderstood his cue. Today, he wanted to discuss magic:

> There are tantrics here. They make things appear. If you ask them, they can show you anything, but it only stays for a short time. After that, it goes away, or you have to pay for it. They can get you so many *notes* from the bank. They can show you hundreds of *notes*, but then they have to return them to the bank. They can just make things appear in your hand. They aren't yours, but it's still fun.

I asked how they do it, and he responded with a wry smile: *jādū* (magic).

While Rajiv's was the only discussion of tantra I encountered during my time in Shiv Camp, young men frequently told each other fantastical stories about the sudden appearance of wealth, commodities, and money in the contemporary city, frequently suggesting that these objects of fancy sprung from the landscape itself. On one occasion, Rajesh and Sanjay, boys in their early twenties with slicked back hair who liked to race around the neighborhood streets on Sanjay's motorbike, approached me, saying that Sanjay had found a bill worth "one lakh" (100,000) on the ground. One lakh what? Rupees? I asked. It was a foreign note, Sanjay said, not a dollar, but he was sure it was real: "It was lost by somebody and is very valuable [*kimtī*]," he offered in response to my skeptical look. "*Bhaiyā*, take a look!" Rajesh implored, as they ran off to collect it.

They delivered the note to me. The bill looked and felt real, with "100,000" written on its corners. A large, pillared building appeared on one side and an owl on the other. The note was written in a script that I could not recognize, had no Roman text, and was free of political imagery (see Figure 6.1). I had no idea where the note was from and told the boys that it was certainly not a dollar or a pound, but that it could be real.[11] They looked content with my response, moving on to explain how it landed in Sanjay's hands. Not interested in a genuine assessment of its exchange value, to Sanjay and Rajesh, I would soon learn, marveling at its appearance and sudden materialization in their hands was enough.

Sanjay had been walking along the street one day when the note hit his foot [*per lag gayā*]. He picked it up, put it in his wallet, and told nobody about it for an entire year. He began showing it to others only after Rajesh had noticed it when he opened his wallet one day. Over the year of wear, however, the note had developed a slight tear down the middle. Only

Figure 6.1. 100,000 Greek drachmas (circa 1944), the same note Sanjay held. Reproduced courtesy of Ron Wise.

after Rajesh saw it and encouraged him to take it to a local moneyman did he attempt to assess its worth. Rajesh interrupted Sanjay's narrative, adding that the moneyman had told them that the note was worth "lots of money. Lots!" However, because of the tear, the moneyman would not accept it.[12]

If he had thought of it earlier, Sanjay said, he would have taken the note to the moneyman right away, but by putting it in his wallet, it "went bad." Both boys continued to assert the value of the note, holding onto it like a curio, an artifact that emerged from the landscape and into Sanjay's grips.[13] Was this damaged note a symbol of value, or of its spontaneous and fleeting appearance?

A few days later, while having chai with Uncle Ji at his shop, Rajesh and another friend joined us in conversation. After recounting the story of Sanjay's note, Rajesh said that he had similarly happened upon a wad of money one day, lying on a crowded street. Bound upon itself, Rajesh picked it up, surprised that so many people had walked by without even noticing it. He did not recognize the bills' provenance, so started distributing them to children, thinking they must have been play money [naklī paisā]. Why else would so many others fail to pick up so much cash? He gave away almost all the bills, keeping just one as a souvenir. Later on, his uncle saw him fiddling with the bill and asked where he had found what turned out to be a dollar! By this time, it was too late; Rajesh had already given his fortune away. Rajesh told this story jovially, expressing no regret for his loss. Luck [kismat] brought him this wealth, but he did not recognize its value [kīmat], so he squandered it.

Value in these stories was fleeting, always slipping away, out of reach. Such was the experience of money for many Shiv Camp residents, especially its young. Laboring boys and men would occasionally earn good money in a single day, but might go weeks after without a day of work. Even when work was good, residents were constantly reminded of their inability to access higher circuits of value represented in and conveyed through the new urban infrastructures and speculative projects emerging around them, which they could witness but rarely use.[14] Such stories of the magical appearance and disappearance of wealth in the landscape were widespread in Shiv Camp, and I initially thought they were part of a game: an effort to trick the gullible listener, or the ethnographer with his silly questions begging for silly responses. I therefore (too hastily) dismissed Sanjay's claim that his note was real. Such stories often generated disbelief among listeners, though, and only later did I recognize that they were mobilized not to convince others of fundamental truths, but rather to evoke shared reactions and collective responses from an audience—that is, to try to identify a common experience.[15]

For example, after Uncle Ji and I had marveled at Rajesh's story of the lost dollars, Rajesh continued to explain the uncanny: "Just like in the village, there are *shaitān*s [devils] here. They do not always do bad [*burāī*]; sometimes their work is to deceive," he said. To Uncle Ji, this was going too far: "Shaitans don't exist!" But Rajesh persisted: "Uncle Ji, if you believe in god, you must also believe in shaitans." Uncle Ji then changed his tactic; no longer interested in truth or falsity, he used *shaitans* to make his own point about the changing city: "When there's not even room for people to live in this world, then where is there room for shaitans?" The three of us burst into laughter. There is no room for *shaitans* in Delhi. They'd be evicted too!, we joked.

Over time and after having recorded numerous stories and rehearing iterations of the same ones, I came to consider them to be narrative testaments to their speakers' experience of seeing but not holding wealth—that is, their ability to visually participate in the speculative landscape around them, but not reap its rewards.[16] [Land was producing wealth, but those in *basti*s could not capture it.] While such stories were especially prominent among youth, other people captivated by the new, property-driven economy also shared in them, including people living outside of *basti*s. For example, my middle-class landlord, a retired postal worker who rented me a one-bedroom flat above his home in a nearby private, gated apartment complex, used a metaphor similar to Rajesh's to describe wealth in the contemporary city: "There is money just lying on the streets in Delhi. People smart enough can pick it up and become rich; everyone else will be left behind."[17]

Huddled in front of the *pān* stalls (where betel nut and cigarettes are sold) and in shaded areas of the *basti*, groups of boys in Shiv Camp excitedly mixed their discussions of money, wealth, and work with another symbol of value: the shiny new buildings springing up around them. Early in my fieldwork on a dull February afternoon, Sanjay and Dhaniram competed to see who could name the most malls in the city. Ansal Plaza came first, but now DLF is bigger, Sanjay shouted. Dhaniram replied: Yes, DLF is bigger, but which DLF mall is biggest? Out of such repartee—which took place as much over world-class urban icons, such as Metro station names, as more common aspirational commodities, like the newest motorbike models—a set of enduring questions emerged.[18] What explained the sudden appearance of these immense concentrations of wealth in the city? How might they reap the rewards of this transfiguring landscape? How might they, in other words, possess the bank notes, the foreign currency, and the wads of money that Rajiv, Sanjay, and Rajesh had so enthusiastically described? And what might possessing such wealth mean for who they are and what they might become?

On a hot May afternoon, I joined three college-aged boys—Sanjay, Uday Prakash, and Dhaniram—for flavored ice from an itinerant vendor. Sitting on the edge of a pushcart, the boys began to recall how they used to beg their mothers for the two rupees necessary to get the best ice flavors in nearby Sanjay Camp: "Chacha's masala grape was the best," but, now that Sanjay Camp had been demolished, the nearest ice option—when a vendor did not show up—was in the district center. Housing a multiscreen movie theater, branded retailers like Adidas and Lee, and overpriced *chāṭ* cafes and hukka bars, the ice cones sold there cost twenty-five rupees, five times what we'd paid. Taking the boys' mention of the increased price of their favorite syrupy treat as a critique of such upscale developments, I asked what was so great about the castle-esque district center. But I misread Sanjay's cue, who replied, dripping in cherry, "no, *bhaiya*. It is something you have to go and see, especially in the evening. Women dance there every night, and you can go and watch. It is the best place to go to pass time." Ignoring the younger Uday Prakash's disagreement about the presence of regular dancing women, he continued: "One has to go and see these places." Uday Prakash again interjected, noting that one cannot roam there without purpose and that one must pay to go inside for it to be fun. Sanjay disagreed: "No, you can even enjoy looking from the outside: just being there and walking around and seeing."

For Sanjay, "just being there and seeing" was an important, albeit qualified, way of grasping and participating in the emerging world-class spatial order. Yet even while young men like Sanjay aligned their visions with the world-class urban imaginary, they rarely ventured out to experience the sites and sights they so admired. Although I heard stories of the local RWA closing down a smaller neighborhood park due to "misuse" by Shiv Camp children, such transgressions of the boundary between slum and world-class city were uncommon. Youth rarely ventured into the large parks and commercial spaces nearby, and none of them had been to the malls they described: not Ansal Plaza and not DLF, although they could tell you about the smooth pink sandstone and white marble of each, the latter "brighter than even the Taj Mahal," Dhaniram had once said. Following the boys' discussion of the District Center and its dancing women, I proposed we go have a look, but we only made it halfway: "I feel like another ice," Uday Prakash suggested as we turned back to the *basti*.

The spatiality of dwelling had greater imaginative than material reach in Shiv Camp, and young men experienced nothing of the "incessant mobility and incipient translocality" that scholars celebrating the creative powers of the informal city tend to emphasize.[19] Young men's experience of simultaneous inclusion and exclusion, of distancing themselves from the topoi they admired, was built into the increasingly commodified landscape where simple city pleasures like consuming flavored ice became increasingly class segregated, but it equally had to do with changing conceptions of value [*kīmat*] and its imagined sources. I soon learned that *basti* and world-class city represented differently valued spaces, which residents understood to imbibe their occupants with different value-coding. Accessing the world-class city was not a simple matter of walking into an air-conditioned shopping mall; it rather required, according to the Shiv Camp youth I came to know, a fundamental reorientation of the self, one that they understood to potentially require relocation to a different place and into a different value system.] *This is a story of class quiescence*

VALUE, OLD AND NEW

While the puzzle of value in the world-class city was complex, working-age boys in Shiv Camp recognized that finding secure jobs and accessing higher circuits of value required, at the very least, moving beyond the manual labor and construction-based professions of their parents' generation. Ravi, an eighteen-year-old who was enrolled in a correspondence course to earn his BA, told me, "without education, people have no value [*kīmat*]. Without education, you can't do anything but masonry here. And that's not good. You can get at best 3–4,000 rupees, which is nothing." Ravi said that 90 percent of boys in Shiv Camp were *bekhār* [useless, without value]. They just "roam around; some do little jobs, but most don't do anything. Most don't study and can't get jobs. They don't want to be construction workers, so they live off their parents. See, there are two types of people here: *old minds* and *new minds*."

Old minds, Ravi and his sidekick Uday Prakash went on to explain, are usually those who, like their parents, are uneducated and have what Ravi called a village mentality—a belief that individuals are rewarded according to their effort, that steady employment from and loyalty to a single employer is the pathway to success, and that money earned provides money to be spent. But based on the new desires and aspirations that come with city life, even old minds do not want to do manual labor [*mazdūrī*] like their parents. Instead, Ravi noted, they seek out low-level security jobs, work as bus conductors, or are sales boys—the bottom end of the retail food chain. More often, they do not work at all and instead depend on their families for income. As Manoj, a nineteen-year-old "old mind" who had become a regular at the card games, said soon after, "*maiṁ free rahtā hūṁ* [I remain free/unoccupied]."

Prior to Ravi and Uday Prakash's explanation of the new mind–old mind divide, Ravi's brother-in-law, the older Rajesh, whose story about the wad of cash I described above, had been trying to explain his work life to me using verbless English. Ashok, a younger, more educated boy with a single, bleached red tuft of hair crossing his brow, was interrupting Rajesh's sentences with witty phrases that rhymed with and played with Rajesh's words. His verbal dexterity and prowess in turning Rajesh's words against him proved he was sharper and funnier than Rajesh, and the laughter of the other boys confirmed Ashok's verbal triumph over this old mind rival. Ashok closed with a final quip, echoing Rajesh: "If *school* is useless, then why are you still a *fool*?" This led Ravi to offer Rajesh as an example of his point about old minds: "See Rajesh, he only drinks and plays cards. He's not educated. He's married, has two children, and he's not *independent*. He completely *depend*s on his parents." Rajesh agreed, resigning himself to Ravi's far more balanced assessment in the face of Ashok's taunts, saying in English, "I not independent."

In contrast to these old minds, Ravi, Uday Prakash, and Ashok considered themselves new minds: educated youth who had hopes of earning salaries well above the 3,000 to 4,000 rupees the old minds could at best receive and who were committed to finding salaried jobs involving *dimāg* (brains), not *hāth* (hands). Their imagined pathway to income and wealth varied, but they emphasized the necessity of being strategic in job decisions, cultivating middle-class style, and breaking from what they considered the *jhuggi* lifestyle [*jīvanshelī*], which they took to constrain their potential for economic mobility and self-improvement. Most self-professed new minds cycled through jobs, sticking with one for a few weeks or months, before moving on in hopes of finding something with better career potential.

In the autumn of 2007, while I was maintaining daily contact with this group, Ashok had a weekly assortment of new work options he seemed to be considering, the same type of jobs that were regularly advertised on telephone polls outside the nearby for-profit IT college. Within two weeks of our first discussions of work, he had described a variety of low-level clerical and service jobs available to him—a bill collector for a bank, a Hindi-based call center worker, a door-to-door advertisement salesman for a local magazine, an airplane cleaner for Jet Airways—but he had yet to begin any work. Every few days, Ashok recited a list of jobs, work responsibilities, and pay scales, methodically weighing the positives and negatives of each opportunity, but as he explained it, "the problem is I just can't decide which job to do!"

Due to their higher level of education but restricted employment prospects, new minds such as Ashok experienced considerable pressure to find work that justified their additional years of education. Faced with the potential embarrassment of taking up lower-skilled jobs like the old minds, Ashok chose unemployment, criticizing the old minds' jobs for their lack of *career* scope, as when he said of Sanjay: "He was just married, but he has a job as a guard [*caukīdār*] that only pays 2,000 rupees. What good is that?

How can he start a family?" Sanjay, whose ear had become infected after a home piercing inspired by the Hindi film star Salman Khan's latest look, responded nonchalantly, "I get by," displaying a contented freedom in sharp contrast to Ashok's regular work-related anxiety.

For many new minds, such as Dhaniram, it was the *basti* that held them back: "I went for a job in a call center office. The advertisement said that the salary was 6,500 rupees per month. When I wrote my address, they saw where my home is and offered only 4,000, motherfuckers." Dhaniram's older brother, who worked nights in an English call center, avoided the other boys altogether, insisting that Dhaniram's English would never improve if he spent time only with "*yahāṁ ke lāyak* [those worthy of here/ the slum]." Despite their labor insecurity and shared structural position with old minds, Shiv Camp's self-described new minds actively portrayed themselves as modern workers poised to capitalize on the city's shifting economy, an effort that often led the *basti* itself to be cast as holdover from a previous system of value, one they had to exit if ever they were to become "big." As I discuss in later sections, as the territorialized stigma of the slum increasingly became attached to its residents, resettlement came to bear an increasing burden of transforming residents' fates and inner potential. First, however, allow me to introduce how the perceived value-coding of place shaped theories of the inherent social worth—or *value* to use Shiv Camp residents' own language—of their occupants.[20]

Consider, for example, a conversation between Dhaniram and the older Mukesh, a trained electrician who told me he earned 9,000 rupees per month. Mukesh suggested that Dhaniram—considered one of the smartest boys from Shiv Camp—work in an office that plays the "share market." Mukesh insisted that even the most basic workers in such offices, "where people just push buttons buying and selling gold, copper, and *shares*," earn at least 15,000 rupees per month.

Dhaniram's home had been destroyed in the April demolition, but his father, a well-established contractor, had purchased a vacant plot of land in a not-too-distant, but poorly serviced, unauthorized colony a few years earlier. After the demolition, Dhaniram's family began construction in haste and a few months later settled in their new colony. Mukesh admonished Dhaniram for continuing to spend most days in the *basti*, unlike Dhaniram's older brother, who rarely visited Shiv Camp after the demolition. Mukesh found Dhaniram's current business plan—to set up a DVD/VCD shop in a rented *jhuggi* in Shiv Camp—uninspired. The slum held him back, Mukesh suggested.

Mukesh was working at the time wiring rooms in the Hilton Hotel being constructed nearby, and he spoke with great pride about his role in building the new city: "New buses will be running all over, and people from all countries will come visit Delhi for the Commonwealth Games and stay in places like this. You see, we're building a new city." I asked him if Delhi really would look so different in the coming years, and he replied affirmatively: "Only educated people will remain. *Mazdūr* [laborers] will have no *value*. They'll have to leave." Mukesh went on to complain about rising costs in Delhi, describing how ordinary people were being pushed out as earnings shrank relative to costs. But just as he began to critique wider economic conditions in the city, Mukesh returned to the new, high cost–high reward economy: "But, the main problem is all these people coming from UP and Bihar. Because of them the wages are falling. That is the problem: someone earns twelve rupees for something, then a cousin from the village comes and asks for only eleven rupees for the same job, then nine, then seven. *Mazdūrī* [labor] has no *value* today."

Mukesh further detailed his conception of *value* by describing fixed deposit schemes, emphasizing the importance of saving money bit by bit and letting it grow with time: "Anyone working can save something. If you earn 3,000 rupees per month and can't save 500 rupees, what's the point in earning? You should save that money and it will grow. See, I got a 20,000 rupee check from my LIC [the Life Insurance Corporation, which offers a variety of insurance and savings schemes], but I didn't take it; I put it back in. It will be worth three lakh [300,000] in fifteen years." He brought his discussion of value back to the *basti*: "People here earn only a hundred rupees per day, but still they spend thirty rupees at night on booze or games. Jhuggi people cling to their jhuggis like they are all that matter. They don't look beyond. They don't understand *value* today."

If new minds like Mukesh celebrated the earning potential of the new economy, at times associating the downfall of the *basti* with the declining *value* of manual laborers ill-suited to the world-class city, many elder men and women mourned the loss of a more communal time when residents shared working habits and aspirations. Ramlal, a grizzle-haired Rajasthani man with a thick moustache and hands worn from brick work, for example, told me:

> There used to be good *society* here. People were together. . . . But now, nobody listens to anyone anymore. They all think of themselves as the prime minister of the place. When people came from villages, they were used to getting together for meetings. After being in the city for so long, people don't care about each other as much. Also, people drink too much, and gambling is a big problem. People just waste their money.

"Why do people gamble so much?" I asked.
"People don't think like they used to," he replied.
"Is it because there is less work?"
"No, it is the youth. The youth don't respect earnings. They don't know how to run a home. Older people play cards, but not with money. It is only

timepass for us. It is the youth that have ruined unity here. People here are themselves ruining the basti. . . . Everything is only about themselves. Unity has been broken."[21]

Ramlal's sense of value clearly differed from Mukesh's, reversing the determination of value between *basti* and its residents. Like many others, he considered *value* to be respect for work and an overall attachment to community and place. Many old-timers disagreed with what they saw as the youth's infatuation with "big things," like motorcycles, fancy mobile phones, and lavish lifestyles beyond the *basti*. "They are busy looking at the sky, while losing the ground [*āsmān meṁ lage haiṁ, jaise zamīn kho jā rahī hai*]," Motilal said to me one day.

Mukesh and Ramlal's statements affirmed socially differentiated value-codings of work and community, but they also indexed differentially valued spaces. By contrasting his own values ("good society" and unity) with those leading to the ruin of the settlement, Ramlal affirmed Shiv Camp's inherent *value* as a place of community. By criticizing those who "cling to their jhuggis like they are all that matter," Mukesh, in contrast, located value in processes and places beyond Shiv Camp: five-star hotels, shopping malls, air-conditioned offices, and as he would later assert, distant resettlement plots. Value in these places somehow accrued more rapidly and took on a more enduring form.

For Mukesh, saving, allowing money to grow, all this was necessary so that he could one day buy a plot: "If we can buy land—our own property [*sampattī*]—we will be able to stay in Delhi. Like the LIC, it will become more valuable [*zyādā kimtī*] with time." For Motilal, who in the previous chapter affirmed his attachment to Shiv Camp, this power of self-expanding value was equally compelling. Describing the neighboring *kothis* to me one afternoon, he said: "These people bought the land when it was cheap. Now they have one family living here and they rent out to three renters and ask for lots of money. They just sit and make money. They can work for a month, or sit and earn the same money [through rent]." Land produced rent automatically and became *zyādā kimtī* (M–M'), whereas labor seemed to be decreasing in *value*, lost (bracketed out) in M–M'—a speculative value system in which the process of surplus value creation disappears from view. The question was how to enter this circuit of self-expanding value, how to partake in this first mystery of property.

FATE

Although old-timers lamented deepening social divisions within the *basti*, many—like Motilal—also found compelling the world-class value regime and its spectacular accomplishments. Thus while many residents shared Ramlal's affirmation of the inherent *value* of the Shiv Camp community, the decreasing value-coding of labor in the world-class city profoundly challenged residents' sense of place and home, in some instances forcing them to rethink where they fit into society and what their fates might entail.

Although Shiv Camp had evolved from its early days as a labor camp, most of its men and many of its women were still involved in the construction industry, working primarily as bricklayers, carpenters, contractors, or suppliers of construction materials. Among these, only contractors and specialist carpenters had regular work. The rest were day laborers who maintained highly flexible work schedules. When unattached to a contractor involved in a larger job, residents would trudge out to a street corner in front of a nearby brick godown, waiting for contractors in need of head loaders or more specialized masons: 150 rupees a day for healthy male bricklayers and concrete mixers; 120 rupees a day for women at the time of my research. But even this work was irregular. As a man too old to work told me, lamenting what had become of men in the *basti*, "three out of four men here have become total drifters [*ekdam avārā*]. They have no work at all."

In contrast, women bore increasing income-earning responsibilities, primarily as maids in the nearby *kothis* or selling vegetables in the surrounding neighborhoods during lulls in regular domestic duties. Meanwhile, men woke up early each morning to try their luck, arriving at the laborers' corner by the time the first contractor showed up to collect bricks. When unsuccessful, they returned to Shiv Camp, many to try their luck differently—through the card games that peppered the *basti*'s open spaces. Most of my days of fieldwork in Shiv Camp began when a group of such men, huddled together along the *basti*'s main paths playing cards, gambling, or gossiping, called me over to join them (see Figure 6.2). These men often referred to their daily *timepass* activities as *chuṭṭī*, which literally means "holiday" or "day off." Despite this suggestion that not working was a willed choice, not an imposed condition, men intimately felt what Mukesh had described as labor's loss of value. As Ramdas explained of daily routines in Shiv Camp: "The boys wander, the men sit around home; lots of people gamble and play cards. We sweep the floor and take care of the home, and the women go and work."

In Shiv Camp residents lived in constant anticipation of their displacement, waiting for the slum-free future to arrive and take them away. As buildings grew and neighborhoods improved around them, residents lived in parentheses, waiting for the stream of history to pick them up and carry them forward. As Shambu said, "our future isn't here," although when that future would arrive remained uncertain. In this context, everyday life increasingly acquired the temporality of the card game: whether or not

Figure 6.2. Shiv Camp men taking *chuṭṭī*. Photograph by author.

one won a hand of cards, whether or not one secured employment on a given day, whether or not one's home was demolished seemed, to many unemployed Shiv Camp men, sealed by their fate, built into a pregiven time series. As Rajiv told me one day when explaining yet another failed job lead, "whatever is in someone's fate [*kismat*], that is what they get."

The Hindi word *kismat* means both fate and luck, relaying differences in meaning ranging from one's destiny, in the sense of a predetermined outcome, to one's lot, as in the likelihood that chance will serve one well, to one's share, as in one's place within the social division (*le partage*, which Rancière reminds us is always also *le partage du sensible*).[22] When residents would refer to something as "written in fate [*kismat kā likhā*]," they were expressing more a sense of destiny. But fate was also something to be tempted, something that could be influenced by action. Despite the frequency with which residents criticized gambling as a social pathology and sign of residential decay, the game itself often affirmed the courage, even masculinity, of the gambler. Thus, while the unemployed gambler was resigned to his fate, he could play the game of chance in hopes that a better future or a new opportunity might arise.[23] Perhaps this was escapism, or perhaps an attempt to leap back into history—to turn the card instead of having it turned for you, to establish a sense of agency in an uncertain world. Shambu, for example, once said, while stepping into a card game, that he was going to "test his fate [*kismat āzmānā*]," while someone benefiting from a favorable turn of cards, or a man who landed a multiweek job might be called *kismat kā dhanī*, literally meaning a man rich in luck. Following Rajiv's above profession of fate, he said, "in the village, there are still gold coins that people sometimes find. Whoever has it in their fate gets crores of rupees. But he never knows what he might find if he doesn't go looking!"

In the lead-up to the April demolition, Shiv Camp residents were constantly speculating about when the bulldozers would return to clear the remaining *jhuggis*. A few weeks before the municipal elections, which took place in the first week of April 2008, one among a group of men wagered, "after the election, this [basti] will definitely be broken. We are just waiting for the elections, then we are gone. We'll be thrown somewhere on the outside of the city." The indeterminacy of work, of tenure, and of the timing of displacement led many to see their life trajectory through the lens of chance, and discussions of fate saturated everyday attempts to make sense of residents' economic and political vulnerability. In this context, games of chance served as a means to accommodate the uncertainties of the day, almost mimicking the vagaries of slum life: walking to the street corner each morning in search of work resembled the indeterminacy of each hand of cards. In each, the outcome of the present operation was independent of the outcome of the previous one—experience did not matter—leading men to occasionally blur their descriptions of the two in conversation (Would the dealer hand him a high card? Would the contractor pick him from the crowd?). For example, while discussing work prospects with a group of men playing "cut," a version of the card game "war," a man, enraptured by the game, would raise his voice when his next card was coming: "give it, give it," egging on the dealer and anticipating a high card. Overhearing our discussion of work in the middle of a hand, he quickly looked to me, saying, "oh *bhaiya*, I sit here unoccupied everyday. Give me some work. I'll do anything," before returning his gaze to the game, as if his hand of cards determined the fate of not just his bet, but work too.

The ease with which fate was introduced into conversations to explain future and past indicates that the prevalence of gambling in Shiv Camp ought to be read not only in relation to increased idleness or the shortage of work, but also as a particular experience of sociospatial change, or what Georg Simmel called a "structuring of experience."[24] Indeed, invocations of fate, I found, often did not index a state of resignation or fatalism, as has often been attributed to low-caste Hindus or outcastes, or as is often assumed of popular Hinduism and the more fatalistic interpretations of karma doctrine it is sometimes seen to proffer.²⁵ Residents rather invoked fate to register profound struggles over value—both their own social values and inner potentialities, as well as deeper conceptions of the origins of economic value. Like Sanjay and Rajesh's stories about fleeting value in the city's streets, and like residents' broader experience of being unable to capture and hold onto wealth in the contemporary city, men used stories of fate to pose questions about what personal transformations might be necessary to become full participants of the future city—to be the type of subjects to whom value might become attached.²⁶

One day, while a group of boys were asking me about how they could get a work visa to move to the United States, Lakshman began describing his experience working in Mauritius as a clerk for the Indian Foreign Service, where he had lived for six years: "I had a great boss; work was easy; and I earned 5,000 rupees per week!" Lakshman had fallen in love with a Muslim girl there, who he had met while helping her complete tax forms: "She loved me very much, and there was no difference between us. . . . But, her family said I had to become Muslim to marry her, and I couldn't give up on my India. So I didn't marry this beautiful woman." A boy joked that she must have left him, and Lakshman replied, "even today she would send me lakhs of rupees if I asked; that's how much she loved me."

Lakshman used this story to suggest that the fleeting nature of certain experiences is a product of one's fate. He was able to live in a foreign country, find love, and earn good money, but those things were not in his fate: "I got in a fight with a top official and had to leave that place." He returned to "his India," where his fate guided him. A differently fated person might have done something else in that situation. Even the right knowledge, he went on to say, could not ensure success and fortune, a point he made through his description of another missed opportunity:

> I was offered a visa to work in America. The passport, visa, and even airplane ticket were ready. There were six days before my departure, so I went to Pune to see a relative. I had a hundred rupees with me. I bought food and took a taxi and was left with only thirty rupees. I didn't have enough money to go to Mumbai, so I asked a friend for money, who laughed, saying, "you're going all the way to America and can't even buy a train ticket to Mumbai!" I got angry and said, "forget it! I don't want to go to America anyway," and I returned. It wasn't in my fate to go there, otherwise I too would be living in one of these kothis. I would have had lakhs of rupees and a car here. Where our fate takes us, we must follow.

Looking back at the events that had befallen him, Lakshman signaled that his return to the *basti* after failed attempts to journey abroad were due to his inner tendency—his own values and dispositions (e.g., an unwillingness to request assistance) that, had they differed, may have led to a different fate: "Now, all I do is *beldārī* [manual labor]."

Shambu shared a similar story. When he first came to Delhi, he met a British man with whom he worked to build a road: "We used to joke with each other and became good friends. At that time, work was good, so I didn't even think about it, but I should have had that man get me work in England. He told me I could work with him there. Who knows where I would have been today? But then, work was good and I was happy here, so I told the man: 'I don't want to become the slave of England.'" The man left, and Shambu never saw him again.

Dhaniram, who was sitting beside me on the cot in Shambu's smoke-filled *jhuggī*, remarked, "God gives everyone one chance in their lives. If they see it and take it, they can become millionaires [*karoḍpati*]." Both Shambu and Dhaniram here indicated that one's fate is produced through the combination of inner dispositions, how one locates and defines value, and external opportunity.[27] These were the same terms on which many Shiv Camp residents made sense of their potential resettlement, an outcome that appeared increasingly unlikely after the April demolition, when none of the 122 displaced families received resettlement plots.

In October, having just returned from spending three months in his village, Motilal asked me about the status of the Shiv Camp legal case. Hearing my ambiguous response, he replied, "this [the basti] could break anytime." Motilal's wife had fallen extremely ill while in the village: "I spent 5,000 rupees for a cure, but she's in [the hospital]. Now what can I do? We've spent money; now everything is in god's hands." He had suggested the same idea of fate when referring to the demolition process: "Who knows if we'll get anything." Motilal continued describing the relationship between resettlement and fate: "In the past, we were offered resettlement in Kali Basti, but we refused. Now that people have built there, they could sell the plots for five lakh rupees. They have twenty-five gaj [square yards]. . . . Anywhere in Delhi with that much [land] will get at least one and a half lakh [rupees]. . . . We could have had that all, but we didn't act. Now we are too late."

In the months after the April demolition, this became a common refrain throughout the *basti*. As Lalaji said, "at that time [~five years ago], sarkar was offering twenty-five gaj plots, but we refused. Our pradhan said we wanted bigger plots, so they left, and nothing happened. Now, we will be lucky to get eighteen gaj plots. We had the opportunity to have a good plot there, but we lost it." Bhagavati, having made a similar statement, followed by saying *sarkar* had surveyed Shiv Camp like all the other *bastis*. Even though these other settlements were not as old as Shiv Camp, she noted, they had already been resettled and had become well off: "They received nice plots . . . only six kilometers away. When will our fate change?"

In each of these narratives, an opportunity to capitalize on an external event—the offer of resettlement, the chance to work in England, the opportunity to marry a rich, beautiful woman—did not align with the inner tendency or values of the protagonist, who was unwilling to leave "home," defined either as one's house or neighborhood, country, or religion and family. Whether or not these were indeed available options, the narrator interpreted them as such, appropriating these external conditions as self-defining: in each case, by attributing chance encounters/outcomes to individual choice or disposition, they used the language of fate to affirm their attachment to place. Looking back, often with regret, the narrators were also registering alternative value regimes: Maybe they should have acted differently? Maybe Shambu should have left India? Maybe Lakshman should have converted to Islam? As the promise of property ownership, and its promise of capturing ever-expanding value, seemed to lie in locations beyond the *basti*, maybe they had mis-valued home and should have submitted to relocation? Maybe their jhuggis could have been converted into five-lakh-rupee plots, as had happened with Kali Basti, and maybe they still could.

VALUE IN DISTANCE

Ghar (home) versus *plot*: these were the terms on which Uday Prakash and Sanjay framed the resettlement process in front of the *pān* stall one March afternoon, a few weeks before Holi—when women would make *pyāz pakoḍīs* and other fried snacks to share with neighbors, men would get drunk and sing, and children would douse one another, and everyone around them, in the bright powdered colors that would leave *jhuggi* walls bespeckled for weeks. When I joined the boys, they were already talking about resettlement, and Sanjay was describing how sad it would be if they were removed from Shiv Camp: "How would we celebrate Holi? We know everyone here and celebrate together. Everyone is open." Sanjay had recently visited Bawana, where a friend from another *basti* had recently been resettled. What he saw of Delhi's largest resettlement colony, situated more than thirty kilometers north of Shiv Camp (see Map), did not fit the image of resettlement presented by government officials. Instead of a well-serviced plot and paved roads, his friend's family was living in a makeshift, shoulder-height *jhuggi* with a mud floor in an open field awaiting an official land allocation: "They live beside a canal; there are snakes there, and people are scared to go out at night."

Uday Prakash disagreed with this summary of resettlement, but he used terms quite different from those of Sanjay: "Everyone sent there receives a *plot*. If not immediately, then after some time they will have their own *plot*, their own land."

Sanjay replied, "even if everyone receives a *plot*, they are only eighteen gaj," far too little space. "Do you know how much those *plots* cost?" Uday Prakash asked rhetorically, before answering his own question: "They cost one and a half to two lakh rupees now and will cost even more soon! But, yes, they don't have *ghar* yet, only *plot*."

In replying to Sanjay, Uday Prakash had introduced two unequal entities, which had to be equated for the resettlement process to make sense: *ghar* is a place that provides comfort and security—a particular use value—whereas *plot* is a piece of land defined by its exchange value. Uday Prakash agreed with Sanjay that eighteen gaj plots were too small for a comfortable life, but wondered if the *value* of the plot was enough to compensate for the loss of *ghar*: "If we are going to *shift* from here, we should receive good compensation [*muāvzā*]. Eighteen gaj is small, but it will grow with time. Two lakh rupees will someday become five."

Shiv Camp residents often framed resettlement as a question of compensation, which they understood as an exchange of *ghar*—including the sense of community and the social networks they had built over the years—for something of monetary value—a piece of property, something first possessed and only later fully lived in. By their very nature, plots were understood to have the power to produce value—"two lakh will someday become five"—which Uday Prakash and many of the other boys saw as a highly desirable trait. *This* was value, the kind that grows automatically with time: M–M′, money produces more money without the necessity of labor.

Sonu, who had earlier in the day been telling me about Shiv Camp's increasingly fraught relationship with the neighboring *kothi*s, added his perspective, stating how he would smash the *kothi* windows if his *jhuggi* were removed: "But, if we get compensation, then we will be happy and they will be happy. We will get what we want [plot] and they will get what they want: more space, more cleanliness." Sonu, Sanjay, and Uday Prakash's statements here evoked the conundrum of exchange: could the qualitative value of *ghar* (C), a concrete particularity built personally for a family's use, be measured in monetary terms (M)? To Sonu, such a transaction—giving up *ghar* (C) for *plot* (M)—seemed fair, even if strange, a point with which Sanjay sympathized when he said that although he would prefer to stay in Shiv Camp, resettlement was acceptable to him: "Bawana will slowly be built. It will improve. It takes time to build *ghar*"—to give *plot* more than just monetary value. As Sonu said of a hypothetical resettlement plot, "its price will go up with time. You see, if you look anywhere in Delhi . . . you can't find anything, even the smallest plot, for less than one and a half lakh. So, this area in Bawana, which is central and has all these services, will have a lot of value [*uskī kīmat bahut hogī*]."

The Peruvian economist and global development celebrity Hernando de Soto describes the "mystery of capital" as the power of formal property within a capitalist bureaucracy to give assets that serve "immediate physical purposes," such as "houses used for shelter," a "parallel life as capital outside the physical world." Formal property allows for the coordination of use and exchange value by mobilizing the "dormant value," "the potential energy," of a commodity "to produce surplus value over and above its physical assets."[28] Such surplus value, which de Soto posits is an inherent property of landed property, is realizable through land titling, the practice of legalizing the physical asset and thereby allowing its owners to use (and potentially lose) that asset as collateral for loans and credit. This story of the power of formal property to generate surplus value by representational means—"capital is born by representation in writing," de Soto writes—underpins the promise of the world-class city: the promise that property can morph penury into plenty.[29] In this representational sorcery we also see the implicit property form of M–M′, or the fetish claim: "Give land a piece of paper and it will grow money."[30] Yet while de Soto represents—and is indeed the global representative of—this first mystery of property, he neglects the second mystery that accompanies it: property's promise to transform the inner tendencies of its possessor. This is the notion of property in the sense of its symantically correct root, being a resource "proper" to a person, and it is at the same time the reciprocal promise that *that* person will be made "proper" to the conditions of property.[31] How does this promise find expression in the devalued space of the slum, and how might residents' continual reminder of and sacrifice for this second promise also operate as a claim to the city?

One day in November, Pappu began describing a *basti* that had recently been resettled. Although in the April Demolition, just seven months earlier, many of his neighbors had been displaced without compensation, his tone evinced a faith in the trusteeship of the state: "Those people now have their own land. They have houses in Bawana." At the time, Bawana had unpaved roads, irregular bus service and electricity supply, and no schools or medical dispensaries. Many men spent only weekends in Bawana, sleeping at their work sites in the main city for the remainder of the week to minimize the arduous and costly commute, a common practice in Bawana to this day. Most women had stopped working outside of the home completely, a condition they bemoaned.[32] Pappu's image of Bawana differed from what Sanjay had seen: "Bawana is really nice. It is like a field. There is open air, a canal, and big, wide roads. It has a factory atmosphere [*factory kā māhaul*]. It is a planned area." I asked if people's lives there are better than in Shiv Camp. "Oh yes," he responded, "there, everything is clean; you have 24-hour electricity, good clean water at any time; there are factories all over."

Sensing that Pappu saw Bawana more as an imagined landscape than a physical locale, I asked him what Bawana would look like in five to ten years. Would it look like the rest of Delhi? He stared at me, confused, before rejecting the basis of my question: "Bawana *is* in Delhi." Noting that it is far away from central Delhi and its conveniences, he affirmed that it would look like the rest of Delhi: "It has factories and good roads." Insistent, I asked if Bawana would look more like the *basti* or the neighborhoods with *kothis*. Sonu had joined our conversation, and both he and Pappu agreed that Bawana homes would look more like the *kothis*. As Sonu explained:

> People will have permanent [*sthāyī*] and finished [*pakkā*] houses. It will be *nishcit* [guaranteed] there. You can have all of your family in one place. If someone gets married, they too can stay there. You'll have a permanent address. . . . Here, if you want to have nice things, you are always worried because the government could come and break this place. Then you'll lose all that. There is no such worry in Bawana.

For Sonu, it was the permanence of resettlement plots that would allow individuals to acquire nice things. His suggestion was that *jhuggi* residents and *kothi* owners did not fundamentally differ; it was the impermanence of tenure that prohibited the former from transforming their homes into *kothis*, from investing their wealth into a permanent asset. Sonu, like many of the youth, saw wealth around him, but believed that without a plot, that wealth could never be fully grasped. Here was de Soto in the *basti*, making a standard neoliberal argument for the importance of clear property rights and the transformational power of this simple form of representational work.

Tenure security was only a piece of the puzzle, however. In many residents' accounts, there was something particular to property ownership and the sacrifice required to achieve it, something that fundamentally changed the fate of its owner. As Pappu went on to say, describing how individuals were transformed through the resettlement process, "there [in Bawana], I saw someone with a cart of ice that spilled over. Nobody stole the ice; they just let it stay or picked it up [for the absent owner]. Here, these people would have taken it all." Bawana, it seemed, instilled its residents with social "rightness" and civility. When I asked Ramkali, Pappu's wife, what a plot in Bawana would offer, she said, as I quoted at the beginning of the chapter, "if we receive a plot, all our problems will go away. We will become big people, like the *kothi* owners." Sonu also read aspirational qualities into resettlement, although he first explained the transformative power of resettlement through its demarcation of a clear boundary between public and private:

> When people have their own land, then they make their own houses and gates. If someone is bothering you there, you can have them removed from your land. . . . But, here you can't stay away from those people. People just sit around and gamble. They get drunk every day and then fight in the night. You can't escape that here. In Bawana, people don't do that. If people gamble, they do it in their own homes, not in the open. They don't bother people like here. Here, the atmosphere is dirty. The men play cards all the time. If they don't want to go to work, they just stay and gamble. Then, what are the children going to do? Of course they are going to gamble and drink, too. In Bawana it isn't like that. Even if people don't have good work, even if they only earn fifty rupees a day, they still go to work. The system is better there.

While Sonu here explained the habits of individuals through institutional arrangements and social norms, he also considered certain "natural" inclinations to arise from the land itself. As he went on to say, "see, here, there is no reason for a child to get educated. He is in an atmosphere that won't let him improve. But, there, other people study. People work hard, they aren't dirty like here; they aren't thieves and they don't try to harm others. There, people will be able to do more."

Jagdish, a newly married man who worked for a company installing security cameras, also fell in this camp: "Going to Bawana, people improve a lot. Once jhuggi residents [*jhuggīvāsī*] arrive there, they don't drink so much; they stop gambling. All these bad habits go away. . . . If we get plots there, we'll be better off. Our children will go to school, and we will find good work." This is the propriety of property; this is what Marx called the fetishistic transformation of social relations "into properties of these things themselves."[33] This is the transposition of rightness from the power bestowed on property owners by the legal system to define "the proper" into the practical struggle for belonging under conditions of dispossession. This also seems to be a clear case of *jhuggi* residents acting as governable subjects, a population whose conduct aligns with the overall rationality of slum removal and land privatization.

However, while many Shiv Camp residents invested in the transformative power of resettlement, speculating on their futures and aligning their horizons with those of the speculative economy, they also saw the requirements for accessing private property in starkly different terms than de Soto. In particular, acquiring *plot*-as-exchange value required relinquishing *ghar*-as-use value. That is to say, acquiring the power to generate surplus value was not an additive process, but a substitutive one: one had to give up home to access property. This was more than a mere representational transformation "outside the physical world," as de Soto suggests. It is closer to what Marx describes through the equation C–M, the exchange of a commodity (C) that has a certain use value for an exchange value (M), and I suggest that we think of the exchange of *ghar* for *plot* on these same terms.[34] Use value and exchange value are usually considered different attributes/representations of a single commodity—that is, the usefulness of a thing on the one hand, and its value relative to other things of potential use on the other: commodities appear to us as objects "with a dual character, possessing both use-value and exchange-value."[35] This is what de Soto means when he says assets have a "parallel life" "outside the physical world" of "immediate physical purpose" (or use). In resettlement, however, the exchange process (C–M, *ghar*–plot) is spatially displaced. That is, there is a spatial transposition in which the acquisition of an exchange value requires geographic dislocation—the representation of *value* in an "elsewhere." Here, exchange takes place through the loss of *ghar* (use value, the *value* of community Ramlal described) in one's neighborhood for the realization of *plot* in a distant locale. The distance in C–M thus acquires geographical expression, and accessing M, with its seeming power to become M′, or to generate surplus value, means accepting displacement. But resettlement plots have an intimate association with *ghar*, since they represent *ghar*'s associated exchange value, even while remaining geographically distant. This distant presentness of housing—the potential energy of one's present home to become a distant plot—inspired sometimes speculative imaginaries about life in resettlement colonies, but it also meant that residents understood well the sacrifices necessary to traverse this distance. In exchange for these sacrifices, residents expected not just M′—not just the first promise of property—but also property's second promise, the promise of propriety.

PROPERTY'S PROMISE

As the chasm in value between residents' homes and resettlement plots deepened in millennial Delhi, discourses of social worthiness that associated differentially valued individuals with the differentially valued spaces of *basti* and private colony simultaneously rose in prominence. Such discourses assigned the attributes of world-class citizenship and middle-class civility to the occupants of private property, casting those on public land as backward, degraded, and socially unworthy of the world-class city. In this context, many Shiv Camp residents saw the key to transforming their fate from low-value workers to high-value property owners to lie in affirming a linkage between self-propriety and the implicit value of property. To pursue property was to pursue a life of propriety. But in conjoining the inner tendency of the self to settlement, such linkages also invested land itself with the power to improve subjects: acquiring more valuable land implied a more valuable personhood. In addition to de Soto's mystery of capital, the mystery of land's self-expanding value, the property fetishism of the world-class city, also carries this second mystery of the mere thing transforming social relations and individual subjectivities. Rather than reject the fetish, Shiv Camp residents got with it, imagining their own futures on its very terms.

In his close reading of Marx's notion of fetishism, Rancière notes: "What is lost in fetishism is the structural implication that founds the distance of the thing from itself [M from M′], a distance which is precisely the site at which the economic relations are in play."[36] In most treatments of fetishism, this distance is presumed to be lost through the concealment of the underlying processes of dispossession from those being dispossessed.[37] Shiv Camp residents, however, show the experience of fetishism to be less a response to ideological concealment and more a practical response to a condition in which society, the law, and economic relations attribute to property the power of value creation. In other words, it is not that Shiv Camp residents misrecognize the origin of value; it is that society is organized as though property is in itself value producing. In this regard, their efforts to conjure a mental image of a better future through the lens of property ownership are simultaneously efforts to align themselves with the speculative promises of world-class development. The speculative landscape, that is to say, opens itself to a speculative disposition, enjoining residents to identify resettlement as a source of fortune, but also providing a foundation for them to make political claims for a better life.

Ironically, in the wake of the slowdown in Indian real estate over the past few years, world-class city making has sought to capitalize precisely on the urban poor's demand for propriety via property. The urban poor, including *jhuggi* dwellers such as Mukesh struggling to gradually build up their savings, have become the new frontier of world-class development, as a whole new affordable housing and micromortgage industry has emerged to bank on what business guru C. K. Prahalad calls "the fortune at the bottom of the pyramid."[38] The promise of the world-class city today is increasingly the promise of the *jhuggi* dweller as speculative investor, and in this promise lies the potential to demand propriety: proper services, proper health care, proper sanitation, and infrasturucture—a proper city for the urban majority. While Mukesh, Uday Prakash, and other residents of Shiv Camp pursuing resettlement may not have articulated these demands on such concise terms, their expectations about property and their refusal to accept resettlement as mere dispossession were also expectations for the world-class city and what it would, and should, offer them.

Conclusion

This book began with the paradox of a state encumbered by its own vast calculative apparatus, Like most postcolonial cities around the world, urban territory in Delhi had been administered over the twentieth century through a set of linked calculative and inscriptive practices—including slum surveys, paper-based land records, land-use maps and zoning, and identity cards—that together were intended to collate complex ground realities into simplified trends and patterns from which deficiencies could be identified and programs of progressive improvement devised. By the late 1990s these calculative instruments had lost their functional efficiency, such that by the time the new chief minister, Sheila Dikshit, affirmed the goal of making Delhi a world-class city, they had become increasingly prone to manipulation. Slum dwellers in particular were able to deftly implicate themselves into the inscriptive apparatus of the state, manipulating records, appropriating lists, and mobilizing lower-level bureaucrats and elected political leaders to modify or ignore plans to secure shelter and livelihood. As the existing system of rule by records began to correspond less and less to the realities it purported to represent, a gap formed between plans and the more mundane bureaucratic procedures through which city making actually took place. In this gap arose millennial Delhi's calculative crisis.

While various efforts to improve the calculative instruments of the state had been attempted over the previous decades, the millennial project of transforming Delhi into a world-class city soon called for more drastic measures. Like other aspiring world-class cities, Delhi began its world-class city-making project by formulating plans for infrastructure investment, slum rehabilitation, environmental improvement, and good governance.

(183)

While different plans and programs came and went, this broad project of speculative real estate, slum clearance, and spectacular infrastructure development was sustained more by an aspirational vision of what the world-class urban future should look like. Skyrocketing land prices, hubristic government proclamations of the glorious city yet to come, and carefully crafted image work by real estate firms, the media, and international consultants gave further impetus to what had seemed but a pipe dream a few years earlier: the decades-old promise of making Delhi look like Paris—of transforming this old Mughal city into a globally competitive, aesthetically appealing metropolis—seemed suddenly realizable.

Rule by Aesthetics has examined the aftermath of Delhi's calculative crisis and the novel ways in which its various governors were able to turn what appeared to be a weakness into a strength. Forgoing the statutory mandate that urban space be carefully monitored and recorded, rule in Delhi became increasingly aesthetic, governed more by that diffuse, aspirational vision of the world-class city than by the imprecise, outdated, and tamper-prone maps and records that undergirded rule by records.[1] A. K. Jain, the commissioner of planning in the Delhi Development Authority (DDA), demonstrated this at the very outset of the book: instead of conducting a comprehensive civic survey to draw up the new Delhi Master Plan that he and his massive team was preparing, he used what he called "a windshield survey," a purely visual inspection of urban space. By the time of my interview with Jain in 2005 the visual underpinnings of rule by aesthetics were well established, allowing the DDA to flout its own calculative mandate without notice.[2] As I argued, the judiciary in the early 2000s had dispensed with the requirement that slum legality be assessed on the basis of survey-based records. It instead drew upon a new interpretation of nuisance law—a set of colonial-era statutes that define nuisances on essentially aesthetic grounds—to put in place a system for adjudicating slum legality on the basis of world-class aesthetic codes. For the first time in postcolonial India, slums were deemed illegal because they *looked* illegal.

I have called this mode of partitioning space on the basis of codes of appearance "rule by aesthetics" and the sensory knowledge that undergirded it in millennial Delhi the "world-class aesthetic." In doing so, I have insisted that the world-class aesthetic was not the outcome of the ideas or actions of a discrete set of actors: not the commissioner of planning, the Delhi High Court, the chief minister, or the resident welfare associations representing elite property owners, although I traced the story of how each of these actors helped translate the world-class aesthetic into a governing vision for ordering the city. Rather, the world-class aesthetic emerged through the more diffuse normative consensus around the look of a world-class city. As it garnered institutional backing through its incorporation into state programs, and as it gained discursive authority through its incorporation into mass speech, this aesthetic normativity acquired increasingly map- and plan-like objective standing, such that diverse city residents could refer to it—this *look*—and know that others shared in its knowledge, even if they disagreed with or disliked it. In this sense, I argued that the world-class aesthetic operates as a particular form of what Rancière calls "the distribution of the sensible," or a system of self-evident facts of sense perception that informs how those who make up its "community of sense" see and make sense of the social world. The aesthetic, in other words, is a form of power/knowledge that operates on sensory, nonideational grounds, even while it shapes and is shaped by cognitive faculties and reason. In this sense, the world-class aesthetic elicits a form of public viewership premised on taken-for-granted criteria for identifying what belongs and what is out of place, and it solicits membership in that public—a "community of sense"— by asking potential members to partake in its ways of seeing and saying.

Throughout the book, I have used the term "rule by aesthetics" in two ways. The first use refers to the deployment of standardized aesthetic codes for partitioning and ordering things. It is this power to differentiate and administer from afar without the need for the complicated inscriptive and calculative instruments—such as map, survey, and census—that enabled Jain sitting in his air-conditioned office, judges confined to their benches, and elite property owners who had never ventured into the slums they so despised to assess and act upon space from a distance. My second use of the term "rule by aesthetics" sought to attend to the complex ways in which the self-evident facts of sense perception—the map-like objectivity of slum unsightliness and unbelonging—were taken up and negotiated by slum dwellers. In other words, I used it to ask how and why those with seemingly no part in the world-class city took part in the world-class aesthetic. As a particular aesthetic form of governmentality—a term that Foucault famously described as "the conduct of conduct"—rule by aesthetics, I showed, successfully conducted the conduct of the slum population in millennial Delhi. Residents of the *jhuggi* colony I called Shiv Camp, for example, described their own settlement and similar settlements around the city as nuisances to the world-class city and aligned their expectations for the future with state plans to resettle them on the outskirts of the city. Yet I also showed that the ability to effectively conduct the conduct of subject populations does not imply that those populations consent to programs of rule.

Too often in scholarship on political rule and governmentality, analysis stops at the point when populations are considered governable. Scholars are then left with little means of explaining how and why governmental programs and ruling rationalities experience the crises that they do. As I have shown, the shift in the mode of government from calculative rule to aesthetic rule in millennial Delhi was precipitated not just by outdated records and inefficient bureaucracy, but also by slum dwellers' appropriation and manipulation of the state's very calculative techniques. Similarly, as I show in the following sections, the crisis of aesthetic rule in the wake of millennial Delhi and the more recent return to a more calculative form of government was precipitated not just by failed systems of accountability, but also by slum dwellers' transformation of the world-class aesthetic into a demand for improved shelter and livelihood. The larger lesson is that conduct must be understood as a more diverse field of everyday practice in which the successful cultivation of governable subjects does not imply an absence of politics. In millennial Delhi, by being conducted toward accepting government resettlement, residents also appropriated the vision of resettlement, harnessing the promise of formal property ownership that resettlement ostensibly offered and transforming resettlement from a geography of banishment into a geography of hope.

All successful projects of rule consist of the cultivation of forms of popular conduct conducive to the goals of government: slum removal, land privatization, speculative real estate, urban clean-up, and beautification in millennial Delhi. But they also consist of the diverse means by which those forms of conduct are invested with political force, ascribed diverse meanings, and inhabited and reworked by those being governed. The world-class aesthetic—that preeminent apparatus for casting slums as self-evidently out of place—acquired just such a reworked political force and renewed meaning once taken up by slum dwellers. I conclude this book by considering the politicization of the world-class aesthetic and the manner in which slum dwellers began to hold the government accountable for the promises of the world-class city.

AESTHETIC CRISIS

The Commonwealth Games arrived in Delhi on October 3, 2010, laden with controversy and scandal. Two weeks before the opening ceremony, Scottish officials described their athletes' housing as "unsafe and unfit for human habitation." Days later, a number of prominent athletes pulled out of the competition altogether, while a wider set of national delegates declared that the "Commonwealth Games Village is severely compromised."[3] The collapse of a footbridge outside the Jawaharlal Nehru Stadium, home to the opening and closing ceremonies, along with the Australian Olympic Committee's public statement of regret for having supported India's bid for the games, further called into question Prime Minister Manmohan Singh's claim that the mega-event would demonstrate how India "is rapidly marching ahead with confidence."⁴

The games eventually took place with fewer hiccups than anticipated: foreign athletes praised India's hospitality, and the host nation won the second most gold medals, its best ever showing. However, the event magnified larger concerns with world-class city making. Before the games, it came to light that over nine billion (900 crore) rupees had been diverted from state pensions, social welfare programs, and basic services in resettlement colonies to fund infrastructure projects linked to the games.⁵ After the games, the *Hindustan Times* ran a story titled "Glitzy Hotels Built on Subsidized Land Reported Very Low Tourist Turn Out" as news broke that only ninety-one of the 2,500 newly constructed high-end hotel rooms had been booked during the event.⁶ The glimmering Hilton Hotel in west Delhi, which the Shiv Camp resident Mukesh had helped wire (see chapter 6), received no Commonwealth Games guests, and overall foreign tourism numbers were 25 percent lower than official predictions.⁷

In response to widespread reports of corruption, the central government announced the day after the closing ceremony that it would form a special committee to investigate government graft. The committee, headed by the auditor general of India, found that sweetheart deals had delivered two and a half billion rupees of profit to private contractors. It further observed that Delhi's lieutenant governor had inflated the agreed upon sales price of the Games Village, allowing the Dubai-based developer Emaar-MGF to pocket one billion rupees in excess earnings.⁸ Combined with an audit report that discovered that this famed builder of the world's tallest building, the Burj Khalifa, had used inferior construction materials, this news gave new meaning to Emaar-MGF's tagline "Creating a New India" and called into question the celebrated role of the public–private partnership, long considered the standard-bearer of world-class urban development.

A series of national corruption scandals involving land and telecommunication giveaways before the games had already shaken the Congress Party-led central government, and the deep, systemic faults of world-class city making became indisputable when in 2011 Delhi's Corruption Ombudsman found the chief minister, Sheila Dikshit, also of the Congress Party, guilty of having made false campaign promises to slum dwellers; her 2008 claim that 60,000 flats were being allotted to the urban poor was proven an outright lie when it was later revealed that the project had not even been allocated land for development.⁹

As millennial Delhi wound to a close, the world-class city had lost its luster. Thus, while Delhi's 2012 Budget reiterated the goal of "making Delhi a good, beautiful, world-class city . . . comparable to any other city in the world," it emphasized that city planning would have to embrace a more "humanistic approach" going forward.¹⁰ Reflecting this need, a year earlier Delhi's three members of parliament, all from the Congress Party, had initiated and passed the Delhi Special Laws Act, a national-level law to provide *jhuggi* and unauthorized colonies with protection against "punitive action by any local authority" in Delhi.¹¹ Chief Minister Dikshit soon after rebranded Delhi "The Caring City," stating that "economic growth per se will not guarantee eradication of poverty and hence inclusive growth has to be a 'guiding philosophy' in all development paradigms."¹²

INCLUSIVE GROWTH

Inclusive growth was not an innovation of the Delhi-based Congress Party. It had already become a buzzword in international development circles in the wake of the 2008 global financial crisis, and it had been introduced as a the core principle of the Rajeev Awas Yojana (RAY), India's ambitious national-level housing program aimed at creating a slum-free India.¹³ Joined by Hernando de Soto, the Peruvian economist celebrated for his property-based approach to urban poverty alleviation, at the opening of a 2010 "Conference on Inclusive Growth" in Delhi, the minister of housing and urban poverty alleviation described the preparations for RAY in distinctly de Sotoian terms: "Our Ministry is intensively working on preparing the blueprint for a Slum-free India based on the foundation of property rights to the slum dwellers and the urban poor."¹⁴ When RAY guidelines were published a year later, they echoed activists' and community organizers' long-standing critique of master planning:

> City master plans follow an exclusionary model that reserves land for housing high and middle income groups, commercial, institutional, recreational and other uses, with no ear-marking for Economically Weaker Sections and Low Income Groups. These factors, coupled with sky-rocketing urban land prices, have squeezed the urban poor out of formal urban land markets. Slums are an inevitable outcome of this deficiency in urban policy and planning.¹⁵

RAY won widespread praise for including what it called "those who are forced to live in extra-formal spaces," and well-known planners hailed "slum-free cities" as "a new deal for India's urban poor" and a policy that "seek[s] to integrate rather than render surplus marginal populations."¹⁶ Yet slum-free city planning, the process through which city governments could access RAY funds, included and integrated the poor through the very speculative urbanism I have described throughout this book—a model of development that depends on sky-rocketing urban land prices and the squeezing out of those who cannot afford to pay them. Thus, while slum-free city planning required cities to devise plans for providing tenure security to *jhuggi* dwellers, tenure security was framed almost universally through the narrow de Sotoian logic of land titling, property ownership, and converting public land into a commodified asset.[17] Inclusion, in other words, was to take place through what residents of Shiv Camp called *plot*, an asset won only through the forfeiture of *ghar* (home) (see chapter 6). This is evidenced by the fact that a central focus of slum-free city planning is the compensation package, which sets the terms on which slum dwellers can receive de Soto's celebrated legal title—not to centrally located land in the neighborhoods they have occupied for generations, but rather to peripheral resettlement plots and fee-based flats. Slum-free cities and the inclusive growth discourse through which they are framed, in other words, are built on a model of propertied citizenship premised on spatial displacement, the very same terms Shiv Camp residents were struggling to reconcile when I left in 2008. Planning in postcolonial India had previously sought to engineer inclusion through mixed-income housing: in Delhi, the Master Plan required that 25 percent of all housing in 100,000-person blocks be reserved for the urban poor, a provision that lasted until 2007. Inclusive growth, in contrast, dispenses with the spatial logic of inclusion altogether, recasting it as the ability to participate in market mechanisms.[18]

While the inclusive growth agenda arose alongside a budding consensus around the need to implement a comprehensive urban social security framework, it must also be seen as a response to the realization that the bold, millennial projection that urban poverty would gradually disappear—crafted through the speculative poverty projections I described in chapter 1—was not coming to pass.[19] The persistence of urban poverty mattered in part because of mounting disaffection with a political machine that sacrificed welfare programs for speculative real estate development: slum-based organizations had increasingly mobilized to ask where their inclusion would come from. But in addition to the promise that urban poverty would disappear, the world-class city also promised that those exiting poverty would fill up the speculative housing complexes driving the Indian property boom. The failure to fulfill this second promise signaled a far deeper crisis of world-class city making.

While property prices continued to climb nationally after the 2008 global financial meltdown, India's housing market eventually lost steam in 2011, the same year the rate of overall economic growth dipped below the 8 percent mark economists have long deemed necessary to absorb the country's expanding workforce.[20] Things worsened in 2013 and 2014, with economic growth falling below 5 percent annualized growth, the result in part of a stagnant construction industry that grew less than 2 percent a year—down from over 10 percent in 2012.[21] Housing prices in India's major cities fell in the summer of 2013 for the first time since the National Housing Bank's residential property index was established, and in Delhi, speculators' share of new home purchases spiked to 65 percent as vacancy rates climbed.[22]

Inclusive growth emerged in this context as a renewed promise to engineer a way to transform those priced out of the world-class city into an engine of growth, while simultaneously offering to wrench the urban poor out of poverty. As signs of a real estate cool-down were setting in, the minister of housing and urban poverty alleviation claimed: "A critical issue is: how to bring the urban poor engaged in the informal sector into the formal system so that they can benefit from the growing urban economies to both, *create and share in the wealth of the nation.*"[23] The CEO of Infosys, India's software giant, similarly described at the 2011 World Economic Forum the urgent need to "leverage growth in a manner that will benefit people at the bottom of the pyramid"—that is, the poorest strata of society—and incorporate them into the process of wealth creation.[24] Yet in contrast to claims that the poor are leveraged up the income ladder via economic growth, I have argued in this book that the bottom of the pyramid is leveraged *out* of the world-class city to sustain speculative real estate. In millennial Delhi, this took place through mass slum demolitions and the privatization of public land—a form of accumulation by dispossession that did not directly incorporate the urban poor as economic subjects. This was a process sustained through the exclusionary form of aesthetic rule that I have described in this book. As millennial Delhi wound to a close, the problem was not the inability to remove the unwanted—a task at which aesthetic rule had been more than effective—but rather how to capitalize on them. Thus, while inclusive growth continues the logic of transforming public and undercapitalized central city land into globally integrated real estate, it does so using new instruments of finance and governance to instrumentalize, not abandon, the urban poor. This has meant seeking to enhance and capitalize on their hopes for formal property, and it has required a return to a more calculative form of government, along with a shift in the role of the world-class aesthetic.

AFFORDABLE HOUSING

The twin logics of land capitalization and financial inclusion that make up the inclusive growth agenda are being brought together today most directly through India's newly conceived affordable housing market, which has been engineered to tap into the urban poor's aspiration for formal property—an aspiration enhanced through the criminalization of public land occupation and the banishment of the urban poor I have described in this book.[25] According to US-based consultancy Monitor Deloitte, there is a vast pool of low-income households in India—twenty-one million to be precise—that can afford homes priced between 300,000 and one million rupees, a price that real estate developers had long considered too low to achieve the industry standard 40 percent internal rate of return.[26] Since the late 2000s, the Mumbai-based Monitor Inclusive Markets group has been seeking to design and promote this affordable housing market by publishing market information, producing and disseminating a business prototype for "building a scalable low-income housing company," developing risk assessment models and advising nonconventional "micromortgage" lending firms on how to target informal sector workers, and hosting workshops on the challenges of low-cost housing construction.[27] Throughout these efforts, Monitor has been arguing that the affordable housing market has unique advantages—including faster turnover and the opportunity to turn cheap, peri-urban land undesirable to the luxury segment into fully capitalized real estate—that allow developers to overcome its lower profit margins.[28] These arguments have led to a steady rise in the list of social enterprises, business celebrities, and multinational corporations investing in and praising the growth potential of this estimated eleven trillion rupee (~$180 billion) market.[29]

The central government, via RAY and the Finance Ministry, has also latched its engine to the affordable housing train. In 2011, the Finance Ministry proposed offering tax deductions for developers who successfully launched affordable housing projects, and in 2012 a twelve billion rupee Credit Risk Guarantee Fund was approved under RAY to "facilitate credit enablement of the urban poor and the flow of institutional finance for affordable housing."[30] RAY further offered a 1 percent interest rate subsidy for mortgages smaller than 500,000 rupees and allowed cities to use RAY funds to offer land and construction subsidies to incentivize such private developments. While state-provided resettlement housing continues to have a place in RAY, the dominant slum-free cities strategy in the early phase of RAY—up until the Congress Party was defeated nationally in 2014—was the public–private partnership model, in which the local state provided land, infrastructure, subsidies, and development rights, while private firms constructed, marketed, and sold projects. Affordable housing, either via heavy state subsidy to house former slum dwellers or through outright market purchase, has become the new hope of inclusive growth.

According to Monitor, more than 130 affordable housing projects had been launched in twenty-two Indian cities by 2014, while more than a dozen new nonbanking financial institutions emerged to peddle micromortgages, small home loans that do not require the same strict income verification procedures as standard mortgages and that carry interest rates 3 to 4 percent higher than those offered by traditional lenders—what might be termed India's new subprime.[31] However, despite widespread celebration of affordable housing, early evidence suggests that this still-emerging market is experiencing an investor rush that is pricing out the lower-income households it is imagined to serve.[32] Only projects with a designated social mission have been able to successfully book more than a few token units for lower-income families. This is in part due to the fact that the definition of affordable housing has gradually stretched: from a maximum ticket price of 900,000 rupees in 2009 to 2.5 million in 2012. Even in smaller market cities, standard, one-bedroom 400-square-foot units rarely sold for less than 800,000 rupees in 2014, a price that only comfortably middle-income households could afford. And there is little evidence that local housing boards have moved beyond what a Ministry of Housing-sponsored report found in 2010: "While some state housing boards have been performing their duties, in recent times many of them have shifted their focus to merely selling land for profit and sitting on cash surpluses."[33] For the vast majority of India's lower- and even middle-income households, and thus for the vast majority of urban India, affordable housing remains out of reach.

INCLUSIVE DELHI?

I returned to Shiv Camp in 2010. As in 2008 when I left, resident were still wrestling with the question of formal property. Kishani, who had taken the risk of investing her life savings in building a second floor to her *jhuggi*, was operating the busiest *kirānā* (provisions) store in the settlement out of her ground floor. Motilal's construction business had slowed down, he had become a regular at the card games, and he complained to me about the high fee he would have to pay should his family be allotted a resettlement plot. Dhaniram still visited the *basti*, but less frequently than before. He had started working for a property dealer in the unauthorized colony his family had been living in since their *jhuggi* was demolished in 2007. When he did visit Shiv Camp, he often bragged about the three-story home his father had constructed, embellished with molded concrete columns, like those on the nearby *kothis*. For Dhaniram, the promise of *plot* had been fulfilled: "We bought our land for only 25,000 rupees. Now our house is worth twenty-five lakh," he boasted.

In 2009, the legal case filed by the neighboring Krishna Garden resident welfare association (RWA) against Shiv Camp was closed. Shiv Camp residents had convinced the court commissioner in the High Court mediation hearings that most of the land they occupied belonged to the long-absent land colonizer Chaudhury, who had moved away after having sold off the plots he had built up in Krishna Garden. The RWA had not stopped trying to evict its less-fortunate neighbors, however. Instead of filing a fresh court petition, it took a more piecemeal approach: lobbying its political representatives, using Bhagidari contacts in the local bureaucracy, and pressuring the Municipal Corporation to deliver the amenities listed on the tattered layout plan created by the colonizer Chaudhury in 1968, which had been declared official in the High Court mediation hearings.

In the winter of 2010, the Municipal Corporation demolished fifteen Shiv Camp *jhuggis* for being too close to an inner colony road. In 2011, the RWA used its Member of the Legislative Assembly (MLA) from the opposition Bharatiya Janata Party (BJP) to submit a letter to the Municipal Corporation, which had been taken over by the BJP in the 2008 municipal elections, requesting the demolition of Shiv Camp's toilet block to make way for the community hall shown in the 1968 layout plan, and confirmed as Municipal Corporation land.

In late 2011, the toilet block was locked and in its place a trailer unit with fourteen toilets, a third of the previous number, was installed at the far corner of the settlement. When I visited Shiv Camp in 2012, queues to use the toilets were so long that adults were forced to defecate in the open, an act only small children had been willing to endure previously. As Kishan explained to me: "[The MLA] told us it would benefit us. He said we could hold weddings and festivals there [in the community hall], but how will this benefit us [*iskā kyā fāydā*]? Now, we have to go to the public taps and bathe in the open. How long can we live like this? Delhi has improved so much. We also want improvement [*Dillī itnā sudharī hai. Ham bhī sudharnā cāhte haiṁ.*]."

Despite ongoing pressure against slums, demolitions have slowed in Delhi, in part due to the fact that most large settlements had been cleared in millennial Delhi, and in part because of legal protection offered by the Delhi Special Laws Act and a 2010 High Court judgment that ruled that "every eligible slum dweller had to be relocated to a place with proper civic amenities before being evicted from a piece of public land."[34] This judgment reinstated the Delhi government's resettlement policy requiring that resettlement take place before *jhuggi* demolition, which had been ignored since 2003. In doing so, it reaffirmed the requirement that survey- and land records-based procedures be carried out prior to demolition and thereby called for the more thorough calculative administration of space that nuisance law had sidestepped.[35]

Despite the reduction in nuisance-driven demolition orders, however, nuisance continues to shape the organization and management of urban space in Delhi, albeit in a way that has shed its underlying logic of environmental improvement. This is evidenced by a clear shift in how property owners have used nuisance in recent years. In the first fifty years of postcolonial Delhi, challenging slum-based nuisance was a mechanism for improving the sanitation and public health of local neighborhoods. Before the millennial moment, this took place through judicial orders that required the local state to reduce slum-based nuisance via the provision of sanitation services. This is the context in which the Municipal Corporation constructed Shiv Camp's toilet block in the mid-1990s.[36] In the millennial moment, nuisance jurisprudence shifted, leading to a flurry of judicial orders that demanded that improper sanitation in slums, especially open defecation, be remedied through slum removal (see chapter 4). Despite this innovation, which for the first time in postcolonial India equated entire slum settlements with nuisance, the rationale behind nuisance law was still to make neighborhoods cleaner. Today, we witness a form of sanitary malevolence in which property owners mobilize nuisance not to improve sanitation, but rather as a weapon to stigmatize and degrade those who must live in a degraded environment.[37] In this context, the degradation of the local environment is the product not of neglectful municipal government, but a condition engineered by property owners and the local state. No longer able to cast out their unwanted neighbors, property owners continue to cast *jhuggi* dwellers down, rendering them abject, their settlements increasingly stigmatized as places of open defecation and filth that cannot but be seen as nuisances.[38]

With little hope that life in their settlement would improve, Shiv Camp residents, when I again visited in 2012, were enthusiastic about the inclusive promise of Delhi's new slum-free city plan, launched under RAY with the widely publicized goal of relocating 125,000 *jhuggi* residents into multistory, fee-based flats. The procedures under RAY for identifying beneficiaries, issuing allotment slips, and collecting deposits from those deemed eligible were hindered, however, by a lack of accurate and up-to-date land and population records—the same functional inefficiency that had precipitated the millennial shift to aesthetic rule. RAY guidelines recognized these constraints and echoed a broader, national call for Indian cities to adopt cutting edge information technology and geographical information systems for governance and land monitoring. This was an agenda inspired by the idea popularized by the Indian software mogul Nandan Nilekani that the "new India" of 8 percent annual growth, which Nilekani argued was made possible by India's successful IT and software industry, was being choked by the paperwork of "old India."[39]

The first step of slum-free city planning under RAY guidelines followed this logic and required that cities use aerial photography and geo-referenced ground surveys to form a comprehensive geographic information system of all slum households. The Delhi government signaled a broader return to calculative government when it passed the ambitious Geo-Spatial Data Infrastructure Act in 2011 aimed at establishing an integrated geo-spatial information system for maintaining all land, population, and property records. In 2011, the Survey of India, in coordination with the state Revenue Department, carried out a new comprehensive land survey of Delhi. In 2012, the newly formed Delhi Urban Shelter Improvement Board (DUSIB), tasked with the maintenance and delivery of low-income housing, completed its "fresh comprehensive socioeconomic survey of all the JJ [*jhuggī jhompḍī*] clusters in Delhi," its first order of business.[40] Since 2013, the Revenue Department has been carrying out door-to-door household surveys of all properties in Delhi to update tax and land registration records. Enrollment is ongoing in India's new—and the world's largest—biometric identification card system, *Aadhaar*, a national program chaired by Nandan Nilekani intended to track individual's welfare payments, financial records, and, maybe one day, land rights and tenure history. Calculative government in the form of high resolution land surveys and digital maps, e-governance, biometric ID cards, and an integrated, statewide IT infrastructure has returned with a vengeance. And what of the world-class aesthetic?

When I visited Shiv Camp a few months after the new socioeconomic survey had taken place, Motilal and Kishan told me that residents had enthusiastically paid the one hundred-rupee fee necessary to complete their applications to participate in the RAY flat scheme, which, if approved, would later require a 66,000-rupee down payment. While residents were hopeful that they would finally receive a secure flat, the settlement was given an allotment number they considered unlikely to bear fruit—"bad fate" according to Motilal, but something he suggested might change if their candidate from the upstart Aam Aadmi Party were to win the coming Legislative Assembly elections. Residents anxiously awaited their number, hopeful that these flats would finally fulfill the promise of the world-class city.

THE DEMAND FOR THE WORLD-CLASS CITY

By the beginning of 2013, no allotments had been made in Delhi for the planned 125,000 flats. Slum residents who had deposited the 66,000-rupee fee for their flats, along with those yet to receive allotment, had begun agitating, and the urban poor's broader demand for formal property had begun to reverberate more broadly through the city's political machinery. In the lead-up to the State Assembly elections, from which the chief minister is selected, the Aam Aadmi Party began to work with slum-based organizations in *nukkaḍ sabhās*, or street corner meetings, to consolidate the demand for better resettlement terms. The Aam Aadmi Party had formed in the aftermath of a national, cross-class anticorruption movement that had shaken the city and the national government the summer before. Its leader, Arvind Kejriwal, a long-time right to information activist, had gained visibility for his hunger strike alongside Anna Hazare, the Gandhian figurehead of the protests, and Kejriwal had begun attacking the Congress Party at the time for falsely promising flats to *jhuggi* dwellers. Twisting the language of inclusive growth, he stated in his "Letter to jhuggiwasi [*jhuggi* dwellers]": "If you honestly look, Delhi can't run for even one day without *jhuggi* dwellers."[41]

Ramping up her populist appeal, incumbent Chief Minister Sheila Dikshit responded by promising to build 300,000 low-cost houses for the urban poor, yet the Aam Aadmi Party claimed victory, winning enough seats—most by first-time candidates who were chosen by local constituents—to form a coalition government by capturing its largest vote share in slum areas, the first party to win Delhi's slum vote over the Congress Party.[42]

Soon after his inauguration as chief minister, Kejriwal stated: "People living in jhuggis live there out of compulsion, not out of interest [*jhuggī meṁ rahnevāle log mazbūrī se rahte haiṁ, shauk se nahīṁ*] and until an *improved alternative* is provided for them, they should be allowed to remain there." He soon after put forward a Swaraj Bill for Delhi, *swarāj* being the term Gandhi had used during the Indian independence movement to signal the will to cast off hierarchal forms of government employed by the British in favor of self-governance through community bodies.[43] The Delhi bill would have institutionalized *mohallā sabhās*, or neighborhood committees: small collectives of residents who would have decided on local civic matters by consensus and would have sent elected representatives to larger ward committees, where ward-level governance decisions were to take place and be coordinated with the state government. The mohalla sabhas promised deep political inclusion and would have devolved extensive power to the *aam aadmi*, or "the common man," by giving sabhas the power to authorize expenditure for development or welfare programs, a power previously centralized in the state government and Municipal Corporation and captured locally by property owners through Bhagidari (see chapter 2).[44]

However, only a month after his inauguration, Kejriwal suddenly resigned from office, citing obstinacy among the Congress-led national government, which is responsible for land administration in Delhi, and whose support was needed to modify the state acts necessary to implement the Swaraj Bill. At the time of writing, Delhi has a hung government and is under president's rule, yet the demand for formal property and an improved alternative continues to build among the urban poor and middle classes.

While it is premature to suggest that the rise of the Aam Aadmi Party marks a moment of the urban poor's political inclusion in the project of world-class city making, it is clear that its world-class aspirations will not be easily contained. Whereas the world-class aesthetic long operated as a vision of a sanitized, slum-free city imposed by elite property owners and an antipoor judiciary, in recent years it has emerged increasingly as the foundation and vehicle for a popular demand. The visual stigma of living in settlements with stagnant water, inadequate drainage, mud lanes, and locked or clogged toilet facilities that long served as the sign of slums' status as abject outsiders is now being reversed. Appropriated by the *jhuggi* dweller, the world-class aesthetic operates as a visual index of the failed promises of the world-class city: deficient infrastructure, irregular services, and shoddy housing stock on which the urban majority depends. Thus while urban government in Delhi, as in much of India, has shifted away from the more exclusionary form of aesthetic rule that characterized the millennial hype about the world-class city, the world-class aesthetic endures as a platform for new claims for a more inclusive city. Inclusive growth is certainly one response to this, but so is Aam Aadmi's success in Delhi. Whether through the market-based populism of the former, or the promised bureaucratic efficiency and political devolution of the latter, there is little doubt that the demand for more—for property *and* propriety—has emerged within the popular political imagination. As India's most recent Five Year Plan observes:

> India's 1.25 billion citizens have higher expectations about their future today, than they have ever had before. They have seen the economy grow much faster in the past 10 years than it did earlier, and deliver visible benefits to a large number of people. This has understandably raised the expectations of all sections, especially those who have benefited less. Our people are now much more aware of what is possible, and they will settle for no less.[45]

This refusal to settle is also a refusal to forget the promise of the world-class city. In that promise, however, lies a central tension over the meaning of inclusion and over the terms on which political claims are sayable and hearable. The urban poor's experimentations with dominant ways of seeing and saying suggest that they are prepared politically to force inclusion. The question is whether it will be through formal state channels, in which they long invested faith, or through other means. What I have called the gentrification of the local state (see chapter 2) means that considerable reform will be required to restore this faith. The return to calculative government is in part a promise of improved accountability and benefits delivery; Aam Aadmi's campaign to launch mohalla sabhas offers further hope. But inclusion in existing state programs will not be enough given the deep sacrifices the urban poor have already made in the name of the world-class city. For them, the promise of the world-class city includes the promise of propriety: of dignity and belonging and a "proper" place. It is Shambu's claim "We too should become big [Ham bhī baḍe hoṁ]," or Kishan's statement that "Delhi has improved so much. We also want improvement."

In the 2014 State Assembly Elections, from which members of parliament are chosen, the BJP—a party historically aligned with Delhi's traders and wealthier classes—won in Delhi for the first time in fifteen years, sweeping all seven seats. The BJP, led by prime ministerial candidate Narendra Modi, promised in its election manifesto that it would adopt a "low-cost housing policy that would ensure every family in Asia's third-largest economy has a home by 2022."[46] While the BJP, which cruised into power nationally in May 2014, has abandoned the specific details of slum-free city planning, its promise to further incentivize a private affordable housing market looks likely to deepen the market-based approach of inclusive growth.[47] Modi's home state of Gujarat, after all, has been the leader in affordable housing projects and has offered deeper land subsidies to private developers than any other state: his motto for investors was famously "no red tape, only red carpet."[48] As chief minister, his "Gujarat model" also deemed mass displacement and slum clearance, not to mention communal violence in the form of the 2002 anti-Muslim pogrom, to be economic development's necessary collateral damage.[49] With housing affordability and land access now perhaps the most pressing political issues in India, the question is how the urban poor's appropriation of the world-class aesthetic will translate into action. Will the world-class city follow the inclusion that elite property owners and developers have long clamored for, wherein the social worth of subjects is linked to their ability to pay for property? Or will the urban poor, now subjects of the discourse of the world-class city, bend its trajectory, forging a more inclusive vision of the city to come?

NOTES

INTRODUCTION

1. Žižek (2006, 268). "Planet of slums" is Mike Davis's (2006) phrase. See UN-HABITAT's mission statement for the estimation of the "worldwide slum population" and the global challenge to contain this population: www.unhabitat.org/content.asp?typeid=19&catid=10&cid=928.
2. According to the United Nations (2014), the Delhi urban agglomeration has twenty-five million people, second in the world after Tokyo, a position it is projected to hold at least through 2030, when its population will grow to thirty-six million.
3. Combined demolitions reported by the DDA and Slum and Jhuggi Jhompdi Wing of the Municipal Corporation from 1997–2007 lead to the conservative estimate of 710,000 displaced residents. *The City Development Plan of Delhi*, prepared by private consultants, on the other hand, estimates that 1.8 million residents were displaced in 1997–2001 alone. Government records suggest at least a tripling in the pre-2000 demolition pace (Dupont 2008). The 2011 Census also shows a surprising decrease in the rate of population growth in Delhi over previous decades, leading to 1.7 million fewer residents than had been projected. The director of census operations for the National Capital Territory "attributed the fall to the removal of slum settlements." As *The Times of India* (Srivastava 2011) reported, "of the several lakh [1 lakh = 100,000] people displaced as a result of these demolitions, only 32,000 families, or 1.5 lakh people, have been officially relocated in rehabilitation colonies. This leaves lakhs of people unaccounted for. They may have settled in slums elsewhere or may have left the city." Shopping mall development trends are discussed in Taneja (2007).
4. See *The Hindu*, "SC Stays Construction in Ridge Area in Vasant Kunj," May 1, 2006, for the phrasing in the courtroom and *T. N. Godavarman Thirumulpad v. Union of India and Ors.* ((2006)10 SCC 490), paragraph 8, for the logic supplied in the final judgment.
5. *Jagdish & Ors. v. DDA*, CWP 5007/2002 (Delhi High Court).
6. Interview with A. K. Jain, May 26, 2005.
7. Field note entry, January 15, 2007.
8. According to Timothy Mitchell (2002, 9), "the map signifies the massive production of knowledge, the accuracy of calculation, and the entire politics based upon a comprehensive knowledge of population and territory."
9. Foucault (2007). The phrase "do as they ought" comes from Scott (1995, 202), citing Jeremy Bentham, the great designer of disciplinary and security mechanisms. See Gordon (1991) for the most common Anglophone interpretation of governmentality as "the conduct of conduct."
10. Foucault (2007, 104). By "modern and contemporary governmentality," Foucault meant a form of biopolitical government oriented toward the vitality of the population, premised on a calculative techne, and differentiated from earlier forms of pastoral power.

11. Rose (1999, 221). "In Foucault's account, government is inevitably a technical matter. Practices of government rely on an array of more or less formalised and more or less specialised technical devices from car seat-belts and driving codes to dietary regimes; and from economic instruments to psychotherapy" (Barry 2001, 5).
12. Scott (1998, 11, 124). Geographer Denis Cosgrove (2004, 54) similarly says, "urban legibility becomes the overarching goal of city mapping, to be achieved through precisely measured survey using carefully calibrated instruments." See Sundaram (2009) for the history of how a similar technicity was presumed to underpin postcolonial city planning in India.
13. Joyce (2003, 37), who premises his argument on Edney (1997).
14. Hacking (1990, 112). Rabinow (1989, 15), drawing on Foucault's (2007) same lectures, finds that urban planning emerged as a science only with "a more precise and powerful analysis of milieu." Commenting on Foucault's analysis of space, he (Rabinow 1982) notes that planning has "the need for a precise knowledge of the state of such matters as geology, geography, demography, the market, the dispositions and possibilities of the inhabitants' of trades, the conditions of hygiene, dangers of infection from abroad, and so on."
15. See Hull (2008) for a lucid account of a similar shortage of calculative rigor in land records and plans in Islamabad and Roy (2004) for an account of the "unmapping" of Calcutta. Dupont (2008) and Bhan (2013) detail the lack of aggregate state records on slum demolitions in Delhi and the illegibility, or at least the need for considerable interpretive finesse to make sense of records that do exist.
16. As Foucault (2007, 348) remarks in his concluding lecture on modern and contemporary governmentality, "the knowledge involved [in this governmentality] must be scientific in its procedures. Second, this scientific knowledge is absolutely indispensable for good government. A government that did not take into account this kind of analysis . . . would be bound to fail."
17. As Cohn (1996, 7) writes, "what is observed and reported" in this process "is mediated by particular socio-political contexts as well as historically specific aesthetic principles." In the context of East India Company and subsequently British rule, these were distinctly orientalist principles that objectified and often ossified dynamic native cultural practices, appearances, styles of dress, and language. For more on observational and travel practices in the consolidation of imperial projects, see Gregory (1994), Said (1978), and Stoler (1995).
18. Rancière (2009).
19. The history of city planning in Delhi shows a persistent anxiety about the population slipping out of state control without the accuracy and "scientificity" (Foucault 2007, 350) thought necessary to rationally administer a city. Legg (2006) discusses the pursuit of statistical and cartographic command that influenced the formation of the DDA in the wake of Indian independence. By the mid-1980s, a decade after careful documentary oversight during the Emergency (1975–1977) had facilitated a disciplinary regime that linked resettlement housing for displaced *jhuggi* dwellers to forced sterilization, the DDA commissioned its first ever external institutional review. The report, completed by Tata Consultancy Services, found that DDA data are generally typified by what it called a "lack of accuracy." Related specifically to knowledge of land, the report found information inadequacies in areas including the inventory of the land with the DDA, the status of land development thereupon, and the extent of land misuses, calling for a comprehensive redevelopment of the DDA's information management system (Tata Consultancy Services 1986, 4.6).
20. Simone (2006, 258, 260).
21. Chakrabarty (2000, 8) describes colonial constructions of modernity compellingly as "somebody's way of saying 'not yet' to someone else." See Gupta (1998) for a discussion

of how modernist development projects during Congress Party rule through the first forty-five years of independence were framed in terms of overcoming India's historical lag.
22. The Hindi press, more than the English press, regularly published stories in the 2000s linking Delhi's future appearance to Paris's. This is perhaps because Chief Minister Sheila Dikshit was reported to have said in a number of public speeches that "*Dillī ko Paris banegā.*" At the tail end of Dixit's rule, this same saying started to be used against her. See Gyan Varma, "Dikshit Turned Delhi into a Slum, Not Paris as Promised: Interview with Delhi President, BJP," *Business Standard*, February 23, 2013.
23. See Jervis-Read (2010) for a discussion of how those resettled during the Emergency period understood, and continue to understand, the phrase "making Delhi like Paris" to be part of the modernist impulse to beautify Delhi and remove the poor. She also traces this phrase to Jagmohan, vice-chairman of the Delhi Development Authority during the Emergency, when Indira Gandhi suspended civil liberties and initiated forced urban beautification and clean-up campaigns that would lead to the largest number of *basti* demolitions before the 2000s.
24. Baviskar (2010).
25. Sundaram (2009, 53–54) cites a 1958 Town Planning Organization report that states, "if India is to progress, the living conditions of slum dwellers must be improved." He also notes the prominent view that informed Delhi's first master plan that the problem of the slum was one of rural practices, such as animal rearing, persisting in the city.
26. This is conveyed in the Delhi Master Plan, as I describe in chapter 1: whereas the original 1962 Master Plan and the 1991 revision had included targets for inclusive planning that were intended to integrate lower-income areas into more affluent spaces to achieve a class mix, the 2007 revision deleted such targets. Deshpande (2003) has neatly described this as a change in the representation of the nation as "imagined economy" away from patriotic producer to consumer citizen.
27. FDI inflow into real estate jumped from 467 million to 2.179 billion dollars from fiscal year 2007 to 2008. "India FDI Fact Sheet," Department of Industrial Policy and Promotion, Ministry of Commerce and Industry, January 2010. For a discussion of land banks and speculative property development in Bangalore, see Goldman (2011), and in India's Special Economic Zones, see Levien (2011).
28. Budget documents show that the Delhi government diverted resources for health care and Dalit welfare into bridge building, road widening, and beautification in the three years leading up to the 2010 Commonwealth Games. Internal memos record how state officials justified this reallocation by noting the broad benefit all members of the public would receive, including Dalits, through Delhi's accelerated progress toward world-class city status. See "Delhi Govt Diverted SC Funds for CWG: Document," Rediff News, August 2, 2010, http://news.rediff.com/report/2010/aug/03/delhi-govt-diverted-scs-funds-for-cwg-document.htm.
29. See Ramesh (2008).
30. *New Delhi Pvt. Ltd.*, 2006, Hazards Centre Productions, 64 minutes.
31. Specifically, DDA field officers are required to monitor unauthorized uses of public land and report such uses to the Revenue Department for verification, while "keep[ing] a record of all such reports in the form of a register" (DDA 1987, 1). Officers in the Revenue Department, a state-level agency, are required to simultaneously maintain estate-wise registers that include the nature and extent of the encroachment, the existing land use, the cadastral number, the number of occupants of the land, and the approximate date of encroachment. This assessment register, cross-tabulated with the DDA register, is supposed to be an up-to-date index of all encroachments in Delhi, and it forms the calculative basis for governing public land encroachments according to the Delhi Development Act, 1957.

32. Das (2007). Also see Tarlo (2003, 10), who describes how "people wishing to negotiate with the state not only learn [the language of documents] but also learn to reproduce it through" the acts of accumulating, showing, interpreting, and mobilizing those documents toward their own ends, and Chatterjee (2011, 147), whose "politics of the governed," or the paralegal arrangements that modify and rearrange the law to deliver government services to those otherwise outside the law, often rely on similar documentary processes.
33. Das (2007, 177) notes the regularity with which "the signature of the state can detach itself from its origin and be grafted onto other structures and chains of signification."
34. Benjamin (2008) describes the more patronage-based work of "vote banks," whereas Das (2011) attends more to the inseparability of state and society.
35. "Rule by records" is a term used both by Smith (1985) and Hull (2008) to describe paper-mediated forms of government in different South Asian historical settings. For Smith, records-based rule put in place procedures different from rule by reports, whereas Hull's study emphasizes the material specificities of modern bureaucracies and the different political possibilities that arise within them. I employ the term here more broadly to refer to a calculative form of government in which state records and calculative procedures are assumed and expected to accurately represent or correspond to the population and territory they would govern, regardless of whether or not they actually correspond to that reality. Hull (2012, 246) has more recently called this "a regime of presumptive written truth." What I am calling "rule by aesthetics" operates on a different epistemological premise: dispensing with the presumption of correspondence, or written truth, it relies on aesthetic codes and visual criteria to assess truthfulness. See Appadurai (2002) and Ghertner (2010) for accounts of how activists in Mumbai and Delhi, respectively, were able to self-enumerate and turn the calculative instruments of the state toward their own ends, and Hull (2008) for an example of the more individualized manipulation of state records to facilitate land occupation in Islamabad. Also see McQuarrie, Fernandes, and Shepard (2013) for an example of settlers using the Right to Information Act and judicial petitions to intervene in a developer's acquisition of their land. See Raman (2012) for a discussion of how the low-level state scribes, or *kacceri*, in early colonial South India subverted and compromised the intentions of colonial policy and reform, a process that occurred more broadly in late colonial and postcolonial India (Kaviraj 1984, Yang 1989).
36. For example, in its landmark decision in *Olga Tellis v. Bombay Municipal Corporation* pertaining to the rights of pavement dwellers in 1985, the Supreme Court, after affirming that "the right to livelihood is an important facet of the right to life," argued that the "eviction of the (pavement dwellers) will lead to deprivation of their livelihood and consequently to the deprivation of life." In doing so, the court argued that the state's failure to build the required quantity of low-income housing compelled pavement and slum dwellers to squat on unused public land. In *Chameli Singh v. State of UP* ((1996) 2 SCC 549), the Supreme Court further stated, "right to shelter when used as an essential requisite to the right to live should be deemed to have been guaranteed as a fundamental right." See Ramanathan (2006) for a further discussion of the legal protections enjoyed by squatters through the 1990s. I discuss the history of the low-income housing entitlements enshrined in the Delhi Master Plan in chapter 1.
37. Chakrabarti (2008).
38. "C'wealth Games Top Priority of Govt.," *The Hindu*, February 6, 2008.
39. *Pitampura Sudhar Samiti v. Government of India*, CWP 4215/1995, order dated May 26, 1997. See Ghertner (2010) for additional examples.
40. *Okhla Factory Owners' Association v. GNCTD* (108 (2002) DLT 517), paragraph 22.
41. Affidavit filed by Satish Kumar, under secretary, Ministry of Urban Development & Poverty Alleviation (Delhi High Court), CWP 2253/2001.

42. *Resident Welfare Association v. DDA and Ors.* (Delhi High Court), CWP 6324/2003, order dated August 29, 2007.
43. Scott (1998, 45).
44. Latour (1987).
45. See Municipal Corporation of Delhi affidavit filed in 2006 in *Kalyan Sansthan v. GNCTD* (Delhi High Court), CWP 4582/2003.
46. Biswas (2006). In fact, the Municipal Corporation confronted this dilemma after the Supreme Court had ordered it to close and seal all commercial establishments operating in residential zones of the city in late 2005. This led to the sealing of thousands of businesses with tens of thousands more threatened, citywide protests by traders leading to the death of three young men, the demolition or partial demolition of hundreds of private residences not conforming to building codes as well as a shopping mall under construction in south Delhi, and a political nightmare for the ruling Congress Party. In 2006, the Lower House (Lok Sabha) of the Indian Parliament passed a legislative act postponing all demolitions and sealing drives in Delhi for one year. While this act also included slums, the courts did not acknowledge their protected status and continued with slum clearance apace. The DDA finally modified the Master Plan ex post facto to regularize Delhi's commercial land-use violations in 2007.
47. I use the language of "rule" to point to the specific epistemological underpinnings of governmental programs. I do so following one of Foucault's (2001, 33–34) strongest methodological recommendations that power be studied through an ascending analysis, which he argues requires attention to "the actual instruments that form and accumulate knowledge, the observational methods, the recording techniques, the investigative research procedures, the verification mechanisms." This focus on the micropractices of knowledge formation demands attention to the diverse forms in which knowledge is consolidated and used to craft grids of intelligibility: how governmental programs use carefully selected metrics to assess and assign value and meaning to their targets. This means that the knowledge practices at play in any moment not only establish the technical requirements of government, but also form the epistemological basis on which information is gathered, knowledge assembled, and "truths" verified so as to guide a population's interests.
48. Rancière (2004, 13).
49. Eagleton (1990, 75).
50. Rancière (2004, 12–13).
51. I use the language of "rule" rather than hegemony because I find it more open to the possibility of disagreement among those governable subjects whose conduct is otherwise conducted toward what Foucault (2007) calls the "convenient ends" of government. That is, I find it open to acts that appear compliant but that fall short of consent. Rancière (1998) provides important insight into this terrain in exploring the aesthetic constraints of translating oppositional positions into enunciable and visible forms of disagreement. In other words, one can comply while disagreeing with the compliant act, but to engage in a politics of disagreement requires a redistribution of the sensible, a reconfiguration of the aesthetic field so that acts of disagreement are made visible and heard as more than mere noise. While notions of hegemony inspired by Antonio Gramsci (1971) are open to similar interpretations of consent as a terrain consisting of acts that partake in *and* try to rework dominant ideology, I prefer "rule" so as to avoid the tendency to equate conformance with ideology with ideational consent.
52. See Mechoulan (2004) for this argument. This awkwardness appears in the very definition of the distribution of the sensible in Rockhill's translation, where the "something in common"—the sharing that it offers—appears, in English, as a secondary definition of, rather than as a component internal to, *le partage*/distribution.
53. Rancière (2004, 12); emphasis added.

54. *Olga Tellis v. Bombay Municipal Corporation* ((1985) 3 SCC 545).
55. It did so while also invoking Human Rights law: "Article 25(1) of the Universal Declaration of Human Rights declares that everyone has the right to a standard of living adequate for the health and well-being of himself and his family; it includes food, clothing, housing, medical care and necessary social services." *Ahmedabad Municipal Corporation, Appellant v. Nawab Khan Gulab Khan and Others* (1997).
56. Rancière (2004, 12) introduces his approach to the politics of aesthetics using the language of citizenship: taking up Aristotle's definition of the citizen as someone who takes part in the act of governing, he proposes that another distribution precedes this act of partaking in government, "the distribution that determines those who have a part in the community of citizens" and the terms on which those with no part must cultivate the ability to be recognized as citizens. As I describe in detail in chapter 4, the judiciary explicitly cast out *jhuggi* dwellers from the community of citizens, contrasting them with "legitimate" citizens in millennial Delhi.
57. Dalit is a term for those who have suffered the stigma of untouchability and means "ground down" in Marathi and Hindi. It gained prominence in the 1970s as a term meant to assert a national identity and consolidate a political community defined by historical vulnerability, as distinct from the diverse regional caste names and governmental categorizations that had been applied to former untouchables before (Rao 2009, xiii).
58. Special Leave Petition filed in the Supreme Court "against the interlocutory order passed by the Division Bench of the High Court of Judicature at Delhi dated 05.04.2006 in WP(C) No. 3419 of 1999." The senior advocate in this case, Prashant Bhushan, is a prominent human rights and public interest lawyer who became well known for his probono work to defend settlements. Many of his antidisplacement petitions varied only in the geographical description of the particular settlements they sought to defend. Bhushan has since become a prominent leader in the Aam Aadmi Party (AAP), a party formed in 2012 and that swept into power in the Delhi Legistlative Assembly elections in 2013 on the back of its anticorruption campaign. The AAP's advocacy of a "propoor" slum policy signaled a shift in the ethos of government in the aftermath of Delhi's millennial moment, the implications of which I explore in the conclusion.
59. *Hem Raj v. Commissioner of Police* (Supreme Court of India), CWP 3419/1999. As Datta (2012, 28) notes in her study of a settlement in south Delhi, in the "absence of fundamental rights to shelter, it was harder for squatters to articulate any discourse of rights to housing from the state. Already marginalized within normative legal spaces, simple recourse to law (through courts) was not possible."
60. Agamben (1998).
61. See Davis (2006, 201).
62. Auyero and Swistun (2009, 134).
63. Wacquant (2008, 18).
64. Appadurai (2002), Chatterjee (2004), and Weinstein (2009) are examples, albeit from different perspectives, of studies of the organizational capacities of the urban poor in India that elevate politics as collective resistance. See McQuarrie, Fernandes, and Shepard (2013) for a vivid account of the foreclosure of documentary and judicial channels of redress for residents of Golibar slum in Mumbai, despite collective protests that gained national visibility and clear evidence of fraudulent misdealing by the developer that acquired the Golibar land. For discussions of the generalizability of gentrification as a framework for explaining development-induced displacement, see Lees (2012) and Smith (2002). For my critique of such template models of reading "gentrification" as a universal, generalized phenomenon employable across planning, property, and political contexts, see Ghertner (2014).

65. Chatterjee's (2011, 150) recent reflection on the trappings of the early Subaltern Studies project makes a similar case: "While insurgency is undoubtedly a crucial and revealing moment in subaltern history, it is nonetheless an extraordinary moment which, while throwing light on the daily life of ordinary exisence, cannot ever fully explain it."
66. The conflict between commercial and residential interests that played out through Delhi's 2006 "sealing drive," in which the Supreme Court ordered the Municipal Corporation to close and seal more than 50,000 shops operating in residential zones, represents one such tension within the world-class city-making project (see Mehra 2009). Also see Taneja's (2008) discussion of conflict between the development of a public golf course and a heritage site in Delhi, both of which were identifiably world-class monuments. The link between Delhi and Paris is often invoked due to both cities' rich and abundant architectural heritage, the promise being that Delhi can leverage its heritage to draw in tourists.

CHAPTER 1

1. Presentation by A. K. Jain at the "East Delhi Workshop on Development and the Delhi Master Plan 2021," April 12, 2005.
2. Quotation by A. K. Walia from "We Want to Make Delhi a World-Class City," Project Monitor, New Delhi, March 14, 2005, www.projectsmonitor.com/detailnews.asp?newsid=8876.
3. The former headline was published in the New Delhi issue of the *Hindustan Times* on July 16, 2006. The latter headline was published in the New Delhi issue of *The Hindu* on November 19, 2007.
4. Chatterjee (2004, 143).
5. DDA (1997).
6. This process of fixing capital in property is commonly called, in India and globally, "land monetization" and is the central pillar of urban development policy and infrastructure planning in contemporary India as in many emerging market contexts. It is the key feature of what Goldman (2011) calls "speculative urbanism." See A. K. Jain (2003) for a further discussion of land underutilization and how planners understand the need to align land policy with the economic reform agenda.
7. See Zaloom (2009) for a discussion of bond yield curves as an affective device for organizing market behavior.
8. Lakoff (2008, 401) notes how scenario-based exercises based on biological threats "generate an affect of urgency in the absence of the event itself." See Miyazaki (2006) and Zaloom (2006) for further studies of how affect, hope, and image saturate futures markets and construct value in the present.
9. For an insightful discussion of how modes of social scientific expertise enter into the projection and constitution of markets, while simultaneously obscuring their origins, see Born (2007).
10. Lahiri (2011).
11. See *Delhi Master Plan 1962* (DDA 1962) and *Delhi Master Plan 2001* (DDA 1990), which define low-income classes in terms of the nationally defined income groups "Economically Weaker Sections" and "Lower Income Group."
12. See Kamath and Baindur (2009) and Mahadevia (2003) for discussions of the popularization among Indian administrators of the importance of private investment in financing infrastructure development in India. Much of the policy agenda pertaining to land market reform relates to the aim of the World Bank (2005) and other international financial institutions (e.g., the Asian Development Bank) of making Indian cities more creditworthy ("bankable") so as to increase the flow of private sector lending into municipal government and to align India's historically more closely guarded debtscape with financial markets elsewhere. The Planning Commission's Committee on Infrastructure Financing (Planning Commission of India 2007,

10), for example, states: "Shortage of risk capital in the domestic market is also grounds for seeking larger FDI [foreign direct investment] into infrastructure, which would not only narrow the risk capital gap, but also usher in requisite skills to implement and monitor projects in line with global best practices." McKinsey & Company's (2010) report on urban financing in India states that land monetization must be a primary funding mechanism if India is to avoid prolonged urban crisis. Land monetization, besides attracting capital, also offers to increase municipal governments' tax base (Lall 2003), in some cases by more than 50 percent (World Bank, 2005, 43), allowing them to better leverage private sector money.

13. World Bank (2007, 11), and GNCTD (2004) for the population residing in unplanned neighborhoods in Delhi.
14. World Bank (2007, 3).
15. World Bank (2005, 3, 61).
16. McKinsey & Company (2001, 1, 44).
17. "Putting a Roof Over India: An Interview with the Country's Biggest Developer," *The McKinsey Quarterly*, November 2007. DLF, originally named Delhi Lease and Finance, had purchased large tracts of land in Delhi in the wake of Indian independence, turning some into elite residential colonies to meet growing housing demand and holding others for future use. The principles of socialized land introduced into the first master plan, some argue, were motivated by the speculative practices and growing power of DLF in land development in Delhi, and DLF's return as the largest developer in Delhi today marks nothing less than the reversal of early efforts to curb speculative land practices.
18. International consultants had advocated this perspective since the late 1990s. As the World Bank's (2007, 2) *India 2025* report argued, reflecting this position: "A rapid rise in the Foreign Direct Investment (FDI) will be needed to finance the domestic saving-investment gap. The target is to increase this three times from the current level."
19. Presentation by A. K. Jain at the "East Delhi Workshop on Development and the Delhi Master Plan 2021," April 12, 2005.
20. McKinsey & Company (2010, 70). The *World Development Report 2009*, the first such report to highlight economic geography and urban development, made the same case on a global scale: "Successful cities have relaxed zoning laws to allow higher-value users to bid for the valuable land—and have adopted land use regulations to adapt to their changing roles over time" (Word Bank 2009).
21. This process began in 1998, when the central government repealed the Urban Land Ceiling Act, which had restricted investors' ability to amass large banks of unused land. Also in 1998, the Land Acquisition Act was modified, which drastically reduced the requirements for proof of public good in the exercise of eminent domain, opening the door for the state to acquire land that could be flipped and sold for commercial use.
22. DDA (2007, 2).
23. See Searle (2014) for an ethnographic account of the practices of commensuration necessary for Indian developers and international real estate firms to set the terms for this speculative framing of Indian land's market potential and the different interests such framing serves for these groups.
24. Tsing (2005, 57).
25. Akerlof and Shiller (2009, 55).
26. *Economic Survey of India, 2008–2009*, Ministry of Finance, Government of India.
27. Shukla (2007, 5).
28. Cited in Fernandes (2009, 224).
29. NCAER (2005).
30. McKinsey & Company (2007, 51).
31. Ibid., 54.

32. Ibid., 52.
33. Ibid., 56–57.
34. Searle (2008). Referring to the McKinsey study, the article reports: "As the seismic wave of income growth rolls across Indian society, the character of consumption will change dramatically over the next 20 years." Diana Farrel and Eric Beinhocker, "Next Big Spenders: India's Middle Class," *BusinessWeek*, May 19, 2007.
35. Ila Patnaik and Ajay Shah, "India in the Great Recession," *The Financial Express*, April 15, 2009.
36. Jones Lang and LaSalle, "Strengthening India's Capital Market—Rising Foreign Direct Investment in Real Estate," *Economic Insight*, May 2007.
37. Rajesh Abraham, "DLF IPO to Make India a Property-Driven Stock Market," *The Hindu Businessline*, April 26, 2006. The real estate index of the Bombay Stock Exchange, for example, doubled in just ten months after the government liberalized FDI norms in 2005. Jones Lang LaSalle, "The New Investment Mantra—Understanding Risk and Returns in the Indian Real Estate Sector," April 2006, page 6.
38. "DLF Limited, Speech by the Chairman K. P. Singh at the 42nd General Meeting," printed in the *Hindustan Times*, October 1, 2007.
39. Jones Lang LaSalle press release, Mumbai, April 22, 2008, www.jllm.co.in/India/en-gb/Pages/NewsDetail.aspx?ItemID=7307.
40. "Interview with Anuj Puri," *Bloomberg UK*, air date November 6, 2008, www.jllm.co.in/India/EN-GB/Pages/BloombergInterview.aspx. Also see the report by Merrill Lynch, which in 2006 estimated that "the Indian realty sector will grow from $12 billion in 2005 to $90 billion by 2015," www.terrapinn.com/2007/reiwin/on.
41. The speculative fury in real estate has drawn in a host of new players, such as India's most successful IT firm Infosys, which began to invest its operational profits not in workforce training or new computing campuses, but rather in land banks, which it deemed to be a higher profit avenue than IT (Goldman 2011).
42. Jones Lang LaSalle Meghraj 2007. "The Geography of Opportunity: The 'India 50'," World Winning Cities Series.
43. *Oxford English Dictionary*, Second Edition, 1989.
44. National Commission for Scheduled Castes and Scheduled Tribes, Fourth Report 1996–97 & 1997–98, Volume 1, www.indiastat.com/economy/8/incidenceofpoverty/221/stats.aspx and Lok Sabha Unstarred Question No. 2090, March 16, 2005.
45. Patnaik (2008).
46. Patnaik (2007, 139).
47. Patnaik (2008). See Visvanathan and Meenakshi (2003) as well as Patnaik (2007, 148) for a discussion of why the National Institute of Nutrition considers calorie intake an accurate proxy of overall nutritional status in India.
48. Patnaik (2008) finds the rural and urban poverty lines to be 710 and 840 real rupees in the year 2000, respectively. This also explains why her estimate of overall poverty is lower than mine. I did not receive a reply from her after requesting information on how she derived these numbers.
49. The World Bank's most recent economic estimates show a poverty rate of 42 percent for India in 2005. This is based on the purchasing power adjustment of its global $1.25/day poverty line equaling 21.6 rupees in urban areas and 14.3 rupees in rural areas, both higher than the Planning Commission's estimate (Chen and Ravallian 2010, World Bank 2008). The Bank thus estimates that 455 million people are poor in India, an increase in the number of poor since the 1980s. Field-based studies by the World Bank go further, concluding from long-term case studies that the official poverty line is well below what is necessary to escape poverty (Narayan, Sen, and Hull 2009).

50. While some economists hypothesize that declining calorie intake does not imply a decline in overall nutrition (Deaton and Dreze 2009), the fact remains that the Planning Commission claims to uphold the minimum calorie norms it set in 1973.
51. "More Indians in Extreme Poverty," *BBC News*, August 21, 2009, http://news.bbc.co.uk/go/pr/fr/-/1/hi/world/south_asia/8214061.stm.
52. The Planning Commission assumes, among other things, that people today spend their money on the exact same basket of goods as in 1974, thus making the price adjustment from the 1974 poverty line a reasonable estimate for today. The direct observation method assumes that the National Sample Survey captures all consumption expenditure in surveyed households. In his presidential address at the American Economic Association, Angus Deaton (2010), commenting on the great variation in estimates of global poverty caused by slight changes in estimates of purchasing power, noted that "global trends are relatively secure" only if "we are prepared to ignore the fact that each new set of estimates makes the world look like a very different place."
53. For evidence of the intensely political nature of debates over technicalities like "reporting period" and "survey nonresponse" in poverty studies, see Deaton and Kozel (2005).
54. I follow Hull's (2003) definition and use of "graphic artifacts."
55. Cited in Harriss (2009, 205).
56. Harriss (2009, 210).
57. Barthes (1972, 143).
58. Planning Commission of India (2003, 2); emphasis added.
59. Ibid., 3.
60. "There is no natural or inevitable link between the signifier and the signified" (Culler, 1976, cited in Hall 1997, 31); rather, this link is established through cultural codes or learned conventions of representation. A red traffic light triggers in our heads the signified "stop" only because we have internalized a code tying the two together. In the case of poverty statistics, nutritional data are tied to the signified, "the number of people spending less than 539 rupees a month has decreased," through conventions for representing and reading charts.
61. Barthes (1972, 114) makes it clear that this linguistic sign is not limited to words or text: "The semiologist is entitled to treat in the same way writing and pictures: what he [*sic*] retains from them is the fact that they are both *signs*, that they both reach the threshold of myth endowed with the same signifying function, that they constitute, one just as much as the other, a language-object."
62. Virmani (2006, 8); emphasis in original.
63. Semiotic approaches acknowledge the ways numbers operate beyond single representational systems, becoming signs defined relationally in terms of their objects and interpretants. See, for example, Rotman (1987) and Verran (2010).
64. Barthes (1972, 116).
65. While the absolute poor are measured in terms of consumption (what people spend), and McKinsey's category of the deprived is based on income, these measures can be compared if we assume that those living in extreme poverty (i.e., those unable to meet daily calorie intake norms) spend most of their earned income within the sample period of thirty days on which the National Sample Survey is based: why would someone save money if they are hungry? The deprived represent households that earn 90,000 rupees per year, equal to a per capita monthly income of approximately 1,500 rupees. This figure is nearly triple the official poverty line in rural (356 rupees) and urban areas (539 rupees) in 2005, and it is more than 50 percent greater than the poverty lines I derived using NSS tables. This suggests that a 50 percent increase in earnings would leave most Indians locked in McKinsey's deprived income group, with nowhere near the consumptive power of the middle class.
66. On declining rates of per capita food absorption in India, see Patnaik (2007, 124–125).

67. Barthes (1972, 129). All charts and figures obviously have a graphic/aesthetic function. My point is not to create a false division between different types of signifiers, but to clarify Barthes's point that the secondary signification of myth operates not through reference to already agreed upon meanings (as in language), but rather via cultural codes that supply us with the mythic concept to which the signifier/picture can be associated by us the reader.
68. Buckley, Singh, and Kalarickal (2007, 2).
69. According to the philosopher J. L. Austin, the term "performative" indicates statements that "do something": "In saying what I do, I actually perform the action" (Austin 1970, 235) (e.g., a judge uttering "guilty" in a courtroom). In the social scientific study of markets, models or figures are performative "if practices informed by the model altered economic processes towards conformity with it" (MacKenzie 2007, 67). In this sense, I broadly see McKinsey's figures as performative instruments that induce changes in investor practice and government policy towards conformity with the growth story.
70. Watts (1983).
71. Jason Overdorf, "The Boom from the Bottom," *Newsweek*, February 23, 2009.
72. Searle (2008, 55).
73. This differs from Lakoff's (2008) insightful discussion of rationalities of preparedness in castrophe planning, where public officials learn to define and take responsible action in the face of possible yet necessarily uncertain futures. As I argue in greater detail in chapter 6, preparedness in the context of a prophetically defined world-class future means aligning one's inner self and present disposition with the horizons of the future-oriented city.
74. Roy (2007, 155–156).
75. Calculation by author, using the direct observation method described in Patnaik (2008) and table 3u of NSS report number 513. *The New York Times* also reports that "42.2 percent of children under 5 are stunted, or too short for their age, and 26 percent are underweight" in Delhi. See Somini Sengupta, "As India Grows, Child Hunger Persists," *The New York Times*, March 13, 2009. In contrast, the Planning Commission claims that less than 15 percent of Delhi is poor.
76. See Khan and Sharma (2012) for the estimation of real estate purchase and Subramaniam's (2011) insightful investigative account of real estate sales in the National Capital region.
77. See Subramaniam (2011) for an excellent commentary on mechanisms of soliciting interest in and selling yet-to-be-built flats in the Delhi National Capital Region. According to Searle (2014, 73), the practice of preselling arose due to a historic shortage before the early 2000s of formal finance for land purchase or construction; presales generated the cash to complete construction or expand the scale of development operations. Developers' and landowners' ability to make profit before beginning construction, reinforced by a strong agrarian tradition that emphasizes the social value of land, has shaped Indian real estate into an industry that views land as the principal source of real estate value, and construction as an almost ancillary mechanism for extracting profit from land.
78. These numbers are from the 2011 Indian Census for Gurgaon, reported in Sukhbir Siwach, "1 in 5 City Properties Lying Vacant," *The Times of India*, March 20, 2012.
79. See the Ministry of Housing and Urban Poverty Alleviation's (2007) 11th Five Year Plan report on urban housing shortage and "Over 9 Lakh Empty Houses in Delhi NCR: Report," http://post.jagran.com/over-9-lakh-houses-empty-in-delhi-ncr-report-1372943530, on vacancies. The Delhi Master Plan 2021 estimates a 800,000-unit housing shortfall, 88 percent of which is for the Economically Weaker Sections (EWS) (DDA 2007).
80. Cronon (1991, 32).
81. 2009 Annual Report, Alpine Real Estate Funds, page 10, www.alpinefunds.com/default.asp?P=442562. While Delhi saw a mild drop in real estate prices at the peak of the global recession (7 percent across all zones from 2008 to 2009), prices remained more

than 20 percent above their 2007 levels in 2010. National Housing Bank Residex, Delhi, http://nhb.org.in/Residex/delhires.php.

82. For Marx, the social power of property is a negative power to make land available for the capitalist's use, or not, and to claim a portion of surplus value in return for this use. In *Capital, Volume 3*, Marx (1981 [1894]) distinguishes between differential and absolute rents, the former based on differentials in the productivity of land (e.g., agricultural fertility, depth of mineral deposits), defined in terms of a particular use, and the later on the power of landlords to set monopoly prices under conditions of relative scarcity (e.g., the premium price of land in Manhattan or south Delhi). Whereas in contexts where differential rent predominates it is use that determines the level of rent the landlord is rewarded, with absolute rent, it is rent (set by monopoly powers) that determines use (e.g., when a bank and not a bookstore can afford rent in a given building). Harvey (2009 [1973], 189–190) shows how absolute rent predominates in contemporary capitalist cities, creating conditions in which speculation and artificial scarcity determine the allocation of land uses.

83. I have intentionally defied conventions for depicting significant figures here to show the precision (number of decimal places) necessary for the rich categories to be significant (nonzero). Deciles, a standard way of showing income distribution, would divide the population into ten evenly distributed income groups. If we were to evenly redistribute NCAER data into eight categories (each group representing 12.5 percent of the population) according to income, all four groups of the rich plus the strivers and seekers would be aggregated into a single, upper-income class through 2005, while the deprived would be disaggregated into at least five categories.

CHAPTER 2

1. In an interview with Surendra Kumar, superintendent of the Chief Minister's Office who oversaw the daily operations of the Bhagidari Cell, he said, "before Bhagidari [which began in 2000], less than 5 percent of the population knew what 'RWA' stood for." Interview date: October 9, 2007.
2. For an indicative example of the former position, see Fernandes (2006), and of the latter, see Swyngedouw (2005).
3. For additional perspectives on the differentiated spaces of the Indian state that I do not directly discuss in the following pages, see Chandra (2004), Corbridge et al. (2005), Frankel (1978), and Rudolph and Rudolph (1987).
4. Kaviraj (1991).
5. Saberwal (1996, 150). This divide has a linguistic basis as well, which became a key way in which class and caste differences were reinforced within the structure of the state. The state apparatus inherited from the British was one wherein English was established as the language of administration, even though most state-society (and many state-state) interactions took place in vernacular languages. This "structural bilingualism," as Prasad (2008) calls it, not only created openings for reinterpretation and mis-translation between points of high command and low-level implementation, but also contributed to the uneasy relationship between Indian nationalism, dominated by English, and various regional nationalisms, a tension that continues to play out in postcolonial India over the deferred promise of creating linguistic states.
6. See Witsoe (2011, 75) for a discussion of how colonial forms of governance depended on caste networks and locally dominant groups to penetrate these vernacular spaces, a practice that he argues endures in postcolonial India; see Hansen (2001) and Roy (2002, 2009) on urban patronage networks in India.
7. Kaviraj (1991, 91).
8. Fuller and Harriss (2000, 8).

9. Kaviraj (1984, 227) and Kaviraj (1991, 91). Frankel (1978, 111) makes a similar point in describing the lack of shared goals and willingness to cooperate between the central and state governments and the upper- and lower-level bureaucrats in the early decades of state planning: "But in the last analysis, the local development officers were themselves drawn mainly from the village population, and responsible to superiors in the administrative services and the ministries of state governments, many of whom had very little genuine enthusiasm for the tasks of social education [and reform]."
10. This position contrasts with more conventional approaches to governance capacity that describe "state scarcity" in India, an arrangement that leaves the poor to scramble for the secondary spoils left behind once state resources are allocated to the elite (see Weiner 1962, Rudolph and Rudolph 1987, Bardhan 1990).
11. Chatterjee (2004, 2011) develops this distinction based on an earlier formulation from the Subaltern Studies project that theorized a split during the Indian nationalist movement between a more organized, vertically mobilized, and "controlled" elite domain and an unorganized, or more horizontally mobilized, subaltern domain of "spontaneous" politics (Guha 1982). I do not take Chatterjee to be arguing, however, that the elite or those in civil society do not use the tactics of bribery or coercion employed by those in political society (cf. Coelho and Venkat 2009). I take his point to be, rather, that political society is a subject-position in which these are the principal tactics available.
12. Benjamin (2008).
13. See Datta (2012), Desai (2012), Doshi (2013), Harriss (2005), and Roy (2002) for discussions of how patronage networks in settlements are structured by caste, class, and gender in diverse urban settings in India. See Jha, Rao, and Woolcock (2007) for the role of *pradhans* in Delhi's *bastis*.
14. This commissioner system is in place in most Indian cities, Kolkata being a major exception (Lama-Rewal 2007, 59, note 6). In Delhi in 2008, each municipal councilor had an annual budget of approximately 7.5 million rupees (~$150,000) and each MLA about 20 million rupees (~$400,000) to spend directly on development-related projects in their area. However, because these projects must be approved by the executive wings of the Municipal Corporation, they are usually not fully utilized.
15. Low-income housing here refers to the Economically Weaker Sections (EWS) and Low Income Group (LIG), government-set, income-based classifications (along with Middle Income Group and Higher Income Group) that are periodically updated based on purchasing power. These terms are also used to classify the size of housing units: EWS is typically a one-room flat, LIG two-room, MIG three-room, etc.
16. Batra (2007). The Report of the Committee on Problems of Slums in Delhi, organized by the Planning Commission (2002, 29–30), confirms the gross under provision of land for the poorest segments of the population: "DDA claims that 20 percent of the residential area [of Delhi] is earmarked for Economically Weaker Sections/squatter population under the integrated development project. DDA has not allotted any land to Slum & JJ [*jhuggī jhompḍī*] Department [responsible for slum housing] during 1992–97. . . . Prima facie, the allocation of land for the housing of the urban poor has been insufficient to meet the requirements, and below the proportion of their share [provided through the Master Plan]."
17. Ministry of Urban Affairs (1996), *A Compendium on Indian Slums*, Government of India; Census of India, 2001. According to the Slum Wing of the Municipal Corporation of Delhi, the number of households living in slums increased from 260,000 in 1990 to 480,000 by 1995.
18. See Bhan (2013) and Ramanathan (2005) for an elaboration of how slums are defined in law. The Slum Areas (Improvement and Clearance) Act, 1956 defines slums as "any area [where] buildings . . . (a) are in any respect unfit for human habitation, or (b) are

by reason of dilapidation, overcrowding, faulty arrangement and design of such buildings, narrowness or faulty arrangement of streets, lack of ventilation, light or sanitation, or any combination of these factors, are detrimental, to safety, health or morals." For administrative purposes, though, only areas notified as slums are eligible for various state improvement schemes. In Delhi, no new slum has been notified since 1994, and almost all notified slums are on private land (Bhan 2013). The Census of India, 2001 defines a slum as "(i) All areas notified as 'Slum' by State/Local Government and UT [urban territory] Administration under any Act; (ii) All areas recognised as 'Slum' by State/Local Government and UT Administration, which have not been formally notified as slum under any Act; (iii) A compact area of at least 300 population or about 60–70 households of poorly built congested tenements, in unhygienic environment usually with inadequate infrastructure and lacking in proper sanitary and drinking water facilities."

19. This information is based on interviews conducted with officials in the Municipal Corporation of Delhi and the Delhi Development Authority, as well as on information conveyed to me during preliminary fieldwork in various settlements across Delhi in April–July 2005. Interviews with housing NGO workers and Sajha Manch organizers, as well as fieldwork in Shiv Camp in 2006–2008, subsequently confirmed this information. For more detail on the history of government documentation, surveying, and ration card administration in Delhi, see Ghertner (2010).
20. Krishna Garden is a fabricated name, chosen to conceal the location of Shiv Camp and protect the anonymity of its residents.
21. In a survey of fifty residents of Shiv Camp I conducted, forty-eight residents stated that either upon arrival or after receiving their first ration card, they considered themselves legal occupants of their land, mostly on the basis of the implicit government approval their ration cards provided.
22. Estimates of the overall variance between planned and actually existing land use are rare. See Pethe et al. (2014) for such an estimate from a single ward in Mumbai, where the authors examine the deviation of existing land uses from the Development Plan—both legal, as approved through development control regulations, and illegal, such as residential squatting on non-residential land.
23. Writ Petition No. 4582 of 2003 and CM No. 587 of 2006 filed in the Delhi High Court, order dated January 18, 2006.
24. Verma (2002).
25. Dupont (2008).
26. Chatterjee (2004, 61).
27. Ibid., 140.
28. Ibid., 142, 144.
29. Chatterjee (1993, 5) describing Anderson (1983).
30. Chatterjee (1993, 36).
31. Fernandes (2006, xxii); also see Fernandes (2004).
32. Fernandes (2006, 26).
33. Ibid., xxiii.
34. Fernandes and Heller (2006, 516–517).
35. Quoted from Delhi-based magazine called *Civil Society*, September–October 2005.
36. "Middle class" is the term widely used in the literature on urban politics to describe the category of people imposing a new, bourgois vision on the Indian city (see Baviskar 2003, Fernandes 2006, Mawdsley 2009). This association of the "middle class" (often in quotation marks) with a political and moral leadership role—that is, class more as a form of political agency than an income bracket—is consistent with historiographical research on the Indian nationalist movement (see Chatterjee 1993, Sarkar 1983). As Pandey (2009, 328) writes, "middle classes had to represent and lead into the modern." The middle class

hence becomes synonymous with those who define the ideal nation or, in this case, those who set the urban agenda. I retain usage of the term here to make clear that I am talking about the same actors as these scholars of the Indian urban, although I prefer the term "propertied classes," because, as I show later in this chapter, it is the condition of property ownership that formally empowers RWAs in Delhi and because, as I show in the next chapter, the world-class aesthetic is premised on a notion of the public–private divide conditioned by property ownership.

37. GNCTD (2007).
38. GNCTD (2004a, XIII).
39. Interview with S. Regunathan, November 24, 2006.
40. Asian Centre for Organization Research and Development, Silver Jubilee Year 2006 brochure.
41. Unauthorized colonies are subdivided agricultural lands that fall beyond the urbanizable limits of the city, even though they are administratively part of Delhi. Unauthorized colony plots are sold and purchased via power of attorney sales that are typically registered with the Revenue Department, but are not formally recognized by the Delhi Development Authority because they do not conform with area layout plans and violate the Master Plan. See GNCTD (2006b, 3) for the Delhi government's description of RWAs.
42. Cornwall (2004).
43. "Maken Lashes Out at *Bhagidari*," *The Hindu*, March 10, 2006.
44. Interview in Chief Minister's Office, April 26, 2006.
45. Bhagidari thematic workshop, October 22, 2006.
46. GNCTD (2007, 10).
47. Kiron Wadhera, president and CEO of ACORD, October 13, 2006.
48. GNCTD (2007, 10).
49. GNCTD (2007, 11).
50. GNCTD (2001, 7).
51. GNCTD (2004a).
52. Brenner (2004).
53. Interview with George Koreth, chairman of ACORD, October 13, 2006.
54. Two of the remaining three respondents neither agreed nor disagreed, and only one disagreed. These data were collected in 2007 using a mail-in survey sent out to eighty-five randomly selected RWA members (response rate of 29 percent) using a database provided by the Bhagidari Cell of the Chief Minister's Office. I made initial contact over the phone and sent surveys to those who expressed a willingness to participate. In four instances, upon the respondents' request, I administered the survey over the phone.
55. Interview, November 30, 2006. S. Regunathan confirmed this: "The government has on many occasions consulted RWAs directly on the drafting of civic policy. It sought cooperation on provisions of certain acts and infrastructure provision in general at the neighborhood level."
56. "Govt Faces Heat at RWA Meet," *The Times of India*, July 15, 2006.
57. "Cabinet Meets RWAs to Figure Way Out," *The Times of India*, November 21, 2006.
58. Quoted in Chakrabarti (2007, 62).
59. Ibid.
60. Interview date: February 3, 2007.
61. Rama Lakshmi, "Indian Cities Eye New Delhi's Quiet 'Citizen Revolution,'" *The Washington Post*, A15, March 2, 2008.
62. Only two respondents disagreed or strongly disagreed with these claims, with one respondent in each case neither agreeing nor disagreeing. A public perception survey conducted by the Delhi government shows that RWAs report an overall increase in the quality of service delivery. Forty percent and 43 percent of the 240 RWAs surveyed

found their interactions with the MCD and DDA (which do not fall under the command of the Bhagidari Cell and Delhi government), respectively, to be successful, meaning that these interactions showed a marked improvement thanks to Bhagidari (GNCTD 2006a, 95).

63. Interview with Rashmi Krishnan, deputy commissioner (east), February 3, 2007.
64. Interview with Ravi Bajpai, November 6, 2006.
65. "Delhi Govt., MCD Set for a Clash," *The Hindu*, June 3, 2005.
66. "MCD Chief Faces Corporators' Ire," *The Hindu*, May 16, 2002.
67. "Bhagidari Workshops," *The Hindu*, May 5, 2005.
68. Interview with Monu Chadha, November 17, 2006.
69. "Bhagidari Runs into Rough Weather with MLAs," *The Hindu*, January 2, 2005.
70. "Delhi Budget: RWAs Welcome Hike in Bhagidari Fund," *The Times of India*, May 29, 2012.
71. "Government Bypassing MCD, Says BJP," *The Hindu*, October 30, 2004.
72. "Bhagidari Monitoring System Launched," *The Hindu*, February 2, 2008.
73. "Rs. 50 Lakh," *West Delhi Plus, The Times of India*, September 9, 2006.
74. As a senior MCD officer said: "Under this, we invited registered RWAs to take up the maintenance of municipal parks in their areas. For this, the MCD would pay them Rs 60,000 per acre per year in the first year and Rs 50,000 per acre in every subsequent year. . . . Till now, we have given away 155 sites to private organisations for maintaining the green spaces there." See "Many Schemes, But Few Takers," *Hindustan Times*, June 24, 2006.
75. Office Order No.F. 17/17/AR/02/Vol.11/9988-10137, dated October 10, 2004.
76. Different District Offices seem to call these committees by different names. Some councilors call them ward committees, some zonal committees (e.g., see Leena and Sharma 2007, 45–54).
77. This information was confirmed at the time of research either through direct contact with the Deputy Commissioner's Office, or by information posted on deputy commissioners' websites.
78. Interview date: May 26, 2005.
79. "SC Panel to Hear RWAs on May 2," *Hindustan Times*, May 1, 2006.
80. "Speed Up Process of Enlisting Roads," *The Hindu*, November 24, 2006.
81. "Ministry Directs Changes in New Master Plan," *The Hindu*, August 19, 2006. A. K. Nigam, the commissioner of the MCD, opposed this process, saying that "the RWAs can give their suggestions, but consulting them should not be made mandatory." "What Corporation Wants from Master Plan," *Hindustan Times*, January 16, 2007.
82. "Encroachments Removal Project to Be Launched Soon," *The Hindu*, May 8, 2007, www.thehindu.com/todays-paper/tp-national/tp-newdelhi/encroachments-removal-project-to-be-launched-soon/article1839386.ece.
83. Interview date: May 11, 2007.
84. Interview with Sidharth Mridul, November 30, 2006.
85. Interview date: November 28, 2006.
86. Interview date: February 12, 2007.
87. Interview with Pankaj Agarwal, secretary of the RWA Joint Front, a federation of more than three hundred RWAs, on April 24, 2006.
88. Interview with Uttara Rajinder, November 15, 2006.
89. See Baud and Nainan (2008) for an example of a similar, but less extreme, program in Mumbai, where neighborhood associations are delegated responsibilities for local waste management. Mumbai's ward committees are far more functional and representative than Delhi's, making the risk of gentrified participation less extreme there.
90. Interview with Uttara Rajinder, November 15, 2006.

CHAPTER 3

1. Kristeva (1982).
2. See McClintock (1995) and Ferguson (1999).
3. In this sense, nuisance talk resembles rumor, only with a different spatial relation. Das (2007, 119) argues that rumor's "essential grammatical feature" is that "it is conceived to *spread*," wherein words are not just communication, but become communicable, prone to spreading. But whereas rumor is centrifugal, routed in particular critical events—a riot, an assassination—from which it radiates outwards, creating an "uncanny knowledge" of a central something "embodied in rumor," not known experientially (120), nuisance talk is centripetal: it consolidates a central something. Nuisance talk's circulation, in other words, does not begin with a central event; it is rather strengthened through the enunciative common ground—a shared meaning or mutual knowledge—that it builds up by tying experiences from everyday life into a more general way of speaking. The performative power of the circulation of nuisance stems from the way that a community of feeling is built through the shared experience of what nuisance names and what that naming is intended to do. In rumor, in contrast, "normally functioning words"—the words of everyday life—lose their surety and in their place enters an unassigned, unattributed voice: the voice of rumor (120).
4. See Jain (2005) for a discussion of the relationship between nuisance statutes and environmental law in India, which I discuss more fully in chapter 4.
5. Following the conventions of J. L. Austin (1975), this is perlocutionary force, or a force external to the performer that affects how the audience receiving speech acts is led to do or realize something.
6. In more philosophical language, in garnering a coalition of speakers who agree to the literal, enunciative meaning of certain speech acts, nuisance talk, as a type of mass speech, builds up different, indirect intentionality formed through the conventions for how nuisance is uttered and what such utterances guide others to do. See Searle (1969) for the difference between direct and indirect speech acts.
7. I draw here from McClintock's (1995, 72) differentiation of the abject into abject objects (corpse, domestic dirt), abject states (hysteria, bulimia), abject zones (prisons, camps), agents of abjection (soldiers, nurses), socially abject groups (prostitutes, slum dwellers), and political processes of abjection (mass removals, genocide).
8. This encounter took place in Hindi. All other conversations described in this chapter took place in English unless otherwise noted. While I interacted with RWA activists from diverse neighborhoods and class backgrounds during my research, most of my interlocutors lived in wealthier colonies dominated by English speakers. This was because my initial RWA contacts were through Bhagidari, and because wealthier, English-speaking RWAs were best equipped to garner media and judicial recognition and therefore come to my attention. I would not have encountered the neighbors of Ravi Das Camp had I not already been studying Ravi Das Camp.
9. There is a long history of associating the smell of meat and fish with caste impurity in Hinduism. While physical contact has been understood by Brahmins historically to provide the strongest medium of caste pollution, offensive smells associated with degraded castes and outcastes provided a strong foundation for enforcing caste segregation on the basis of the defense of the five elements of the body (*pancamahābhūte*) in the Vedas, under which air (*vāyu*) is threatened by contamination (including repulsive or corrupting sound). The story of Satyavati (also known as Kali, "the dark one"), mentioned in the *Mahabharata* and told in greater detail in the *Devi Bhagavata Purana*, illustrates the Puranic roots of notions of caste-based olfactory pollution and the Brahminical need to expunge and purify it (see Bhattacharya 2004), as well as the association of lower castes with animals. Satyavati was born from a fish after it had swallowed King Vasu's semen.

When the king received Satyavati, he gave her to a fisherman, bestowing her with the name Matsyagandha ("the one who smells of fish") due to her fishy odor. Raised in the lowly fisherman's household, she was one day ferrying the Brahmin sage Parashara across the Yamuna River when he began lusting for her, despite her smell. In her attempt to dissuade Parashara, she said a Brahmin should not desire a woman who stinks of fish. He persisted, and when she said her body stank, Parashara used his powers to transform her into Padmagandha ("the one who smells of lotus"), elevating her to the status of a Brahmin: "his touch, like sandalwood paste, would leave her untainted and pure" (Bose 2000, 37), before impregnating her with what would become Vyasa, the compiler of the *Mahabharata*.

10. Sant Ravi Das was a fifteenth-century mystic of the bhakti movement venerated for his devotional poetry and for his strong critique of the system of untouchability. While revered across much of north India, he is especially celebrated by Dalits, being himself of the Kutbandhla Chamar caste, what is today a Scheduled Caste.

11. In response to a Right to Information request that I filed in 2006, the Southwest Zone headquarters of the DDA wrote me that in all of Zone G, the zone in which Sant Ravi Das Camp is situated and that has a population of 1.4 million people (DDA n.d., 10), only 808 EWS housing units were built between 1990 and 2006, none before 1998. This is not enough to house even half a percent of the population, whereas the Master Plan mandates that 25 percent of residential plots be for EWS and LIG categories.

12. Almost six months after the demolition of Ravi Das Camp and with the main road clear, this man still did not own a car. He had driven in on a scooter as the shopkeeper introduced me to the others. I take his statement about his inability to purchase a car as an act of boundary-making, in this case along class lines. He was making an argument that his potential for upward mobility (a car is the consumer item that best symbolizes middle-class status in Indian cities today, replacing the scooter or color television of the 1990s) was thwarted by the spatial proximity of the *basti*. Just as Uncle had suggested that the absence of nearby *jhuggis* provides posh neighborhood status, the removal of the *basti* for this man represented the removal of an obstacle to acquiring symbolic capital. Did he no longer need a car to symbolize his status once his neighborhood became slum-free? Was he ever able to afford a car?

13. As Gopal Guru (2013, 41) writes, "in the social construction of ecology, dalits become dirt and dirt is them. The upper-caste imagination thus eliminates the fault line between dirt and dignity on the one hand, severing quality from life on the other. Thus, the social production of such an ecology firmly establishes an ontological link between the dalit and the context (social ecology) of grotesque description."

14. Kristeva (1982, 71).

15. Chakrabarty (1992, 542, 544). See Kaviraj (1998) for a fuller discussion of the uneven mapping of inside/outside and private/public in Indian cities. Kaviraj charts how the attempt to construct a bourgeois public sphere in twentieth-century India followed a trajectory distinct from the Western one, in that it pursued not "a tendency toward universality," but rather an effort to extend the codes of civility found in bourgeois, inside spaces into common spaces and to expel uses of those spaces that did not accord with these codes. Also see Chatterjee (2004).

16. Sibley (1995, 19).

17. Civil Writ Petition No. 593 of 2002 in the Delhi High Court, order dated March 8, 2006.

18. Interview date: May 5, 2007.

19. Safdarjung Enclave's *nālā* is visible on the Map (see front matter of book) as the small black line immediately above the letters "av" in the word "Enclave."

20. Gooptu (2005), Gupta (1998), and Kaviraj (1998).

21. See Yadav (2000) and Jaffrelot (2003) for popular treatments of the regionalization of India's party system and the role of caste in it.
22. Interview date: April 24, 2006.
23. See Caldeira (2001) and Davis (1990).
24. Interview date: April 20, 2006.
25. Between 1998 and 2006 in Delhi, all categories of violent crime decreased in incidence, with the exception of rape, the occurrence of which increased from 441 to 623 cases, and kidnapping for ransom (25 to 32). The number of murders fell from 649 to 476, robbery from 823 to 541, rioting from 195 to 50. Property crimes fell even more drastically, with burglary dropping from 3764 to 1101. Rajya Sabha, Unstarred Question No. 942, dated July 3, 2007. According to the chief of police, the increasing incidence of rape is likely due to "an increase in reporting." Most cases of rape, he said, were "perpetrated by members of the victim's family, or a person known to the victim." "Police Chief Says Crime in India's Capital Under Control," *AP Worldstream*, January 6, 2006.
26. "Unsafe City—3 Cases a Day in 'Rape Capital,'" *Hindustan Times*, May 1, 2008.
27. Elsewhere, it suggested that "Hiring a domestic help, especially a Nepalese or Bangladeshi, is fraught with dangers, say the police." Ravi Bajpai, "Verification Drives Not Being Given Weightage," *Hindustan Times*, October 1, 2007.
28. Ayodhya is the former site of the Babri Mosque, which was destroyed by Hindu nationalists in December 1992. This act and the controversy surrounding it fueled a rise in communal politics that led to rioting in numerous cities across India. While the demolition of the mosque was carried out by Hindu activists, the police chief seems to be making reference to Muslim extremists in this quote.
29. Field notes, November 18, 2006.
30. Interview date: January 6, 2007.
31. Anderson (1992, 17, 4).
32. Ibid., 16.
33. Gidwani and Reddy (2011, 25). Also see Sharan (2014).
34. For example, consider the primarily aesthetic function of the 34-million-rupee Green Delhi Action Plan, which focuses on roadside landscaping, litter removal, and strategic tree planting without attention to broader sources of resource degradation or deforestation. "Delhi Is Gearing Up for a New Green Revolution," *The Hindu*, July 6, 2008. For further discussion of the role of environmental discourse in facilitating slum removal in Delhi, see Ghertner (2011).
35. "Yamuna Pollution Issue: Delhi High Court Summons Top Officials," *Hindustan Times*, February 15, 2007.
36. E. Sridharan, "Restrict Yamuna with Walls and Develop Low-Lying Areas," *The Times of India*, May 20, 2009.
37. "CM Concern for Green Lung, Seeks Expert Panel," *The Times of India*, May 14, 2009.
38. Bourdieu (1991, 105).

CHAPTER 4

1. Jain (2005, 97).
2. Ibid.
3. Sengar (2007).
4. The Code of Criminal Procedure, 1973, Section 133.
5. AIR 1980 SC 1622. Also see, AIR 1979 SC 143, *Govind Singh v. Shanti Sarup*.
6. See, for example, CA No. 1019 of 1992 in the MP High Court, *Dr. K. C. Malhotra v. State of M. P.* Section 133 Cr. P.C. was further supported by state-level policies, such as Delhi's "Scheme of Environmental Improvement of JJ Clusters," which stated that until longer-

term solutions (i.e., either in-situ upgradation or resettlement) for *jhuggi* colonies were reached, the Municipal Corporation was required to provide them "minimum basic civic amenities." This policy was first proposed by the Municipal Corporation in 1990; it was strengthened in 2000 when the Delhi government, with central government support, passed the Rehabilitation and Improvement Scheme.

7. CWP No. 531 of 1990 in the Delhi High Court.
8. 1996 2 SCC 594.
9. 2000 2 SCC 679.
10. Anti poor environmental discourse has circulated widely in India since colonial times (see Prakash 1999, Sharan 2006, Prashad 2001). For historical uses of nuisance law to facilitate industrial development, see Anderson (1995) and Rosen (2003).
11. See notes 32 and 35 from the introduction for summaries of how state records are appropriated and used by the urban poor.
12. CWP No. 2112 of 2002 and CWP No. 689 of 2004, order dated March 23, 2006.
13. Affidavit filed by under secretary, Ministry of Urban Development and Poverty Alleviation, in the High Court of Delhi, CWP 2253/2001. For an example of an order appointing a court commissioner, see the order dated February 16, 2001, in *Samudayik Vikas Samiti v. Government of India* (Delhi High Court), CWP 6553/2000.
14. Civil Misc. Petition No. 6982 of 2007 (Dayavanti & Ors.) in CWP No. 4582 of 2003 (Delhi High Court).
15. Such a diversity of tenure arrangements is common throughout India, providing the basis for economic clustering and dynamic informal growth economies (Benjamin 2005). In Bangalore, Benjamin (2005, 30) identified more than ten forms of tenure.
16. This interim order was cited in *Wazirpur Bartan Nirmata Sangh v. Union of India* and *Okhla Factory Owners' Association v. Govt. of NCT of Delhi*, CWP No. 2112 of 2002, 108(2002) DLT 517, paragraph 22.
17. CM No. 7896 of 1999 in the Delhi High Court, decided under *Pitampura Sudhar Samiti v. Union of India*, CWP No. 4215 of 1995 on September 27, 2002.
18. *Pitampura Sudhar Samiti v. Union of India*, CWP No. 4215 of 1995 on September 27, 2002.
19. CWP No. 6553 of 2000, order issued on February 16, 2001 and ibid. These sixty-three matters were listed under the lead petitions of Pitampura Sudhar Samiti, CWP No. 4215 of 1995, and K.K. Manchanda, CWP No. 531 of 1990.
20. See Verma (2002), for a discussion of Delhi's slum population as what she calls "Master Plan implementation backlog." Verma deftly shows how the current slum population is equal in size to the gap between the EWS housing stock the DDA was supposed to build according to the *Delhi Master Plan 2001* and the DDA's actual EWS housing provision.
21. *Wazirpur Bartan Nirmata Sangh v. Union of India* and *Okhla Factory Owners' Association v. Govt. of NCT of Delhi*, CWP No. 2112 of 2002, 108 (2002) DLT 517.
22. This logic has been applied to subsequent cases as well. For example, see *Federation of Paschim Vihar Group Housing Societies v. MCD*, CWP No.17869 of 2005 in the Delhi High Court, order dated October 6, 2005.
23. During previous cases, judges considered the circumstances leading to the settlement of a slum before making its final decision. In particular, see *Olga Tellis v. Municipal Corporation of Greater Bombay*, AIR 1986 SC 180, and *Ahmedabad Municipal Corporation v. Nawab Khan and Ors.*, AIR 1997 SC 152.
24. Valverde (2011, 295).
25. Gray and Gray (1998, 16).

26. *Olga Tellis v. Municipal Corporation of Greater Bombay*, AIR 1986 SC 180 and *P. G. Gupta v. State of Gujarat*, (1995) Supp. 2 SCC 182. See note 36 in the introduction for additional discussion of Olga Tellis.
27. For various legal analyses of Delhi slum demolitions that emphasize the "right to life" clause in Article 21, see Bhushan (2006), Ramanthan (2006), and Bhan (2009).
28. *Hem Raj v. Commissioner of Police (Supreme Court of India)*, CWP No. 3419 of 1999, discussed in the introduction at note 58.
29. The High Court made the link between slum removal and world-class city status clear when it noted in a 2006 case that, at the current pace, it would "require 1,263 years to demolish the illegal constructions carried out over the last 50 years, and convert Delhi into a world-class city," quoted in "'So, it'll Take You 263 Years to Wash Sins!,'" *Hindustan Times*, August 19, 2006.
30. Valverde (2011, 296) notes a similar use of nuisance law to differentiate categories of citizens in Western common-law countries: "The content of nuisance and nuisance-type provisions (such as noise rules) actively instutionalizes in law the rather illiberal idea that middle-class homeowners deserve greater protection from disorder and disruption, at least when they are at home, than other citizens."
31. Jain (2005, 97).
32. As Anderson (1992, 15–16) notes of colonial nuisance law in British India, "propertied groups were able in many instances to invoke public nuisance provisions against anyone threatening the value of their property." Anderson also found that such claims, in which "public nuisance complaints were blatantly driven by private material interest," "gave rise to some alarm in judicial circles," prompting some judges "to issue warnings of abusive or improper litigation" (1992, 16). Such litigation was dismissed outright in the post colonial period until approximately 2000, when the defense of private property owners' civic sensibilities started to be treated as a matter of public interest. The reintroduction of colonial applications of nuisance law might appear unusual, but Valverde (2011, 306), discussing a variety of cases from the United States and Canada, notes that "nuisance comes back to haunt the courts" from time to time due to the fact that "the premodern knowledge moves contained in nuisance law . . . remain necessary for governing modern cities."
33. *Wazirpur Bartan Nirmata Sangh v. Union of India* and *Okhla Factory Owners' Association v. Govt. of NCT of Delhi*, CWP No. 2112 of 2002, 108 (2002) DLT 517.
34. The judgment goes on to say that the former occupy areas of land adjacent to the latter, making the latter "inconvenienced": "An unhygienic condition is created causing pollution and ecological problems. It has resulted in almost collapse of Municipal services." Thus we come full circle: inadequate municipal services are not the cause of nuisance, but rather the outcome according to the new nuisance discourse.
35. Diwan and Rosencranz (2001, 97).
36. 2000 2 SCC 679.
37. This statement was issued in CWP No. 6553 of 2000 in the Delhi High Court, order dated February 16, 2001, an order banning open defecation, and restated in the final judgment in the Pitampura case, decided on September 27, 2002.
38. *Ahmedabad Municipal Corporation v. Nawab Khan and Ors.*, AIR 1997 SC 152, paragraph 30.
39. This recalls Chatterjee's (2004) distinction between "civil society" and "political society." Only whereas Chatterjee describes these as stable categories springing from postcolonial state form, the analysis here shows how they are actively produced through struggle over the public/private divide.
40. These petitions include those submitted in CWP Nos. 593 of 2002, *K-Block Vikas Puri RWA v. MCD*; 6160 of 2003, *Maloy Krishna Dhar v. Govt. of NCT Delhi*; 8556 of 2005,

Kailash Fraternity v. Govt. of NCT Delhi; 3494 of 2006, *Pawan Kumar v. MCD*; and 9358 of 2006, *Jangpura RWA v. Lt. Governor of Delhi*.

41. Interview conducted at the home of the interviewee on November 17, 2006, pertaining to CWP 8556 of 2005.
42. CWP No. 593 of 2002.
43. CWP No. 9358 of 2006.
44. Ibid.
45. Likewise, nuisance-based petitions were not the only type used to target slums in millennial Delhi.
46. CWP No. 6160 of 2003. I was able to obtain only low-resolution photocopies of these photographs, the quality of which is too poor to reproduce here.
47. CWP No. 531 of 1990 in the Delhi High Court.
48. CWP No. 1869 of 2003 in the Delhi High Court, order dated November 14, 2003.
49. Ibid.
50. CWP No. 593 of 2002, order dated March 8, 2006.
51. Ibid.
52. It should be noted that there is no indication that the slum residents alone were to blame for the improper garbage disposal.
53. *Wazirpur Bartan Nirmata Sangh v. Union of India* and *Okhla Factory Owners' Association v. Govt. of NCT of Delhi*, order dated March 3, 2003.
54. In contrast, research by the non governmental organization the Hazards Centre (Roy 2004) found that Pushta contributed only 0.33 percent of total sewage released into the Yamuna. In a later order (October 19, 2003), the court justified this order by referring to the Pitampura case, which I showed in the previous section to be the case that most strongly equates slums with nuisance.
55. CWP No. 689 of 2004 (Delhi High Court), *The court on its own motion v. Union of India*.
56. *Wazirpur Bartan Nirmata Sangh v. Union of India* and *Okhla Factory Owners' Association v. Govt. of NCT of Delhi*, order dated August 11, 2006; "Yamuna Pollution Issue: Delhi High Court Summons Top Officials," *Hindustan Times*, February 17, 2006.
57. "Yamuna Pollution Issue: Delhi High Court Summons Top Officials," *Hindustan Times*, February 17, 2006.
58. Interview date: January 15, 2007.
59. The fact that the same lawyers represent government departments in multiple cases before the same bench no doubt contributes to such confusion.
60. The fast pace of High Court decisions is a symptom of an incredibly high case backlog, with more than 370,000 cases outstanding in India's High Courts in 2007, and, according to legal experts, an insufficient number of judges. See "77,000 Judges Needed to Clear Backlog: CJI," *The Times of India*, December 22, 2007.
61. A hearing in the court case pertaining to Shiv Camp, the settlement I describe in chapters 5 and 6, produced a similar misunderstanding, where the judge only realized which case he was addressing after he had granted an extension to one of the parties.
62. Cited in Eagleton (1990, 44).
63. CWP No. 1869 of 2003 in Delhi High Court, page 5; also see "Chock-Full of Problems is 'Posh' Safdarjung Enclave," *The Times of India*, August 9, 1999, page 8, a copy of which was included as an annexure to the petition, which includes a photograph of the drain and adjoining *jhuggis* with the caption, "An open drain alongside Block A in Safdarjung Enclave causes a stink and provides a breeding ground for pests, while next to it is a cluster of jhuggis which strain the area's already inadequate civic facilities."

CHAPTER 5

1. Yurchak (2003).
2. Rancière (2009).
3. Appadurai (2004).
4. I first visited Shiv Camp two days after the demolition and recount this event based on what residents explained to me over the ensuing week.
5. Shiv Camp residents referred to their settlement through the name of the larger colony of which they were a part, calling it *Krishna Garden Jhuggi* (Krishna Garden is a fabricated name), although they occasionally called it a *bastī* (settlement) or *jhuggī bastī*. The use of *jhuggi* in the singular to refer to the entire settlement might be translated as "slum," as it clearly indicates housing that differs from that of planned colonies. When quoting speakers, I transliterate the words they spoke to refer to their settlement, although I use *basti*, slum, and *jhuggi* colony interchangeably in my own descriptions for the purposes of clarity and flow. While *basti* means settlement, in Delhi it is a term used almost exclusively to refer to areas predominantly made up of *jhuggis*, and is almost never applied to middle-class neighborhoods. The state and court typically refer to such settlements as slums or JJ (*jhuggi jhompdi*) clusters, the meanings of which are nearly the same. See Rao (2006) and Jones (2011) for insightful discussions of the place and politics of the slum in urban theory.
6. The vast majority of Shiv Camp residents were Dalits (former untouchable castes). Many Shiv Camp elders told me they left their villages due to oppression—a handful said they were bonded laborers—by various types of *baḍe log*, a phrase they used to refer to upper castes. Although they felt a great sense of freedom in Delhi, where they rarely experienced the overt forms of caste discrimination more common in their villages, they often read their wealthier neighbors' disdain for them through this same caste-coded vocabulary.
7. After three days, a leader from the Jan Shakti Party from the neighboring state of Haryana, rumored to be the *pradhan* of more than two hundred villages, announced that his party chief, Ram Vilas Paswan, a charismatic Bihari politician, was aware of the situation and would initiate inquiries into the matter. Shiv Camp residents, gaining mild coverage in local Hindi newspapers, declared victory and broke the strike.
8. The MCD showed no concern with the *jhuggis* when it took charge of the colony. Records of the transfer of the land to the MCD make mention of Chaudhury-the-colonizer's layout plan, but do not mention any *jhuggis*, although they were described in Chaudhury's letter requesting the land conversion.
9. Kuldip Singh, one of the planners involved in the preparation of the first Delhi Master Plan, quoted in Lahiri (2011).
10. Eagleton (1990, 43).
11. Pow (2009, 373–374).
12. Hall and Hubbard's (1996, 162) view is common in literature on urban entrepreneurialism and geographies of exclusion, where invocations of the particularly aesthetic dimensions of urban political projects are treated as an extension of distinct ideological programs (see Duncan and Duncan 2004, Walks 2006, Harvey 1989). Cosgrove's (1986, 47) influential approach to cultural geography interrogates how landscapes are produced through "visual ideology," which gains expression through a combination of a distinct social organization of space and a representational regime that naturalizes that formation. More ethnographic writing on urban regeneration and experiences of dispossession similarly notes the ideological power of notions of "beauty," "progress," and "development" in convincing those subject to dispossesion, in the global North and South, to consent to their displacement (see Harms 2012, Imrie and Huw 1997).

13. See my introduction for a discussion of the sociological literature on urban marginality, which evaluates the politics of the poor largely in terms of collective resistance and visible displays of dissent. The residents of Shiv Camp, as in so many spaces of urban relegation, might be classified according to this literature as resigned to their fate. But my contention is that another, more aesthetic domain of political practice reveals an array of subtler, yet no less significant, forms of struggle and critique.
14. "C'Wealth Games Top Priority of Govt.," *The Hindu*, February 6, 2008.
15. Mazzarella (2003).
16. As Mitchell (1996, 32–33) writes, "the look of the land becomes at least partially determinate in the struggles that are to follow."
17. Bourdieu (1990, 52). I take landscape, following Cosgrove (1986), to mean both the physical reconfiguration of the land and the modes of representation that stem from, reinforce, and naturalize that reconfiguration.
18. GNCTD (2008).
19. Randhawa (2012) shows how land monetization became a central component of the Delhi Metro Rail Corporation's revenue model, with approximately 66 percent of its revenue coming from real estate in 2006. He cites a study that finds that land prices near stations on the peripheries have begun to converge with those in the city center.
20. I discuss this experience in detail in the following chapter, where I describe how shifting perceptions of the value of work and the rise of a speculative property market in Delhi together created the conditions for what I call "land fetishism," a sense that property not only generates value automatically, but also endows its beholder with positive attributes and powers.
21. Buck-Morss (1989, 87).
22. See Bhatia (1994).
23. Broudehoux (2007, 383).
24. See chapter 3 for an extended discussion of historical conceptions of public and private in urban India.
25. See Kaviraj (1998).
26. *K. K. Manchanda v. The Union of India*, CWP No. 531 of 1990 in the Delhi High Court.
27. Bourdieu (1991, 17).
28. Unseen maps were indeed powerful symbolic devices in choreographing Shiv Camp residents' lives. The demolition of the 122 huts in January (and again conclusively in April) was ostensibly based on a land-use map—created in 1967 by the same private land colonizer Chaudhury, who settled Shiv Camp to house the workers he hired to build the surrounding colony—that showed a forty-five-foot road through the middle of the present-day settlement.
29. See Crary (1989, 103) for the attribution of this phrase to Benjamin.
30. Specifically, the Municipal Corporation (MCD) claimed that it had never acquired the land on which Shiv Camp was settled from the land colonizer Chaudhury, who had since moved out of the area. The RWA seeking to have Shiv Camp removed claimed the land was the MCD's.
31. This is the clause in Section 133 of the Code of Criminal Procedure that empowers private property owners to seek remedy against private nuisances, a clause that I argued in chapter 4 was strengthened in millennial Delhi and that had become the primary mechanism of slum demolition.
32. Bourdieu (1991, 20).
33. Bourdieu (1975, 19).
34. Yurchak (2005, 25).
35. Ibid. 80.
36. Yurchak (2003) argues for a view of discourse as situated activity, borrowing from Bakhtin's conception of "voice" as always dialogized and multiple, to critique binary

conceptions of social interaction that divide belief and performance into speakers' "true" or "hidden" transcripts on the one hand, and their "dissimulated" or "public" transcripts on the other (see Scott 1990, Wedeen 1999).

37. For Bourdieu (1991) too, submission to the rules of the game is necessary if one is to modify the institution governing the linguistic field. Bourdieu, however, calls such submission to the rules of the game "misrecognition," which comes too close to implying that the speaker who reproduces hegemonic speech unknowingly reinforces his or her subordination. Motilal was in no way confused about his subordinate position in the courtroom.

38. *Pitampura Sudhar Samiti v. Government of India*, CWP No. 4215 of 1995 in the Delhi High Court, final judgment issued on September 27, 2002. Also see the case of Nangla Machi, *Hem Raj v. Commissioner of Police* (Supreme Court of India), CWP 3419/1999, discussed in the introduction.

39. In the language of linguistic anthropology, all institutions are organized by "representational economies" (Keane 2007), which designate who can talk and about what and, in doing so, establish roles such as party and nonparty to a legal case. In this sense, Motilal upheld and participated in the representational economy of the courtroom, but gained positional advantage (a new role as party to the case) through his ability to make use of the terms of sensibility to perform effective acts of speech. As Carr (2011, 226) argues, acquiring such a role "may have as much to do with learning how to control an interactional text as deploying a denotational one."

40. I draw from Chatterjee (2011, 141) here, who, following Laclau (2005), distinguishes between differential and equivalent demands, the former which can be broken up by the techniques of governmentality to isolate specific groups and benefit-seekers from others, and the latter which establish chains of equivalences that unite a sum total of unfulfilled demands and direct populist energies toward an unresponsive state. For Chatterjee, "the politics of the governed" is successful when it "turn[s] governmental classification of populations into political categories by mining the statistical and ethnographic resources of colonial knowledge and building chains of equivalence to mark out deep faultlines between an ethnic 'people' and its oppressors" (147). I am describing here a politics that does not rely upon the classificatory technologies of governmentality. Chains of equivalence in this case are not inscriptive or calculative chains, but rather chains of signification.

41. Sources for the positive association between resettlement and property ownership are multiple. Thirty-six post-Partition colonies created to house Panjabi refugees arriving from the newly formed Pakistan have since become prosperous south Delhi colonies (Lahiri 2011, Kaur 2005). Targeted resettlement drives during Indira Gandhi's rule in the 1970s and 1980s typically relocated slum dwellers within a five-kilometer radius of their previous settlements and gave them well-serviced and relatively large plots, free of cost, on a permanent leasehold basis (Tarlo 2003, 73). Such resettlement sites have since been developed and integrated into the surrounding residential areas, bearing little visual distinction from the neighboring planned colonies. Resettlement since the early 1990s has been offered on far less favorable terms, with plot sizes having decreased from fifty square meters in the 1970s to 12.5 square meters, resettlement locations now more than twenty kilometers from central Delhi, and five-year licenses now replacing permanent leases. Despite the decrease in tenure security and service provision, the MCD and DDA actively perpetuate the perception of resettlement as a positive process, in part through surveys it regularly conducts of slum dwellers' resettlement eligibility (Ghertner 2010).

42. See Menon-Sen and Bhan (2008) for an account of life around this time in two of Delhi's largest resettlement colonies, Bawana and Narela.

43. Poster design and publishing in India has been dominated by a handful of publishers whose origins lie in devotional imagery (see Jain 2007, Pinney 2004). House posters,

most of which are produced by these same publishers, borrow many of the same aesthetic qualities of these "photos of gods." They typically retain the rich, pastoral landscapes, compressed depth of field, and "increased stress on the surface" found in devotional posters, yet replace the central figure of a deity with a private, bungalow-style house (Pinney 2004, 96).

44. See Willis (1981) for a formative ethnographic account of cultural reproduction.
45. As King writes (1984, 160), "as a symbol of private property the detached and territorially separate bungalow—the irreducible minimum of a house within its own grounds—was patently second to none."
46. Rancière (2010, 139).
47. Compare this with more recent efforts to seek spheres of political possibility within neoliberal projects of development (Ferguson 2010, Lawson 2005, Roy 2010).
48. This is what Bayat (2007) describes as "the habitus of the dispossessed," a form of strategic negotiation the subaltern uses to make the best of a bad situation. This is a view of habitus as the set of dispositions imprinted on bodies through the structure of the field.
49. Rancière (2004, 12).
50. While there is a broad elite consensus on the need to eliminate the slum, even among RWA members actively mobilized against slums, many describe the state's need to provide them with improved housing.

CHAPTER 6

1. Marx (1981 [1894], 256).
2. Marx (1993 [1893], 303); emphasis added. As Marx (2010 [1894], 568) begins his discussion of the trinity formula in *Volume 3*, "however, capital is not a thing, but rather a definite social production relation, belonging to a definite historical formation of society, which is manifested in a thing and lends this thing a specific social character."
3. Ranciere (1976 [1965], 362). In Marx's (1981 [1894], 858) language in *Capital, Volume 3*, the social determinations of production through which surplus is produced are reduced to material determinations of the thing.
4. "Capital is a perennial pumping-machine of surplus-labour for the capitalist, land a perennial magnet for the landlord, attracting a portion of the surplus-value pumped out by capital, and finally, labour the constantly self-renewing condition and ever self-renewing means of acquiring under the title of wages a portion of the value created by the labourer" (Marx 2010 [1894], 572).
5. See Ranciere (1976 [1965]) for a brief discussion of fetishism in relation to Marx's trinity formula of interest, rent, and wages. He, like most, focuses on the capital-interest couple. While studies of property often remark on its aspirational qualities, as far as I am aware, there have been no sustained studies of the fetish character of the property–rent couple, especially of an ethnographic nature.
6. Marx (1981 [1894], 963).
7. World Bank (2005, 3).
8. Marx (2010 [1894], 575) described "the mystifying character that transforms the social relations, for which the material elements of wealth [land, capital, labor-power] serve as bearers in production, into properties of these things themselves (commodities) and still more pronouncedly transforms the production relation itself into a thing."
9. In this way, I reject what Rancière (1976 [1965], 361) calls the treatment of *Verkehrung* as concealment, which he sees "surrounded by a whole anthropological halo, marked by an unreflected and uncriticized reference to an earlier conceptual domain." In contrast to this approach (of which Lucács is taken as a prime example), Rancière prefers a second meaning of *Verkehrung*—reversal—in which M–M' "is a form which becomes alien from the relation that it supports and, in becoming alien to it, becomes a thing and leads to the

materialization of this relation." I follow this approach in rejecting the interpretation that settlers' response to a speculative theory of value is actually a reaction to their ideological concealment from an unfettered, precommoditized conceptual domain. However, I also reject Rancière's dismissal of the significance of understanding how subjects take shape through fetishism. In this regard, I draw more from Taussig (1980) in seeing the production of value as linked inseparably with the production of magic and the magical power of objects—something both subaltern and elite subjects experience.

10. See Foucault (2007) and Gordon (1991), as well as my introduction, on governmentality as "the conduct of conduct."
11. After returning to the United States many months later, I discovered through an Internet search that the note was a Greek drachma issued in German-occupied Greece during World War II, a period of extremely high inflation. See Figure 6.1, which shows the ruins of the Temple of Athena Aphaea on Aegina. This "old" drachma was later converted into "new" drachma once Greece entered the Bretton Woods system in the 1950s, and the drachma ceased being legal tender in 2002 when it was replaced by the euro.
12. Indian banks long had a habit of stapling currency together. When a teller would remove notes from a bunch, it would often leave a hole in one of the corners. With excessive wear such notes often became fragile, and many stores and smaller banks would not accept them. I recall numerous instances in the early 2000s having to cycle through bills in my possession to find one acceptable to merchants. The most damaging wear a note could (and can still today) face, however, was a central tear. Sanjay's suggestion that a tear made his note un-exchangeable was based on this material history of currency exchange in India.
13. A number of boys in Shiv Camp had small foreign currency collections, and I quickly exhausted my supply of US coins by adding to their stock. One boy had a collection of coins from the United Kingdom, the United States, the United Arab Emirates, China, Japan, and Pakistan. It is perhaps no surprise that the stories of wealth the youth often told involved foreign, alien currencies more often than domestic ones. The sudden appearance of new forms of wealth in the city was most easily attributed to foreign processes, either magical or transnational (cf. Taussig 1997).
14. By "circuit of value," I mean value as represented in the fetishized, transformed form: "Landed property, capital and wage-labour are thus transformed from sources of revenue— ... from sources by means of which one portion of value is transformed into the form of profit, another into the form of rent, and a third into the form of wages—into actual sources from which these value portions and respective portions of the product in which they exist, or for which they are exchangeable, arise themselves, and from which, therefore, in the final analysis, the value of the product itself arises" (Marx 2010 [1894], 574).
15. As Walter Benjamin (1968, 161) writes, "it is not the object of the story to convey a happening per se, which is the purpose of information; rather it embeds it in the life of the storyteller in order to pass it on as experience to those listening."
16. This recalls Walter Benjamin's (2002, 805) characterization of the nineteenth-century world exhibitions: "The world exhibitions were training schools in which the masses, barred from consuming, learned empathy with exchange value. 'Look at everything; touch nothing.'"
17. Marx (1990 [1867]: 190) affirms the normalcy of fabulous tales of money when he writes of political economists' own theories: "in its function as measure of value, money ... serves only in an imaginary or ideal capacity. This circumstance has given rise to the wildest of theories."
18. Some of the boys took pride in being able to precisely recite Metro travel times to Karol Bagh, Connaught Place, and Khan Market, vibrant commercial areas in central Delhi that they rarely if ever visited.

19. McFarlane (2011, 651). Shiv Camp youth experiences differed from the "disjointed geographies" or youth efforts to "delink themselves from the familiar social contexts in which they have been embedded" that Simone (2004, 7, 214) observes across African cities, wherein "power increasingly derives from a capacity to transgress spatial and conceptual boundaries" (Simone 2006, 257). The stigma of slum life and the diminishing economic prospects Shiv Camp youth faced were more often lived through physical confinement than outward social experimentation, an everyday mode of habitation that resembles Weiss's (2002, 104) description of Tanzanian young men, who "reflexively display and proclaim their own absence from the world they aspire to inhabit." I also find literature on "dwelling" and assemblage that attempts to move beyond human-centric accounts of the city and that emphasizes radical openness and the "capacity of random connections to generate the possibility of new encounters, spaces, and collectives" limited in accounting for such life-worlds (McFarlane 2011, 654; Venn 2006). For, while assemblage theory very well may orient the researcher to the flows, compositional possibilities, and emergent properties of the city, it suggests little on how those in highly constrained political circumstances might do the same.
20. Urban sociologists and anthropologists have observed how such value-coding constrains, both physically and symbolically, residents of low-income and stigmatized territories' ability to move in and across urban space. See, for example, Wacquant's (2008) discussion of shared experiences of territorial stigma among the youth of the American ghetto and the French *banlieue*, Auyero's (1999) study of reduced economic prospects among Argentine shanty dwellers, and Harms's (2011, 123) examination of the changing relations between "the spatial meaning of land and the ability of people to move across it" among the peri-urban residents of Saigon.
21. Jeffrey (2010) provides an insightful analysis of *timepass* as an entrepreneurial strategy among unemployed youth of forging patronage networks in the city of Meerut, Uttar Pradesh. In Delhi, "timepass" is a word used by Hindi and English speakers across diverse classes to describe various modes of waiting, often with no intended aim.
22. I thank Mazen Labban for pointing out that *kismat* is an Arabic-root word and for helping me identify the sense of *kismat* as "share."
23. Phillips (1997, 239–240) writes of the *reason* in poor people's expenditure on lottery tickets in the United States, "maybe poor people actually have a good understanding of what their life chances are; maybe lottery players are *right*. At issue is not the lottery per se, but the chance of personal mobility, the question of where you can get ahead by saving up money; the lottery should make sense to anyone for whom the answer is nowhere."
24. Simmel (2007 [1913]).
25. Sociological and literary characterizations of Dalit fatalism have a long history, from Christian missionaries—such as J. C. Heindrich, who observed a "mass inferiority complex" among Dalits in *bastis* that was expressed both as ambition to outdo and reject other "untouchables" as well as a fatalism often interpreted as a desire to identify with higher castes (Hebden 2011, 79)—to the literary production of the Dalit character as an inactive object of pity and disdain (Gajarawala 2012), to economic treatments that derive behavioral models from narrow textual sources and that associate popular belief in karma with a deterministic reading of current fate as predestined by deeds in a past life. In justifying his opposition to a separate electorate for "untouchables," Gandhi affirmed that "there is very little political consciousness among them, and they are so horribly treated that I want to save them against themselves" (cited in Roy 2014, 120). The history of interpretations of slum settlements as breeding grounds for despair and a fatalistic approach to life is also long, but for one influential report in the history of Delhi slum policy, see Bharat Sewa Samaj (1958, 217).

26. As anthropologist Lawrence Babb (1983, 173) notes of interpretations of destiny in popular Hinduism, "theories of misfortune that posit human responsibility for destiny"—theories that relate present experience to past action—"are not just rationalizations of the present; they are recipes for human responses to destiny as well."
27. According to Simmel (2007 [1913], 80), fate signals the merging of one's inner tendency and external events, a blurring of the subject and object, as "merely causal events take on *a meaning* [einen Sinn], a retrospective teleology, as it were." According to this framework, fate "expresses the ability of the human being *to adapt*" as "certain elements are integrated into its [the subject's] life as defining occurrences"—returning to "his India" in the case of Lakshman, or rejecting an offer to work abroad for Shambu.
28. De Soto (2000, 39, 40–45).
29. De Soto (2000, 51, 49). Adam Smith (1982 [1776], book 1, chapter 6) described wages, profit, and rent—elements resulting from the distribution of value produced in a certain period—as constitutive elements of this value. In other words, de Soto is distinctly Smithian in seeing rent as a source of value.
30. "Representational sorcery" is Christophers's (2010, 95) term; also see Mitchell (2007) for a robust critique of de Soto's argument. For critiques of the practical limitations of de Soto's approach to property formalization, see Gilbert (2002) and Varley (2002). I engage de Soto here as a theorist and spokesman of the economy of appearances; he is an advocate of the property fetish, although with limited grasp of its full effects for those most subject to them.
31. Gray and Gray (1998).
32. See Menon-Sen and Bhan (2008) for a comprehensive survey of resettlement conditions in Bawana and Narela, two of Delhi's largest resettlement colonies. Also see Ramakrishnan (2014, 2), who observes how residents of resettlement colonies experience spatiotemporal disruption, "where their futures within the city remain stalled and fixed in uncertainty."
33. Marx (2010 [1894], 594).
34. Slum land becomes a fictitious commodity at the point when it is subjected to the "rule of the commodity" and can be exchanged as cadastral property (Polanyi 1944).
35. Marx (1990 [1867], 131).
36. Ranciere (1976 [1965]).
37. In *Capital, Volume 1*, Marx (1990 [1867], 168–9) wrote: "It is . . . precisely this finished form of the world of commodities—the money form—which conceals the social character of private labour and the social relations between the individual workers, by making those relations appear as relations between material objects, instead of revealing them plainly." This narrower interpretation of fetishism was later supplemented, in *Volume 3*, with a more extensive treatment of capital fetishism (M–M'), of which commodity fetishism is a part. Marx describes fetishism in *Volume 3* as something closer to a form of "social misrecognition," not the misrecognition by, or the concealment from, a particular class of workers or the dispossessed (Milios and Dimoulis 2006, 142). What in the Marxian literature are called "anthropological readings" that focus on individual and class misrecognition, rather than the social misrecognition produced in fetishized economic systems that treats capital as itself value producing, tend to be those that emphasize the narrower treatment of fetishism of *Volume 1*, such as Holloway (2002).
38. Prahalad (2006).

CONCLUSION

1. It is not that records stopped being collected, but that the presence or absence of any correspondence between those records and the material realities they were supposed to represent mattered far less than before.

2. This mandate is recorded in the Delhi Development Act, 1957. See note 31 in the introduction for further discussion of its requirements.
3. See "British Teams Raise Delhi Doubts," *BBC News*, September 20, 2010, http://news.bbc.co.uk/go/pr/fr/-/sport1/hi/commonwealth_games/delhi_2010/9018515.stm.
4. Daniel Rossingh and Mehul Srivastava, "Bridge Collapse Adds Safety to Terror Fears Before Delhi Games," *Bloomberg News*, September 22, 2010, www.bloomberg.com/news/2010-09-22/delhi-faces-filth-security-fears-bridge-collapse-at-commonwealth-games.html.
5. Brijesh Pandey, "Wages. Pension. Metro. It's Sinking in Now. Delhi Has Taken Away Money Meant for These and Put it into CWG 2010," *Tehelka*, August 14, 2010, http://archive.tehelka.com/story_main46.asp?filename=Ne140810Metro.asp.
6. Neelam Pandey, "13 CWG Hotels, Only 91 Guests," *Hindustan Times*, March 25, 2011, www.hindustantimes.com/india-news/newdelhi/13-cwg-hotels-only-91-guests/article1-677336.aspx.
7. "At Least 75,606 Tourists Visited Delhi During CWG," *Zee News*, November 25, 2010, http://zeenews.india.com/news/nation/at-least-75-606-foreign-tourists-visited-delhi-during-cwg_670386.html.
8. Raman Kirpal, "CWG Debris: A Costly Fiddle," *Tehelka* 7(47), November 27, http://archive.tehelka.com/story_main47.asp?filename=Ne271110A_COSTLY.asp#.
9. Iftikhar Gilani, "As Poll Promises Go Sour, Sheila to Face Ombudsman," *Tehelka*, July 2011, http://archive.tehelka.com/story_main50.asp?filename=Ws200711As_poll.asp.
10. "Budget Aimed at Making Delhi a World-Class City," *Indian Express*, June 5, 2012, http://archive.indianexpress.com/news/-budget-aimed-at-making-delhi-a-worldclass-city-/957943/.
11. National Capital Territory of Delhi Laws (Special Provision), Second Act 2011, published by the Ministry of Law and Justice in the Gazette of India, March 30, 2011, www.urbanindia.nic.in/programme/dd/dd_notification/k_12016_2_2006_ddib.pdf. The first Special Provisions Act of 2006 was passed while the 2007 Master Plan revision was still in preparation and was launched with a special focus on halting the Supreme Court-ordered sealing of all commercial establishments operating in Master Plan-designated residential areas. It was extended in 2009 and 2010, before the updated Second Act was passed.
12. "Sheila Dikshit Blames Unbridled Influx of Migrants for Delhi's Woes," *India Today*, December 28, 2012, http://indiatoday.intoday.in/story/sheila-dikshit-blames-unbridled-influx-of-migrants-for-delhis-woes/1/239744.html.
13. See, for example, McKinsey's report on building inclusive cities in India (McKinsey & Company, 2010). At the 2011 World Economic Forum, the union minister of urban development, Kamal Nath stated that "this year's message will focus on inclusive growth as developing economies must have healthy growth"; quoted in "'Inclusive India' Everywhere on Davos Agenda," *Business Standard*, January 25, 2011, www.business-standard.com/article/economy-policy/-inclusive-india-everywhere-on-davos-agenda-111012500106_1.html.
14. "Inclusive Paradigms for Inclusive Growth," address by Kumari Selja, minister of housing & urban poverty alleviation and tourism, February 15, 2010, Conference on "A Paradigm for Inclusive Growth," Federation of Indian Chambers of Commerce and Industry, www.ficci.com/events/20323/ISP/kumari_Selja.pdf.
15. "Rajiv Awas Yojana: Guidelines for Slum-Free City Planning," page 8, Planning Commission of India, http://mhupa.gov.in/w_new/RAY%20Guidelines-%20English.pdf.
16. Mathur (2009) and Roy (2014, 8).
17. Kamath (2012, 76) notes in her study of RAY and the Basic Services to the Urban Poor initiated under the earlier Jawaharlal Nehru National Urban Renewal Mission that the

"progressive thrust on security of tenure in the new policies seems associated exclusively with issuing property title." Ananya Roy (2014, 9) observes that "RAY is a policy that seeks to transform urban land, with its multiplicity of occupancy and ownership, into cadastral property, and to then transform cadastral property into a commodity with globally legible value."

18. While RAY guidelines express a strong recommendation for in-situ redevelopment of slum lands, this is more the exception than the norm. The most prominent slum-free cities approach is the transfer of development rights (TDR) model, through which developers are able to access valuable slum land in exchange for an obligation to rehouse the displaced slum dwellers in a portion of the multi-story flats built on the site. Since its early adoption, TDR requirements in many cities have been relaxed so that developers can use prime slum land entirely for luxury housing, as long as they build resettlement housing for displaced slum dwellers elsewhere in the city, usually on peripheral land.

19. Gupta (2012, 291, 294) argues that inclusive growth "has meant taking the higher government revenues obtained from rapid growth in sectors of the economy tied to the global market and redistributing them to indigent sections of the population." Programs such as the National Rural Employment Guarantee Scheme, the National Rural Health Mission, and the Sarv Shiksha Abhiyan (Universal Education Program) have been coupled with similar proposed national missions for health, education, sanitation, and livelihood in urban areas. Gupta argues, however, that "inclusive growth" seeks to "paper over the cracks" of an economic order premised on mass displacement for mining and infrastructure development. I agree with Gupta in noting that the extensive and impressive programs of pro poor resource transfer lumped together as "inclusive growth" must be understood in the context of deepening structural imbalances that orient the economy away from employment generation and towards property-based, infrastructure, and extractive industry growth, areas that have historically led to worsening economic prospects for the poor in rural and urban areas alike. I further point here to how "inclusive growth" in cities aims to incorporate the poor into speculative real estate—to make them speculative investors like any other—but with far greater risk of being made dependent on financial instruments of debt.

20. "India's Economy Grows Slower Than Expected," *BBC News*, February 28, 2014, www.bbc.com/news/business-26385545.

21. Information retrieved from the Planning Commission of India, http://planningcommission.nic.in/data/datatable/0306/table%2017.pdf. The growth rate of fixed capital formation, of which real estate and physical property is a key component, also fell from over 12 percent in 2011–2012 to less than 1 percent in 2012–2013, dipping further into negative territory in 2013–2014.

22. In the April–June quarter of 2013, Delhi real estate prices dropped 1.5 percent and prices fell in twenty-two of the twenty-six cities tracked by the National Housing Bank's residential property index. See "NHB's Residential Property Index to Turn Monthly," *Business Standard*, September 6, 2013, www.business-standard.com/article/companies/nhb-s-residential-property-index-to-turn-monthly-113090500193_1.html.

23. "Inclusive Paradigms for Inclusive Growth," address by Kumari Selja; emphasis in original.

24. Quoted in "'Inclusive India' Everywhere on Davos Agenda."

25. Virendra Pandit, "Push to Affordable Housing," *Hindu Business Line*, March 19, 2011, www.thehindubusinessline.com/money-wise/personal-finance/push-to-affordable-housing/article1553448.ece.

26. Anupama Chandrasekaran, "Affordable Housing Turns Unaffordable," *Mint*, September 10, 2010, www.livemint.com/Politics/PwrF8BndJpPAnCHHTSWdbI/Affordable-housing-turns-unaffordable.html.

27. See Nishant Lalwani, Kushagra Merchant, and Bala Venkatachalam (2010), *Micromortgages: A Macro Opportunity in Low-Income Housing Finance*, Monitor Inclusive Markets, October 2010, and "Market Based Solutions for Affordable Housing in Urban India," June 11, 2008, www.inclusivemarkets.monitor.com/downloads/FGDwithMFIinHyderabad.pdf.
28. As Monitor argued in a 2010 white paper based on market research in Ahmedabad and Mumbai, "Developer project IRRs can be as high as 40%–50% in these locations, with gross margins in the region of 20%–30%." See Animitra Deb, Ashish Karamchandani, and Raina Singh, "Building Houses, Financing Homes: India's Rapidly Growing Housing and Housing Finance Markets for the Low-Income Customer," July 2010, www.mim.monitor.com/downloads/whitepaper-buildinghousesfinancinghomes-final-screen.pdf, page 6.
29. Jerry Rao, the founder and former CEO of the software company Mphasis, is one example of a prominent business leader who has written about affordable housing and launched his own affordable housing venture. Tata Housing, the property development arm of the Tata Group, planned to invest 2.5 billion rupees in its Smart Value Homes venture, which builds homes priced between 500,000 and 3.5 million rupees. "Tata Housing Sets Up Arm to Focus on Affordable Homes," *Economic Times*, October 11, 2010, http://articles.economictimes.indiatimes.com/2010-10-11/news/27631802_1_affordable-homes-shubh-griha-tata-housing-managing-director.
30. "Establishment of the Credit Risk Guarantee Fund Trust for Low Income Housing Under the Rajiv Awas Yojana Scheme," March 23, 2012 press release, http://pib.nic.in/newsite/erelease.aspx?relid=81554.
31. Amy Kazmin, "Developers Spot Chance to Plug India's Affordable Housing Gap," *Financial Times*, July 22, 2013, www.ft.com/cms/s/0/26bd2d64-eead-11e2-b8ec-00144feabdc0.html#axzz36LntyWaG.
32. Anupama Chandrasekaran, "Affordable Housing Turns Unaffordable."
33. "Making Affordable Housing Work in India," Royal Institute of Chartered Accountants Research Report, November 2010, www.ricssbe.org/RICSINDIA/media/rics/PublicationandResources/Making-affordable-housing-work-in-India-Research.pdf?ext=.pdf, 14.
34. Jiby Kattayam, "DDA Continues, High Court Stays Jhuggis' Demolition," *The Hindu*, March 25, 2011, www.thehindu.com/todays-paper/tp-national/tp-newdelhi/dda-continues-high-court-stays-jhuggis-demolition/article1569880.ece.
35. Declaring that the Delhi government's resettlement policy is (again) operative, the judgment states: "The policy for relocation of J.J. clusters w.e.f. 01.04.2000, interalia, provided that slums will be relocated only from project sites where specific requests have been received from the land owning agencies and no large scale removal should be resorted to without any specific use. Relocation land will be identified in Delhi and NCR in consultation with DDA and NCRPB so that it is in conformity with the land use policy under the Master Plan and the NCR Plan." It further states that "Prior to relocation and payment of subsidy by the land owning agency and Delhi Government, a joint survey of the slum cluster will be carried out by the DC of the revenue district, jointly with the land owning agency and Executing Agency." CWP Nos. 8904 of 2009, 7735 of 2007, 7317 of 2009 and 9246 of 2009 in the Delhi High Court, pronounced on February 11, 2010.
36. The requirement to provide adequate sanitation in the form of toilet blocks was often enforced through Section 133 of the Code of Criminal Procedure, or through the "Scheme of Environmental Improvement of JJ Clusters," a state policy that stated that until longer-term solutions for *jhuggi* colonies were reached, the Municipal Corporation was required to provide them with "minimum basic civic amenities." See chapter 4, note 6 for further details on the link between nuisance and environmental improvement.
37. See McFarlane (2012, 1288) for a discussion of municipal byelaws in Mumbai that "reflect the tendency to punish rather than alleviate sanitation inequalities," what he

calls a form of "politico-moral malevolence" that he argues is becoming increasingly prevalent in India and elsewhere. This sanitary malevolence has become widespread throughout Delhi, not least in resettlement colonies, where systemic underfunding of water and sanitation services is the norm. In their evaluation of sanitation programs in Delhi, Agarwala and Panda (2013) found that the newly formed Delhi Urban Shelter Improvement Board has systematically withheld funds from toilet and sanitation infrastructure, leading to a more than 40-million-rupee debt owed to the Delhi Water Board, which builds piecemeal systems based on pressure from local political representatives and leaders.

38. This is Ferguson's (1999, 236) definition of abjection, which he says, "implies not just being thrown out but also thrown *down*—thus expulsion but also debasement and humiliation."

39. As Nilekani (2009, 23) argues, "new IT infrastructure can bypass inefficient public systems and, by bringing improved measurement of government objectives and outcomes, it can also enable greater effectiveness. . . . Information technology is also a key mechanism for addressing the knowledge asymmetry between the government and the governed." The 2010 High Court judgment reinstating the Delhi government's resettlement policy echoed this sentiment in demanding an improvement in the calculative apparatus of the state: "The respondents in these cases were unable to place records to show that any systematic survey had been undertaken of the jhuggi clusters where the petitioners and others resided. There appears to be no protocol developed which will indicate the manner in which the surveys should be conducted. . . . Therefore, the exercise of conducting a survey has to be very carefully undertaken and with great deal of responsibility keeping in view the desperate need of the jhuggi dweller for an alternative accommodation. A separate folder must be preserved by the agency or the agencies that are involved in the survey for each jhuggi dweller with all relevant documents of that jhuggi dweller in one place. Ideally if these documents can be digitalized then there will be no need for repeated production of these documents time and again whenever the jhuggi dweller has in fact to be assigned a place at the relocated site [*sic*]."

40. Delhi Urban Shelter Improvement Board, "Present Policies and Strategies," issued July 1, 2010, http://delhishelterboard.in/main/?page_id=128.

41. "Arvind Kejriwal's Letter to Jhuggi Wasi," https://aamaadmiparty.wordpress.com/2013/06/22/arvind-kejriwals-letter-to-jhuggi-wasi/comment-page-1/.

42. "And So Begins the Pole Dole, Dikshit Decides to Legalise 200 Unauthorized Colonies," *India Today*, January 6, 2013, http://indiatoday.intoday.in/story/sheila-dikshit-decides-to-legalise-200-unauthorised-colonies-in-delhi/1/240999.html. On the Aam Aadmi Party's remarkable capture of the slum vote, see Ramani (2013).

43. See Parel (1997) on Gandhi's use of *swaraj*.

44. As the draft Delhi Nagar Swaraj Bill, 2014, states, "mohalla sabhas shall strive for universal education and healthcare in the mohalla and formulate and implement schemes to eradicate hunger and homelessness and for welfare of senior citizens, disabled and other vulnerable sections of society." See Ambika Pandit, "Mohalla Sabhas for Aam Aadmi Self-Rule," *The Times of India*, February 5, 2014, http://timesofindia.indiatimes.com/city/delhi/Mohalla-sabhas-for-aam-aadmi-self-rule/articleshow/29917180.cms.

45. Planning Commision of India (2013, 1), http://planningcommission.gov.in/plans/planrel/12thplan/pdf/12fyp_vol1.pdf.

46. Aditi Shah, "Narendra Modi's BJP Sells Indian Voters Low-Cost Housing Dream," *Mint*, May 14, 2014, www.livemint.com/Politics/TOX8QpfvVVRTvMT0DKUSVO/Narendra-Modis-BJP-sells-Indian-voters-lowcost-housing-dre.html?utm_source=copy.

47. The Modi government's first budget, issued in July 2014, included an allocation of forty billion rupees (4,000 crore) for low-income housing in urban areas and eighty billion

rupees in rural areas. See "Affordable Housing Top Priority," *The Indian Express*, http://indianexpress.com/article/business/business-others/affordable-housing-top-priority/.
48. "Red Carpet, Not Red Tape for Investors, Is the Way Out of Economic Crisis: Narendra Modi," *Economic Times*, June 7, 2012, http://articles.economictimes.indiatimes.com/2012-06-07/news/32101241_1_narendra-modi-prime-minister-red-carpet.
49. See Desai (2012, 50) for an analysis of how state authorities involved in the Sabarmati Riverfront Development in Ahmedabad, Gujarat's largest city, used "an ambivalent and shifting approach vis-à-vis the poor" to draw slum dwellers into resettlement programs, thereby "allow[ing] for official representation of the project as inclusive," while deepening the scale of displacement and disregarding promises of social justice. In 2013, while overseeing Ahmedabad's new city plan, Modi is reported to have come up with the idea, now in the plan, of building a belt for the poor on the city's periphery, past the ring road. See Ellen Barry, "Local Policies Help an Indian Candidate Trying to Go National," *The New York Times*, May 6, 2014, http://www.nytimes.com/2014/05/07/world/asia/local-policies-help-an-indian-candidate-narendra-modi-trying-to-go-national.html.

REFERENCES

Agamben, Giorgio. 1998. *Homo Sacer: Sovereign Power and Bare Life.* Redwood City, CA: Stanford University Press.

Agarwala, Trisha, and Gyana Ranjan Panda. 2013. "Public Provisioning in Water and Sanitation: Study of Urban Slums in Delhi." *Economic and Political Weekly* XLVIII (5): 24–28.

Akerlof, George, and Robert Shiller. 2009. *Animal Spirits: How Human Psychology Drives the Economy, and Why it Matters for Global Capitalism.* Princeton, NJ: Princeton University Press.

Anderson, Benedict. 1983. *Imagined Communities: Reflections on the Origin and Spread of Nationalism.* London: Verso.

Anderson, Michael R. 1992. "Public Nuisance and Private Purpose: Policed Environments in British India, 1860–1947." *SOAS Law Department Working Papers*, No. 1. University of London, School of Oriental and African Studies.

Anderson, Michael R. 1995. "The Conquest of Smoke: Legislation and Pollution in Colonial Calcutta." In *Nature & Culture and Imperialism: Essays on the Environmental History of South Asia*, edited by David Arnold and Ramachandra Guha, 293–335. New Delhi: Oxford University Press.

Appadurai, Arjun. 2002. "Deep Democracy: Urban Governmentality and the Horizon of Politics." *Public Culture* 14 (1): 21–47.

Appadurai, Arjun. 2004. "The Capacity to Aspire: Culture and the Terms of Recognition." In *Culture and Public Action*, edited by Vijayendra Rao and Michael Walton, 59–84. Redwood City, CA: Stanford University Press.

Austin, J. L. 1970. *Philosophical Papers.* Oxford: Clarendon Press.

Austin, J. L. 1975. *How To Do Things with Words.* Cambridge, MA: Harvard University Press.

Auyero, Javier. 1999. "This Is a Lot Like the Bronx, Isn't It? Lived Experiences of Marginality in an Argentine Slum." *International Journal of Urban and Regional Research* 23 (1): 45–69.

Auyero, Javier, and Debora Alejandra Swistun. 2009. *Flammable: Environmental Suffering in an Argentine Shantytown.* New York: Oxford University Press.

Babb, Lawrence. 1983. "Destiny and Responsibility: Karma in Popular Hinduism." In *Karma: An Anthropological Inquiry*, edited by Charles F. Keyes and E. Valentine Daniel, 163–184. Berkeley: University of California Press.

Bardhan, Pranab. 1990. *The Political Economy of Development in India.* Delhi: Oxford University Press.

Barry, Andrew. 2001. *Political Machines: Governing a Technological Society.* London: The Athlone Press.

Barthes, Roland. 1972. *Mythologies.* New York: Hill and Wang.

Batra, Lalit. 2007. "The JNNURM and Urban Reforms in Globalising India." In *The Urban Poor in Globalising India: Eviction and Marginalisation*, edited by Lalit Batra, 98–110. New Delhi: Vusudaiva Kutumbakam Publications.

Baud, Isa, and Navtej Nainan. 2008. "'Negotiated Spaces' for Representation in Mumbai: Ward Committees, Advanced Locality Management and the Politics of Middle-Class Activism." *Environment and Urbanization* 20 (2): 483–499.

Baviskar, Amita. 2003. "Between Violence and Desire: Space, Power, and Identity in the Making of Metropolitan Delhi." *International Social Science Journal* 55 (1): 89–98.

Baviskar, Amita. 2010. "The City and its Commons." In *48º C: Public. Art. Ecology*, edited by Pooja Sood. New Delhi: Goethe Institute.

Bayat, Asef. 2007. "Radical Religion and the Habitus of the Dispossessed: Does Islamic Militancy Have an Urban Ecology?" *International Journal of Urban and Regional Research* 31 (3): 579–590.

Benjamin, Solomon. 2005. *"Productive Slums": The Centrality of Urban Land in Shaping Employment and City Politics*. Cambridge, MA: Lincoln Institute of Land Policy.

Benjamin, Solomon. 2008. "Occupancy Urbanism: Radicalizing Politics and Economy Beyond Policy and Programs." *International Journal of Urban and Regional Research* 32 (3): 719–729.

Benjamin, Walter. 1968. "On Some Motifs in Baudelaire." In *Illuminations: Essays and Reflections*, edited by Hannah Arendt, 155–200. New York: Schoken Books.

Benjamin, Walter. 2002. *The Arcades Project*. Cambridge, MA: Belknap Press.

Bhan, Gautam. 2009. "'This Is No Longer the City I Once Knew.' Evictions, the Urban Poor and the Right to the City in Millennial Delhi." *Environment and Urbanization* 21 (1): 127–142.

Bhan, Gautam. 2013. "Planned Illegalities: Housing and the 'Failure' of Planning in Delhi: 1947–2010." *Economic and Political Weekly* XLVIII (24): 58–70.

Bhan, Gautam, and Swathi Shivanand. 2013. "(Un)Settling the City: Analysing Displacement in Delhi from 1990 to 2007." *Economic and Political Weekly* XLVIII (13): 54–61.

Bharat Sewa Samaj. 1958. *Slums of Old Delhi: Report of the Socio-economic Survey of the Slum Dwellers of Old Delhi City*. Delhi: Atma Ram and Sons.

Bhatia, Gautam. 1994. *Punjabi Baroque*. New Delhi: Penguin.

Bhattacharya, Pradip. 2004. "Of Kunti and Satyawati: Sexually Assertive Women of the Mahabharata." *Manushi*, No. 142 : 21–25.

Bhushan, Prashant. 2006. "Has the Judiciary Turned its Back on the Poor?" Indian Society for International Law, New Delhi, India, November 4.

Biswas, Soutik. 2006. "Why So Much of Delhi Is Illegal." *BBC News*, February 4.

Born, Georgina. 2007. "Future Making: Corporate Performativity and the Temporal Politics of Markets." In *Cultural Politics in a Global Age: Uncertainty, Solidarity and Innovation*, edited by David Held and Henrietta Moore, 288–296. London: Oneworld.

Bose, Mandakrata, ed. 2000. *Face of the Feminine in Ancient, Medieval, and Modern India*. Oxford: Oxford University Press.

Bourdieu, Pierre. 1975. "The Specificity of the Scientific Field and the Social Conditions of the Progress of Reason." *Social Science Information* 14 (6): 19–47.

Bourdieu, Pierre. 1990. *The Logic of Practice*. Redwood City, CA: Stanford University Press.

Bourdieu, Pierre. 1991. *Language and Symbolic Power*. Cambridge: Polity Press.

Brenner, Neil. 2004. *New State Spaces*. Oxford: Oxford University Press.

Broudehoux, Anne-Marie. 2007. "Spectacular Beijing: The Conspicuous Construction of an Olympic Metropolis." *Journal of Urban Affairs* 29 (4): 383–399.

Buck-Morss, Susan. 1989. *The Dialectics of Seeing: Walter Benjamin and the Arcades Project*. Cambridge, MA: MIT Press.

Buckley, Robert M., Mahavir Singh, and Jerry Kalarickal. 2007. "Strategizing Slum Improvement in India: A Method to Monitor and Refocus Slum Development Programs." *Global Urban Development Magazine* 3 (1): 1–24.

Caldeira, Teresa. 2001. *City of Walls: Crime, Segregation, and Citizenship in Sao Paulo.* Berkeley: University of California Press.
Carr, E. Summerson. 2011. *Scripting Addiction: The Politics of Therapeutic Talk and American Sobriety.* Princeton, NJ: Princeton University Press.
Chakrabarti, Poulomi Dhar. 2007. "How the Rise of Middle Class Activism in Indian Cities Is Changing the Face of Local Governance, Case of Delhi." MA thesis, Department of Urban Studies and Planning, Massachusetts Institute of Technology.
Chakrabarti, Poulomi Dhar. 2008. "Inclusion or Exclusion? Emerging Effects of Middle-Class Citizen Participation on Delhi's Urban Poor." *Institute for Development Studies Bulletin* 38 (6): 96–104.
Chakrabarty, Dipesh. 1992. "Of Garbage, Modernity and the Citizen's Gaze." *Economic and Political Weekly* 27 (10/11): 541–547.
Chakrabarty, Dipesh. 2000. *Provincializing Europe: Postcolonial Thought and Historical Difference.* Princeton, NJ: Princeton University Press.
Chandra, Kanchan. 2004. *Why Ethnic Parties Succeed: Patronage and Ethnic Headcounts in India.* Cambridge: Cambridge University Press.
Chatterjee, Partha. 1993. *The Nation and its Fragments: Colonial and Postcolonial Histories.* Princeton, NJ: Princeton University Press.
Chatterjee, Partha. 2004. *The Politics of the Governed: Reflections on Popular Politics in Most of the World.* New York: Columbia University Press.
Chatterjee, Partha. 2011. *Lineages of Political Society: Studies in Postcolonial Democracy.* New York: Columbia University Press.
Chen, Shaohua, and Martin Ravallian. 2010. "The Developing World is Poorer Than We Thought, But No Less Successful in the Fight Against Poverty." *The Quarterly Journal of Economics* 125 (4): 1577–1625.
Christophers, Brett. 2010. "On Voodoo Economics: Theorising Relations of Property, Value and Contemporary Capitalism." *Transactions of the Institute of British Geographers* 35 (1): 94–108.
Coelho, Karen, and T. Venkat. 2009. "The Politics of Civil Society: Neighbourhood Associationism in Chennai." *Economic and Political Weekly* 44 (26): 358–367.
Cohn, Bernard. 1996. *Colonialism and its Forms of Knowledge.* Princeton, NJ: Princeton University Press.
Corbridge, Stuart, Glyn Williams, Manoj Srivastava, and Rene Veron. 2005. *Seeing the State: Governance and Governmentality in India.* Cambridge: Cambridge University Press.
Cornwall, Andrea 2004. "New Democratic Spaces? The Politics and Dynamics of Institutionalised Participation." *Institute for Development Studies Bulletin* 35 (2): 1–10.
Cosgrove, Denis 1986. *Social Formation and Symbolic Landscape.* Madison, WI: University of Wisconsin Press.
Cosgrove, Denis. 2004. "Carto-City. Mapping and Urban Space." In *Mapping a City*, edited by Nina Montmann, Yilmaz Dziewior, and Galerie fur Landschaftskunst, 48–57. Hamburg: Hatje Cantz Verlag.
Crary, Jonathan. 1989. "Spectacle, Attention, Counter-Memory." *October* 50 (Autumn): 97–107.
Cronon, William. 1991. *Nature's Metropolis: Chicago and the Great West.* New York: W.W. Norton.
Das, Veena. 2007. *Life and Words: Violence and the Descent into the Ordinary.* Berkeley: University of California Press.
Das, Veena. 2011. "State, Citizenship, and the Urban Poor." *Citizenship Studies* 15 (3–4): 319–333.
Datta, Ayona. 2012. *The Illegal City: Space, Law and Gender in a Delhi Squatter Settlement.* Farnham: Ashgate.
Davis, Mike. 1990. *City of Quartz: Excavating the Future in Los Angeles.* London: Verso.

Davis, Mike. 2006. *Planet of Slums*. New York: Verso.
DDA. 1962. *Delhi Master Plan 1962*. New Delhi: Delhi Development Authority.
DDA. 1987. *Handbook for Use and Guidance of Damages Section*. New Delhi: Delhi Development Authority.
DDA. 1990. *Delhi Master Plan 2001*. New Delhi: Delhi Development Authority.
DDA. 1997. *Delhi Development Authority Annual Report, 1996–1997*. New Delhi: Delhi Development Authority.
DDA. 2007. *Master Plan for Delhi 2021*. New Delhi: Delhi Development Authority.
DDA. n.d. *Zonal Development Plan, Zone G (West Delhi)*. New Delhi: Delhi Development Authority.
De Soto, Hernando. 2000. *The Mystery of Capital*. New York: Basic Books.
Deaton, Angus. 2010. "Price Indexes, Enequality, and the Measurement of World Poverty." President's Address, American Economic Association Annual Meeting, Atlanta, GA.
Deaton, Angus, and Jean Dreze. 2009. "Food and Nutrition in India: Facts and Interpretations." *Economic and Political Weekly* XLIV (7): 42–65.
Deaton, Angus, and Valerie Kozel. 2005. "Data and Dogma: The Great Indian Poverty Debate." *World Bank Research Observer* 20 (2): 177–199.
Desai, Renu. 2012. "Governing the Urban Poor: Riverfront Development, Slum Resettlement, and the Politics of Inclusion in Ahmedabad." *Economic and Political Weekly* XLVII (2): 49–56.
Dewan, Neha. 2007. "Check Out the Most Expensive Malls in the Country." *Economic Times*. http://economictimes.indiatimes.com/check-out-the-most-expensive-malls-in-the-country/slideshow/2619951.cms.
Diwan, Shyam, and Armin Rosencranz. 2001. *Environmental Law and Policy in India: Cases, Materials and Statues*. New Delhi: Oxford University Press.
Doshi, Sapana. 2013. "The Politics of the Evicted: Redevelopment, Subjectivity, and Difference in Mumbai's Slum Frontier." *Antipode* 45 (4): 844–865.
Duncan, James S., and Nancy G. Duncan. 2004. *Landscapes of Privilege: The Politics of the Aesthetic in an American Suburb*. New York: Routledge.
Dupont, Veronique. 2008. "Slum Demolitions in Delhi Since the 1990s: An Appraisal." *Economic and Political Weekly* 43 (29): 79–87.
Eagleton, Terry. 1990. *The Ideology of the Aesthetic*. Oxford: Basil Blackwell.
Edney, Matthew. 1997. *Mapping an Empire: The Geographical Construction of British India, 1765–1843*. Chicago: University of Chicago Press.
Ferguson, James. 1999. *Expectations of Modernity: Myths and Meanings of Urban Life on the Zambian Copperbelt*. Berkeley: University of California Press.
Ferguson, James. 2010. "The Uses of Neoliberalism." *Antipode* 41 (s1): 166–184.
Fernandes, Leela. 2004. "The Politics of Forgetting: Class Politics, State Power and the Restructuring of Urban Space in India." *Urban Studies* 41 (12): 2415–2430.
Fernandes, Leela. 2006. *India's New Middle Class: Democratic Politics in an Era of Economic Reform*. Minneapolis: University of Minnesota Press.
Fernandes, Leela. 2009. "The Political Economy of Lifestyle: Consumption, India's New Middle Class and State-Led Development." In *The New Middle Classes: Globalizing Lifestyles, Consumerism and Environmental Concern*, edited by Lars Meier and Hellmuth Lange, 219–236. Dordecht: Springer Netherlands.
Fernandes, Leela, and Patrick Heller. 2006. "Hegemonic Aspirations: New Middle Class Politics and India's Democracy in Comparative Perspective." *Critical Asian Studies* 38 (4): 495–522.
Foucault, Michel. 2003. *"Society Must Be Defended"*: *Lectures at the Collège de France, 1975–1976*. New York: Picador.
Foucault, Michel. 2007. *Security, Territory, Population: Lectures at the Collège de France, 1977–1978*. New York: Palgrave Macmillan.

Frankel, Francine R. 1978. *India's Political Economy, 1947–1977: The Gradual Revolution.* Princeton, NJ: Princeton University Press.

Fuller, C. J., and John Harriss. 2000. "For an Anthropology of the Modern Indian State." In *The Everyday State and Society in Modern India*, edited by C. J. Fuller and Veronique Benei, 1–30. New Delhi: Social Science Press.

Gajarawala, Toral Jatin. 2012. *Untouchable Fictions: Literary Realism and the Crisis of Caste.* New York: Fordham University Press.

Ghertner, D. Asher. 2010. "Calculating Without Numbers: Aesthetic Governmentality in Delhi's Slums." *Economy and Society* 39 (2): 185–217.

Ghertner, D. Asher. 2011. "Green Evictions: Environmental Discourses of a Slum-Free Delhi." In *Global Political Ecology*, edited by Paul Robbins, Richard Peet, and Michael Watts, 145–166. London: Routledge.

Ghertner, D. Asher. 2014. "India's Urban Revolution: Geographies of Displacement Beyond Gentrification." *Environment and Planning A* 46 (7): 1554–1571.

Gidwani, Vinay, and Rajyashree N. Reddy. 2011. "The Afterlives of 'Waste': Notes from India for a Minor History of Capitalist Surplus." *Antipode* 43 (5): 1625–1648.

Gilbert, Alan. 2002. "On the Mystery of Capital and the Myths of Hernando de Soto—What Difference Does Legal Title Make?" *International Development Planning Review* 24 (1): 1–19.

GNCTD. 2001. *Bhagidari Working Report: Phase I.* New Delhi: Government of the National Capital Territory of Delhi.

GNCTD. 2004a. *Bhagidari Working Report: Phase III: November 2002 to December 2003.* New Delhi: Government of the National Capital Territory of Delhi.

GNCTD. 2004b. *Economic Survey of Delhi, 2003–4.* New Delhi: Department of Planning, Government of the National Capital Territory of Delhi.

GNCTD. 2006a. *Delhi Human Development Report: Partnerships for Progress.* Government of the National Capital Territory of Delhi. New Delhi: Oxford University Press.

GNCTD. 2006b. "Glimpses of Partnerships and Progress." New Delhi: Bhagidari Cell, Office of the Chief Minister, Government of the National Capital Territory of Delhi.

GNCTD. 2007. "Delhi Smiles." New Delhi: Bhagidari Cell. Bhagidari Cell, Office of the Chief Minister, Government of the National Capital Territory of Delhi.

GNCTD. 2008. *Economic Survey of Delhi.* New Delhi: Department of Planning, Government of the National Capital Territory of Delhi.

Goldman, Michael. 2011. "Speculative Urbanism and the Making of the Next World City." *International Journal of Urban and Regional Research* 35 (3): 555–581.

Gooptu, Nandini. 2005. *The Politics of the Urban Poor in Early Twentieth-Century India.* Cambridge: Cambridge University Press.

Gordon, Colin. 1991. "Governmental Rationality." In *The Foucault Effect: Studies in Governmentality*, edited by Graham Burchell, Colin Gordon, and Peter Miller, 1–52. Chicago: University of Chicago Press.

Gramsci, Antonio. 1971. *Selections from the Prison Notebooks.* Edited by Qutintin Hoare and Geoffery Nowell Smith. New York: International Publishers.

Gray, Kevin, and Susan Francis Gray. 1998. "The Idea of Property in Land." In *Land Law: Themes and Perspectives*, edited by Susan Bright and John K Dewar, 15–51. Oxford: Oxford University Press.

Gregory, Derek. 1994. *Geographical Imaginations.* Oxford: Wiley-Blackwell.

Guha, Ranajit. 1982. "On Some Aspects of the Historiogrpahy of Colonial India." In *Subaltern Studies I*, edited by Rajajit Guha, 1–8. Delhi: Oxford University Press.

Gupta, Akhil. 1998. *Postcolonial Developments: Agriculture in the Making of Modern India.* Durham, NC: Duke University Press.

Gupta, Akhil. 2012. *Red Tape: Bureaucracy, Structural Violence, and Poverty in India.* Durham, NC: Duke University Press.
Gupta, Narayani. 1981. *Delhi Between Two Empires: 1903–1931.* New Delhi: Oxford University Press.
Guru, Gopal. 2013. "Freedom of Expression and the Life of the Dalit Mind." *Economic and Political Weekly* XLVIII (10): 39–45.
Hacking, Ian. 1990. *The Taming of Chance.* Cambridge: Cambridge University Press.
Hall, Stuart. 1997. *Representations: Cultural Representations and Signifying Practices.* London: Sage.
Hall, Tim, and Phil Hubbard. 1996. "The Entrepreneurial City: New Urban Politics, New Urban Geographies?" *Progress in Human Geography* 20 (2): 153–174.
Hansen, Thomas Blom. 2001. *Wages of Violence: Naming and Identity in Postcolonial Bombay.* Princeton, NJ: Princeton University Press.
Harms, Erik. 2011. *Saigon's Edge: On the Margins of Ho Chi Minh City.* Minneapolis: University of Minnesota Press.
Harms, Erik. 2012. "Beauty as Control in the New Saigon: Eviction, New Urban Zones, and Atomized Dissent in a Southeast Asian City." *American Ethnologist* 39 (4): 735–750.
Harriss, John. 2005. "Political Participation, Representation and the Urban Poor: Findings from Research in Delhi." *Economic and Political Weekly* 40 (11): 1041–1054.
Harriss, John. 2009. "Bringing Politics Back Into Poverty Analysis: Why Understanding Social Relations Matters More for Policy on Chronic Poverty Than Measurement." In *Poverty Dynamics: Interdisciplinary Perspectives,* edited by Tony Addison, David Hulme, and Ravi Kanbur, 205–224. Oxford: Oxford University Press.
Harvey, David. 1989. *The Condition of Postmodernity: An Enquiry into the Origins of Cultural Change.* Oxford: Blackwell.
Harvey, David. 2009 [1973]. *Social Justice and the City.* Athens, GA: University of Georgia Press.
Hebden, Keith. 2011. *Dalit Theology and Christian Anarchism.* Surrey: Ashgate.
Holloway, John. 2002. *Change the World Without Taking Power: The Meaning of Revolution Today.* London: Pluto Press.
Hull, Matthew S. 2003. "The File: Agency, Authority, and Autography in an Islamabad Bureaucracy." *Language & Communication* 23 (3–4): 287–314.
Hull, Matthew S. 2008. "Ruled by Records: The Expropriation of Land and the Misappropriation of Lists in Islamabad." *American Ethnologist* 35 (4): 501–518.
Hull, Matthew S. 2012. *Government of Paper: The Materiality of Bureaucracy in Urban Pakistan.* Berkeley: University of California Press.
Imrie, Rob, and Thomas Huw. 1997. "Law, Legal Struggles and Urban Regeneration: Rethinking the Relationships." *Urban Studies* 34 (9): 1401–1418.
Jaffrelot, Christophe. 2003. *India's Silent Revolution.* New Delhi: Permanent Black.
Jain, A. K. 2003. "Making Planning Responsive To, and Compatible With, Reforms." *Cities* 20 (2): 143–145.
Jain, Ashok K. 2005. *Law and Environment.* Delhi: Ascent.
Jain, Kajri. 2007. *Gods in the Bazaar: The Economies of Indian Calendar Art.* Durham, NC: Duke University Press.
Jeffrey, Craig. 2010. *Timepass: Youth, Class, and the Politics of Waiting in India.* Redwood City, CA: Stanford University Press.
Jervis-Read, Cressida. 2010. "'Making Delhi like Paris': Space and the Politics of Development in an East Delhi Resettlement Colony." PhD disssertation, Department of Anthropology, University of Sussex.
Jha, Saumitra, Vijayendra Rao, and Michael Woolcock. 2007. "Governance in the Gullies: Democratic Responsiveness and Leadership in Delhi's Slums." *World Development* 35 (2): 230–246.

Jones, Gareth. 2011. "Slumming About: Aesthetics, Art, Politics." *City* 15 (6): 696–708.
Joyce, Patrick. 2003. *The Rule of Freedom: Liberalism and the Modern City*. London: Verso.
Kamath, Lalitha. 2012. "New Policy Paradigms and Actual Pracitces in Slum Housing: The Case of Housing Projects in Bengaluru." *Economic and Political Weekly* XLVII (47–48): 76–86.
Kamath, Lalitha, and Vinay Baindur. 2009. *Reengineering Urban Infrastructure: How the World Bank and Asian Development Bank Shape Urban Infrastructure Finance and Governance in India*. New Delhi: Bank Information Center.
Kaur, Ravinder. 2005. "Claiming Community Through Narratives: Punjabi Refugees in Delhi." In *The Idea of Delhi*, edited by Romi Khosla, 54–67. Mumbai: Marg Press.
Kaviraj, Sudipta. 1984. "On the Crisis of Political Institutions in India." *Contributions to Indian Sociology* 18 (2): 223–243.
Kaviraj, Sudipta. 1991. "On State, Society and Discourse in India." In *Rethinking Third World Politics*, edited by James Manor, 72–99. London: Longman.
Kaviraj, Sudipta. 1998. "Filth and the Public Sphere: Concepts and Practices About Space in Calcutta." *Public Culture* 10 (1): 83–113.
Keane, Webb. 2007. *Christian Moderns: Freedom and Fetish in the Mission Encounter*. Berkeley: University of California Press.
Khan, Sobia, and Ravi Teja Sharma. 2012. "How Southern Cities Escaped the Real Estate Bubble." *Economic Times*. http://articles.economictimes.indiatimes.com/2012-05-27/news/31860919_1_property-prices-realty-prices-realty-sales.
King, Anthony D. 1984. *The Bungalow: The Production of a Global Culture*. London: Routledge.
Kristeva, Julia. 1982. *Powers of Horror: An Essay on Abjection*. New York: Columbia University Press.
Laclau, Ernesto. 2005. *On Populist Reason*: London. Verso.
Lahiri, Nayanjot. 2011. "A Capital Century." *Caravan* 3 (1): 12–16.
Lakoff, Andrew. 2008. "The Generic Biothreat, or, How We Became Unprepared." *Cultural Anthropology* 23 (3): 399–428.
Lall, Somik V. 2003. "Property Taxes and Local Government Finances." Paper for India: Urban Governance and Finance Review. Washington, DC: The World Bank.
Lama-Rewal, Stephanie Tawa. 2007. "Neighborhood Associations and Local Democracy: Delhi Municipal Elections 2007." *Economic and Political Weekly* 42 (47): 51–60.
Latour, Bruno. 1987. *Science in Action: How to Follow Scientists and Engineers through Society*. Cambridge, MA: Harvard University Press.
Lawson, Victoria. 2005. "Hopeful Geographies: Imagining Ethical Alternatives." *Singapore Journal of Tropical Geography* 26 (1): 36–38.
Leena, D., and Anuradha Sharma. 2007. *Government by the People: Analysing the 74th Constitutional Amendment Act, 1992*. New Delhi: Hazards Centre.
Lees, Loretta. 2012. "The Geography of Gentrification: Thinking Through Comparative Urbanism." *Progress in Human Geography* 36 (2): 155–171.
Legg, Stephen. 2006. "Post-Colonial Developmentalities: From the Delhi Improvement Trust to the Delhi Development Authority." In *Colonial and Post-Colonial Geographies of India*, edited by Saraswati Raju, M. Satish Kumar, and Stuart Corbridge, 182–204. New Delhi: Sage.
Levien, Michael. 2011. "Special Economic Zones and Accumulation by Dispossession in India." *Journal of Agrarian Change* 11 (4): 454–483.
MacKenzie, Donald. 2007. "Is Economics Performative? Option Theory and the Construction of Derivatives Markets." In *Do Economists Make Markets? On the Performativity of Economics*, edited by Donald MacKenzie, Fabian Muniesa, and Lucia Siu, 54–86. Princeton, NJ: Princeton University Press.
Mahadevia, Darshini. 2003. *Globalisation, Urban Reforms and Metropolitan Response, India*. New Delhi: Manak Publishers.
Marx, Karl. 1990 [1867]. *Capital, Volume 1*. New York: Penguin Classics.

Marx, Karl. 1981 [1894]. *Capital, Volume 3.* New York: Penguin.
Marx, Karl. 1993 [1893]. *Capital, Volume 2.* London: Penguin.
Marx, Karl. 2010 [1894]. *Capital, Volume 3.* New York: International Publishers.
Mathur, O. P. 2009. *Slum-Free Cities: A New Deal for the Urban Poor.* Report Submitted to the Ministry of Housing and Urban Poverty Alleviation, National Institute of Public Finance and Policy, New Delhi.
Mawdsley, Emma. 2009. "'Environmentality' in the Neoliberal City: Attitudes, Governance and Social Justice." In *The New Middle Classes—Globalising Lifestyles, Consumerism, and Environmental Concern,* edited by Hellmuth Lange and Lars Meir, 237–252. London: Springer.
Mazzarella, William. 2003. *Shoveling Smoke: Advertising and Globalization in Contemporary India.* Durham, NC: Duke University Press.
McClintock, Anne. 1995. *Imperial Leather: Race, Gender and Sexuality in the Colonial Context.* New York: Routledge.
McFarlane, Colin. 2011. "The City as Assemblage: Dwelling and Urban Space." *Environment and Planning D: Society and Space* 29 (4): 649–671.
McFarlane, Colin. 2012. "From Sanitation Inequality to Malevolent Urbanism: The Normalisation of Suffering in Mumbai." *Geoforum* 43 (6): 1287–1290.
McKinsey & Company. 2001. *India: The Growth Imperative.* New Delhi: McKinsey Global Institute.
McKinsey & Company. 2007. *The "Bird of Gold": The Rise of India's Consumer Market.* Washington, DC: McKinsey Global Institute.
McKinsey & Company. 2007. "Tracking the Growth of India's Middle Class." *The McKinsey Quarterly* (3): 51–61.
McKinsey & Company. 2010. *India's Urban Awakening: Building Inclusive Cities, Sustaining Economic Growth.* Washington, DC: McKinsey Global Institute.
McQuarrie, Michael, Naresh Fernandes, and Cassim Shepard. 2013. "The Field of Struggle, the Office, and the Flat: Protest and Aspiration in a Mumbai Slum." *Public Culture* 25 (1): 315–348.
Mechoulan, Eric. 2004. "Introduction: On the Edges of Jacques Rancière." *SubStance* 33 (1): 3–9.
Mehra, Diya. 2009. "Campaigning Against Its Eviction: Local Trade in New 'World-Class' Delhi." In *Dissent and Cultural Resistance in Asia's Cities,* edited by Melissa Butcher and Selvaraj Velayutham, 148–167. New York: Routledge.
Menon-Sen, Kalyani, and Gautam Bhan. 2008. *Swept off the Map: Surviving Eviction and Resettlement in Delhi.* New Delhi: Yoda Press.
Milios, John, and Dimitri Dimoulis. 2006. "Louis Althusser and the Forms of Concealment of Capitalist Exploitation." *Historical Materialism* 14 (2): 135–148.
Ministry of Housing and Urban Poverty Alleviation. 2007. "Report of the Technical Group on Estimation of Urban Housing Shortage 2007–2012," *11th Five Year Plan.* New Delhi: Government of India.
Mitchell, Don. 1996. *The Lie of the Land: Migrant Workers and the California Landscape.* Minneapolis: University of Minnesota Press.
Mitchell, Timothy. 2002. *Rule of Experts: Egypt, Techno-Politics, Modernity.* Berkeley: University of California Press.
Mitchell, Timothy. 2007. "The Properties of Markets." In *Do Economists Make Markets? On the Performativity of Markets,* edited by Donald MacKenzie, Fabian Muniesa, and Lucia Siu, 244–275. Princeton, NJ: Princeton University Press.
Miyazaki, Hirokazu. 2006. "Economy of Dreams: Hope in Global Capitalism and its Critiques." *Cultural Anthropology* 21 (2): 147–172.
Narayan, Deepa, Binayak Sen, and Katy Hull. 2009. *Moving Out of Poverty in India: An Overview.* Washington, DC: The World Bank.

NCAER. 2005. *The Great Indian Market: Results from the NCAER's Market Information Survey of Households.* New Delhi: National Council of Applied Economic Research.

Nilekani, Nandan. 2009. *Imagining India: The Idea of a Renewed Nation.* New York: Penguin.

Pandey, Gyan. 2009. "Can There Be a Subaltern Middle Class? Notes on African American and Dalit History." *Public Culture* 21 (2): 321–342.

Parel, Anthony J., ed. 1997. *Gandhi: Hind Swaraj and Other Writings.* Cambridge: Cambridge University Press.

Patnaik, Utsa. 2007. *The Republic of Hunger.* New Delhi: Three Essays.

Patnaik, Utsa. 2008. "Neoliberal Roots." *Frontline* 25 (6). http://www.frontline.in/static/html/fl2506/stories/20080328250601700.htm.

Pethe, Abhay, Ramakrishna Nallathiga, Sahil Gandhi, and Vaidehi Tandel. 2014. "Re-Thinking Urban Planning in India: Learning from the Wedge Between the de Jure and de Facto Development in Mumbai." *Cities* 39 (August): 120–132.

Phillips, Kim. 1997. "Lotteryville, USA." In *Commodify your Dissent: Salvos from The Baffler,* edited by Thomas Frank and Matt Weiland, 234–246. New York: W. W. Norton.

Pinney, Christopher. 2004. *Photos of the Gods: The Printed Image and Political Struggle in India.* London: Reaktion Books.

Planning Commision of India. 2002. *Report of the Committee on Problems of Slums in Delhi.* New Delhi: Government of India.

Planning Commission of India. 2003. *India Vision 2020.* New Delhi: Government of India.

Planning Commission of India. 2007. *Report of the Committee on Infrastructure Financing.* New Delhi: Government of India.

Planning Commision of India. 2013. *Twelfth Five Year Plan: Faster, More Inclusive and Sustainable Growth.* New Delhi: Sage.

Polanyi, Karl. 1944. *The Great Transformation: The Political and Economic Origins of Our Time..* New York: Farrar & Rinehart Inc.

Pow, Choon-Piew. 2009. "Neoliberalism and the Aestheticization of New Middle-Class Landscapes." *Antipode* 41 (2): 371–390.

Prahalad, C. K. 2006. *The Fortune at the Bottom of the Pyramid: Eradicating Poverty through Profits.* Upper Saddle River, NJ: Prentice Hall.

Prakash, Gyan. 1999. *Another Reason: Science and the Imagination of Modern India.* Princeton, NJ: Princeton University Press.

Prasad, M. Madhava. 2008. "Surviving Bollywood." In *Global Bollywood,* edited by Anandam P. Kavoori and Aswin Punathambekar, 41–51. New York: New York University Press.

Prashad, Vijay. 2001. "The Technology of Sanitation in Colonial Delhi." *Modern Asian Studies* 35 (1): 113–55.

Rabinow, Paul. 1982. "*Ordonnance,* Disipline, Regulation: Some Reflections on Urbanism." *Humanities in Society* 5 (3–4): 267–278.

Rabinow, Paul. 1989. *French Modern: Norms and Forms of the Social Environment.* Cambridge, MA: MIT Press.

Ramakrishnan, Kavita. 2014. "Disrupted Futures: Unpacking Metaphors of Marginalization in Eviction and Resettlement Narratives." *Antipode* 46 (3): 754–772.

Raman, Bhavani. 2012. *Document Raj: Writing and Scribes in Early Colonial South India.* Chicago: University of Chicago Press.

Ramanathan, Usha. 2005. "Demolition Drive." *Economic and Political Weekly* 40 (27): 3607–3612.

Ramanathan, Usha. 2006. "Illegality and the Urban Poor." *Economic and Political Weekly* 41 (29): 3193–3197.

Ramani, Srinivasan. 2013. "The Aam Aadmi Party's Win in Delhi: Dissecting it Through Geographical Information Systems." *Economic and Political Weekly* XLVIII

(52): Web Exclusive, http://www.epw.in/web-exclusives/aam-aadmi-partys-win-delhi-dissecting-it-through-geographical-information-systems.htm.

Ramesh, Randeep. 2008. "Delhi Cleans Up for Commonwealth Games But Leaves Locals Without Sporting Chance." *The Guardian*, January 8.

Rancière, Jacques. 1976 [1965]. "The Concept of 'Critique' and the 'Critique of Political Economy' (from the *1844 Manuscript* to *Capital*)." *Economy and Society* 5 (3): 352–376.

Rancière, Jacques. 1998. *Dis-agreement: Politics and Philosophy*. Minneapolis: University of Minnesota Press.

Rancière, Jacques. 2004. *The Politics of Aesthetics*. New York: Continuum.

Rancière, Jacques. 2009. "Contemporary Art and the Politics of Aesthetics." In *Communities of Sense: Rethinking Aesthetics and Politics*, edited by Beth Hinderliter, William Kaizen, Vered Maimon, Jaleh Mansoor, and Seth McCormick, 31–50. Durham, NC: Duke University Press.

Rancière, Jacques. 2010. *Dissensus: On Aesthetics and Politics*. London: Continuum.

Randhawa, Pritpal Singh. 2012. "Delhi Metro Rail: Beyond Mass Transit." *Economic and Political Weekly* XLVII (16): 25–29.

Rao, Anupama. 2009. *The Caste Question: Dalits and the Politics of Modern India*. Berkeley: University of California Press.

Rao, Vyjayanthi. 2006. "Slum as Theory." *International Journal of Urban and Regional Research* 30 (1): 225–232.

Rose, Nikolas. 1999. *Powers of Freedom: Reframing Political Thought*. Cambridge: Cambridge University Press.

Rosen, Christine. 2003. "Knowing Industrial Pollution: Nuisance Law and the Power of Tradition in a Time of Rapid Economic Change, 1840–64." *Environmental History* 8 (3): 565–597.

Rotman, Brian. 1987. *Signifying Nothing: The Semiotics of Zero*. New York: St. Martin's Press.

Roy, Ananya. 2002. *City Requiem, Calcutta: Gender and the Politics of Poverty*. Minneapolis: University of Minnesota Press.

Roy, Ananya. 2004. "The Gentleman's City: Urban Informality in the Calcutta of New Communism." In *Urban Informality*, edited by Nezar AlSayyad and Ananya Roy, 147–170. Lanham, MD: Lexington Books.

Roy, Ananya. 2009. "Civic Governmentality: The Politics of Inclusion in Beirut and Mumbai." *Antipode* 41 (1): 159–179.

Roy, Ananya. 2010. *Poverty Capital: Microfinance and the Making of Development*. New York: Routledge.

Roy, Ananya. 2014. "Slum-Free Cities of the Asian Century: Postcolonial Government and the Project of Inclusive Growth." *Singapore Journal of Tropical Geography* 35 (1): 136–150.

Roy, Arundhati. 2014. "The Doctor and the Saint." In *The Annhilation of Caste*, by Bhimrao Ramji Ambedkar, 15–180. London: Verso.

Roy, Dunu. 2004. *Pollution, Pushta, and Prejudices*. Delhi: Hazards Centre.

Roy, Srirupa. 2007. *Beyond Belief: India and the Politics of Postcolonial Nationalism*. Durham, NC: Duke University Press.

Rudolph, Lloyd I., and Susanne Hoeber Rudolph. 1987. *In Pursuit of Lakshmi: The Political Economy of the Indian State*. Chicago: University of Chicago Press.

Saberwal, Satish. 1996. *Roots of Crisis: Interpreting Contemporary Indian Society*. New Delhi: Sage.

Said, Edward W. 1978. *Orientalism*. New York: Vintage Books.

Sarkar, Sumit. 1983. *"Popular" Movements and "Middle Class" Leadership in Late Colonial India: Perspectives and Problems of a "History from Below."* Calcutta: K. P. Bagchi.

Scott, David. 1995. "Colonial Governmentality." *Social Text* 43 (Autumn): 191–220.

Scott, James C. 1990. *Domination and the Arts of Resistance: Hidden Transcripts*. New Haven, CT: Yale University Press.

Scott, James C. 1998. *Seeing Like a State: How Certain Schemes to Improve the Human Condition Have Failed.* New Haven, CT: Yale University Press.
Searle, John R. 1969. *Speech Acts.* Cambridge: Cambridge University Press.
Searle, Llrena Guiu. 2008. "Betting on Growth." *Seminar* 582: 51–56.
Searle, Llerena Guiu. 2014. "Conflict and Commensuration: Contested Market Making in India's Private Real Estate Development Sector." *International Journal of Urban and Regional Research* 38 (1): 60–78.
Sengar, Dharmendra S. 2007. *Environmental Law.* New Delhi: Prentice-Hall India.
Sharan, Awadhendra. 2006. "In the City, Out of Place: Environment and Modernity, Delhi 1860s to 1960s." *Economic and Political Weekly* 41 (47): 4905–4911.
Sharan, Awadhendra. 2014. *In the City, Out of Place: Nuisance, Pollution, and Dwelling in Delhi, c. 1850–2000.* New Delhi: Oxford Univesity Press.
Shukla, Rajesh. 2007. "How India Earns, Spends and Saves: Results from the Max New York Life-NCAER India Financial Protection Survey." New Delhi: Max New York Life Insurance Limited.
Sibley, David. 1995. *Geographies of Exclusion.* London: Routledge.
Simmel, Georg. 2007 [1913]. "The Problem of Fate." *Theory, Culture & Society* 24 (7–8): 78–84.
Simone, AbdouMaliq. 2004. *For the City Yet to Come: Changing African Life in Four Cities.* Durham, NC: Duke University Press.
Simone, AbdouMaliq. 2006. "Pirate Towns: Reworking Social and Symbolic Infrastructures in Johannesburg and Douala." *Urban Studies* 43 (2): 357–370.
Smith, Adam. 1982 [1776]. *The Wealth of Nations: Books 1–3.* London: Penguin.
Smith, Neil. 2002. "New Globalism, New Urbanism: Gentrification as Global Urban Strategy." *Antipode* 34 (3): 427–450.
Smith, Richard Saumarez. 1985. "Rule-by-Records and Rule-by-Reports: Complementary Aspects of the British Imperial Rule of Law." *Contributions to Indian Sociology* 19 (1): 153–176.
Srivastava, Rukmini. 2011. "Delhi's Population Grows Slowest in 100 years." *The Times of India,* April 5.
Stoler, Ann Laura. 1995. *Race and the Education of Desire: Foucault's History of Sexuality and the Colonial Order of Things.* Durham, NC: Duke University Press.
Subramaniam, Samnath. 2011. "Lifetime Opportunity." *Caravan* 3 (10): 42–49.
Sundaram, Ravi. 2009. *Pirate Modernity: Delhi's Media Urbanism.* New York: Routledge.
Swyngedouw, Erik. 2005. "Governance Innovation and the Citizen: The Janus Face of Governance-Beyond-the-State." *Urban Studies* 42 (11): 1991–2006.
Taneja, Amitabh, ed. 2007. *Malls in India: Shopping Centre Developers and Developments.* New Delhi: Images Multimedia.
Taneja, Anand. 2008. "History and Heritage Woven Into the New Urban Fabric: The Changing Landscapes of Delhi's 'First City.'" In *Patterns of Middle Class Consumption in India and China,* edited by Christopher Jaffrelot and Peter van der Veer, 157–169. London: Sage.
Tarlo, Emma. 2003. *Unsettling Memories: Narratives of the Emergency in Delhi.* Berkeley: University of California Press.
Tata Consultancy Services. 1986. "Delhi Development Authority Organizational Review Study, Vol. 1: Proposed Management Information System." New Delhi: Tata Consultancy.
Taussig, Michael. 1980. *The Devil and Commodity Fetishism in South America.* Chapel Hill: University of North Carolina.
Taussig, Michael. 1997. *The Magic of the State.* New York: Routledge.
Tsing, Anna. 2005. *Friction: An Anthropology of Global Connection.* Princeton, NJ: Princeton University Press.
United Nations. 2014. *World Urbanization Prospects: The 2014 Revision.* New York: Department of Economic and Social Affairs.

Valverde, Mariana. 2011. "Seeing Like a City: The Dialectic of Modern and Premodern Ways of Seeing in Urban Governance." *Law & Society Review* 45 (2): 277–312.

Varley, Ann. 2002. "Private or Public: Debating the Meaning of Tenure Legalization." *International Journal of Urban and Regional Research* 26 (3): 449–461.

Venn, Couze. 2006. "The City as Assemblage: Diasporic Cultures, Postmodern Spaces, and Biopolitics." In *Negotiating Urban Conflicts: Interaction, Space, and Control* edited by H. Berking, S. Frank, L. Frers, L. M. Low, S. Steets, and S. Stoetzer, 41–52. Piscataway, NJ: Transaction.

Verma, Gita Dewan. 2002. *Slumming India: A Chronicle of Slums and their Saviours*. Delhi: Penguin Books.

Verran, Helen. 2010. "Number as an Inventive Frontier in Knowing and Working Australia's Water Resources." *Anthropological Theory* 10 (1–2): 171–178.

Virmani, Arvind. 2006. "Poverty and Hunger in India: What Is Needed to Eliminate Them." Planning Commission Working Paper No. 1/2006-PC. New Delhi: Planning Commission, Government of India.

Visvanathan, Brinda and J. V. Meenakshi. 2003. "Calorie Deprivation in Rural India, 1983–1999/2000." *Economic and Political Weekly* XXXVIII (4): 369–375.

Wacquant, Loïc. 2008. *Urban Outcasts: A Comparative Sociology of Advanced Marginality*. Cambridge: Polity.

Walks, R. Alan. 2006. "Aestheticization and the Cultural Contradictions of Neoliberal (Sub) urbanism." *Cultural Geogrpahies* 13 (3): 466–475.

Watts, Michael. 1983. *Silent Violence: Food, Famine and Peasantry in Northern Nigeria*. Berkeley, University of California Press.

Wedeen, Lisa. 1999. *Ambiguities of Domination: Politics, Rhetoric, and Symbols in Contemporary Syria*. Chicago, University of Chicago Press.

Weiner, Miron. 1962. *The Politics of Scarcity: Public Pressure and Political Response in India*. Chicago, University of Chicago Press.

Weinstein, Liza. 2009. "Democracy and the Globalizing Indian City: Engagements of Political Society and the State in Globalizing Mumbai." *Politics and Society* 37 (3): 397–427.

Weiss, Brad. 2002. "Thug Realism: Inhabiting Fantasy in Urban Tanzania." *Cultural Anthropology* 17 (1): 93–124.

Willis, Paul. 1981. "Cultural Production Is Different from Cultural Reproduction Is Different from Social Reproduction Is Different from Reproduction." *Interchange* 12 (2–3): 48–67.

Witsoe, Jeffrey. 2011. "Corruption as Power: Caste and the Political Imagination of the Postcolonial State." *American Ethnologist* 38 (1): 73–85.

World Bank. 2005. "Urban Land Markets in India: Analytical Background Papers." New Delhi: The World Bank.

World Bank. 2007. *India 2025: Inputs for an Urban Strategy. Presentation to the Planning Commission*. The World Bank India Country Management Unit, New Delhi.

World Bank. 2008. "New Data Show 1.4 Billion Live On Less Than $1.25 a day, But Progress Against Poverty Remains Strong." news release: 2009/065/DEC, Washington, DC: The World Bank. http://go.worldbank.org/QDSYZU1AR0.

Word Bank. 2009. *World Development Report 2009: Reshaping Economic Geography*. Washington, DC: The World Bank.

Yadav, Yogendra. 2000. "Understanding the Second Democratic Upsurge: Trends of Bahujan Participation in Electoral Participation in the 1990s." In *Transforming India: Social and Political Dynamics of Democracy*, edited by Francine Frankel, Zoya Hasan, Rajeev Bhargava, and Balveer Arora, 120–145. New Delhi: Oxford University Press.

Yang, Anand. 1989. *The Limited Raj: Agrarian Relations in Colonial India, Saran District, 1793–1920*. Berkeley: University of California Press.

Yurchak, Alexei. 2003. "Soviet Hegemony of Form: Everything Was Forever, Until It Was No More." *Comparative Studies in Society and History* 45 (3): 480–510.

Yurchak, Alexei. 2005. *Everything Was Forever, Until It Was No More: The Last Soviet Generation*. Princeton, NJ: Princeton University Press.

Zaloom, Caitlin. 2006. *Out of the Pits: Traders and Technology from Chicago to London*. Chicago: University of Chicago Press.

Zaloom, Caitlin. 2009. "How To Read the Future: The Yield Curve, Affect, and Financial Prediction." *Public Culture* 21 (2): 245–268.

Žižek, Slavoj. 2006. *The Parallax View*. Cambridge, MA: MIT Press.

INDEX

Aadhaar (biometric identification card system), 195
Aam Aadmi Party (AAP), 195–98, 204n58
abjection, 79–81, 85–86, 88–89, 95, 194, 231n38. *See also* nuisance
Agarwal, Pankaj, 92, 94
Agarwala, Trisha, 231n37
Akerlof, George, 29
Almrita Patel v. the Union of India, 104–5, 107, 111, 113
Anderson, Benedict, 55
Anderson, Michael R., 219n32
Appadurai, Arjun, 127
Aristotle, 204n56
Ashok Vihar RWA, 102–3
Asian Centre for Organisation Research and Development (ACORD), 58, 62–64
Asian Development Bank, 26
Austin, J. L., 209n69, 215n5
Auyero, Javier, 19

B. L. Wadehra v. the Union of India, 103–4
Babb, Lawrence, 227n26
Bakhtin, Mikhail, 222–23n36
Bangalore, 218n15
Barry, Andrew, 200n11
Barthes, Roland, 36, 39, 208n61
basti. *See jhuggi* colonies (Delhi)
Baviskar, Amita, 9
Bawana (resettlement colony), *151*, 178–180
Bayat, Asef, 224n48
Benjamin, Solomon, 48, 202n34, 218n15
Benjamin, Walter, 145–46, 225n15, 225n16
Bentham, Jeremy, 199n9
Bhagidari: criticism of, 75–76; membership workshops and, 59–62; monthly meetings and, 60, 65–66, 68–70; "new state space" in, 66–73, *67*; power of property and, 73–77; role and goals of, 14, 46, 57–59; thematic workshops and, 60–61, 62–65

Bhagidari Cell, 58, 60–61, 70, 71, 72
Bhan, Gautam, 200n15
Bharatiya Janata Party (BJP), 75, 193
Bhushan, Prashant, 204n58
Biswas, Soutik, 203n46
Bombay Municipal Corporation, 17
Bourdieu, Pierre, 97–98, 142, 145, 148, 152, 223n37
Brenner, Neil, 66
Buck-Morss, Susan, 143
BusinessWeek (magazine), 33

calculative governmentality (rule by records), 5–8, 12–14, 100, 105–6, 183, 186, 195–96
Calcutta (Kolkata), 55, 211n14
Carr, E. Summerson, 223n39
caste: Indian state and, 47; purity and pollution and, 83, 85–86, 91. *See also* class habitus; Dalit (former untouchable)
Census of India (2001), 212n18
Census of India (2011), 199n3
Chakrabarty, Dipesh, 85–86, 200n21
Chambers, Robert, 36
Chameli Singh v. State of U.P., 202n36
Chatterjee, Partha: on civil society and political society, 48, 54–56, 219n39; on differential and equivalent demands, 223n40; on politics of the governed, 202n32; on subaltern history, 205n65, 211n11; on world-class aesthetic, 23–24
Chaudhury (land colonizer), 132–33, 192–93, 222n28, 222n30
China, 28, 29
Christophers, Brett, 227n30
The City Development Plan of Delhi (report), 199n3
civil society, 48, 54–55, 219n39

(247)

class habitus: purity and pollution and, 85–86, 91; state access and, 46–49; world-class aesthetic and, 42, 144–46
Clean Delhi, Green Delhi (campaign), 95
Cohn, Bernard, 6–7, 200n17
Commonwealth Games (2010), 8, 12–13, 95, 141–42, 186–87
Commonwealth Games Village, 11
community of sense, 7, 126, 185
Congress Party, 75, 187, 196
Cooperative Housing Society Policy, 28
Co-Operative Societies Act, 12
corruption, 187–88
Cosgrove, Denis, 200n12, 221n12, 222n17
Credit Risk Guarantee Fund, 191
Cronon, William, 43

Dalit (former untouchable): fatalism and, 226n25; origin and use of term, 204n57; Sant Ravi Das Camp and, 83, 85–86; Shiv Camp and, 221n6; slum removal and, 12. *See also jhuggi* colonies (Delhi)
Das, Veena, 12, 48, 202n33, 202n34, 215n3
Datta, Ayona, 204n59
Davis, Mike, 199n1
DDA. *See* Delhi Development Authority (DDA)
De Soto, Hernando, 178, 180–81, 182, 188–89
Deaton, Angus, 208n52
Delhi: administrative structure in, 49–54, 50; housing market in, 43–44, 188–195; land market in, 10, 24–29, 143, 160–61; population of, 51; rise of new middle classes in, 54–57. *See also* Bhagidari; *jhuggi* colonies (Delhi)
Delhi Development Act (1957), 25, 201n31
Delhi Development Authority (DDA): DLF Emporio and, 2; government housing and, DP; land market and, 28; petitions by RWAs and, 122–23; Ravi Das Camp and, 81, 83; removal of slums and, 11–12; role of, 51–52, 106; slum removal and, 2–3, 99
Delhi High Court: Pitampura judgment and, 107–14; Ravi Das Camp and, 86–87; RWAs and, 74; Shiv Camp and, 146–48; slum removal and, 13–14, 106, 114–123, *118*, 193

Delhi Master Plan: Delhi Development Authority and, 106; DLF Emporio and, 2; Jain on, 3; land market and, 25–26, 28–29; origins and status of *jhuggi* colonies and, 51–54; Shiv Camp residents' view of, 145–46; world-class aesthetic and, 10–11, 23–24
Delhi Special Laws Act, 188, 193
Delhi Urban Shelter Improvement Board (DUSIB), 195
Desai, Renu, 232n49
Deshpande, Satish, 201n26
Dikshit, Sheila, 57, 183, 187–88, 196, 201n22
district development committees, 73
Diwan, Shyam, 113
DLF (real estate firm), 27–28, 33–34
DLF Emporio, 2–3, *2*
Dupont, Veronique, 200n15

Eagleton, Terry, 139–140, 141, 154
East India Company, 5
Economically Weaker Sections (EWS), 83, 211n15
Electricity Act (2003), 119
Emaar-MGF, 187

fate and fatalism, 170–76, *172*
Ferguson, James, 231n38
Fernandes, Leela, 56
fetishism, 158–161, 181–82
Finance Ministry, 191
Foucault, Michel, 5, 185, 200n14, 200n16, 203n47, 203n51
Frankel, Francine R., 211n9
Freehold Conversion Program, 28

Gandhi, Indira, 201n23
Gandhi, Mohandas Karamchand, 226n25
Geo-Spatial Data Infrastructure Act (2011), 195
ghar (home), 176–181, 189
Goldman, Michael, 205n6
government housing, 12, 26, 51–54, 83–84, 108, 211n15
governmentality, 5–8, 180, 185, 203n51. *See also* rule by aesthetics; rule by records (calculative governmentality)
Gramsci, Antonio, 203n51
Gray, Kevin, 111
Gray, Susan Francis, 111

Green Delhi Action Plan, 217n34
Gupta, Akhil, 229n19
Guru, Gopal, 216n13

habitus, 224n48. *See also* class habitus
Hacking, Ian, 5–6
Hall, Tim, 140, 221n12
Harriss, John, 36
Harvey, David, 210n82
Hazards Centre, 19
Hazare, Anna, 196
Heindrich, J. C., 226n25
Heller, Patrick, 56
Higher Income Group (HIG), 211n15
The Hindu (newspaper), 71–72, 74–75
Hindustan Times (newspaper), 46, 93, 96, 187
Hindustan Times Live (weekly supplement), 70
house posters, 152–56, *152, 154*
housing market, 43–44, 188–195. *See also* government housing
Hubbard, Phil, 140, 221n12
Hull, Matthew S., 202n35

Imagined Communities (Anderson), 55
inclusive growth, 188–195, 197–98
India: rise of new middle classes in, 54–57; state access in, 46–49. *See also* Delhi
India Vision 2020 (Planning Commission), 37
India: The Growth Imperative (McKinsey & Company), 27
Indonesia, 28
Infosys (IT firm), 190, 207n41
inside/outside, 79, 85–86, 88–89

Jagmohan, 201n23
Jain, A. K.: governmentality and, 6; on land privatization, 28; on RWAs, 74; on world-class aesthetic, 3, 4–5, 23, 184
Janshakti Party, 131, 221n7
Jeffrey, Craig, 226n21
Jervis-Read, Cressida, 201n23
jhuggi colonies (Delhi): origins and status of, 1, 51–54; population of, 6, 51; ration and voter ID cards and, 52–53, 133–34, 149–150; removal of, 11–14, 54, 57, 70–71; V. P. Singh token and, 132. *See also* nuisance; resettlement; Sant Ravi Das Camp (*jhuggi* colony); Shiv Camp (*jhuggi* colony)

JJ clusters. *See jhuggi* colonies (Delhi)
Jones Lang LaSalle (real estate firm), 33

K. K. Manchanda v. the Union of India, 102–3, 105, 107–8, 145. *See also* Pitampura judgment
Kailash Fraternity RWA, 115, 121
Kamath, Lalitha, 228–29n17
Kant, Immanuel, 15–16
Kaul, Sanjay, 91–92
Kaviraj, Sudipta, 47, 216n15
Keane, Webb, 223n39
Kejriwal, Arvind, 196
Keynes, John Maynard, 33
King, Anthony D., 224n45
Kolkata (Calcutta), 55, 211n14
Kristeva, Julia, 79
Kumar, Surendra, 210n1

Laclau, Ernesto, 223n40
Lakoff, Andrew, 205n8, 209n73
Land Acquisition Act (1894), 26, 110, 206n21
land market, 10, 24–29, 143, 160–61. *See also* housing market
Latour, Bruno, 13
Legg, Stephen, 200n19
Legislative Assembly, 49–51
Lower Income Group (LIG), 83, 211n15

magic, 161–66, *162*
Mahabharata, 215–16n9
Marx, Karl, 44, 159–160, 180–81, 182, 210n82, 225n17
Mazzarella, William, 142
McClintock, Anne, 215n7
McFarlane, Colin, 230–31n37
McKinsey & Company, 24, 26–27, 31–33, *32, 34,* 38–42, *39–40,* 206n12
media, 92–93. *See also specific newspapers*
middle classes, 24, 29–33, 38–44, 54–57. *See also* resident welfare associations (RWAs)
Middle Income Group (MIG), 83, 211n15
Ministry of Urban Development, *50, 66,* 74
Ministry of Urban Housing and Poverty Alleviation, 21
Mitchell, Don, 222n16
Mitchell, Timothy, 199n8
Modi, Narendra, 198

mohalla sabhas, 197–98
Monitor Deloitte, 191–92
Monitor Inclusive Markets, 191–92
Moretti, Franco, 124
Mumbai, 214n89
Municipal Corporation of Delhi (MCD): Bhagidari and, 65, 67, 68–73; on land use, 13–14; role of, 50, 51; Shiv Camp and, 19–20, 53–54, 126, 128–133, 140, 150, 159, 193–94; slum removal and, 11, 103–7, 121–22
My Delhi, I Care fund, 72–73
myth, 36–42, 38

Nangla Machi (*jhuggi* colony), 18
Nath, Kamal, 228n13
The Nation and its Fragments (Chatterjee), 55
National Council of Applied Economic Research (NCAER), 30–33, **30**, 34
National Sample Survey Organization (NSSO), 34–35
New Economic Policy, 10
Newsweek (magazine), 41
Nilekani, Nandan, 194, 195, 231n39
nuisance: abjection and, 79–81, 194; DLF Emporio and, 2–3; legal definition of, 101; performative dimension of, 97–98, 110–11; private property and, 94–96, 96; Sant Ravi Das Camp as, 81–87; world-class aesthetic and, 14–15, 87–93, 97–98
nuisance law: Pitampura judgment and, 107–14; roots of, 99–107; slum removal and, 114–123, *118*, 184, 193–94

Olga Tellis v. Bombay Municipal Corporation, 111–12, 202n36

Panda, Gyana Ranjan, 231n37
Pandey, Gyan, 212n36
Paris, 9
Paswan, Ram Vilas, 221n7
Patnaik, Utsa, 34–36, 207n48
People's Action (RWA), 91
Phillips, Kim, 226n23
Pitampura judgment, 107–14, 220n54. See also *K. K. Manchanda v. the Union of India*
Planning Commission, 34–38
plot, 147, 176–181, 189

police, 92–93
political society, 48, 49–51, 54–55, 68, 71, 219n39
pollution, 85–86, 91, 95–97, 103, 120
poverty: inclusive growth and, 189; measurement of, 33–36; myth of, 36–42, *38–40*; projections for, 24–25, 29–33, 32
Pow, Choon-Piew, 140
Prahalad, C. K., 182
Prasad, M. Madhava, 210n5
private property: De Soto on, 178, 180–81, 182; in Delhi, 26, 160–61; Marx on, 159–160, 180–81, 182; propriety and, 21, 94–96, 96, 111–12, 158, 180, 181; resettlement and, 158–59; world-class aesthetic and, 181–82. See also land market
propriety, 21, 94–96, 96, 111–12, 144–45, 158, 180–181, 198
public interest, 110–13
public interest litigations (PILs), 12–13, 86–87, 112
Public Premises Act (1971), 110

R. L. Kaushal v. Lt. Governor of Delhi, 118
Rabinow, Paul, 200n14
Rajeev Awas Yojana (RAY), 188–190, 191, 194–95
Ramakrishnan, Kavita, 227n32
Rancière, Jacques: on aesthetic politics, 15–17, 155–57; on citizenship, 204n56; on community of sense, 7, 126, 185; on disagreement, 203n51; on the distribution of the sensible/*le partage du sensible*, 16–17, 172; on fetishism, 182, 224n5; on *Verkehrung*, 224–25n9
Randhawa, Pritpal Singh, 222n19
Rao, Jerry, 230n29
ration cards, 52–53, 133–34, 149–150
Ratlam Municipal Council v. Vardichan, 101–2, 103
Ravi Das Camp (*jhuggi* colony), 81–87, *81–82, 85*, 118–19
Ravi Das (Sant), 216n10
Regunathan, S., 58, 213n55
resettlement: *ghar* (home) versus *plot* and, 176–181; property and, 158–59; Shiv Camp residents and, 150–56, 158–59, 175–181; terms of, 223n41

resident welfare associations
(RWAs): antislum views of, 70–71,
74–75, 78–79; nuisance talk and,
87–93; petitions by, 102–3, 107–8,
110–11, 114–123, *118*; private
property and, 94–96; role of, 45–46;
Sant Ravi Das Camp and, 85–87; Shiv
Camp and, 130, 137, 146–48, 192–93;
slum removal and, 12–13, 99, 114–123,
118; world-class aesthetic and, 97–98.
See also Bhagidari
right to life, 17, 111–12, 116
right to shelter, 18
Rosencranz, Armin, 113
Roy, Ananya, 228–29n17
rule by aesthetics: aesthetic politics and,
15–17; crisis of, 186–88; definition of,
4–5, 125, 184–86; governmentality
and, 5–8, 101. *See also* world-class
aesthetic
rule by records (calculative
governmentality), 5–8, 12–14, 100,
105–6, 183, 186, 195–96
RWA Joint Front, 92

Saberwal, Satish, 47
Sajha Manch (Joint Platform), 19
Sanjay Camp (*jhuggi* colony), *81*
Sant Ravi Das Camp (*jhuggi* colony), 81–87,
81–82, 85, 118–19
Satyavati (Kali, "the dark one"), 215–16n9
Scott, David, 199n9
Scott, James, 5
Searle, Llerena Guiu, 33, 207n34, 209n77
settlements. *See jhuggi* colonies (Delhi)
Shiller, Robert, 29
Shiv Camp (*jhuggi* colony): Delhi Master
Plan and, 145–46; demolition of
(January 2007), 125–26, 128–131,
133, 222n28; demolition of (April
2007), 145–46, 173; demolition of
(winter 2010), 193; fate and, 170–76,
172; fetishism and, 181–82; fieldwork
in, 18–20; "grassroots battle" (strike)
and, 131–32, 135–37; history of, 53,
132–34; magic and, 161–66, *162;*
"paper battle" (legal case) and, 131,
137–38, 146–48, 192–93, 220n61;
photographs of, *129, 133, 138–39,
172;* Rajeev Awas Yojana and, 194–96;
resettlement and, 150–56, 158–59,

175–181; unbelonging and, 126–28,
134–141, 143–46, 148–150; value and,
164–170; world-class aesthetic and, 4,
134–141, 143–46, 148–150, 155–57
Simmel, Georg, 173, 226n19, 227n27
Simone, AbdouMaliq, 7–8
Singh, Manmohan, 30, 186–87
Singh, Rajiv, 27–28
Singh, V. P., 132
Slum Areas (Improvement and Clearance)
Act (1956), 211–12n18
slums and squatter settlements, 1. *See also
jhuggi* colonies (Delhi)
Smith, Adam, 227n29
Smith, Richard Saumarez, 202n35
social order, 6, 17, 79, 125
speculative urbanism, 10, 29–30, 43–44,
159, 205n6
statistics, 5–6
structural bilingualism, 210n5
Sundaram, Ravi, 201n25
Supreme Court of India: DLF Emporio and,
2–3; Nangla Machi and, 18; nuisance
law and, 101–5, 114; right to life and,
17; RWAs and, 69, 74
Survey of India (2011), 195
Swistun, Debora Alejandra, 19

Tarlo, Emma, 202n32
Tata Consultancy Services, 200n19
Tata Housing, 230n29
Taussig, Michael, 225n9
terms of sensibility, 127–28,
146–49, 155–56
The Times of India (newspaper), 73, 76, 77,
199n3, 220n63
Town Planning Organization, 201n25
transfer of development rights (TDR)
model, 229n18

UN Public Service Award (2005), 76
unbelonging, 126–28, 134–141, 143–46,
148–150
United Nations (UN), 199n2
Universal Declaration of Human
Rights, 204n55
untouchability. *See* Dalit (former
untouchable)
Urban Land Ceiling Act (1998), 206n21
US Agency for International Development
(USAID), 26

value, 95, 164–170
Valverde, Mariana, 111, 219n30, 219n32
Verma, Gita Dewan, 218n20
voter ID cards, 52–53, 133–34

Wacquant, Loïc, 19
Weiss, Brad, 226n19
World Bank, 26, 28, 160, 205n12, 206n18, 207n49
World Economic Forum (2011), 190
world-class aesthetic: Bhagidari and, 57, 60; as codified in law, 123–24, 141–42; Delhi Master Plan and, 23–24; as future-oriented technology, 8–11, 42–44, 183–85; inclusive growth and, 188–195, 197–98; land market and, 24–29; nuisance and, 87–93, 97–98, 100; poverty projections and, 29–33; private property and, 181–82; removal of slums and, 11–14, 57, 142–43; scenes from Delhi and, 1–5; Shiv Camp residents and, 4, 134–141, 143–46, 148–150, 155–57; as symbol of progress and modernity and object of desire, 141–42; unbelonging and, 126–28

Yamuna River, 96, 106, 120–21
Yurchak, Alexei, 148–49, 155